AYEEN AKBERY

OR, THE

INSTITUTES

OF

THE EMPEROR AKBER

AYEEN AKBERY

OR, THE

INSTITUTES

OF

THE EMPEROR AKBER

TRANSLATED FROM THE ORIGINAL PERSIAN

Translated By

FRANCIS GLADWIN

IN TWO VOLUMES

VOL. II

GYAN

Published by

GYAN

Gyan Publishing House
5, Ansari Road
Daryaganj, New Delhi-110002
Phone: 011-47034999, 9811692060
E-mail: books@gyanbooks.com

Distribution Network
gyanbooks.com
India, USA, Canada, UK, Australia, France

ISBN: 978-81-212-9667-0 (Set)
ISBN: 978-81-212-9665-6 (PB)
First Published, 1800

2nd Impression 2023

Printed at: Gyan Press, Delhi.

AYEEN AKBERY OR, THE INSTITUTES OF THE EMPEROR AKBER (VOL. II)

Translated by: FRANCIS GLADWIN

AYEEN AKBERY;

OR, THE

INSTITUTES

OF

THE EMPEROR AKBER.

TRANSLATED FROM THE ORIGINAL PERSIAN

By FRANCIS GLADWIN.

IN TWO VOLUMES.

VOL. II.

1800.

THE Tranflator embraces this opportunity of returning thanks to his friend Colonel Polier, for having enabled him to give the particulars of the *Tukseem Jumma*, or *Rent Roll*, in a ftate of greater perfection than he otherwife could poffibly have done. This gentleman was at the pains to collate, with feveral ancient manufcripts, the copy from which this part of the tranflation is made.

Although it be poffible that fome few of the names, in the diftricts leaft known to us, may not be completely correct, yet, upon the whole, we may venture to affert, that nothing of the kind, even fo perfect as this, has ever appeared in any European language; and we therefore hope it will prove an acceptable addition to hiftorical and geographical learning.

Since the publication of the firft volume of this work, the honourable Board have favoured the tranflator with the following recommendation to the Court of Directors:

Extract of a general letter from the Governor-General and Council, to the Honourable the Court of Directors, dated the 23d *October*, 1783, *and dispatched per Nerbudda.*

" A propofal having been made to us by Mr. Francis Gladwin, for the publication of a complete tranflation from the Perfian language, of a book well known by the name of the AYEEN AKBERY, and this being a work which may prove of the utmoft utility to the Company, as it contains the original inftitutes of the Sultan Akber, the founder of the empire, we refolved, as well on this account, as for the promotion of the knowledge of Indian literature, to fubfcribe, in the Company's name, for

150

150 ſets of three quarto volumes each, at 40 rupees per volume. Soon afterwards, Mr. Gladwin finding that objections were entertained againſt the payment of ſo large an amount in our preſent ſituation out of the treaſury, declined to receive the ſubſcription, and conſented to leave the matter in reference to you. Impreſſed with the ſame favourable opinion of the undertaking, in which we originally viewed it, we beg leave to recommend it to your conſideration, either to make or authoriſe the ſubſcription we intended on the Company's account."

CONTENTS.

CONTENTS

OF THE

SECOND VOLUME.

General

CONTENTS.

The

CONTENTS.

AYEEN

AYEEN AKBERY.

THE

HISTORY

OF THE

TWELVE SOOBAHS.

IN the fortieth year of his majesty's reign, his dominions consisted of one hundred and five Sircars(1), subdivided into two thousand seven hundred and thirty-seven Kusbahs (2), the revenue of which he settled for ten years, at the annual rent of three Arribs, sixty-two Crore, ninety-seven Lacks, fifty-five thousand two hundred and forty-six Dams (3), or Sicca Rupees, 9,0743881. 2. 5.

The empire was then parcelled into twelve grand divisions, and each was committed to the government of a Soobadar (or Viceroy), upon which occasion the Sovereign of the world distributed twelve Lacks of beetle. The names of the Soobahs (or Viceroyalties) were Allahabad, Agra, Owdh, Ajmeer, Ahmedabad, Bahar, Bengal, Dehly, Cabul, Lahoor, Multan, and Malwa: when his majesty conquered Berar, Khan-

(1) Provinces. (2) Townships.

(3) One hundred thousand make one Lack, one hundred Lacks one Crore, one hundred Crore one Arrib. A Dam is the fortieth part of a Rupee.

deefs, and Ahmednagur, they were formed into three Soobahs, increafing the number to fifteen (4).

I fhall give a fuccinct defcription of the moft remarkable countries; as alfo of their feveral princes, together with the periods in which they lived.

The SOOBAH of BENGAL.

Since I propofe to begin my defcription of thefe poffeffions from Bengal, which is the loweft extremity of Hindoftan, and to carry it to Zabuliftan, I hope that, while I am writing, not only Turan and Iran, but alfo other countries may be added to the account.

After having defcribed the country which lies to the eaft, I fhall proceed to the north, from thence defcend to the fouth, and conclude with the weftern divifions.

The Soobah of Bengal is fituated in the fecond climate. From Chittagong to Kurhee is four hundred Cofe difference of longitude; and from the northern range of mountains to the fouthern extremity of Sircar Madarun, comprehends two hundred Cofe of latitude. And when Oriffa was added to Bengal, the additional length was computed to be forty three Cofe, and the breadth twenty Cofe (5).

Bengal (including Oriffa) has the fea on the eaft, is bounded by mountains on the north and fouth, and on the weft joins to the Soobah of Bahar. Efau Afghan

(4) Soobah is frequently, but improperly, ufed for Soobahdar by European authors: Soobah is properly the Vice-royalty, and Soobahdar the Viceroy.

(5) The Cofe is different in the feveral provinces; but we fhall be fufficiently exact if we reckon it to be two Englifh miles.

carried

carried his conqueſts towards the eaſt into a country called Bhatty, which is reckoned a part of this Soobah, and cauſed the Kootbah (or prayer) to be read, and coin to be ſtruck in the name of his preſent majeſty. Nothing remarkable is related of this country, excepting that the mangoe trees, which produce very delicious fruit, are not ſo high as the ordinary ſtature of a man.

Bordering upon Bhatty is a very extenſive country, ſubject to the chief of Tiprah; him they ſtyle Yeyah Manick; and whoever are poſſeſſed of Rajahſhips bear the title of Manick at the end of their names, and all the nobility are called Narain. Their military force conſiſts of a thouſand elephants, and two hundred thouſand infantry, but they have few or no cavalry.

To the northward of Bengal is the province of Coach, the chief of which commands a thouſand horſe, and one hundred thouſand foot. Kamroop (which is alſo called Kamroo and Kamtah) makes a part of his dominion. The inhabitants of Kamroop are ſaid to be extremely handſome; and they are reported to be very ſkilful in magic. Many incredible ſtories are told of the natural productions of this place; ſuch as flowers that retain their colour and ſmell many months after being gathered, and of which they make chaplets; trees that being cut ſend forth ſtreams of delicious liquor; and mangoes that grow upon a kind of vine.

The dominions of the Rajah of Aſham join to Kamroop: he is a very powerful prince, lives in great ſtate, and when he dies, his principal attendants, both male and female, are voluntarily buried alive with his corpſe.

Adjoining to Aſham is Tibet, bordering upon Khatai, which is properly Mahacheen, vulgarly called Macheen. The capital of Khatai is Khan Baleegh, four days journey from the ſea, to which there is a large artificial canal, lined with ſtone. Alexander of Greece is reported to have entered that country by this canal. And it is ſaid that there is another paſſage, by which you may reach the ſea in four days and four nights.

To the ſouth-eaſt of Bengal is a large country, called Arkung (or Aracan) to which the Bunder (or port) of Chittagong properly belongs. Here are plenty of elephants, but great ſcarcity of horſes: alſo camels and aſſes are very high priced. Neither cows nor buffaloes are found in this country; but there are animals of a middle ſpecies between thoſe, whoſe milk the people drink; they are pied and of various colours. Their religion has no kind of agreement either with the Mahommedan or Hindoo. Twin brothers and ſiſters may intermarry, and only mother and ſon are prohibited from it. They pay implicit obedience to the will of their prieſts, whom they ſtyle Wallee. When the prince holds a court, the ſoldiers wives attend, whilſt their huſbands remain in their houſes. The complection of theſe people is dark; and the men are beardleſs.

Near to this tribe is Pegu, which former writers called Cheen, accounting this to be the capital city. Their military force conſiſts of elephants and infantry. Some of their elephants are white. Cloſe to this country are ſome mines of metals and precious ſtones, which are the ſubject of continual contention betwixt the chiefs of Pegu, Aracan, and the Mugs.

Bungaleh, originally, was called Bung; it derived the additional Al from that being the name given to the mounds of earth which the ancient Rajahs cauſed to be raiſed in the low lands, at the foot of the hills; their breadth was uſually twenty cubits, and height ten cubits.

The

The air of Bengal is very temperate. The periodical rains commence in April, and continue for somewhat more than six months. During this season the low lands are sometimes entirely overflowed, excepting the mounds of earth described above. For a long time past the air of Bengal had been unhealthy at the leaving off of the rains, afflicting both man and cattle; but under the auspices of his present majesty this calamity has ceased (6).

This Soobah abounds with rivers, the finest of which is the Gung (or Ganges), whose source has never been traced. The Hindoo priests say that it flows from the hair of Mahadeo. From the northern mountains it runs through the Soobah of Dehly, Agra, Allahabad, and Bahar, into Bengal. Near the town of Cazyhuttah, in the Sircar of Barbuckabad, at which place it is called the Pudhawutty, it sends a branch to the east, which empties itself into the sea at Chittagong. The main river in its course to the southward forms three streams, the Sirsutty, the Jown, and the Gung; which three streams are collectively called, in the Hindovee language, Tirpunny, and they are all held in high veneration by the Hindoos. The Gung, after having divided into a thousand channels, joins the sea at Satagong, and the Sirsutty and Jown discharge themselves in like manner. The learned amongst the Hindoos have composed volumes in praise of these waters, all parts of which are said to be holy, but some particular places are esteemed more so than others. The great people have the water of the Ganges brought to them

(6) In the beginning of April (and sometimes earlier in the southern parts of Bengal) there are frequent storms of thunder, lightning, wind, and rain, from the north-west quarter: these squalls moderate the heat very much, and they continue till the setting in of the periodical rains, which generally commence in the beginning of June, and by which the country is in many parts overflowed. If the rains break up early in September, the weather is intensely hot, and the inhabitants are very sickly.

from

from vaſt diſtances, it being eſteemed neceſſary in the performance of ſome religious ceremonies. The water of the Ganges has been celebrated in all ages, not only for its ſanctity, but alſo on account of its ſweetneſs, lightneſs, and wholeſomeneſs, and for, that it does not not become putrid though kept for years.

There is another very large river, called Berhumputter, which runs from Khatai to Coach, and from thence through Bazoohah to the ſea.

The ſea of Bengal, which is a bay of the ocean, goes on one ſide to Baſrah, and on the other to Kulzum of Egypt, and from thence to Perſia, where, by the natives, it is called the ſea of Oman, and the ſea of Perſia.

Moſt of the rivers of Bengal have their banks cultivated with rice, of which there a variety of ſpecies. The ſoil is ſo fertile in ſome places, that a ſingle grain of rice will yield a meaſure of 2 or 3 Seer. Some lands will produce three crops in a year. Vegetation is here ſo extremely quick, that as faſt as the water riſes the plants of rice grow above it, ſo that the ear is never immerſed. Men of experience affirm that a ſingle ſtalk will grow ſix cubits in one night.

The ſubjects are very obedient to government, and pay their annual rents in eight months by inſtalments, themſelves bringing Mohurs and Rupees to the places appointed for the receipt of the revenues, it not being cuſtomary in this Soobah for the huſbandman and government to divide the crops. Grain is always cheap, and the produce of the lands is determined by Nuſſuk (7). His majeſty has had the goodneſs to confirm thoſe cuſtoms. The food of the inhabitants is for the moſt part fiſh and rice; wheat and barley not being

(7) Vide Vol. I.

eſteemed

esteemed wholesome here. Great numbers of men and women go quite naked, except a covering for the loins. In this country women are allowed to transact business in public.

Their houses are chiefly made of bamboos, some of which however will cost five thousand Rupees and upwards, and are of a very long duration. They travel chiefly by water, especially in the rainy season. They construct boats for war, burthen, and travelling. Particularly for besieging places, they make them of such a form that, when they run ashore, they are higher than the fort, which is thereby easily entered. For their journies by land they make use of Sookhasens. This is a machine supported upon the shoulders of men, by a pole formed of a number of straight pieces of wood joined together by iron rings. The sides of the machine are ornamented with different metals, and over the top is thrown an arched covering, made of woollen cloth, for defence against the sun and rain. In these machines you sit or lie down, and sleep as conveniently as in a room of a house. Some also ride upon elephants. Horses are very scarce. In some parts of this Soobah are manufactured hempen carpets, so beautiful, that they seem to be made of silk. The inhabitants of Bengal are exceedingly fond of salt, which is scarce in some parts of this Soobah.

Diamonds, emeralds, pearls, agates, and cornelians are brought from other countries to the sea-ports of this Soobah.

Their flowers and fruits are fine and in plenty. The beetlenut stains the lips of those who eat it quite red (8).

Jennutabad

(8) As it may not be displeasing to the naturalist to see a passage, which I have not inserted in the text, on account of its being rather indecent,

Jennutabad is a very ancient city, and was once the capital of Bengal. Formerly it was called Lucknowty, and ſometimes Gowr, the name it now bears was given by the late emperor. Here is a fine fort, to the eaſtward of which is a large lake, called Chutteahputtea, in which are many iſlands. If the dams break during the heavy periodical rains, the city is laid under water. To the northward of this fort, at the diſtance of a coſe, is a large building, a work of great antiquity, where there is a reſervoir of water called Peazbarry, which is of a very noxious property. It was uſual when a criminal was capitally condemned, to confine him in this building, where, being allowed no other drink than this water, he expired in a very ſhort time; but his majeſty has ordered this puniſhment to be diſcontinued.

indecent, I ſhall here ſubjoin it both in the original language and in Latin.

خواجه سرا ازين ديار بر آيد و آن سه گونه
بود صندلي بادامي كافوري نخست را هر
سه عضو از بيخ برند واطلسي نيز گويند دو
يمين را قدري الت فعلي باشد سيو يمين
آنكه خصيين اورا هنگام خوردي بمالش
نابود سازند يا بر آرند چنان بر گزارند جز
آدمي هر جانداري كه خصي كنند ازان سر
كشي فرو نشيند و مردم زادرا بر افزيد

Tria inde genera eunuchorum veniunt, quos Sundâlos, Budâmos et Cafooros nuncupant: Priores, partibus genitalibus radicaliter exſectis, Atleeſes etiam nominant. Budâmis pars ſolum Penis relinquitur. Câfooros adhuc teneræ ætatis Teſtes vel compreſſi conficiuntur vel exſecantur: tamen notatum eſt, caſtrationem, quæ veneris deſiderium cæteris omnibus animalibus tollit, hominibus ſolis excitare.

Mah-

Mahmoodabad. The fort is surrounded by a marsh. When Sheer Khan conquered this country, some of the Rajah's elephants fled into the wilds, where they have increased to great numbers. This Sircar produces long pepper.

The Sircar of Khaleefutabad abounds also with elephants, and long pepper.

Sircar Bokla is upon the banks of the sea. The fort is situated amongst trees. On the first day of the moon the water begins to rise, and continues increasing till the fourteenth, from which time to the end of the month it decreases gradually every day. In the 29th year of the present reign, one afternoon at three o'clock, there was a terrible inundation, which deluged the whole Sircar. The Rajah was at an entertainment, from whence he embarked in a boat: his son, Parminund Roy, with many people, climbed to the top of a Hindoo temple; and the merchants betook themselves to the high lands. It blew a hurricane, with thunder and lightning for five hours, during which time the sea was greatly agitated. The houses and boats were swallowed up, nothing remaining but the Hindoo temple and the heights. Near two hundred thousand living creatures perished in this calamity.

Sircar Ghoraghaut produces raw silk, gunneys, and plenty of Tanghion horses. Here are abundance of fruits in high perfection, amongst the rest is one called the Lutken, of the size of a walnut, but to the taste is somewhat like the pomegranate; it contains three seeds.

Sircar Barbuckabad is famous for a fine cloth, called Gungajel, and great abundance of oranges.

Sircar Bazooha. The forests of this Sircar supply timbers fit for building boats, and for the beams of houses: and here is an iron mine.

Sircar

Sircar Sunargong. In this Sircar is fabricated a very beautiful cloth, called Cassah. In the town of Catarehsoonder is a large reservoir of water, which gives a peculiar whiteness to the cloths that are washed in it.

Sircar Silhet is very mountainous. It furnishes many eunuch slaves for the serais (or seraglios). Here grows a delicious fruit, called Soontara, in colour like an orange, but of an oblong form. China root is produced here in great plenty, which was but lately discovered by some Turks. In these mountains is abundance of lignum aloes. They fell the trees at the end of the rains, and leave them exposed to the weather for some time; after which they reject all those that are anywise rotten. The Bunraj is a bird with a black body, red eyes, a long tail, and wings beautifully variegated, measuring a cubit when extended; they are easily tamed, and will imitate the voice of any animal. The Sheergunj is another bird, which differs from the former but in the colour of its legs and bill, which are red. They both eat flesh, and prey upon small birds.

Chittagong is a large city, situated amongst trees upon the banks of the sea, and is a great emporium, being the resort of christian and other merchants.

Shereefabad produces very beautiful white bullocks, of a great size, who will carry a burden of fifteen maunds, and, like camels, they bend the knees to be loaded. It is also noted for large goats and fighting cocks.

Satgong. There are two emporiums, a mile distant from each other; one called Satgong, and the other Hoogly, with its dependancies; both of which are in the possession of the Europeans. Satgong is famous for pomegranates.

Madarun.

Madurun. In this Sircar, at a place called Huneyeh, is a diamond mine, where are ſound only ſmall ſtones.

ORISSA.

This formerly was an independent country. The climate is very healthy. It conſiſts of five Sircars, viz. Jalaſor, Buderuck, Cuttek, Kullengdundpaut, and Rajemahindrah. Theſe five Sircars are now added to Bengal.

Oriſſa contains one hundred and twenty-nine brick forts, ſubject to the command of Gujeputty.

The periodical rains continue here eight months; and they have three months of winter, and only one month that is very hot.

Rice is cultivated here in great abundance. The inhabitants live upon rice, fiſh, and vegetables. After boiling the rice, they ſteep it in cold water, and eat it the ſecond day.

The men are very effeminate, being exceedingly fond of ornaments, and anointing their bodies with Sandal-wood oil. The women cover only the lower parts of the body, and many make themſelves dreſſes of the leaves of trees. They live in huts made of the leaves of the Tewar tree.

Here are many idolatrous temples built of ſtone, and of great height.

Their women, contrary to the general cuſtom of Hindoos, may marry two or three times.

Paper and ink are ſeldom uſed here: for the moſt part

part they write with an iron ſtyle on the leaf of the Taar tree, and they hold the pen with the fiſt clenched.

Here are manufactures of cloth. Some elephants are found in this province.

The fruits and flowers of Oriſſa are very fine, and in great plenty. The Nuſreen is a flower delicately formed, and of an exquiſite ſmell; the outer ſide of the leaves is white, and the inner is of a yellow colour. The Kewrah grows here quite common, and they have great variety of the beetle leaf.

They reckon all their accounts in Cowris, which is a ſmall white ſhell, with an aperture in the middle, and they are found on the ſea-ſhore. Four Cowries they call a Gundah, five Gundahs a Boory, four Boories are a Pun, ſixteen Pun one Khawun (ſometimes they reckon 20 Pun to the Khawun) and ten Khawuns are a Rupee.

CUTTEK.

At the capital bearing this name is a ſtone fort, ſituated between two rivers, the Mahanuddy and the Gunjoory, the former of which is held in great veneration by the Hindoos. Within the fort are many magnificent buildings, and it is the reſidence of the governor of the province.

The country, for five or ſix coſe round the fort, is ſo low, that in the rainy ſeaſon it is entirely under water.

Here is a fine palace built by Rajah Muckund Deo, conſiſting of nine ſtories. The firſt ſtory is for the elephants, camels, and horſes. The ſecond, for the artillery and military ſtores; where are alſo quarters for the guards and other attendants. The third is occupied

pied by the porters and watchmen. The fourth is appropriated for the feveral artificers. The kitchens make the fifth range. The fixth contains the Rajah's public apartments. The feventh is for the tranfaction of private bufinefs. The eighth is where the women refide. And the ninth is the Rajah's fleeping apartments. To the fouth of this palace is a very ancient Hindoo temple.

In the town of Purfotem, on the banks of the fea, ftands the temple of Jagnaut, near to which are the images of Kifhen, his brother and their fifter, made of fandal-wood, which are faid to be four thoufand years old.

It is related that Rajah Inderdummun, of Neelkurburbut, fent a learned Brahmin to pitch upon a proper fpot for the foundation of a city. After a long fearch, he arrived upon the banks of the fea, which he thought, on many accounts, preferable to any place he had yet feen. Whilft he was debating with himfelf whether to fix upon this fpot, or to continue his journey in queft of a better, he faw a crow dive into the water, and after having wafhed it's body, it made obeifance to the fea. The Brahmin ws aftonifhed at this fight, and as he underftood the language of birds, he afked the crow the reafon of this ftrange procedure. The crow anfwered, "I was formerly of the tribe of the Dewtah*, and from the curfe of a religious man, was transformed into this fhape; know that this fpot is highly favoured by the Creator of the univerfe; and whoever abides here, and applies his mind to the worfhip of God, he fhall quickly profper. It is a long time that I have been worfhipping in this place, and the feafon for the accomplifhment of my defires is near at hand. If you are of the number of the righteous, remain here a fhort

* Celeftials.

period,

period, and behold and comprehend the wonders of this land." The Brahmin, in conformity to the words of the crow, remained on that ſpot, and after a ſhort time, what the crow had foretold was revealed unto him, and of which he apprized the Rajah, who built a large city and a place of worſhip upon the ſpot where the crow had appeared. The Rajah one night, after having diſtributed juſtice, heard in a dream a voice ſaying, "On a certain day caſt thine eyes upon the ſea ſhore, when there will ariſe out of the water a piece of wood fifty-two inches long, and one and a half cubits broad: this is the true form of the deity, take it up, and keep it hidden in thine houſe ſeven days, and in whatever ſhape it ſhall then appear, place it in the Temple, and worſhip it." It happening juſt as the Rajah had dreamt, he, as inſtructed by the revelation, called the image Juganaut, and having ornamented it with gold and precious ſtones, he placed it in the Temple, when it became the object of worſhip of all ranks of people, and is reported to have performed many miracles. It is pretended that when Callapahar conquered this country for Soliman Goorzany, he threw the wooden image of Juganaut into a fire, which having no effect upon it, he ordered it to be caſt into the ſea, from whence it was again recovered. And in order to give credit to theſe images, they relate a number of ſuch incredible ſtories.

The Brahmins waſh the images of Juganaut ſix times every day, and dreſs them every time in freſh clothes; as ſoon as they are dreſſed, fifty-ſix Brahmins attend them, and preſent them with various kinds of food. The quantity of victuals offered to theſe idols is ſo very great, as to feed twenty thouſand perſons. They alſo at certain times carry the image in proceſſion upon a carriage of ſixteen wheels, which in the Hindovee language is called Ruhth; and they believe that whoever

ever aſſiſts in drawing it along obtains remiſſion of all his ſins.

Near to Juganaut is the temple of the Sun, in the erecting of which was expended the whole revenue of Oriſſa for twelve years. No one can behold this immenſe edifice without being ſtruck with amazement. The wall which ſurrounds the whole is one hundred and fifty cubits high, and nineteen cubits thick. There are three entrances to it. At the eaſtern gate are two very fine figures of elephants, each with a man upon his trunk. To the weſt are two ſurpriſing figures of horſemen, completely armed; and over the northern gate are carved two tigers, who having killed two elephants, are ſitting upon them. In the front of the gate is a pillar of black ſtone, of an octagonal form, fifty cubits high. There are nine flights of ſteps; after aſcending which, you come into an extenſive encloſure, where you diſcover a large dome, conſtructed of ſtone, upon which are carved the ſun and the ſtars, and round them is a border, where are repreſented a variety of human figures, expreſſing the different paſſions of the mind; ſome kneeling, others proſtrated with their faces upon the earth; together with minſtrels, and a number of ſtrange and wonderful animals, ſuch as never exiſted but in imagination. This is ſaid to be a work of ſeven hundred and thirty years' antiquity. Rajah Nurſing Dĕo finiſhed this building, thereby erecting for himſelf a laſting monument of fame. There are twenty-eight other temples belonging to this pagoda, ſix before the northern gate, and twenty-two without the encloſure; and they are all reported to have performed miracles.

Many pretend that at this place is the tomb of Kebeer Mowehhed, and to this day they relate many ſtories of his ſayings and actions. He was revered both by Mahommedans and Hindoos, on account of his wiſdom and exemplary virtue. When he died, the Brahmins

 wanted

wanted to carry his body to be burned, and the Mahommedans insisted on burying it, but when they lifted up the sheet from the bier, the corpse could not be found.

The Soobah of Bengal consists of twenty-four Sircars, and seven hundred and eighty-seven Mahls. The revenue is fifty-nine crore, eighty-four lacks, fifty-nine thousand three hundred and nineteen dams, or sicca rupees, 1,49,61,482—15—2 in money; and the Zemindars (who are mostly Koits) furnish also 23,330 cavalry; 801,158 infantry, 170 elephants, 4260 cannon, and 4400 boats.

A summary Account of the Princes of Bengal.

Four thousand and ninety-six years prior to the date of this book, Rajah Bhugrut having come to Dehly, to the assistance of Rajah Jirjoodhun, gallantly fell in the war of the Mahabahrut.

Rajah Noe, when the cup of life was filled to the brim, was succeeded in the government by Luckmeenyah, the son of Luckmen. At that time Nuddea was the capital of Bengal, when it abounded with wisdom; but now it is thinly inhabited, although it be still conspicuous for learning.

The astrologers foretold Rajah Luckmeenyah of the loss of his kingdom, and of the establishment of another religion; both which points, they said, would be accomplished in the person of Mahommed Bukhtyar Khuljee; yet the Rajah was so infatuated, that he would not listen to their predictions: however many of his people fled into distant countries for safety.

At this time Shahĕbeddeen had sent into Hindostan Koteb-eddeen Ibek, whose general, Mahommed Bukhtyar Khuljee, possessed himself of the Soobah of Bahar, and

and then marched towards Bengal; upon which the Rajah made his escape in a boat. Khuljee having plundered and entirely destroyed the city of Nuddea, made Lucknowty the capital of Bengal; from that period Bengal began to be subject to the kings of Dehly.

During the reign of Towghluck Khan, Kudder Khan was employed by him in Bengal, till Fukhireddeen Sillahdar revolted, put him to death, assumed the government, and refused obedience to the kings of Dehly.

Mullick Aly Mobarick, who had been one of the generals of Kudder Khan, took the title of Allaheddeen, and made war upon Fukhireddeen, whom having taken in battle, he slew, and then caused himself to be proclaimed king.

Hajee Alyas Alla-ey, who was one of the nobles of Bengal, entered into a confederacy with some other chiefs, and having killed Allaheddeen, he usurped the kingdom under the title of Shumseddeen, and he is sometimes also called Bungereh. Sultan Feeroz marched from Dehly to punish him, and for some time carried on a brisk war; but the rainy season approaching, he accepted of a submission, and returned to Dehly.

When Shumseddeen died, the chiefs of the army placed upon the throne his eldest son, whom they styled Secunder Shah. Upon this occasion Feeroz came again into Bengal, and was reconciled in like manner to Secunder Shah, as he had been to his father.

Secunder was succeeded in the government by his son Ghiasseddeen. Hafiz of Shiraz sent him an ode, in which is the following verse: "All the parrots of Hind will enjoy the sweets of the Persian sugarcandy, which is now going to Bengal."

An Hindoo Zemeendar, named Kanſy, having fraudulently obtained a victory over Ghiaſſeddeen, uſurped the kingdom.

When Kanſy died, his ſon became a Mahommedan, and obtained the throne, with the title of Jilaleddeen.

It was the cuſtom in thoſe times, for the palace to be guarded by ſeveral thouſand pykes, who are a kind of infantry. An eunuch entered into a confederacy with theſe guards, who one night killed the king, Futteh Shah, when the eunuch aſcended the throne, under the title of Barbuck Shah.

Feeroz Shah was alſo put to death by theſe guards, and his ſon Mahmood Shah raiſed to the throne.

He was by the like intrigue murdered, and ſucceeded by his Ethiopian ſlave, named Mozuffer.

This Mozuffer met with the ſame fate as his maſter, through the management of one of his ſervants, named Allaheddeen, who likewiſe aſſumed the kingdom, and reigned with great juſtice. He diſbanded the pykes, but ſubſtituted in their ſtead low Sirhengs.

Nuſſeeb Shah, his ſon, was alſo of a very upright and charitable diſpoſition, and behaved with great kindneſs to his brothers.

When Sultan Baber had ſlain Sultan Ibrahim in battle, his brother, and the other chiefs of the army, put themſelves under the protection of Nuſſeeb Shah, and found ſafety.

Hemayun raiſed to the Soobadary of Bengal, Jehangeer Kuly Khan Beg, whom Sheer Khan, when he again gained the victory, drew to him by protestations of safety, and then slew him.

During the reign of Seleem Khan, (at Dehly) this kingdom was ruled with strict justice by Mahommed Khan, one of his relations, and when he was killed in war by Mumraze Khan, he was succeeded in the kingdom by his son Khysir Khan, who took the title of Behader Shah, and he slew Mumraze Khan in battle.

Taje Khan, who was one of the nobles of Seleem, killed Jilaleddeen, and succeeded him in the kingdom.

Taje Khan's younger brother, Soleeman, although a tyrant, reigned some time, and afterwards the names of his children, Bazeed and Daoud, dishonoured the coin and the pulpit. Thus concludes my abstract.

God be praised, that out of his mercy, this populous kingdom will now be made glorious by the royal justice.

TABLES

Of the Successions of the ancient Rajahs, and of the Mahommedan Princes who have reigned in Bengal.

TABLE I.

The family of Bhugrut, of the Kehtry cast, twenty-four Princes, reigned 2418 years.

	Reigned years.		Reigned years.
Bhugrut - -	218	Runbheem - -	108
Annungbheem -	175	Gujbheem - -	82

Deodut

	Reigned years.		Reigned years.
Deodut - -	95	Owdeyſingh -	85
Jugſingh - -	106	Biſſuſingh - -	88
Birmahſingh -	97	Beermath - -	81
Mohundut - -	102	Ruckdeo - -	83
Benowdſingh -	97	Rakhnuud - -	79
Seylerſein - -	96	Jugjeevun - -	107
Suthajeet - -	101	Kalloodund -	85
Bhooput - -	90	Kamdeo - -	90
Suddruck - -	91	Bejykeren - -	71
Jeedruck - -	102	Sutſingh - -	89

TABLE II.

The Family of Bowjgorya, of the Koyth cast, nine Princes, reigned 250 years.

	Reigned years.		Reigned years.
Bowjgorya - -	75	Pert-hoo - -	52
Lallſein - -	70	Gurrer - -	45
Rajah Madhow -	57	Luckhmun - -	50
Summuntbowj -	48	Nundbowj - -	53
Jennet - -	60		

TABLE III.

The Family of Udsoor, of the Koyth cast, eleven Princes, reigned 714 years.

	Reigned years.		Reigned years.
Udſoor - -	75	Girdher - -	80
Jamennybhan -	73	Pirtehydehr -	68
Anrood - -	78	Shiſhtdehr - -	58
Pertaub Rooder	65	Pirbahker - -	63
Bhowadet - -	69	Jydehr - -	23
Rekhdeo - -	62		

TABLE

TABLE IV.

The Family of Bhowpaul, of the Koyth cast, ten Princes, reigned 698 years.

	Reigned years.		Reigned years.
Bhowpaul - -	55	Biggenpaul - -	75
Dheerpaul - -	95	Jypaul - - -	93
Deopaul - -	83	Rajpaul - - -	98
Bowputpaul - -	70	Bhowgpaul, his brother	5
Dhunputpaul -	45	Jugpaul, his fon -	74

TABLE V.

The Family of Sookhsein, of the Koyth cast, seven Princes, reigned 160 years.

	Reigned years.		Reigned years.
Sookhfein - -	3	Madhowfein -	10
Billalfein (he built the fort of Gowr) -	50	Kyfoofein - -	15
Lukhenfein - -	7	Suddafein - -	18
		Nowjeh - -	3

Sixty-one Rajahs reigned for the fpace of 4544 years, when Bengal became fubject to the kings of Dehly. From the time of Sultan Kotebeddeen Ibek, till the reign of Sultan Mahommed Towghlich Shah, includes 17 Princes, who reigned about 150 years.

TABLE VI.

Of the Mahommedan Princes of Bengal from the time of Towghlich Shah.

	Reigned years.
Mullick Fekhreddeen Sillahdar - - -	2 years and fome months.
Sultan Allaheddeen	1 ditto and fome ditto.
Shumfeddeen Bungerah	16 ditto and fome ditto.

Secunder,

	Reigned years.
Secunder, his ſon	9 years and ſome months.
Sultan Ghiaſſeddeen, his ſon - - -	7 ditto and ſome ditto.
Sultan-ul Sulateen, his ſon	10 years.
Shumſeddeen, his ſon	3 years and ſome months.
Kanſy Bhowmy -	7 years.
Sultan Jilaleddeen -	17 years.
Sultan Ahmed, his ſon	16 years.
Naſſer, his ſlave -	a week, or according to others only half a day.
Naſſer Shah, a grandſon of Shumſeddeen Bun-gerah - -	2 years.
Barbuck Shah -	17 years.
Youſef Shah - -	7 years 6 months.
Secunder Shah -	half a day.
Futteh Shah - -	7 years 5 months.
Barbuck Shah -	2½ days.
Feeroz Shah - -	3 years.
Mahommed Shah, his ſon	1 year.
Mozuffer, an Ethiopian	3 years and 5 months.
Allaheddeen - -	27 years and ſome months.
Nuſſeeb Shah, his ſon	11 years.
Sheer Khan.	
Hemayun.	
Sheer Khan again.	
Mahommed Khan.	
Bahader Shah.	
Jilaleddeen, his brother.	
Ghiaſſeddeen.	
Taje Khan.	
Soliman.	
Baizeed.	
Daoud.	

THE

The SOOBAH of BAHAR.

IT is ſituated in the ſecond climate. The length from Gurhee to Rhotas is 120 coſe, and the breadth from Tirhoot to the northern mountains, includes 110 coſe. It is bounded on the eaſt by Bengal, has Allahabad and Owdh on the weſt, and on the north and ſouth are large mountains.

The principal rivers of this Soobah are the Ganges and the Sown; whatever wood, or leather, or any thing of that kind, which is ſoft, and does not ſoon periſh, is thrown into the Sown, becomes petrified. The Sown, the Nerbuddah, and the Cheleh (or Chelum), all three ſpring from one ſource, near Kurrah. The water of the Sown is cool, pleaſant to the taſte, and wholeſome; having run to the ſouth as far as Muneyr, it then unites with the Ganges. The river Gunduck comes from the north, and empties itſelf into the Ganges near Hajeepoor. Thoſe who drink this water are afflicted with wens in their necks, which continue to increaſe till they become as large as a cocoa-nut. Young people are the moſt ſeverely afflicted with this diſorder.

Salgram is a black ſtone, which the Hindoos hold ſacred, paying great adoration to it. The criterions of it's excellence are roundneſs, ſmallneſs, and an oily appearance. According to the difference of their forms, they have various names and properties aſcribed to them. Some of theſe ſtones are perforated with one or more holes, and ſome are quite perfect. They contain ſome gold ore. Some pretend that a worm is bred in the ſtone, which eats it's way through; and others ſay that a worm makes a paſſage into the ſtone. The Hindoos have written a large book upon the properties and virtues of this ſtone. It is a tenet of their religion, that any idol which is mutilated, thereby loſes all ſanctity,

tity, excepting theſe ſtones, which although broken, retain their efficacy. They are found in the river Sown, at the diſtance of forty coſe from the ſource.

Kerumnaſſa is a river, which, after running from the ſouth to Chowſa, then empties itſelf into the Ganges; it's water is greatly diſcommended. The river Poonpoon runs from the ſouth, and enters the Ganges at Patna. There are a number of ſmaller rivers in this Soobah, of which I take no notice.

The ſummer months here are very hot; but the winter is very temperate. The rains continue for ſix months.

The country is continually covered with verdure, and the ſoil is ſo hard, that, during the ſtormy winds which blow here, you are not much incommoded with duſt. Agriculture is here in the higheſt perfection, the rice being ſo excellent, and of ſuch a variety of ſpecies, as are no where to be equalled.

Keſaree is a ſmall grain, reſembling peaſe, which is eaten by the lower claſſes of people, but it is very unwholeſome.

Sugar-cane is cultivated here in great abundance, and in high perfection.

Mughee is that ſpecies of the beetle leaf which is moſt eſteemed; it is of a very thin and delicate texture; of a fragrant ſmell, with a beautiful colour, and the flavour is delicious.

At Muneyr grows a flower, called Mujgund, reſembling the Dehtoorah, and which for fragrance excels that of every other place.

Milk

Milk is here very good, and to be procured at a cheap rate.

It is not cuſtomary in Bahar to divide the crops. The huſbandman brings the rents himſelf, and when he makes his firſt payment, he comes dreſſed in his beſt attire.

Moſt of their houſes are rooſed with tiles. Plenty of good elephants are to be procured here. The inhabitants are famous for building boats. Horſes and camels are ſcarce. Bahar is famous for parrots and goats, and they have cut goats ſo fat as not to be able to walk, being carried about upon litters. Their fighting cocks are remarkable for affording great ſport; there are alſo plenty of different kinds of hawks. Gilded glaſs is manufactured here.

In Sircar Bahar, near a village called Rajgurh, is a quarry of ſtone, reſembling marble, of which they make ornaments. Good paper is manufactured here. Geya, the place of Hindoo worſhip, is in this Sircar; they call it Birhm Geya, being conſecrated to Brahma. Here is carried on a traffick of precious ſtones, which are brought from other countries.

In Sircar Mungeer is raiſed a ſtone wall, extending from the Ganges to the mountains; and this wall is conſidered to be the boundary between Bengal and Bahar.

In Sircar Hajypoor, there are great plenty of the fruits called Kuthul, and Budhul; ſome of the firſt are ſo large as to be too heavy a load for one man to carry.

In Sircar Chumparun, they ſow a grain called maſh, without ploughing the ground, and it requires no further attention. Long pepper grows here in the wilds.

Tirhoot has from old time been the reſidence of Hindoo

Hindoo learning. The water and air of this place are much celebrated. The inhabitants have a method of preserving milk curds for a year. If those who sell milk adulterate it, some unforeseen accident befals them. Buffaloes are here so fierce, that they will attack a tiger. Here are many lakes, the bottom of one of which is unfathomable, and the water never decreases. There are delightful groves of orange trees, which extend thirty cose. In the rainy season, the deer and tigers repair to the high spots, where the inhabitants hunt them; the deer they surround with an enclosure, and take them when they please.

Rhotas is a very strong fortress, situated upon a lofty mountain, of most difficult access; it is fourteen cose in circumference. The enclosed land is cultivated, and within this space are many springs; and water may be procured in any part, by digging three or four ells below the surface of the earth. There are several lakes within the fort. In the rains there are not less than two hundred delightful cataracts. This Soobah contains seven Sircars, subdivided into 199 Pergunnahs. The gross amount of revenue is twenty-two crore, nineteen lacks, nineteen thousand four hundred and four dams and a half, or sicca rupees 55,47,985 1 3.

One hundred and thirty-eight of these Pergunnahs are measured, and amount to twenty-four lacks, forty-four thousand one hundred and twenty beegahs, which yield to the state 18,268,1774½ dams, or sicca rupees 43,160044.

The unmeasured lands, consisting of 61 pergunnahs, are rated at 49,237,630½ dams, or sicca rupees 1,23,0940 12 5; out of which sum, 22 lacks, 72 thousand, and 149 dams, or sicca rupees 55,803 8 10 are Seyurghal.

The Soobah of Bahar furnishes 11,415 cavalry, 449,350 infantry, and 100 boats.

THE

THE SOOBAH OF ALLAHABAD.

IT is ſituated in the ſecond climate. In length from Sunjooly Jownpoor to the ſouthern mountains are 160 coſe, and the breadth, from Chowſa Ferry to Ghatempoor, includes 122 coſe. To the eaſt it has Bahar; on the north Owdh; Bundhoo lies on the ſouth; and Agra on the weſt.

The principal rivers in this Soobah are the Ganges, and the Jown (or Jumna), beſides which there are the Arund, the Geyn, the Seroo, the Birnah, and ſeveral other ſmaller ones.

Variety of fruits, flowers, and eſculent plants grow here; and it produces abundance of melons and grapes.

Agriculture is here in great perfection; but they do not cultivate any Jewary, nor Ludereh; and Mowth is ſcarce.

They fabricate here Jhewnah, Meergool, and other cloths; the moſt beautiful of which are thoſe made at Benaris, Jemalabad, and Mow. At Jownpoor, Nerwal, and ſome other places are manufactures of woollen carpets.

There are great variety, and plenty of game.

The ancient name of Allahabad was Piyaug. His majeſty gave it the name of Allahabad, and built a ſtone fort, in which are many magnificent edifices. The Hindoos call this ſpot *the king of worſhipped places*, becauſe that near to it is the junction of the Ganges, the Jumna, and the Sirſootty; although there be not any diſtinct branch of the latter viſible here.

Near

Near the town of Kuntut are caught a great number of elephants.

It is aſtoniſhing that, when the planet Jupiter enters the conſtellation Leo, a hill ariſes out of the middle of the Ganges, and remains for a month; ſo that people go upon it and perform divine worſhip.

Baranaſſey, commonly called Banaris, is a large city, ſituated between two rivers, the Birnah and the Aſſey. In ancient books this city is called Kaſſy. It is in the form of a bow, and the river Ganges reſembles the bowſtring. Formerly here was an idolatrous temple, to which the Hindoos uſed to make pilgrimages, encompaſſing it in the manner of Mecca, and performing many ceremonies like thoſe obſerved by the Hajees. It has from old time been the capital ſeat of Hindoo learning, multitudes of people flocking hither from great diſtances; and they proſecute their ſtudies and devotions with indefatigable application. Some particulars hereof ſhall be related in the ſequel of this hiſtory.

In A. H. 410, Sultan Mahmood Guznevy came hither, and gained a few converts to the faith. He viſited it a ſecond time in 413. He blockaded the fortreſs of Gauliar, but raiſed the ſiege upon terms of compromiſe. Then he formed a deſign of taking Kalinjer; but, after much entreàty, he accepted from Nund, the governor of the fort, three hundred elephants, and ſome complimentary verſes, with which he was ſo much pleaſed, that he not only continued him in that government, but alſo put fourteen other places under his command.

Jownpoor is a large city; it was founded by Sultan Feeroz, king of Dehly, who named it after his couſin Fukhered-

Fukhereddeen Jowna. Its longitude is 109 degrees and 6 minutes, and latitude 26 degrees 15 minutes.

Chunar is a ſtone fort, of incomparable ſtrength, ſituated upon a hill; and the river Ganges runs at the foot of it. Near this fort are a race of people who go quite naked, living in the wilds, and ſubſiſting by the uſe of their bows and arrows. In thoſe wilds are alſo elephants.

Kalinjer is a ſtone fort, ſituated upon a very lofty mountain. No one can tell by whom it was founded. Within it are many idolatrous temples. Here is an idol, called Kalbihroon, 18 cubits in height; and of which they relate many marvellous ſtories. In the compaſs of this fort are many ſprings and lakes, and near it are thick foreſts, where they catch elephants; the Lacheen, the Baſheh, and other birds. Ebony is found here: and a variety of wild fruits. In this neighbourhood is an iron mine. At the diſtance of 20 coſe from the fort, the huſbandmen ſometimes find ſmall diamonds; and it is ſaid that Rajah Keerut Sing, a former governor of this fort, had ſix very valuable ſtones. During his government, there lived a Brahmin who had a parrot, which returned rational anſwers to all queſtions that were put to him; and ſome aſſert that this bird remembered every thing that he heard. There lived alſo at that time a ſinger, named Bukhſhoo, who was unequalled for ſkill in the art of muſic; and the rajah had alſo two beautiful female bond-maids, who were likewiſe ſine ſingers. Sultan Bahader Gujeratty, having formed an intimacy with the rajah, wanted to have one of the three, and the rajah generouſly ſent him Bukhſhoo. Then Sheer Khan ſent and demanded the other two melodious ſingers; and, when his meſſenger returned with a refuſal, he ſurrounded the fort and cut off its ſupplies; whereby the beſieged were reduced to great diſtreſs. The rajah deſpairing of preſerv-

ing

ing his reputation, which the Hindoos hold facred, burnt his women to afhes, and then deftroyed himfelf. But God did not fuffer the wicked defigns of Sheer Khan to go unpunifhed, for no fooner had he poffeffed himfelf of the fort, but fire fell upon the magazine of powder and deftroyed him.

This foobah contains ten fircars, divided into one hundred and feventy-feven pergunnahs. Revenue 21,24,27119 dams, or ficca rupees 53,10,695—7—9, and 12,00000 beetle leaves.

It furnifhes 11,375 cavalry, 237,870 infantry, and 323 elephants.

A summary History of the Kings of Allahabad.

THIS foobah was early fubject to the emperors of Dehly; and Sultan Mahommed, fon of Feeroz Shah, upon his afcenfion of the throne, appointed to this government Mullick Sereer, a eunuch of the palace, and dignified him with the title of Sultan-ul Sherk. This eunuch had been given to Sultan Mahommed by his grandfather Khan Jehan.

At the death of Sultan-ul Sherk, his adopted fon, Mobarak Kerunfool, with the affiftance of the chiefs of the foobah, affumed the government, ftruck coin, and had the Khotbah read in his own name. When advice thereof was brought to Dehly, the emperor marched at the head of a large army, and encamped on the banks of the Ganges; where both armies came to an engagement, in which, neither having gained any fuperiority, they returned to their refpective kingdoms.

When Sultan Mahommed died, he was fucceeded in the empire of Dehly by his younger brother Ibraheem; who

who was an active and a good prince, and he punished the rebellion of Kerunfool and some others. During his reign flourished Cazy Shahebeddeen, one of the most renowned names in Hindostan for wisdom and learning. At the time Timoor came to Dehly, Shahebeddeen arrived at Jownpoor with his master Mollana Khojahgee, who was the successor of Sheikh Nasseereddeen Cheragh of Dehly. Shahmuddar who was esteemed a saint in Hindostan, was cotemporary with Shahebeddeen. But the saint and the philosopher have seldom had an affection for each other, so the Cazy and Shahmuddar did not much agree.

Upon the demise of Sultan Ibraheem, his eldest son, Bheekun Khan, mounted the throne, under the title of Mahommed. But, proving to be a bad prince, he was deposed, and his brother Hussein raised to the empire. The beginning of his reign was the admiration of every one, for justice and mildness. But, when he thought himself firmly established on the throne, he began to be proud and arrogant, when having been put to flight in battle by Sultan Behlole, this prince left in the government of Allahabad his son Barbuck, and possessed himself of the empire of Dehly.

When Sultan Behlole died, he was succeeded by Sultan Secunder. At this time Sultan Hussein, having formed alliances, and raised an army, made several attempts upon Dehly; but in him ended the Sherkyan dynasty.

The SOOBAH of OWDH.

IT is situated in the second climate. The length from Sircar Gowreckpoor to Kinoje, includes 135 cose; and the breadth, from the northern mountains of Seddehpoor to the Soobah of Allahabad, comprises

115

115 cofe. To the eaft it has Bahar; on the north lie mountains; Manickpoor bounds it on the fouth; and Kinoje on the weft.

The water and air are good. The fummer and winter are both temperate.

The large rivers are the Gehgher (or Gograh), the Gowdy (or Goomty), and the Sy. In the two firft rivers are a variety of extraordinary aquatic animals.

Agriculture is here in great perfection; the rice, in general, is excellent; but thofe called Sukdofs, Mudchker, and Chunwah, are incomparable for whitenefs, delicacy, odour, and digeftivenefs. They fow their rice three months earlier than in any other part of Hindoftan. By the time the rice is in ear, the rivers Sy and Gograh begin to overflow their banks; and by the commencement of the periodical rains, the country in general is inundated. The ftalks of rice rife as faft as the water, unlefs the inundation be very rapid before the grain is in ear, in which cafe the crops are deftroyed.

Here are great variety of fruits and flowers. Of game there are many kinds, and plenty of wild buffaloes. When the plains are inundated, the wild animals refort to the high lands, and the hunting of them affords great diverfion. Some animals remain all day in the water, juft keeping their nofes above the furface to breathe, and coming on fhore only at night.

Owdh, which is one of the largeft cities of Hindoftan, is fituated in longitude 118 degrees 6 minutes, and latitude 27 degrees 22 minutes. In ancient times this city is faid to have meafured 148 cofe in length and 36 cofe in breadth. It is efteemed one of the moft facred places of antiquity. Upon fifting the earth which is round about the city, fmall grains of gold are fometimes ſometimes obtained from it. In the Tereetah Jowg, this city was the reſidence of Rajah Ramchund, who enjoyed the twofold office of king and prophet. At the diſtance of a coſe from the city the river Goghar unites with the Sy, which confluence runs at the foot of the fort.

Near this city are two ſepulchral monuments, one ſeven and the other ſix cubits in length. The vulgar pretend that they are the tombs of Seth and Job; and they relate wonderful ſtories of them. Some alſo conjecture that in the town of Ruttenpoor is the tomb of Kobeer-unitarian, who lived in the reign of Sultan Secundur Lowdy, and to whom the door of truth having been partly opened, he ſecluded himſelf from the world, and has left behind him a great many verſes in the Hindovy language, upon the ſubject of futurity.

Biratch is a large city, delightfully ſituated, amongſt a number of gardens, upon the banks of the river Sy. Sultan Maſſaood and Rejeb Sillar are both buried here. The common people of Hindoſtan, who are Mahommedans, hold them in great veneration, making pilgrimages to them from great diſtances, going together in large bodies, and carrying banners of cloth of gold. Sultan Maſſaood was a relation of Mahmood Guznevy. Rejeb Sillar, the father of Sultan Feerooz, king of Dehly, gained renown by his auſtere life and martyrdom. Near this city is a village called Dugown, which, for a great length of time, has had a mint for copper coinage.

From the northern mountains are imported a number of articles of commerce, which are brought upon the backs of men, and by horſes and goats. The principal articles imported are the following, viz. gold, copper, lead, muſk, cowtails, honey, chook (which is an acid made of lime and lemon juice boiled

 to

to a confiftence), pomegranate feeds, grapes, dried ginger, pepper, redwood, tincar, civet, zedoary, wax, woollen cloths, wooden ware, and various fpecies of hawks, together with amber, rock-falt, afafœtida, and glafs toys. In return, they carry back earthen ware.

Neemkhar is a famous large fort, and a place of great religious refort; the river Gowdy runs near it. Here are a great number of idolatrous temples. In the neighbourhood of this place is a refervoir of water, called Brahma Wurt Koond, which bubbles up fo violently, and has fuch a circular motion, that a man cannot force his way down into it, it ejecting whatever is thrown into it. Near this place there is alfo a hill, with a very fmall fpring of water, whofe ftream runs into the Gowdy. The fpring is only four inches deep, and an ell in breadth. The Brahmins refort hither to pay their devotions. The fand, which is the bed of the ftream, fometimes affumes the form of Mahadeo, which vanifhes again fuddenly. If rice, or any other light fubftance, be thrown into this fpring, it difappears entirely. Here is alfo a place called Cheramutty, where, during the feaft of the Hooly, flames iffue out of the ground in a moft aftonifhing manner.

Luckhnow is a large city, pleafantly fituated upon the banks of the Goomty, and the fuburbs are alfo very delightful. Sheikh Meena, whom the people of this country confider as a faint, lies buried here.

Soorej Koond is a place of religious worfhip, whither numbers of people refort from far.

Khurry is a town fituated upon the banks of the river Sy, upon which people go in boats to ftrike fifh.

Belgram is a little town, very healthy, and famous for producing men with lively imaginations and melodious

dious voices. Here is a well, of which whosever drinks for forty days continuance, it enlivens his understanding and brightens his eyesight.

In this soobah are five sircars, divided into one hundred and thirty-eight pergunnahs. The measured lands are one crore, one lack, seventy-one thousand and eighty beegahs. The amount of revenue is 20,17,58,172 dams, or sicca rupees 50,43,454—4, including of Seyurghal 85,21,658 dams, or sicca rupees 2,13041—15, it supplies 7660 cavalry 168,250 infantry, and 59 elephants.

The SOOBAH of AGRA.

IT is situated in the second climate. In length, from Ghatimpoor, which confines it on the side of Allahabad to Pulwul, the boundary towards Dehly, it measures 175 cose; and its breadth is from Kinoje to Chundery, in Malwah.

It is bounded on the east by Ghatempoor; on the north by the river Ganges: on the south lies Chundery; and Pulwul confines it on the west.

In this soobah are many rivers, the chief of which are the Jown (or Jumna,) and the Chumbul. The first comes from the northern mountains; the other has its source at Hasselpoor, in Malwah; and near Calpee it unites with the Jown.

A great many situations, in the southern mountainous parts of this soobah, are remarkably pleasant and healthy.

Agriculture is here in perfection. Here is abundance

dance of flowers and ſweet-ſcented oils; and very excellent beetle-leaf.

They have melons and grapes, as fine as are produced in Iran and Turan.

Agra is a large city, the air of which is eſteemed very healthy. The river Jown runs through it for five coſe, and on both ſides are delightful houſes and gardens, inhabited by people of all nations, and where are diſplayed the productions of every climate. His majeſty has erected a fort of red ſtone, the like of which no traveller has ever beheld. It contains alone five hundred ſtone buildings, of ſurpriſing conſtruction, in the Bengal, Gujerat, and other ſtyles; and the artificers have decorated them with beautiful paintings. At the eaſtern gate are carved in ſtone two elephants, with their riders, of exquiſite workmanſhip. In former times Agra was a village, dependant upon Byaneh, where Sultan Secunder Lowdy kept his court. Here his majeſty has founded a moſt magnificent city. On the oppoſite ſide of the river is the Charbagh (or four gardens), a monument of the magnificence of the inhabitant of paradiſe (Hemayun). The author of this book was born on that ſide of the river, and there are the tombs of his anceſtors, together with that of his elder brother Sheikh Fizu, Sheikh Allaheddeen Mujzoob, Meer Ruffyeddeen Sufvy, and many other eminent perſonages are alſo interred there.

Near the city of Agra, upon the banks of the river Jown, in a village called Rungleh, is a famous place of Hindoo worſhip.

Futtehpoor was formerly a village dependant on Byaneh, and then called Sickery. Upon Agra being made the ſeat of government, it alſo became a city. It is ſituated at the diſtance of twelve coſe from the

the city of Agra. It has a ſtone fort, containing magnificent buildings, and over one of the gates are two aſtoniſhing elephants, carved in ſtone. The royal palace and the houſes of the nobility are built upon the mountain, but the plains are alſo decorated with many houſes and gardens. His majeſty has cauſed to be erected upon the top of the mountain a moſque, a college, and a monaſtery for Sooſees, which are the admiration of travellers. Adjoining to the city is a lake, extending twelve coſe, and upon the edge of it his majeſty has built an amphitheatre with high minarets. The amphitheatre is uſed for the game of chowgong; and here are alſo exhibited the elephant fights. In this neighbourhood is a quarry of red ſtone, out of which they cut pillars and ſlabs of any dimenſion.

In Agra they manufacture blankets and fine ſtuffs; and here are aſſembled artificers of every denomination.

Byaneh, in former times, was a capital city. It has a large fort, containing many buildings and ſubterraneous caverns, where there are now found warlike weapons and kitchen utenſils. And here is a very high tower. The mangoes of this place are excellent, and ſome of them weigh above two pounds. This town is famous for very white ſugar. Here is a well, with the water of which they knead the ſugar into a paſte like flour, and form it into cakes, which they call Gundoreh, and it is carried to great diſtances as a rarity. It cannot be made with any other water. The indigo of this place is very fine, ſelling from ten to ſixteen rupees per maund. Excellent henna, of a high colour, is alſo to be procured here. This town is the burial place of many illuſtrious men. Toodeh Bheem is a place, at the diſtance of three coſe, where there is a cave full of water, whoſe depth is unfathomable. Mines of copper and torquoiſes have been diſcovered here,

here, but they will not defray the expence of being worked.

Mehtrah is a city upon the banks of the river Jown, where are many idolatrous temples, to which the Hindoos resort.

Calpee is also a city upon the banks of the Jown, and where are the tombs of many great personages. Very good sugar is to be procured here. At the time that the Sherkyan dynasty first established themselves, the princes of Calpee were tributary to Dehly. When Kudder Khan, who governed here, rebelled, Sultan Howshung came from Malwah, received his submission, and then reinstated him in his government. Sultan Mahmood, of the Sherkyan dynasty, took it from Nuffer Khan, the son of Kudder Khan.

Kinoje, in ancient times, was the capital city of Hindostan.

Gauliar is a famous fort, in which are many stately buildings, and there is a stone elephant over the gate. The air and water of this place are both esteemed good. It has always been celebrated for fine singers and beautiful women; here is an iron mine.

Allore has considerable manufactures of woollen carpets and glass.

At Beerat are several copper-mines, so profitable, that, out of a maund of ore, they extract thirty-five seers of metal. Here has also been discovered a silver mine, but it is not worth working.

Near the mountains of Narnole is a well, which the Hindoos worship; and when the Tith of Amavus *

* Vide Vol. I.

happens

happens upon a Friday, the water flows over at sunrise.

There are alſo copper mines at Singhoneh Dadypoor, and at Kotepotely. And at the town of Kanwery are many cold and hot ſprings.

This ſoobah contains thirteen ſircars, ſubdivided into two hundred and three pergunnahs. The meaſured lands are two crore, ſeventy-eight lacks, ſixty-two thouſand one hundred and nine beegahs, and eighteen biſwahs. The amount of revenue is ſixty-four crore, ſixty-two lacks, fifty thouſand three hundred and four dams, or ſicca rupees 1,61,56,257—9—6; out of which there are of Seyurghal dams, one crore, twenty-one lacks, five thouſand ſeven hundred and three and a half, or ſicca rupees 2,55,392—9—3. It furniſhes 50,600 cavalry, 577,570 infantry, and 221 elephants.

The SOOBAH of MALWAH.

It is ſituated in the ſecond climate. The length, from Kurrah to Banſwareh, compriſes 245 coſe; and the breadth, from Chundery to Nuderbar, includes 230 coſe. It is bounded on the eaſt by Bandhnoo; on the north by Nerwer and mountains; on the ſouth by Boklaneh; and on the weſt by Gujerat and Ajmeer. The rivers Nerbuddah, Soopera, Calyſind, Neem, and Lowdy, flow through this ſoobah; and you cannot travel two or three coſe, without meeting with ſtreams of good water, whoſe banks are ſhaded by the wild willow, and other trees; and decorated with the hyacinth, and other beautiful and odoriferous flowers.

Here are abundance of lakes and verdant plains, ornamented with innumerable magnificent and elegant buildings.

buildings. The climate is so temperate, that in winter there is no occasion for warm clothing; nor is it necessary in summer to cool the water with saltpetre. But in the four rainy months, the night air is cold enough to render a quilt necessary.

The situation of this soobah, compared with the other parts of Hindostan, is somewhat high, and all the land is arable. Both harvests are very good. Wheat, poppies, sugar-cane, mangoes, musk-melons, and grapes, are here in high perfection.

In Hasselpoor the vine bears fruit twice a year. The beetle-leaf is very fine. Here are manufactured very good cloths.

The people of this soobah give their children opium to eat till they are three years old. The peasant, and even the market people of this soobah, are never without arms.

Owjain is a large city, on the banks of the Soopera, which is held in high veneration by the Hindoos. It is astonishing that sometimes this river flows with milk.

In the 40th year of the present reign, the author of this book was going to the Dekhan, by order of his majesty, and when he arrived at Owjain, he was assured that a week before, or the sixteenth of the month Ferverdeen, after eight o'clock at night, this prodigy happened; and people of all ranks, Mussulmen and Hindoos, took up some of the milk*. In this

* It is impossible to reconcile this fable to reason. Had our author only said that the water of this river sometimes resembles milk, it might have been accounted for, by supposing that it was then accidentally impregnated with chalk. POPE, in his Windsor Forest, says of one of our rivers,

"And chalky Wey, that rolls a milky wave."

this city and its suburbs are 360 buildings, for the religious worship of Brahmins, and other Hindoos. Also in its vicinity is a well, called Kalbadeh, the water of which flows incessantly into a cistern, which is continually running over, and yet remains full. On all sides of it the ancients had erected delightful seats.

Gurreh was formerly independent of this soobah. It abounds with forests, in which are great numbers of wild elephants. The husbandmen here pay the revenues in gold mohurs and elephants. This province is so fertile, that it supplies both the Dekhan and Gujerat with grain.

Chundery is a very large ancient city, in which is a stone fort. It contains fourteen thousand stone houses, three hundred and eighty-four markets, three hundred and sixty caravanseras, and twelve thousand mosques.

Toomur is a town situated on the banks of the river Butmah, in which are seen mermaids. Here is an idolatrous temple, in which, if you beat a drum, it makes no noise.

In sircar Beejagurh there are many wild elephants.

Mundoo is a large city, whose fortress is 12 cose in circuit, and in the centre of it is a minaret of eight stories. This city was formerly the capital of the Soobah, and here are many monuments of ancient magnificence. Here are the tombs of the Kuljyan Sultans. From the dome, which is over the sepulchre of Sultan Mahmud, the son of Howshung, there drops water in the height of summer, to the great astonishment of the ignorant; but men of understanding know how to account for it. Here is a species of tamarind as big as the cocoa-nut, the pulp of which is very white.

The

The learned amongſt the Hindoos relate that in this ſoobah there was diſcovered a ſtone, which, upon touching any metal, immediately converted it into gold; and they call this ſtone *Paris*. The following is the ſtory they tell of the manner in which it was diſcovered. Before the time of Bickermajeet, there reigned in this ſoobah Jyſing Deo, who was a very upright and juſt prince. During his reign, this *Paris-stone* accidentally ſtruck againſt the ſickle of a graſs-cutter, who was aſtoniſhed at the change which it effected in his ſickle; and, ſuppoſing it to be injured by the accident, he carried it to one Mondun, a blackſmith, to have it put to rights. The blackſmith diſcovering the property of the *Paris-stone*, took it from him, and by making a proper uſe of it, acquired immenſe wealth. At laſt, he thought ſuch an ineſtimable prize ought only to belong to the monarch of his country, and therefore carried and preſented it to him. The Rajah, out of the wealth which he obtained by this acquiſition, in the ſpace of twelve years built a fort; and at the requeſt of the blackſmith, many of the ſtones of the walls thereof were cut into the form of an anvil. Some time after the fort was completed, the Rajah gave a public entertainment on the banks of the Nerbuddah, and having determined with himſelf to beſtow a conſiderable largeſs upon his family Brahmin, put the *Paris-stone* into his hands. The ignorant Brahmin, diſpleaſed with ſuch a gift, threw it with indignation into the river. When he was informed of what he had done, he was confounded with ſhame, and overwhelmed with grief, and jumped into the river, to endeavour to recover it, but the water was ſo deep that he could not reach the bottom. And they ſay that to this day, that part of the river is unfathomable.

Dehar was the ſeat of government during the reign of Rajah Bhowj, and ſeveral of his ſucceſſors. The vine bears fruit here twice in a year. Firſt in the month

month of Auguſt, and the ſecond in December; but the firſt vintage is the beſt.

In Sircar Hatundyah are plenty of wild elephants.

Nuderbar is famous for muſk-melons and grapes.

This ſoobah contains 12 ſircars, ſubdivided into 301 pergunnahs, The meaſured land is 44,66,221 beegahs, and 6 biſwahs. The amount of revenue, twenty-four crore, ſix lack, ninety-five thouſand and fifty-two dams; or ſicca rupees 617,376—4—15, out of which eleven lacks, fifty thouſand, four hundred and thirty-three dams, or ſicca rupees 28,760—13, are Seyurghal. It contains 280,816 cavalry, 68,000 infantry, and 90 elephants.

A summary History of the Kings of Malwah.

IT is ſaid that two thouſand three hundred and fifty-five years, five months, and twenty-ſeven days, prior to the date of this book, which is the fortieth year of the reign, a man named Mahahmah, who was famed for the auſterity of his manners, built in this ſoobah a Fire-Temple, and worſhipped in it; and other pious perſons uniting themſelves with him, performed their religious rites: And many devoting themſelves for righteouſneſs ſake, threw themſelves into the flames. The tribe of Boodh, diſpleaſed with this cuſtom, complained againſt it to their prince; ſetting forth that many people were deſtroyed in this temple, and recommending the abolition of fire-worſhip amongſt the Brahmins, as the only means of aboliſhing this abuſe. The prince, in conſequence, prohibited men from ignicoly. Whereupon a number of the inhibited beſought Heaven to ſend them a mighty perſon, to puniſh the tribe of Boodh,

Boodh, and re-establish the religion of the Brahmins. The holy fire had been extinguished for some time, but, at the command of God, there issued from the temple a person under a human form, with a divine countenance, and carrying in his hand a bright sword. This person, who was called Dhunjy, in a short time became king, and gave new lustre to the religion of the Brahmins. He afterwards left the Dekhan, and made Malwah the seat of his government. He lived to a great age, and the kingdom was inherited by his children, till that Putraj, the fifth in descent from him, dying without children, the nobles made Adutpunwar his successor. He was the founder of the Punwar dynasty. When Heymert was killed in battle, Gundrup was raised to the throne. The Hindoos believe that God caused the soul of Heymert to transmigrate into the body of Gundrup, who was a just and a munificent prince, and made his kingdom flourish. He had a son named Bickermajeet, who upon his death succeeded to the throne; and greatly extended his dominions. The Hindoos to this day make use of the commencement of his reign for an æra, and they relate many wonderful stories of him. It is certain, that by the knowledge of talismans and necromancy, he performed feats that astonished the vulgar.

Chunderpaul obtained the kingdom, and conquered all Hindostan.

Beejehnund, once when he was hunting, found a dropt infant near a Munj plant*, who from that circumstance was called Munj; and he educated him like his own son. When Beejehnund died, his own son Bhowj was an infant; on which account Munj was raised to the throne, and he was killed in the wars of the Dekhan. After him, in the 541st year of the æra

* A species of henbane.

of

of Bickermajeet, Bhowj ſucceeded to the kingdom. He made conſiderable additions to his dominions by conqueſt; his reign was celebrated for his juſtice and liberality, and he gave ſuch encouragement to men of learning and wiſdom, that no leſs than five hundred ſages were to be found in his palace. He made trial of the abilities of them all, and found the moſt eminent among them were Beruj, and Dhunpaul, whoſe compoſitions are highly eſteemed to this day. It is related, that upon the birth of Bhowj, through the miſtake of the aſtrologers, or by the fault of thoſe whoſe buſineſs it was to mark the hour of his nativity, his father was convinced from his horoſcope, that he would never come to any good, and therefore ordered him to be expoſed in a diſtant part of the kingdom. He was here nouriſhed by the friendly hand of Divine Providence, for there could not poſſibly have been any intervention of human aid. The philoſopher Beruj, juſt mentioned, had not then become conſpicuous.

He now aſſiſted the fortune of Bhowj. He calculated his horoſcope with great care. He then wrote down a prediction of his future greatneſs and longevity; and threw the paper in the way of the rajah, who no ſooner beheld it, than paternal affection began to riſe in his breaſt. He again aſſembled together all the wiſe men, and made them ſcrutinize Bhowj's horoſcope, when it was diſcovered from whence the error in the former calculation had ariſen. He then went himſelf and ſought out Bhowj, who ſoon gave ſigns of future greatneſs. When he was eight years old, Munj (who on account of his minority at the death of his father, had been raiſed to the throne) entertained jealouſies of him, and employed perſons to deſtroy him ſecretly; but theſe agents taking compaſſion upon Bhowj, contrived his eſcape. At his departure he gave them a paper, containing what he would have them to ſay to the rajah, when he ſhould enquire about him. The ſubſtance of the writing was this, "What kind of man "art thou who, from the darkneſs of thy ſoul, ſtaineſt "thy hands with the blood of the innocent. No mo- "narch hath carried with him, at his death, either king- "dom or treaſure; but you ſuppoſe that your reign "is to be immortal, and that you will experience no- "thing but happineſs." When this was read to Munj, he repented of what he had done, and ſhowed evident ſigns of contrition. When his confidents found him thus diſpoſed, they diſcovered the truth. The rajah, at theſe tidings, returned thanks to the Almighty, and nominated Bhowj his ſucceſſor in the kingdom.

At the death of Bhowj, his ſon Jy ſucceeded to the kingdom. When Jy died, there was not found any one of the Punwar tribe worthy to wear the crown; on which account Chytepaul, an eminent Zemeendar, was choſen king. He founded the Tenore dynaſty. After Kenwerpaul, the Chowhan dynaſty poſſeſſed the kingdom. In the reign of Maldeo, Sheikh Shah came from Ghuzneen, and conquered Malwah, where he enjoyed a long reign. When he died, his ſon Allaheddeen was an infant, whereupon his vizeer, Dherumraj Soud poſſeſſed himſelf of the kingdom. But when Allaheddeen came to years of maturity, he made war upon Dherumraj, and put him to death. Chytepaul, a deſcendant of Manickdeo Chowhan, and who was in the ſervice of Kemaleddeen, became his murderer, and aſſumed the kingdom. In the reign of Beerſein, an Afghan entered into a confederacy with ſome others, who laid themſelves in ambuſh, and killed the rajah whilſt he was hunting. He then ſeized the kingdom, and took the title of Jelaleddeen. Kerukſein, the ſon of Beerſein, having rendered many eminent ſervices to his maſter, the king of Kamroop, the king in return gave him his daughter in marriage, and appointed him his heir. When he had obtained the kingdom of Kamroop, by the death of his father-in-law, he led an army into Malwah

Malwah, to revenge the murder of his father, and Alum Shah was killed in battle. In the reign of Suckut Singh, Bahader Shah, king of the Dekhan, brought an army againſt him, and having killed the rajah, proceeded to Dehly, where he fell into the hands of Sultan Shahaheddeen. When Sultan Ghiaſſeddeen Baleen poſſeſſed the kingdom of Dehly, he was engaged in war with Sultan Mahommed, the ſon of Feeroz Shah. At the death of Ghiaſſeddeen, there was great confuſion in the kingdom of Dehly; upon which Dilawer Khan Gowry, the viceroy of Malwah; Zuffer Khan, viceroy of Gujerat; Khyzir Khan, viceroy of Mooltan; and Khowjah Sereer, viceroy of Jownpoor, all four rebelled, and made themſelves independent princes. Some of the nobles of Ghiaſſeddeen raiſed to the throne of Dehly his ſon Alrup Khan, and gave him the title of Howſhung. It is ſaid that his father had been poiſoned by his order. Sultan Mozuffer Gujeratty attacked Howſhung, and took him priſoner, and made his own brother Nuſſeer Khan king of Dehly. But he proving a tyrant, was depoſed, and Mouſa, Howſhung's couſin, raiſed to the throne. Upon this Sultan Mozuffer releaſed Howſhung from his confinement, and ſent him to Dehly along with his ſon Ahmed Khan. Howſhung gained the victory, which replaced him upon the throne. After the death of Mozuffer, Howſhung ſeveral times carried his arms into Gujerat, and had ſeveral battles with Ahmed, but was always unſucceſsful. At length he attempted to effect his purpoſe by artifice, and diſguiſing himſelf as a merchant, went to Gujnagur. But the governor of that fortreſs being apprized thereof, came himſelf to the caravan, and made the king priſoner. But Howſhung declaring that he came only to purchaſe elephants, the governor preſented him with ſome very fine ones, and ſet him at liberty. Howſhung carried on wars againſt Mobarek Shah, ſon of Khyzir Khan, king of Dehly; and alſo againſt Ibraheem Sherkee; and Sultan Ahmed of the

Dekhan.

Dekhan. At his death the nobles, conformably to his last will, made his son Hussein Khan his successor, under the title of Mahommed Shah. But Mahommed Khan, his relation, bribed the cupbearer to put poison into his wine. The generals of his army kept his death secret, wishing to raise to the throne his son Massaood Khan. And they sent a messenger to invite to court Mahommed Khan. He returned for answer, that if they had any business to deliberate upon, they must come to him. They inconsiderately went to him, and being seized, were obliged to consent to his being made king, under the title of Sultan Mahmood.

This prince maintained wars against Sultan Mahommed, son of Mobarek Shah, king of Dehly; and Sultan Ahmed, king of Gujerat; and Hussein Sherkee; and Ranna Gownho. What greatly contributed to the glory of his reign, was an embassy from Sultan Abusyed Mirza, who sent him to Khowjeh Jemaleddeen Astarabady, with valuable presents. He was afterwards deposed by some of his ungrateful courtiers; but was restored to his kingdom by the assistance of Sultan Mozuffer, king of Gujerat. He was taken prisoner in battle by the Ranna, who generously sent him back to Malwah. In another battle he fell into the hands of Sultan Bahader of Gujerat, and he died as they were conveying him to Chumpaneer, upon which Malwah was annexed to Gujerat. When the late emperor Hemayun conquered these provinces, he added them to Agra. After that, one Mulloor, who was of the family of Sultan Mahmood, possessed himself of Malwah, and assumed the title of Cader Khan. During the usurpation of Sheer Khan, his governor of Malwah was named Shujahut Khan. He refused obedience to Dehly, under the reign of Seleem Khan. During the government of Mobarez Khan, this Soobah again became tributary to Dehly. But upon the death of Mobarez Khan, the eldest son of Cader Khan, named Bazeed, ceed, rebelled, and reigned under the title of Bahader Shah.

But when the auſpicious ſtar of royalty ſhed it's reſplendent influence, this ſoobah again became a part of the empire.

TABLES

Of the Princes who have reigned in the Soobah of Malwah.

TABLE I.

The Family of Dhunjy, five Rajahs reigned 387 years, 7 months, and 3 days.

	Ys.	Ms.	Ds.		Ys.	Ms.	Ds.
Dhunjy -	100	0	0	Nerbahen -	100	0	0
Jeetchunder	86	7	3	Putraj -	100	0	0
Salbahen -	1	0	0				

TABLE II.

Eighteen Princes, of the Punwar Cast, reigned 1062 years, 11 months, and 17 days.

	Ys.	Ms.	Ds.		Ys.	Ms.	Ds.
Adutpunwar	86	7	3	Chunderſein	86	3	2
Birmahraj	30	7	3	Kurrekſein	85	0	0
Atbirmah	90	0	0	Chutterkote	1	0	0
Sudhrowſheneh	80	0	0	Kenckſein	86	0	0
Heymert	100	0	0	Chunderpaul	100	0	0
Gundrup	35	0	0	Mehinderpaul	7	0	0
Bickermajeet	100	2	3	Kurrumchund	1	0	1

 Bejynund

	Ys.	Ms.	Ds.		Ys.	Ms.	Ds.
Bejynund	60	0	0	Bhowj	100	0	0
Munj	—			Jychund	10	2	0

TABLE III.

Eleven Rajahs, of the Tenore Cast, reigned 142 *years, and* 3 *days.*

	Ys.	Ms.	Ds.		Ys.	Ms.	Ds.
Jeetpaul Tenore	5	0	0	Rana Buketmull	5	0	0
Rana Raju	5	0	0	Roy Sukenpaul	5	0	0
Rana Baju	1	2	0	Roy Keyretpaul	5	0	0
Rana Jalu	20	0	0	Roy Anunpaul	60	0	0
Rana Chundra	30	0	0	Konwerpaul	1	0	0
Rana Bahader	5	0	0				

TABLE IV.

Eleven Rajahs, of the Chowhan Cast, reigned 140 *years.*

	Years.		Years.
Rajah Jugdeo Chowhan	10	Bhuldeo - -	10
Jugernaut, his nephew	10	Nanekdeo - -	9
Herdeo - -	15	Keyrutdeo -	11
Baſſdeo - -	16	Pihtowra - -	21
Sirrydeo - -	15	Maldeo - -	9
Dirhemdeo -	14		

TABLE V.

Twelve Princes reigned 77 *years.*

	Years.		Years.
Sheikh Shah -	70	Kemaleddeen -	12
Dirhemraj Soud	20	Jeetpaul Chowhan	20
Allaheddeen, ſon of Sheikh Shah	20	Hurchund -	20
		Keyrutchund -	2

Oogerſein

	Reigned years.		Reigned years.
Oogerſein - -	13	Tipperſein - -	10
Soorejnund -	12		

TABLE VI.

Eight Princes reigned 205 *years.*

	Reigned years.		Reigned years.
Jilaleddeen -	22	Beerſal - -	16
Alum Shah -	24	Purenmull -	32
Kehruckſein -	8	Hurnund - -	62
Nurbahen -	20	Suckutſingh	60

TABLE VII.

Ten Princes reigned 142 *years,* 2 *months, and* 4 *days.*

	Reigned.
Bahader Shah -	ſome months.
Dilawer Khan Ghowry	20 years.
Howſhung Shah -	30 years.
Mahommed Shah -	1 year and ſome months
Sultan Mahmood, Howſhung's uncle -	34 years.
Sultan Ghiaſſeddeen	32 years.
Sultan Naſſereddeen	11 years 4 months & 3 days
Sultan Mahmood -	26 years 6 months & 11 days
Cader Shah - -	6 years.
Shujahut Khan -	12 years.

The SOOBAH of DANDEES.

THIS ſoobah was originally called Khandees. Upon the conqueſt of the fortreſs of Aſſeer, and when this ſoobah

soobah made a government for Sultan Daniel, the name was changed into Dandees. It is situated in the second climate. In length from Poorgong, which joins to Hindiah, to Lelung, bordering upon the territory of Ahmednagur, it measures 75 cose; and the breadth from Jamood, which confines it towards Berar and Pall, joining to Malwah, is 50 cose. It is bounded on the north and west by Malwah; Kalneh confines it on the south; on the east lies Berar; and on the north large mountains. It abounds with rivers and rivulets. The principal river is the Talee, which has it's source between Berar and Gowndwaneh, and it is also called the Poorny. The air of this soobah is delightful; and the winter is very temperate. Jewary is the grain chiefly cultivated here, and in several places they have three crops of it in a year. Their esculent plants are remarkably fine; their rice is excellent; and they have great plenty of flowers and fruits, together with beetle-leaf in abundance.

This soobah is famous for the manufacture of a fine stuff called Abusteh; and at Dehrungong are fabricated Seerrysaf and Bhiroon.

Asseer is a fort where the governor of the province resides. It is situated upon a lofty mountain; there are three other forts encompassing it; and it is incomparably strong. At the foot of the fort is a very large city.

Burhanpoor is a large city, situated on the banks of the river Tapty, and at three cose distant from Asseer. It lies in latitude twenty-one degrees forty minutes. It has many gardens, in some of which is found sandal-wood. The city is inhabited by people of all nations, and abounds with handicraftsmen. In the summer this city is covered with dust, and during the rains, the streets are full of mud and slime.

Adelabad

Adelabad is a good town, and near it is a lake which the Hindoos hold in great veneration. They ſay that Rajah Jefferut expiated his crime here. This lake is always full of water, and it's banks are highly cultivated.

Changdavy is a village, near which the rivers Tapty and Poorna unite their ſtreams; which confluence, held ſacred by the Hindoos, is by them called *Jiggerteerut*, or *the liver of adored places*. There is alſo in this neighbourhood an image of Mahadeo, of which they relate the following ſtory: There was a blind man, who always carried about him an image of Mahadeo, to which he uſed to pay daily adoration. It happened that he loſt it at this place, upon which being greatly diſtreſſed, he formed of ſand an image reſembling it, which he worſhipped as he had done the original. By the will of the Almighty the figure of ſand became ſtone, and is ſaid to be the one above-mentioned. Near it is a ſpring, which the Hindoos believe to be the Ganges. They ſay that, by the power of God, a certain devout man uſed to go conſtantly to the Ganges, and return again the ſame day. One night the river Ganges appeared to him in a dream, and ſaid, "Ceaſe from all this labour, for I will ſpring up here in your cell." Accordingly, in the morning the ſpring appeared, and is running at this day.

Jamood is a very fine pergunnah: near it is a very lofty fort, upon a mountain.

Damerny is a populous town, in the vicinity of which is a reſervoir, the water of which continually boils. The Hindoos worſhip it.

Chowpurreh is a large town, well inhabited. Near it is a place of worſhip called Ramiſſer, being the confluence of the rivers Kurney and Tapty. The Hindoos

doos come here from great diſtances to pay their adorations. The fort of Melunga is ſituated near this place.

Thalny was for ſome time the reſidence of the Feerookyan dynaſty. Although the fort is ſituated upon a plain, it nevertheleſs is of great ſtrength.

In this ſoobah are thirty-two pergunnahs, which are all in high cultivation. The huſbandmen are dutiful ſubjects, and very laborious. They are of the following tribes, viz. Koony, Bheib, and Gownd. Thoſe laſt named tame lions, ſo as to make them do any thing they pleaſe, and many wonderful ſtories are told of them.

The amount of the revenues of this ſoobah is 1,264,762 Berary tungahs, and the conqueſt of Aſſeer made a ſmall addition to the ſum. The tungah is reckoned at 24 dams.

A summary History of the Kings of Dandees.

FORMERLY this country was deſolate, except that a few people inhabited Aſſeer, which was their place of worſhip, and called Aſootahma. It is ſaid that Mullick Rajee, from whom Bahader was the ninth in lineal deſcent, through the verſatility of fortune, came from Bundur to this country, and ſettled in the village of Keerandeey, dependant upon Tahleenir. But being moleſted by the natives, he went to Dehly and entered the ſervice of Sultan Feeroz. As he was an expert huntſman, the king was pleaſed with him, and told him he ſhould have any thing he could wiſh for. Upon this he obtained a grant of the village of Keerandeey. By his prudent management, he peopled the deſerted lands, and brought them into cultivation. In A. H.

784

784 he ſat on his throne at Tahleenir, under the title of Adel Shah, and reigned 17 years. He was ſucceeded by his ſon, Ghereeb Khan, called Nuſſeer Shah. From the commencement of his reign, this kingdom was called Khandees. He reigned 40 years, 6 months, and 26 days. After him reigned 3 years, 8 months, and 3 days, his ſon Meeran Shah, who ſome alſo call Adel Shah. Then came to the throne his ſon Mobarek Shah Chowkundy Sultan, who reigned 17 years, 6 months, and 29 days. Next his ſon Adel Shah Jva, whoſe name, before he came to the throne, was Aſen Khan, reigned 46 years, 8 months, and 2 days. He marched to Burhanpoor, and after making himſelf maſter of Aſſeer, married the daughter of Sultan Ahmed Gujeratty, who founded the city of Gujerat. When Adel Shah died, his brother Daoud Shah obtained the throne, and reigned 7 years, 1 month, and 17 days. Adel Shah, the ſon of Aſen Khan, took refuge in Gujerat. Sultan Mahommed, Bungerah Rajee, king of Gujerat, gave him his daughter in marriage, went with him to Khandees, and conquered the kingdom for him, after which he returned to his own territory. Adel Shah reigned 13 years. He left behind him two ſons, Meeran Mahommed Shah, and Mobarek Shah. Sultan Bahader, king of Gujerat, nominated for the heir of his kingdom Meeran Mahommed, and made him guardian of his ſon Mahommed, and of his own brother Mobarek. Meeran, being a wiſe and upright prince, put Mahommed in poſſeſſion of the kingdom of Gujerat, and contented himſelf with Khandees. He reigned 16 years, 2 months, and 3 days. At his death the nobles raiſed to the throne Rajee, the ſon of Meeran Shah; but Mobarek depoſed him, and reigned 31 years, 6 months, and 5 days. He was ſucceeded by his ſon Meeran Mahommed, who reigned 9 years, 9 months, and 15 days. He had for his ſucceſſor his youngeſt brother Rajah Aly Khan, who aſſumed the title of Adel Shah. He was killed in the wars in the Dekhan, fighting

fighting under his majeſty's victorious ſtandards. His body was interred at Burhanpoor, after a reign of 21 years, 3 months, and 20 days. At his death the throne devolved to his ſon Khyzir Khan, who, upon his inauguration, took the title of Bahader Shah; but, proving a bad prince, his kingdom was taken from him, in the 45th year of our emperor's reign.

The SOOBAH of BERAR.

THE ancient names of this ſoobah are Durdatut, Ruddaroodyut, and Tittkener. It is ſituated in the ſecond climate. The length, from Putaleh to Beeragurh, is 200 coſe; and the breadth, from Bunder to Hindiah, meaſures 180 coſe. On the eaſt it joins to Beeragurh; on the north lies Settara; on the ſouth Hindiah; and on the weſt Telinganeh.

Mekhur is a populous country, ſituated between two of the ſouthern mountains of this ſoobah, one of which is called Bundeh, and on the top of it are the following forts, viz. Kaweel, Nernaleh, Meelgurh, Berooſha, Mehawer, and Ramgurh.

The air of this ſoobah is very temperate. It is highly cultivated. Here are many rivers, the principal of which is called the Gungkotemy, and ſometimes the Godawery. The Hindoos have dedicated this river to Kotum, in the ſame manner as the Ganges to Mahadeo; they relate wonderful ſtories regarding it, and hold it in great veneration. The ſource of this river is in the mountains of Sihya, near Turneek, and paſſing through the territory of Ahmednagur, it enters Berar, and from thence runs into Telinganeh. When the planet Jupiter enters the ſign of Leo, people come from great diſtances to worſhip this river. The Talee and the Tapty

Tapty are alſo ſacred ſtreams. The river Poorna takes its riſe near Deywalgong; the Sirowda has its ſource ten coſe higher up the country than the Talee. The Nupta alſo ſprings up near Deywalgong.

The following are particular idiomatical appellations in this ſoobah. A Chowdry * they call Deyſmuck; a Cannoongou, with them, is Deyſpandeh; a Mokuddem (or principal huſbandman) they ſtyle Puttiel †; and a Putwary * they name Kulkurnee.

Eletchpoor is a large city, where the governor of the ſoobah reſides. Here grows a very fragant flower, called Boohenchunpah, which reſembles the violet in colour, and it has hardly any ſtalk.

At the diſtance of ſeven coſe, from the fort of Kaweel, is a very ſtrong fort, where there is a ſpring with which they water ſteel.

Punnar is likewiſe a ſtrong fort, which is watered on three ſides by two rivers.

Kheyrleh is a plain, and in the centre of it is a hill which is held ſacred. At the diſtance of four coſe from this is a well, which petrifies any bone that is thrown into it. To the eaſt of this fort is a zemeendar named Chatwa, who commands 2000 cavalry, 50,000 infantry, and 100 elephants. Daddher Row is a Zemeendar, whoſe territory lies to the northweſt of this fort; he commands 200 cavalry and 5000 infantry. To the north of it reſides Naher Row, a zemeendar, commanding 2000 cavalry and 5000 infantry. Near to his territory is another zemeendar, called Huſleea Row, whoſe country is at preſent overrun by the tribe of Gownd. Here are wild elephants. He is tributary

* Vide Vol. I.

† This is one of the appellatives given to Madhowjee Scindia.

to Malwah. Chatwa is tributary to Gurreh, and the other zemeendars abovementioned are dependant upon Sircar Hindiah.

Nernaleh is a large fort, containing many buildings, and ſituated on the top of a mountain.

Beeja Row is a zemeendar of this ſoobah, who commands 50 cavalry and 3000 infantry. Doongur Khan is likewiſe a zemeendar, who commands the ſame number of troops, and they are both of the Gownd tribe.

Near Ballapoor are two rivers, amongſt the ſands of which are found ſtones variegated with beautiful colours, which the people cut into various forms. At the diſtance of ſix coſe from Ballapoor, Sultan Morad built a palace, which has now become the centre of a city.

Near Meelgurh is a ſpring called Shapoor, the water of which petrifies wood, and other ſoft ſubſtances.

Kullem is an ancient city: it is famous for buffaloes. Near it is a zemeendar named Bubjeo, of the tribe of Gownd, and he is alſo called Chanda. He commands 1000 cavalry and 40,000 infantry.

In Beeragurh is a diamond mine; and here are manufactured flowered ſtuffs. It is dependant upon Bubjeo, who has but lately conquered it. Near it are found wild elephants in great number. The former inhabitants now reſide near Baſſem, and they are called Hutkeran. They formerly commanded 1000 cavalry and 50,000 infantry. They are in general a refractory and perfidious race.

The Bunjerah zemeendary has 100 cavalry and 10,000

10,000 infantry. The present zemeendar is a woman. The two last-mentioned zemeendars are rajpoots.

The fort of Mahore is very pleasantly situated upon a mountain, and near it is a Hindoo temple, called Jugdeena, dedicated to Doorga. Here are buffaloes that give abundance of milk. The zemeendar of this territory is of a particular tribe of rajpoots, called Ranna.

Manick Durg is a fort upon a mountain, surrounded with wilds. It is near Chanda, and is an independent territory.

In Sircar Pahtery is a town called Chitore, which is a great mart for precious stones and other valuable articles.

Sircar Telinganeh was subject to Koteb-ul-Mulk. The natives are called Telingeh. It has lately been annexed to Berar.

In Indore and Neermul there are steel mines. These places are also famous for very neat stone vessels. Their oxen are very fine. The house cocks, which are bred here, have black blood and bones.

Ramgurh is a strong fort, situated upon a mountain, surrounded with wilds. His majesty has not yet got possession of it. Here are elephants.

Lenar is a part of the Mekhur division. It is a great place of religious resort, and is called Bishen Gyah. The Hindoos say there are three places where, if charity be bestowed, it obtains pardon for the deceased. The first is the Gyah of Bahar, which is dedicated to Brahma. The second Gyah is this which is dedicated to Rooder, or Bishen. And the third is near Beeja-

Beejapoor, being a reſervoir of water, with a very deep ſpring in it. The reſervoir meaſures a coſe in length, and the ſame in breadth, and it is encompaſſed by high mountains. On theſe mountains is a ſpring of ſalt water; but the water which is taken up from the centre and near the edges is perfectly freſh. Theſe mountains produce all the requiſites for making glaſs and ſoap. And here are ſaltpetre works, which yield a conſiderable revenue to the ſtate, from the duties collected upon them. Alſo, on the top of theſe mountains is a ſpring, upon the mouth of which is carved the figure of an ox. When Amavus falls upon Monday, the water of this fountain runs into the reſervoir at Beejapoor, as deſcribed above. Here are great numbers of monkeys.

In the neighbourhood of this place is a zemeendar, called Wayilleh, who is a rajpoot, and commands 100 cavalry and 10,000 infantry. There is alſo another zemeendar of the ſame tribe, and who commands a like number of troops.

Puttyaleh, of which Puttyalnagry is a dependancy, is a ſtrong fort on the top of a mountain. In Puttyaleh are four idolatrous temples, in which are ſome aſtoniſhing idols.

In this vicinity is a rajpoot zemeendar, named Midnee Row, who commands 200 cavalry and 2000 infantry. Kamajeo is another rajpoot zemeendar, with 100 cavalry and 1000 infantry.

This ſoobah contains 13 ſircars, ſubdivided into 142 pergunnahs, the revenues of which are collected by Nuſſuk (or a valuation of the crops.) The tungah of this country is equal to eight of thoſe of Dehly. Originally the amount revenue was three crore and a half of tungahs, or 56 crore of dams. Some of the princes to of the Dekhan exceeded this ſum by 25 lacks, 25,350 tungahs; the groſs amount of which was 37,525,350 tungahs. During the government of Sultan Morad, there was a further increaſe of 26 lacks, 37,454 tungahs; raiſing the amount up to 4,162,704 Berary tungahs, being equivalent to 642,603,262 dams.

Eight pergunnahs, which properly belong to Sircar Kullern, are now poſſeſſed by Chanda, and yield no revenue to the ſtate. Neither are any collections obtained from 22 pergunnahs in Sircar Kehrleh, they being in the poſſeſſion of Chanya, and other independent zemeendars.

This ſoobah originally formed a part of the Dekhan, and during the reign of Sultan Mahmood, it was committed to the care of Futtehullah Amad-ul-Mulk, and he enjoyed the government four years. At his death, his ſon, Allaheddeen Amad-ul-Mulk, ſucceeded to the government, and lived in it 40 years. He was ſucceeded by his ſon, Dirya Khan, who governed 15 years. When he died, the government was conferred upon his ſon, Burhan, a minor. At length it was conquered by Mortaza Nizam-ul-Mulk, and annexed to Ahmednagur.

THE SOOBAH OF GUJERAT.

IT is ſituated in the ſecond climate. The length from Burhanpoor to Jugget is 302 coſe: and the breadth from Jalore to the part of Dummun meaſures 260 coſe; and alſo from Ider to the port of Cambayet it is 70 coſe broad. On the eaſt lies Dandees; on the north Jalore and Ider; on the ſouth are the ports of Dummun and Cambayet; and on the weſt Jugget, which is ſituated upon the ſea-ſhore. In the ſouthern parts of this ſoobah are many mountains. It is watered ed by the ocean, and the following rivers: the Sabermutty, the Bateruck, the Mehindery, the Narbudda, the Tapty, and the Sirfooty. There are two other ſprings, called Gunga and Jumna. The air of this ſoobah is very temperate. The ſoil is ſandy, on which account the rain does not occaſion any mud.

Jewary and Bajera are the grain principally cultivated here; and they are the chief food of the inhabitants. The ſpring harveſt here is inconſiderable. Wheat and barley are imported from Malwah and Ajmeer; and they are ſupplied with rice from the Dekhan. The revenues are for the moſt part collected by Nuſſuck, meaſurement being ſeldom uſed here.

They encloſe their fields and gardens with hedges of the zekoom tree, which is a ſtrong defence from cattle, and makes the country almoſt impenetrable by an army. There are ſuch abundance of mangoes and other fruit trees, that the whole country ſeems a perfect garden.

From Putten to Berodeh, the diſtance of 100 coſe, both ſides of the road are lined with mangoe trees, whoſe fruit are remarkably large and moſt delicious. There is one ſort which is ſweet whilſt it is green. This ſoobah alſo produces abundance of very fine figs. Here are muſk-melons in winter and ſummer, which continue in ſeaſon for two months each time. Their grapes are indifferent. They have other fruits and flowers in abundance. The country is ſo much covered with fruit trees, that is impoſſible to hunt. Here are many wild leopards.

The houſes are for the moſt part covered with tiles, with walls of brick and chunam. Some build themſelves large houſes of ſtone, with cavities in the walls, to which they have private ways of entrance.

A great

A great many people in this ſoobah ride in carriages drawn by oxen. It is famous for painters, carvers, and other handicraftsmen. They cut out letters in ſhells, and inlay with them very curiouſly. They alſo make beautiful inkſtands and ſmall boxes. They manufacture gold and ſilver ſtuffs, velvets, &c. And they imitate the ſtuffs of Turkey, Europe, and Perſia. They alſo make very good ſwords, jemdhers, kewpwehs, and bows and arrows. Here is likewiſe carried on a traffic in precious ſtones. Silver is brought hither from Room and Irak.

At firſt Putten was the ſeat of government, then Chumpaneer, and now Ahmedabad. This laſt is a large, well-formed city, ſituated upon the river Sabermutty. It lies in latitude 23 degrees. The ſituation is remarkably healthy, and you may here provide yourſelf with the productions of every part of the globe. There are two forts, on the outſide of which is the town, which formerly conſiſted of 360 pooras (or quarters), but now only 84 are in a flouriſhing condition. In theſe are 1000 ſtone moſques, each having two large minarets, and many wonderful inſcriptions. In Poora Ruſſoolabad is the tomb of Shah Alum, of Bokhara.

Putteweh is a town three coſe from Ahmedabad. Here is the tomb of Koteb Alum, the father of Shah Alum. It is built in a garden, with accommodations for people who have bidden adieu to the world. Over the ſepulchre is a covering, about a cubit ſquare, part of which is wood, another part ſtone, and the reſt iron. And of this many wonderful ſtories are related.

At the diſtance of three coſe from Putteweh is a place called Sirgunj, where are the tombs of Sheikh Ahmed Khuteo and Sultan Ahmed, after whom Ahmedabad is named. Here alſo reſt many of the Ghaurian Sultans.

Sultans. Here grows very fine indigo, which is exported to Room and other diſtant places.

At the diſtance of twelve coſe from Ahmedabad, ſtands the city of Mahmoodabad, founded by Sultan Mahmood. It contains many grand edifices, and is ſurrounded with a wall ſeven coſe ſquare; at every half coſe of which is erected a pleaſure houſe, with an encloſure, in which are deer and other game.

The zemeendar of Ider, who is named Narain Doſs, lives with ſuch auſterity, that his only food is grain, which has paſſed through oxen, and been ſeparated from their dung; and this kind of aliment, the Brahmins conſider as pure in the higheſt degree. This Narain Doſs is one of the principal chiefs of the Rahtore tribe; and he commands 500 cavalry and 2000 infantry.

The ports of Cambayet (Cambay) and Ghogeh are dependant upon this ſircar. Ghogeh is a large port, well built, and inhabited by merchants of various kinds. Ships come to, and others are fitted out from this place. The cargoes of the ſhips are put into ſmall veſſels, called Tahwery, which tranſport them to Cambayet. At Kurry are very fine oxen, ſome of which are ſold for three hundred rupees a pair and upwards, according to their beauty and ſpeed.

Chalawareh formerly was an independent territory, containing 2200 villages, which extended 70 coſe in length and 40 coſe in breadth; and it had 10,000 cavalry, with the ſame number of infantry. Now it has 200 cavalry and 3000 infantry; is ſubject to the governor of Gujerat, and inhabited by the tribe of Chalah. Although now formed into four diviſions, it is only reckoned as a ſingle pergunnah of Ahmedabad. It has a great number of towns.

Putten has a ſtone fort and another of brick. It is ſituated in longitude 117° 10′, and latitude 23° 30′. It produces oxen that will travel 50 coſe in half a day. Here are manufactures of cotton cloths, which are tranſported to great diſtances.

Siddahpoor is a town on the banks of the Sirſooty, and is a great place of religious reſort.

Beernagurgh, an ancient city, has in it three hundred idolatrous temples, each of which has a reſervoir of water. The inhabitants are principally Brahmins.

Chumpaneer is a fort upon a lofty mountain, the acceſs to which, for upwards of two coſe, is exceedingly difficult, and there are gates at ſeveral parts of the defile. At one place they have excavated near ſixty ells in length, which ſpace is covered with planks, that can be removed when occaſion requires. Here grow very fine fruits.

Sooret (or Surat) is an emporium. The river Tapty runs paſt it, and at the diſtance of ſeven coſe from thence joins the ſea. Raneer, which is ſituated on the oppoſite ſide of the Tapty, is a port dependent upon Surat. In ancient times, it was a large city. The ports of Kundery and Bulſar are alſo belonging to Surat. Here are very fine fruits, eſpecially pine-apples. The followers of Zerduſht, when they fled from Perſia, ſettled at Surat, where they practiſe the doctrine inculcated by the Zend, and its commentary the Pazend. They make uſe of ſepulchres. From the liberality of his majeſty's diſpoſition, every ſect exerciſes its particular mode of worſhip, without ſuffering the leaſt moleſtation. Through the negligence of ſoobahdars and their officers, ſeveral of theſe ſircars are in the poſſeſſion of the Europeans; amongſt the number are Dum-

 mun,

mun, Surjaun, Tarapoor, Mahum, and Buffy, which are cities and emporiums.

Beroatch has a fine fort; the river Nerbuddah runs paſt it, and then unites itſelf with the ſea. It is a great emporium, to which the ports of Kawee, Cundhar, Bhalwut, and Bhigooreh alſo belong.

Near the town of Hanſoot is a park, abounding with deer and other game. It is ſituated on the banks of the Nerbuddah, meaſures eight coſe in length, and four coſe in breadth, is perfectly level, and continually covered with verdure.

Sircar Surat was formerly an independent territory; the chief was of the Ghelote tribe, and commanded 50,000 cavalry, and 100,000 infantry. Its length, from the port of Ghogeh to the port of Aramroy, meaſures 125 coſe; and the breadth, from Sindehar to the part of Diu, is a diſtance of 72 coſe. On the eaſt lies Ahmadebad; on the north the territory of Cutch; and on the ſouth and the weſt is the ſea. The climate is healthy. Fruits and flowers are here in great plenty; amongſt the former are grapes and muſk-melons.

Surat is now formed into nine diviſions, each inhabited by a different tribe.

The *First Division*, which is commonly called *New Surat*, had not been explored for a long time, on account of the thickneſs of the foreſts and intricacy of the mountains. A perſon was carried through it by accident, who informed others of his diſcoveries. Here is a ſtone fort, called Chunahgurh, which was conquered by Sultan Mahmood, who built another ſtone fortreſs at the foot of it. Adhum is another fort, eight coſe diſtant from Chunahgurh. It is ſituated upon a mountain,

tain, but is now abandoned, although it might easily be put into repair. In its vicinity is a fort upon the mountain of Kernal, and surrounded with many large springs. Maabidcheen and Bunder Goondyluckyat are two places in its neighbourhood. At the distance of a cose are two other places called Bunder. Behind Chunahgurh is an island, called Syalkookh, being a square of three cose, where grow various kinds of wild fruits, and the inhabitants are mostly of the Kookyan tribe.

Near the town of Nowgongshah is a river, called Bhader, which empties itself into the sea. The fish of this river are so delicate, that, if they are exposed to the sun for a short time, they melt. At this town are to be procured very fine camels, and horses somewhat taller than those called Coote.

The *Second Division* is Putten. It is a large town, on the sea shore, and has a stone fort, in a plain. It is also called Putten Soomnaut.

The town of Owraneh is situated at the distance of three cose from the sea, and has a stone fort on a plain. Here are made good swords, near it being a well which sharpens any blade that is watered with it.

The source of the Nerbuddah, which is held very sacred by the Brahmins, is near Soomnaut. This city also is a great place of religious resort, as well as Beranjy and Gowreener. About four thousand years ago, in this neighbourhood, at a place situated between the rivers Burn and Sirsootty, there were assembled together an immense multitude of the Jadoon tribe, who, after sporting together, at length fought, and every soul of them perished in the conflict.

At the distance of half a cose from Putten Soomnaut,

naut, a perſon, named Bhalkateerut, came to Kiſhenteer, on the bank of the river Sirſooty, where, at the root of a Peepul tree, he threw himſelf into the river; and that ſpot is now called Peepulſir. Both theſe places are accounted holy. In the town of Moolmahadeo is a temple dedicated to Mahadeo, where, every year, on a certain day, there appears a bird called, in the Hindovy language, Beekh, ſomewhat ſmaller than a pigeon, with a blunt bill, and whoſe body is pied black and white; and, having perched and ſported on the top of the temple, for a ſhort time, it then falls down and dies. The people of the town, who are aſſembled together upon this day, take up the bird and fumigate it with various perfumes, and from examining the marks of the bird, they can from thence predict whether, in the enſuing year, there will be plenty of rain, or a drought: a great degree of blackneſs promiſes rain, and on the contrary, a white plumage portends a drought. In this place they have three crops of jewar in a year. Near a place called Oonah are two ſprings of water, which they call Gungah and Jumnah. The water of theſe reſervoirs bubbles up, and flows over. The fiſh of both theſe ſprings are ſaid to have each three eyes, two in their proper place and one in the forehead.

Between Mangalore and Joorwar is a ſpot which is waſhed by the ſea, but, on a certain day in the year, the water is quite freſh. The reaſon they aſſign for it is, that, in ancient times, a perſon being in want of Ganges water, a holy man directed him to this ſpot, where he found freſh water; and, to this time, on the ſame day every year, the water is freſh. The chiefs of theſe two diviſions are rajpoots, of the Ghelote tribe, as are the other inhabitants: each chief commands 1000 cavalry and 2000 infantry, together with a number of Aheers (or cowherds.)

The

The *Third Division.* At the foot of the mountains of Sironj is a large city, now out of repair, although the situation is very desirable. Maabidcheen and the port of Ghogeh are dependant upon it. The island of Birum is also in this division: it is a square hill, of nine cose, in the midst of the river, and formerly was the seat of government. The zemeendar of this division is of Gowhil tribe, and commands 2000 cavalry and 4000 infantry.

The *Fourth Division* includes the ports of Meheweh and Telaja. The inhabitants are of the Walch tribe. This division has 300 cavalry and 500 infantry.

The *Fifth Division* is Jugget, which is also called Daurka. Kishen came from Mehtra and dwelt at this place, and died here. This is considered as a very holy spot by the Brahmins. The island of Singhoodehar, which measures four cose square, is also reckoned in this division. Near Aramroy is an island 70 cose in circuit. Here is a spot mostly stone, half a cose in extent, from whence, when excavated, there issues out salt water on all sides. Mullick Jyaz, of the tribe of Khaseh Kyel, who was governor on the part of Sultan Mahmood Gujeratty, has excavated about a fourth part of it. The port of Aramroy is a very strong place, inhabited by the tribe of Badhil. This division has 1000 cavalry and 2000 infantry.

The *Sixth Division* has such large rivers, the mountains are so lofty, and the country in general so woody, as to be impervious for an army. It is inhabited by the tribe of Cheetore. It has 1000 cavalry and 2000 infantry.

The *Seventh Division* is inhabited by the Bagheyleh tribe, who command 200 cavalry and the like number of infantry.

Here

Here are alſo many of the Kathy tribe, who are of the Aheer caſt, and whoſe buſineſs it is to look after horſes. Their military force is 6000 cavalry and the like number of infantry.

Some people conſider this tribe to be of Arabian origin. They are very ſagacious, and extremely hoſpitable, and they will eat with perſons of every religion. Many of them are exceedingly beautiful. When a Jagheerdar comes amongſt them, they firſt exact an engagement that neither man nor women of them ſhall be called to account for incontinency. In the vicinity of this tribe, on the banks of the river Doondy, dwell a tribe of Aheers, who are called Poorunjah, and command 3000 cavalry and the like number of infantry. They are perpetually at war with the tribe of Jam.

The *Eighth Division.* Here is a ſeaport called Jhanjeer, inhabited by the tribe of Watchee. This diviſion has 200 cavalry and the like number of infantry.

The *Ninth Division* is inhabited by the Charun tribe. The Hindoos ſay that Mahadeo created, out of the ſweat of his forehead, a human form, whom he called Charun, and gave him charge of his own ox. This Charun compoſed verſes, ſang the praiſes of Mahadeo, and revealed to mankind paſt and future events. This tribe, who bear his name, are his deſcendants. The greateſt part of them employ themſelves in ſinging hymns of celebration, and in reciting genealogies: and in battle they repeat warlike fables, to animate the troops. They are alſo famous for diſcovering ſecret things. Throughout Hindoſtan there is hardly a great man who hath not ſome of this tribe in his ſervice. Here are 500 cavalry and 4000 infantry. There is alſo another tribe, called Bhawt, who at leaſt equal the Charuns in animating the troops by martial ſongs, and

in

in chronology excel them: but the Charuns are better soldiers. They say that Charun was created from the will of Mahadeo, and that Bhawt issued from his spine: and wonderful stories are told of these miracles, the relation of which would cause prolixity.

Between Chalwareh, Sircar Ahmedabad, Putten, and Surat is a low tract of country, 90 cose in length, and in breadth from 7 to 30 cose, which is called Run. Before the commencement of the periodical rains, the sea swells and inundates this spot, and leaves it by degrees after the rainy season. When it becomes dry, great quantities of salt are manufactured there, the duties upon which are collected in the pergunnah of Chalawar. Ahmedabad is situated to the east of this tract of land. To the west of it is a very large separate territory, called Cutch, the length of which is 250 cose, and the breadth 100 cose. The territory of Sind lies to the west of Cutch. The greatest part of Cutch is composed of woods and uncultivated sands. Their horses are very fine, and are supposed to be of Arabian extraction. They have also remarkably good camels and goats. Their chief is of the tribe formerly called Jadown, and now named Charunjeh. The men are tall and handsome, and wear long beards. The military force of this country is 10,000 cavalry and 50,000 infantry. The capital city is Tahej, which has two strong forts, called Jhareh and Kuntkote. To the south of Tahej, on the Gujerat quarter, is a considerable zemeendar, named Jam, who is related to the rajah of Thej. Sixty years ago, one Rawel, after a war of two months, drove him out of the country. He then settled in Sircar Surat, between the territories of Chatwah, Badhil, and Nowneel; and possessing himself of other choice lands, founded the city of Nowanagur, and his new-acquired country obtained the name of *Little Cutch*. Sutterſal, the present rajah, is his grandson. He has 7000 cavalry and 8000 infantry. This

country

country is alſo famous for camels and goats. The Mahommedan religion has prevailed here a long time.

Near to Merow and Mungreetch is a territory, called Pall, through which runs the river Mehindery. On the Gujerat ſide of this territory is an independent zemeendar, who reſides at Doongurpoor. On the Malwah ſide of this country is Banſwaleh, whoſe chief is independent. Thoſe two laſt mentioned chiefs have each 5000 cavalry and 1000 infantry; and they were both of the Seeſoodyah tribe, and relations to the Ranna, but now the poſſeſſors are of another tribe.

In the vicinity of Sircar Putten is a country, of which Serowhy is the capital. The chief commands 1000 cavalry and 5000 infantry. He has a fort, on the top of a mountain, called Iyugurh, encompaſſing twelve villages, with great plenty of water and paſturage. There is alſo another territory, ſituated to the eaſt of Nudeebar, to the north of Mendow, to the ſouth of Madowt, and to the weſt of Chumpancer, meaſuring 60 coſe in length and 40 in breadth. The chief is of the Chowhan tribe, and his capital is Almyohan. Here are many wild elephants. The military force is 600 cavalry and 15,000 infantry.

Between the ſircars of Surat and Nuderbar is a mountainous country, well inhabited, called Buglana. The chief is of the Rahtore tribe, and commands 3000 cavalry and 2000 infantry. Here are apricots, apples, grapes, pine-apples, pomegranates, and citrons in great perfection. Buglana has ſeven forts, of which number Mowleer and Saleer are exceedingly ſtrong.

Between ſircar Nadowt and Nuderbar is a hilly country, meaſuring 50 coſe in length, and 40 coſe in breadth. It is inhabited by the Gowhil tribe of rajpoots. At preſent the management of public affairs is in the hands of of one Tewary, a Brahmin; and the rajah, who poſſeſſes nothing but the name, reſides ſometimes at Rajpeeplah, and ſometimes at Ghoolwa. He has 3000 cavalry and 7000 infantry. The water of the latter place is very bad; but there is produced very good rice and honey.

Gujerat contains nine ſircars, ſubdivided into 198 pergunnahs, of which 13 are ports. The amount of revenue is 43 crore, 68 lacks, 2301 dams; together with 1 lack, 62,628½ dams of port duties. The whole being equivalent to ſicca rupees 1,096,123—3—11.

The meaſured lands, (beſides Surat, which is paid by eſtimate), amount to 1 crore, 69 lacks, 36,377 beegahs, and 3 biſwahs; out of which 4 lacks, 20,274 dams are Seyurghal.

This ſoobah has 67,375 cavalry, and 8900 infantry.

A summary History of the Kings of Gujerat.

IN the books of the Hindoos it is written, that in the year 802 of the æra of Bickermajeet, correſponding with A. H. 154, Bunſraj was the firſt king who made Gujerat an independent monarchy, which happened after the following manner: Rajah Sirry Bhowrdeo, who reigned in Kinoje, put to death one of his ſubjects, named Samunt Singh, for being of a baſe and turbulent diſpoſition, and then plundered his family. The wife, who was pregnant, fled into Gujerat, and there in the wilds was delivered of a ſon, who is this Bunſraj. By chance Syeldeo, a hermit of Owjain, happening to paſs that way, took compaſſion upon the woman, and gave the child in charge to one of his pupils, who carried him to Radhunpoor, where he was brought

brought up. When he came to manhood, he associated himself with a gang of highway robbers, whose number increasing, they at length seized the royal treasure which was going to Kinoje. Chumpa, a market-man, was one of his confederates, and they raised and disciplined troops, by whose means Bunsraj was enabled to establish himself in the kingdom of Gujerat in the fiftieth year of his age. Putten is one of the cities that he founded. It is related that, being in doubt where to fix the seat of his government, one Anhul, a cowherd, said, "I have seen a place, such as you desire, which I will discover, upon condition that you call it after my name." Upon the rajah promising to do so, Anhul directed him to the spot, adding, "such is the superior excellency of every thing produced here, that a dog, who came from another country, attacked a hare of this place, who by the exertion of her strength overpowered the dog, and set herself free." The rajah having founded a city here, called it after the cowherd Anhulpoor. The astrologers have predicted that this city shall be destroyed, when there shall have elapsed, from the day of it's foundation, 2500 years, 7 months 9 days, and 44 ghurries. It was founded on Sunday the sifth of Soodder Shukulputch, in the month of Bysack, of the year of Bickermajeet 802, after sunrise 22 ghurries and 45 puls. After a long course of time, the reason for it's name having been forgotten, it was called Nehrwaleh; and, lastly, on account of the excellency of the soil, Putten, which in the language of that country signifies *chosen*.

Rajah Samunt Singh gave his daughter in marriage to Sirrydunduck Soolunky, a descendant of the rajahs of Dehly. She became pregnant by him, and died in labour; but the child was taken alive out of her womb. The moon happening then to be in the 16th stage, which the Hindoos call Mool, the child was, from that circumstance, named Moolraj. His maternal grandfather,

Samunt

Samunt Singh, educated him as his own ſon. When he was arrived at manhood, Samunt, in a fit of inebriation, abdicated the kingdom in his favour, but when he recovered his ſenſes, denied the fact. Moolraj engaged in a confederacy ſome wicked people, by whoſe means he ſlew his benefactor, and aſſumed the kingdom.

During the reign of Jamund in A. H. 416, or A. B. 1064, Sultan Mahmood Ghuznevy conquered Gujerat, and, in conſideration of a certain annual tribute, placed upon the throne a deſcendant of the ancient rajahs, and then returned by the way of Sind, carrying captive with him, by the deſire of the new monarch, another prince of the ſame family. Some time after, the new king, either through prudence or dread, deſired the Sultan to ſend back the captive prince. When he was arrived near Putten, the king went out himſelf to meet him, apprehenſive that otherwiſe deſigning people might inſinuate themſelves into his friendſhip, and occaſion miſchief. Accidentally the very day that they met, the king fell aſleep under a tree, when a wild beaſt, or bird, plucked out his eyes. Since, according to the laws of the land, a perſon who was blind could not hold the kingdom, his troops ſeized him, and in his ſtead raiſed to the throne him who had before been priſoner.

Kemaderpaul Soolunky, from the dread of loſing his life, made choice of a private ſtation, during the reign of Jyſingh. But at the death of Jyſingh he obtained the kingdom, which he extended by conqueſt. He was poiſoned by Ajeelpaul, who ſucceeded him.

Luckmool dying without iſſue, the nobles elected a king out of the Bagheyleh tribe. In the reign of Rajah Kurren, the army of Sultan Allaheddeen, conquered Gujerat, when the rajah fled into the Dekhan. Before this period, Moozeddeen Sam, and Kotebendeen Ibek, had

had made incurſions into Gujerat, but it had never till now been annexed to the empire of Dehly.

Sultan Mahommed, ſon of Feeroz, appointed viceroy of Gujerat Nizam Muſtuckrej, called alſo Rafty Khan; but he proving oppreſſive to the people, the Sultan diſmiſſed him from the office, and nominated in his ſtead Zuffer Khan, ſon of Wejeeh ul Mulk Tanick, who, from being a Brahmin, had embraced the Mahommedan religion. Upon this Nizam rebelled, and was killed. At the death of Sultan Mahommed, the empire of Dehly was in ſome confuſion, when Zuffer Khan made choice of retirement, and Tatar Khan, the ſon of Nizam, made himſelf king of Gujerat, and marched towards Dehly, but was poiſoned on the way. Hereupon Zuffer Khan cauſed the Kotbah to be read, and coin ſtruck in his own name, aſſumed the title of Sultan Mozuffer, and thus Gujerat became again an independent kingdom. Tatar Ahmed, one of his grandſons, put him to death, and got poſſeſſion of the throne. He built the city of Ahmedabad. During a feaſt, when every one was unſuſpicious of danger, he put to death twelve paternal uncles, thus ſinning paſt forgiveneſs. However he governed the kingdom with juſtice and munificence.

Daoud was put to death on account of his tyranny, and the kingdom conferred upon Futteh Khan, ſon of Mahommed Shah, who aſſumed the title of Mahmood: he was a very good prince. Mullick Shaban, ſtyled Amad ul Mulk, was of the utmoſt ſervice to Mahmood; but ſome evil-minded people, jealous of his exaltation, contrived to eſtrange the king's mind from him, by artful inſinuations, hoping thereby to deprive him of his life. The Sultan, from the dread of being dethroned, ordered Amad ul Mulk into confinement, and was very near putting him to death. But Mullick Abdullah, the maſter of the elephants, who was admitted to

conferences

conferences with the king, discovered to him the plot, and convinced him of the innocence of Amad ul Mulk. The king contrived means to set him at liberty, which so alarmed those who had aimed at his destruction, that they immediately took up arms. On the part of the king were the Kasseh Khyel (a tribe of Pattans) the slaves of the palace, and the master of the elephants, which animals were of great service in the engagement. At length the rebels were defeated, upon all of whom proper punishments were inflicted.

When Sultan Mahmood died, his son Mozuffer, with the assistance of the nobility, reigned under the title of Sultan Mozuffer, and proved a good prince. Shah Seffy of Ispahan sent him presents of the curiosities of Persia, and they contracted together a strict friendship. Upon the death of Sultan Mozuffer, his son took the title of Secunder, and mounted the throne, but Amad ul Mulk, forsaking the paths of virtue, soon put him to death, and in his stead raised to the kingdom his brother Nusseer. The nobles, displeased at these practices of Amad ul Mulk, sought to destroy him secretly. He then applied for succour to our late emperor, and promised that if he would afford him assistance and establish Nusseer in the kingdom, he would cede to him the port of Deeb, with a present of a crore of tungahs. But his majesty, disapproving his conduct, rejected the proposal. At this interval the Babiyan tribe invited to the throne Sultan Bahader, son of Sultan Mozuffer, who thereupon came from Dehly, and obtained the kingdom, with the consent of the nobility. His brother, envying his promotion, fled to the court of Sultan Ibraheim at Dehly, but did not meet with any encouragement. The Omrahs of Jownpoor invited him to be their chief; but when he intended to have gone there, his friends wrote him letters dissuasive from that purpose, and calling him to Gujerat. He consented to their proposal, went to Gujerat, and obtained the kingdom

kingdom, which he governed with honour to himſelf, and happineſs to his ſubjects. But he imprudently entered upon a war with our late emperor, and was defeated in battle. When he died, the Omrahs of Gujerat read the Kotbah, and ſtruck coin in the name of Meeran Mahommed, king of Khandees, nephew of Sultan Mozuffer, and who had appointed him his heir: but he died ſoon after his arrival in Gujerat. Then Mahommed, grandſon of Sultan Mozuffer, who had been priſoner at Pyawel, was raiſed to the throne. But one Burhan, a wicked wretch, entering into a confederacy, ſlew him, together with ſome of his nobles, and placed on the throne Rezee ul Mulk, of the family of the firſt Ahmed, under the title of Sultan Ahmed; but Burhan enjoyed all the power. When Sultan Ahmed came of age, Etahmad Khan ſlew him in the houſe of one of his generals, and in his ſtead placed on the throne another minor, whom he declared upon oath to be the ſon of Sultan Mahmood; and he gave him the title of Sultan Mozuffer. Etamad Khan had the entire command of the kingdom, till our auguſt monarch annexed it to the empire.

TABLES

Of the Princes who have reigned in the Soobah of Gujerat.

TABLE I.

The Family of Bunsraj, seven Princes, reigned 196 years.

	Years.		Years.
Bunſraj - -	60	Behirſingh -	25
Jowgraj - -	35	Reſhadut - -	15
Bheemraj - -	25	Samunt - -	7
Bhowr - -	29		

TABLE

TABLE II.

Ten Princes, of the Soolunkhy Tribe, reigned 244 years.

	Ys.	Ms.		Years.
Moolraj Soolunkhy	56	0	Jyfingh, alfo called Sudhraj -	50
Jamund -	13	0	Kemaderpaul -	23
Beyfer -	0	6	Ajiepaul - -	3
Durlebh -	11	6	Luckhmool -	8
Bheem -	42	0		
Kurrun -	31	0		

TABLE III.

Six Princes of the Bagheyleh Tribe, reigned 126 years.

	Ys.	Ms.	Ds.		Ys.	Ms.	Ds.
Birdmool	12	0	0	Arjun Deo	10	0	0
Beildeo -	34	6	10	Sarung Deo	21	0	0
Bheem -	42	0	0	Kurrun -	6	10	15

TABLE IV.

Fourteen Mahommedan Princes, reigned about 160 years.

	Ys.	Ms.	Ds.
Sultan Mahommed - - -	3	8	16
Sultan Ahmed - - - - -	32	6	20
Mahommed Shah - - -	7	9	4
Kotebeddeen Ahmed Shah - -	7	0	13
Daoud Shah - - - - -	0	0	7
Mahmood Shah, fon of Mahommed Shah	55	1	4
Sultan Mozuffer - - - -	14	9	0
Sultan Secunder - - - -	0	10	16
Nuffeer Khan, brother of Secunder -	0	4	0
Sultan Bahader, fon of Sultan Mozuffer	11	9	0
Mahommed Shah, nephew of Sultan Bahader	0	1	15

Sultan

	Ys.	Ms.	
Sultan Mahmood, grandſon of Sultan Mozuffer	18	2	& ſome days.

Sultan Ahmed, of the family of Sultan Ahmed I. 8 mths.
Sultan Mozuffer, 12 years & ſomething more.

The SOOBAH of AJMEER.

IT is ſituated in the ſecond climate. The length, from Bekhur and the dependencies of Umbeer to Beykaneer of Jelmeer, is 168 coſe; and the breadth, from the extremity of Sircar Ajmeer to Banſwareh, includes 150 coſe. On the eaſt lies Agra; on the north, part of Dehly; it has Gujerat on the ſouth; and Deybalpoor of Multan confines it on the weſt. The ſoil of this ſoobah is ſandy, and you are obliged to dig to a great depth before you come at water, ſo that the ſucceſs of the harveſt depends entirely upon the periodical rains. Their winter is temperate; but the ſummer is intenſely hot. The ſpring harveſt is very inconſiderable. Jewary, lehdereh, and mowth, grow here in plenty. The revenue is in general a ſeventh or an eighth of the produce of the harveſt; little being paid in ready money.

The common people live in houſes with pitched roofs, built of bamboos and ſtraw.

To the ſouth are mountains; and this ſoobah abounds with ſtrong holds. This ſoobah is compoſed of Meywar, Marwar, and Hadowty.

Meywar contains ten thouſand villages; and the whole of ſircar Chitore is dependent upon it. It is 40 coſe long, and 30 broad, and has three very celebrated forts, viz. Chitore, Cowmblere, and Mandel. The governor of the ſoobah reſides at Chitore. In Chowra, a dependency of Gowkondeh, is an iron mine. In Jainpore, and ſome places dependent upon Mandel, are copper mines. The preſent poſſeſſors of theſe lands are native zemeendars, who anciently were named Rawel; but for a long time paſt are called Ranna. They are of the Ghelote tribe, and conſider themſelves to be deſcendants from Noorſhirvan. One of their anceſtors, meeting with misfortunes in his own country, came to Berar, and at length became chief of Bernaleh. Eight hundred years prior to the date of this book, Bernaleh was plundered, and many of the inhabitants fell in battle. During the confuſion, one Patta, an infant, was carried by his mother from that ſcene of diſtreſs to Meywar, and received protection from Rajah Mundeleek Bheyl. When Patta was grown up to manhood, he followed the occupation of a ſhepherd, and his ſkill in hunting was ſuch that the fame thereof recommended him to the rajah, who at length made him one of his court and his confident. Upon the death of the rajah, four of his brother's ſons diſputed the kingdom with each other. At laſt they unanimouſly agreed to reſign their ſeveral pretenſions to the rajahſhip in favour of Patta; but he then refuſed to accept of their offer. Through ſome accident, blood iſſued from a finger of one of the brothers, and he immediately applied it to Patta's forehead, and drew upon it a keſhkeh*; and the other brothers concurred in this election. This cuſtom of drawing a keſhkeh with human blood, upon the forehead of him whom this tribe acknowledge for their rajah, obtains to the preſent time. When Patta found himſelf firmly eſtabliſhed in the rajahſhip, he ungratefully put to death the four brothers, who had been the cauſe of his exaltation. It is related, that ſome time before Patta obtained the

* A mark which the Hindoos make upon their foreheads, uſually with clay, at the time of prayer: and which will be fully deſcribed afterwards.

rajahſhip, one day paſſing through a deſert, he was going to draw his bow againſt Herbunj, the hermit, miſtaking him for ſome wild animal; but upon the hermit calling out, he ſtopped his hand, and ran to him, to aſk forgiveneſs for what he was about to have done. After this he frequently went to viſit Herbunj, who one day predicted his preferment. Many wonderful ſtories are told of thoſe adventures. As Patta ſettled in the village of Seeſoodeeah, this tribe is ſo called; and becauſe that he was at firſt educated by a Brahmin, he is alſo ſtyled the Brahmin.

When Rawel Rutten Sein died, Arſee, his ſon-in-law, was raiſed to the rajahſhip; and they gave him the title of Ranna. The preſent Ranna Omra is the tenth in lineal deſcent from Arſee. Their names are as follows: Jemeer, Salakha, Sokul, Goonha, Roymul, Sanka, Owdyſingh, Pertaub, and Omra.

Ancient hiſtorians relate that Sultan Allaheddeen Khuljee, king of Dehly, hearing that Rawel Rutten Sein, rajah of Meywar, was poſſeſſed of a woman of incomparable beauty, ſent a perſon to demand her. Rutten Sein refuſed his conſent; upon which the Sultan led an army, to force him to compliance. The fort of Chitore was beſieged for a long time, till Allaheddeen, being convinced that he could effect nothing by force, had recourſe to artifice, and offered peace. The rajah readily acquieſced, and invited him to be his gueſt. The king went to Chitore with a hundred choſen followers, accompanied by three hundred ſoldiers habited like common attendants. The interview had at firſt every appearance of cordiality; but the king and his party, watching their opportunity, ſeized the rajah; and before his troops could aſſemble for his relief, carried him off to their camp. The rajah was put into confinement, and the king took, what he thought, effectual meaſures for obtaining his beloved. The rajah's jah's family entreated that he would not ill treat their prince, and wrote letters, with assurances, that not only the beauty whom he sought, but many others, should repair to his presence. The Sultan, being quite delighted with his flattering prospects, treated the rajah in a favourable manner. Seven hundred soldiers having placed themselves in women's doolees, set out from Chitore for the camp of Allaheddeen, and sent news on before, that the ranny was coming to his presence, attended by a great number of handmaids. When they were come to the camp, they sent word that the ranny wished to speak with the rajah, previous to her going to the sultan's apartments. The sultan being thrown off his guard, permitted the rajah to visit her. The soldiers instantly seized the opportunity, threw off their disguise, and bore away their prince. The rajpoots, who were placed at different stations, fought manfully, and before the rajah reached the fort many were slain. The Chowhan tribe had the defence of the last stage, which they supported with the utmost valour, till the rajah was safely returned to Chitore. Thus the sultan being able to effect nothing, returned to Dehly. He, however, soon came again with the same intentions, and returned with the same success as before. But Rawel was so much disheartened by these repeated incursions into his country, that he at length resolved to go himself to the sultan, and court his friendship. The interview was contrived by a base mediator, to be at the distance of seven cose from Chitore; where the sultan, in a cowardly manner, had the rajah put to death.

At the breaking out of these troubles, the nobles raised to the rajahship, Rawel Arsee, the son-in-law of their late prince. The sultan renewed the siege of Chitore, and conquered it. Arsee was killed defending the place, and all the women destroyed themselves with fire. Jemeer, the son of Arsee, fled from the field of battle, and ſettled in the mountainous parts of Meywar. When Sultan Mahommed Jownee gave the government of Chitore to Maldeo Chowhan, the rajah of Jelore, all his endeavours to repeople the country were in vain, till he ſent for Jemeer, and made him his ſon-in-law; when, through his means, the country was reſtored to a ſtate of proſperity. After the death of Maldeo, all his ſons were murdered by Jemeer, who made himſelf rajah. This diviſion has ſixteen thouſand cavalry, and forty thouſand infantry. But the zemeendars of Meywar poſſeſſed themſelves of many other lands, ſo that Sanka had eighteen thouſand cavalry and a conſiderable force in infantry.

Marwar is in length 100, and in breadth 60 coſe. Sircars Ajmeer, Jewdehpoor, Sirowhy, Nagore, and Beykaneer, are dependent upon it. The Rahtore tribe have inhabited this diviſion for ages paſt. When Moezeddeen Sam had conquered Rajah Pithora, he next turned his arms towards Jychund, the rajah of Kinoj, who, in attempting to eſcape, unfortunately periſhed in a boat in the Ganges; and his family were all driven out of the country. Seeka, his brother's ſon, who was at that time at Shumſabad, fell in battle, together with many of his troops. His three ſons, named Sooteek, Aſhotahma, and Bawej, ſet out for Gujerat, but ſettled at Pelly near Soochet. In this city reſided a number of Brahmins, who frequently ſuffered oppreſſions from the tribe of Munneych. It happened juſt at this time, that this tribe were making their depredations, but they were valiantly oppoſed by the three brothers, and at length defeated. The Brahmins, in return, loaded the young heroes with rich preſents, and treated them with very great reſpect. At length their reputation and power became ſo great, that they were enabled to attack the tribe of Gohil, and poſſeſs themſelves of the territory of Coombhir. This conqueſt added greatly to their wealth and renown. Sooteek

teek made an incurſion upon the tribe of Munneyeh, and ſeized from them the diſtrict of Ider. Bawej drove out the tribe of Gooly from Boglana, and Aſhootahma eſtabliſhed himſelf in Marwar; and to this day his deſcendants inhabit that country.

The affairs of the deſcendants of Aſhootahma went on proſperouſly; and Maldeo, who was after him, the ſixteenth in lineal deſcent, was ſo powerful a prince, that he was near proving an overmatch for Sheer Khan. Here are many forts, of which the following are the moſt famous, viz. Ajmeer, Jewdehpoor, Beykaneer, Jelmeer, Amerkote, and Jyugurh.

Hadowty, called alſo Sircar Nagore, is inhabited by the Hadeh tribe.

This ſoobah contains ſeven ſircars, ſubdivided into 197 purgunnahs. The meaſured lands are 21,435,961 beegahs, and 7 biſwahs. The amount of revenue is 22,841,507 dams; out of which 2,326,336 dams are Seyurghal. It has 86,500 cavalry and 347,000 rajpoot infantry.

The SOOBAH of DEHLY

IS in the third climate. The length, from Pulwul to Lodyaneh upon the banks of the Sutulej, is 165 coſe; and the breadth, from ſircar Rewary to the mountains of Kemaoon, meaſures 140 coſe; and again, from Hiſſar to Khyzirabad, it is 130 coſe broad. On the eaſt lies Agra; on the north-eaſt quarter is Khyerabad in the ſoobah of Oudh; to the north are mountains; on the ſouth the boundaries are Agra and Ajmeer; and Lodyaneh confines it on the weſt. The principal rivers

rivers are the Ganges and the Jumna, both of which have their sources in this soobah. Here are also many lesser streams, and amongst them the Kenkher (vul. Cagger). The climate is very temperate. Most of the lands are inundated during the periodical rains. Some places produce three harvests in a year. Here grow most of the fruits of Persia, Tartary, and Hindostan; and there are a great variety of flowers. In this soobah are many grand buildings, of stone and brick; and here are to be procured the productions of every part of the globe.

Dehly is a very ancient city, which was formerly called Inderput. It is situated in long. 114° 38′, and lat. 28° 15′. Some place this soobah in the second climate, making it to begin from the southern mountains; but the latitude shows that they are mistaken. Sultan Kotebeddeen, and Sultan Shumseddeen, both resided in the fort built by Rajah Pithowra. Sultan Ghiasseddeen Baleen erected another fort, containing many magnificent buildings; and he made it a law, that any criminal, who took refuge in it, should escape punishment. Moezeddeen Kaicobad built another city, called Gunglookhery, which is situated on the banks of the Jumna. Emeer Khosru, in his poem entitled Kerain Assaadain, celebrates this city. Here is the sepulchre of the late emperor, which is a very sublime edifice. Sultan Allaheddeen founded a new city and fort, which is called Sirry. Towghluckabad was founded by Sultan Towghluck. His son, Sultan Mahommed, built another city, with a palace, in which is a very high building. In this palace are a thousand marble pillars. Sultan Feeroz also founded a large city, and named it Feerozabad. He dug a canal from the Jumna to this city, near to which the water passes. At the distance of three cose from Feerozabad, he built another palace, to which he gave the name of *Jehanama* (the director of the world.) The late emperor built the

the fort of Inderput, and called it Deenpenah, or, *the asylum of religion.* Sheer Khan deſtroyed the city of Dehly, founded by Allaheddeen, and built another; but now this new Dehly is for the moſt part in ruins. Here are many ſepulchres, among which are the following of religious perſons, viz. Kajah Kotebeddeen Ooſhy; Sheikh Nizameddeen Oulya; Sheikh Nuſſureddeen Mahmood, Cheragh Dehly; Mullickyar Purren; Sheikh Saleh; Mullick Kobeer Oulya; Molana Mahommed; Hajy Abdulwaheb; Sheikh Abdullah Koreiſhy; Sheikh Shums Owta; and Emeer Khoſru. Here are alſo interred the following princes, viz. Sultan Shahabeddeen Ghowry; Sultan Shumſeddeen; Sultan Nuſſeereddeen Ghazi; Sultan Ghiaſſeddeen; Sultan Allaheddeen; Sultan Koetebeddeen; Sultan Towghluck; Sultan Mahommed Adel; Sultan Feeroz; Sultan Belole; and Sultan Secunder Lowdy. Alſo many, who are now living, have built ſepulchres for themſelves, in the midſt of pleaſant gardens. On the mountain of Iſlamabad is a very deep ſpring, of hot water; it is called Purbhaſs, and is a great place of Hindoo worſhip. Puſſoo, one of the nobles of Rekheyſir, made a very deep excavation in this mountain, of three beegahs extent, and which he dedicated to religious purpoſes; it remains to this day in it's original ſtate, and is a proof of the antiquity of this city.

Budawun is an ancient city, in which are the tombs of many ſaints.

A part of the northern mountains of this ſoobah is called Kamaoon, where there are mines of gold, lead, ſilver, iron, copper, orpiment, and borax. Here are alſo found abundance of muſk-deer, ketaſs-cows, ſilk-worms, falcons of various kinds, goot-horſes, and plenty of honey.

The rhinoceros is frequently hunted in ſircar Sembhel.

hel. This animal resembles a small elephant without a proboscis. It has a horn in his forehead, which he uses offensively against other animals. Of his skin are made shields, and his horn is applied to the ends of bows, where the string is fastened. In the city of Sembhel is a Brahmin place of worship, called Hurmundel, and here the tenth Owtar will make his first appearance.

Hansy is an ancient city, where reposes Sheikh Jemal, the successor of Sheikh Fereed Shucker Gunj.

Near the town of Sehnah is a spring of hot water, upon a mountain. This certainly is occasioned by a mine of brimstone.

Hissar was founded by Sultan Feeroz; he dug a canal which brings the water of the Jumna near the city. A Derveish predicted his accession to the throne, and at the instance of this Derveish he dug the canal. This canal passes near the town of Sirsa; and loses itself in the lake Bhedar, in a wonderful manner, and of which many strange stories are related. Hissar has very few rivers; and in order to make wells, they are obliged to dig to a great depth.

Sehrind is a famous city, where are the delightful gardens of Hafez Rekhneh.

Tahnesir is held sacred by the Hindoos. The river Sirsutty, to which the Hindoos pay great adoration, runs near it. In it's vicinity is a lake, called Koorkhet, to which people come from far to pay their adorations, and to bestow charity. This was the scene of the war of the Mahabarut, which was carried on in the latter end of the Duaper Jowg.

The city of Hustnapoor was the residence of Rajah Behrut,

Behrut, a prince renowned for his juſtice, and love of his ſubjects. In return for his virtues, heaven continued the throne in his family for a long ſucceſſion of years. Rajah Koor was the eighth monarch in lineal deſcent from Behrut, and the lake Koorkhet is named after him. Then, after ſix deſcents, reigned Chutterbeerj. Of him were born two ſons, one named Dhertraſhter, and the other Pundoo. Dhertraſhter had one hundred and one ſons, the eldeſt of whom was Durjowdhen. The hundred and one brethren are called the Kowrewan. Pundoo had five ſons, viz. Jewdiſhter, Bheemſein, Arjun, Nekul, and Sehdeo, and thoſe are called the Pundoowan. Pundoo ſucceeded to the kingdom, becauſe his elder brother, Dhertraſhter, was blind. However, upon the death of Pundoo, Dhertraſhter was made king, but Durjowdhen poſſeſſed all the power; and dreading that the government might paſs into the family of the Pundoowan, contrived means to deſtroy them. Dhertraſhter, to put an end to the ſeuds which were increaſing daily, built the city of Narnaweh for the reſidence of his nephews. Durjowdhen, who had workmen devoted to his will, contrived that, in the palace where the Pundoowan were to have dwelt, there ſhould be hidden pitch and other combuſtible materials, which, at a fit opportunity, was to have been ſet on fire to deſtroy them. But if God be for us, what availeth the machinations of the enemy? In ſhort, the Pundoowan, after having entered the houſe, diſcovered the plot, ſet fire to the combuſtibles themſelves, and departed to a deſert ſpot, ſo ſecretly, that nobody knew what had befallen them. It happened that the fire conſumed a woman and her four ſons, whoſe houſe adjoined to the palace. Durjowdhen, miſtaking their aſhes for thoſe of the Pundoowan, was perfectly ſatisfied, and gave a feaſt upon the occaſion. The Pundoowan, after having encountered various adventures, came forth from the deſerts to the city of Cumpela. Here they ſoon became renowned for their valour and munificence;

munificence; but they took care to conceal their family and name from every one. But when Durjowdhen heard every circumſtance concerning them, he began to entertain ſuſpicion of having been deceived in the accounts of their deſtruction. At length, having learnt the truth, he profeſſed to be rejoiced at the diſcovery, and having invited them to court, he there gave up to their dominion one half of his kingdom, including Dehly; and reſerved for himſelf the other half, of which Huſtnapoor was the capital. Jewdiſhter, the eldeſt of the Pundoowan, proved very fortunate, and with the aſſiſtance of his brethren, made conqueſt till at length even ſome of the Kowrewan joined them. Durjowdhen, filled with envy thereat, made a feaſt, and, under the falſe appearance of friendſhip, invited the Pundoowan to partake of it; when, having engaged them to play at the game of chowper, he, by the means of falſe dice, won from them all that they poſſeſſed. For the laſt ſtake it was propoſed, that if the Pundoowan won, all they had loſt ſhould be reſtored to them; and provided Durjowdhen proved conqueror, the Pundoowan were to quit all inhabited places, and wander in the deſerts for the ſpace of twelve years, in the dreſs of beggars; that, after the expiration of this term of abſence, when they returned to ſociety, they ſhould ſo conceal themſelves for another year, that nobody ſhould be able to diſcover them; or, in caſe they ſhould be found out, they were to return to the deſerts again for twelve years more. The Pundoowan, unſuſpicious of any fraud, accepted the propoſal, and were again duped by Durjowdhen's falſe dice.

The Pundoowan faithfully fulfilled their part of the agreement; but, at their return, Durjowdhen treated them with ſuch cruelty, that although they offered to be ſatisfied with the poſſeſſion of five villages, he refuſed them, and made preparations for war, fixing upon a ſpot near the lake Koorkhet for the field of battle.

1 But

But since the reward of deceit is disappointment, Jirjowdhen and his adherents were slain, Jewdishter obtaining the victory, after having fought for the space of eighteen days.

This war happened in the end of the Duaper Jowg, one hundred and five years prior to the commencement of the Kul Jowg, being 4831 years anterior to the fortieth year of the present reign.

It is said, that in this war the army of the Koorewan consisted of eleven kooney, each kooney being twenty-one thousand eight hundred and seventy men mounted on elephants; together with the like number of charioteers; besides sixty thousand three hundred and ten cavalry, and one hundred and nine thousand, three hundred and fifty infantry. Out of this immense multitude of forces on one side, and the troops of Jewdishter on the other, only twelve persons survived the slaughter, of which number four were of the army of Jirjowdhen, who fled from the field of battle, and implored protection from Jewdishter. These four were, 1. Keerpacharij, a Brahmin, who had been preceptor to both the Kowrewan and the Pundoowan. 2. Ashotahman, who had also exercised the same office. 3. Keerut Birman, of the Jadown tribe. 4. Sunjeey, who, notwithstanding his renown for wisdom and learning, drove the chariot of Dirterashter. The other eight survivors were of the Pundoowan army, viz. the five Pundoowan brothers; Satick, of the Jadown tribe, renowned for valour; Hujtush, who was Jirjowdhen's brother by another mother; and Kishen, whose fame is too universal to render necessary any account of him here.

Summarily, Jewdishter, after gaining this victory, reigned thirty-six years. Then his righteous disposition made him despise the perishable vanities of this world,

world, and ſeek for retirement, accompanied by his brothers.

The hiſtory of this war is related moſt circumſtantially in the Mahabarut, comprifed in one hundred thouſand couplets. By the command of his majeſty it has been tranſlated into the Perſian language, and entitled Rezemnameh (or the book of war).

The hiſtory of the Mahabarut is divided into eighteen purbhs, or books, containing as follows: 1ſt Purbh, the hiſtory of the Kowrewan and Pundoowan. A table of contents. 2d Purbh, Jewdiſhter ſends his brother to make conqueſts. The ſacrifice called Raj Sewey. The Kowrewan make a feaſt for playing at dice, &c. 3d Purbh, the departure of the Pundoowan to the deſerts; their adventures. 4th Purbh, the Pundoowan return to the city of Beratt, without diſcovering themſelves. 5th Purbh, the Pundoowan diſcover themſelves; appoint Kiſhen mediator between them and the Kowrewan; Jirjowdhen rejects their propoſal. Both armies arrive at Koorkhet. Preparations for battle. 6th Purbh, the firſt battle, which continued for ten days. Beekhum is wounded; and many of the ſons of Dirteraſhter ſlain. 7th Purbh, Jirjowdhen holds a council of war, and appoints Derown his general, who is afterwards ſlain. A deſcription of the battle, which laſted five days. 8th Purbh, a deſcription of the battle of two days. Jirjowdhen appoints for his general Kurren; the heroic exploits of Kurren. The flight of Jewdiſhter. The death of Kurren by the hands of Arjun, on the ſecond day's encounter. 9th Purbh, Sul appointed general; his aſtoniſhing ſtrength; is ſlain. Jirjowdhen hides himſelf in a reſervoir. He dies, with many heroes of his party. 10th Purbh, the concluſion of the war. Keerutpirman, Keerpacharej and Aſhotaman, join Jirjowdhen upon the field of battle, whilſt he has remains of life. They propoſe a ſally upon the

the enemy at night. 11th Purbh, lamentations of the women on both ſides. Gundhary, the mother of Jirjowdhen, curſes Kiſhen. 12th Purbh, the tranſactions of Jewdiſhter after the victory. Wiſhes to reſign his kingdom, and retire from the world; but is comforted and diſſuaded from his intention by the advice of Byaſs, Kiſhen, and Beekhum. This book contains ſublime maxims of religion and morality, with wiſe rules for the government of a kingdom. 13th Purbh, Beekhum's advice to Jewdiſhter. In my opinion theſe two laſt books might better have been compriſed in one, as they both contain the advice of Beekhum to Jewdiſhter. And I think that the 9th purbh ought to have been divided into two; one to have conſiſted of the hiſtory of Sul, and the other to have contained the deſcription of the death of Jirjowdhen*. 14th Purbh, Dirtraſhter, Gundhary his wiſe, and Koonty the mother of the Pundoowan, go into retirement. 16th Purbh, the deſtruction of the tribe of Jadoon. 17th Purbh, Rajah Jewdiſhter, with his brother, retire from the world: ſink into a bed of ſnow. 18th Purbh, deſcription of the aſcenſion of Jewdiſhter into heaven in his own body, and an account of the diſſolution of the bodies of his brethren. The concluſion, called Herbuns, contains the hiſtory of the Jadoowan tribe. Although in this work there are found many extravagant deſcriptions, it is nevertheleſs delightful and inſtructive in a very high degree.

This ſoobah contains eight ſircars, ſubdivided into 232 pergunnahs. The meaſured lands are 28,546,816 beegahs, and 16 biſwahs. The amount of revenue 601,616,666 dams; out of which 33,075,739 dams are Seyurghal.

* In the courſe of the hiſtory, he is indifferently called Jirjowdhen and Dhurjowdhen.

TABLES

TABLES

Of the Princes who have reigned in the Soobah of Dehly.

TABLE I.

Twenty Princes, of the Family of Anungpaul, reigned 437 years, 1 month, and 28 days.

	Ys.	Ms.	Ds.
Anüngpaul Tenore - - -	18	0	0
Bassdeo - - - - -	19	1	18
Gungoo - - - - -	21	3	28
Peert-hy Mull - - - -	19	6	19
Jy Deo - - - - -	20	7	28
Nirpaul - - - - -	14	4	9
Adereh - - - - -	26	7	11
Bitchraj - - - - -	21	2	13
Beek - - - - - -	22	3	16
Rekhpaul - - - - -	21	6	5
Sookpaul - - - - -	20	4	4
Gopaul - - - - -	18	3	15
Selekhen - - - - -	25	10	2
Jypaul - - - - -	16	4	13
Koonwerpaul - - - -	29	3	11
Anungpaul - - - -	29	6	18
Bejsal - - - - - -	24	1	6
Mehetsal - - - - -	25	2	23
Aksal - - - - - -	21	2	15
Peert-hy Raj - - - - -	22	2	16

TABLE II.

Seven Princes, of the Family of Bil Deo, reigned 83 years and 7 months.

	Ys.	Ms.	Ds.
Bil Deo Chowhan - - - -	6	1	4

Amer

	Ys.	Ms.	Ds.
Amer Gungoo - - - -	5	2	5
Khirpaul - - - - -	20	1	5
Soomeer - - - - -	7	4	2
Jahir - - - - - -	4	4	8
Nag Deo - - - - -	3	1	5
Pithowra - - - - -	48	5	1

TABLE III.

Eleven Princes, of the Ghuarian dynasty, reigned 96 years, 6 months, and 8 days.

	Ys.	Ms.	Ds.
Sultan Moezeddeen Sam -	14	0	0
Kotebeddeen Ibek - -	4	0	0
Aram Shah - - - - -	1	0	0
Shumfedden Altumfh - -	26	0	0
Rokeneddeen Ferooz Shah -	0	6	28
Rezeah - - - - -	3	6	6
Sultan Mozeddeen, Bahram Shah	2	1	15
Sultan Allaheddeen Maffaoud Shah	4	1	1
Sultan Nafeereddeen - -	19	0	0
Sultan Ghiaffeddeen Baleen -	20 & fome mths.		
Sultan Moezeddeen Kaicobad - - - -	3 & fome mths.		

TABLE IV.

Thirteen Princes, of the Kuljean dynasty, reigned 129 years, 10 months, and 19 days.

	Ys.	Ms.	Ds.
Sultan Jilaleddeen Kuljy -	7 & fome months.		
Sultan Allaheddeen - -	20 & fome months.		
Sultan Shahabeddeen -	0	3 & fome days.	
Sultan Kotebeddeen -	14	4	0
Sultan Naffeereddeen -	0	6	0

Sultan

	Ys.	Ms.	Ds.
Sultan Ghiaffeddeen Towghluck Shah - - -	4 & fome months.		
Sultan Mahommed - - -	27	0	0
Sultan Feeroz Shah - -	38 & fome months.		
Sultan Towghluck Shah -	0	5	3
Abubeker Shah - - - -	1	6	0
Sultan Mahommed Shah -	6	7	0
Sultan Allaheddeen Secunder	0	1	11
Sultan Mahmood - -	10	2	0

TABLE V.

	Ys.	Ms.	Ds.
Khizer Khan - - -	7	2	2
Mobarck Shah - - -	3	13	16
Mahommed Shah - -	10 & fome months.		
Sultan Alaheddeen - -	7 & fome months.		
Sultan Bhehlole Loody -	38	8	8
Sultan Secunder - -	28	5	0
Sultan Ibraheem - -	7 & fome months.		
Sultan Baber - - -	5	0	0
Sultan Hemayun - -	9	8	1
Sheer Khan Soor - -	5	0	0
Seleem Khan - - -	8 & fome days.		
Feeroz Khan - - -	0	0	3
Adely			
Ibraheem - - -	fome months.		
Secunder - - -	fome months.		
Hemayun, a fecond time -	1	3	0

A summary History of the Princes who have reigned in Dehly.

IN the year 429, of the æra of Bickermajeet, Anungpaul, of the Tenore tribe, governed with juftice; and

and he founded the city of Dehly. In the 848th year of the same æra, in the vicinity of that city, a battle was fought between Peert-hraj Tenore and Beeldeo Chowhan, who, gaining the victory, transferred the kingdom to the Chowhan tribe. In the reign of Rajah Pithowra, Sultan Moozeddeen Sam made several incursions from Ghuzneen into Hindostan, but never gained any victory. In the Hindoo histories it is said, that Rajah Pithowra gained, from the sultan, seven pitched battles; after which, in A.H. 588, the eighth battle was fought near Tahnesir, when the rajah was taken prisoner, and they give the following account of the manner in which it happened. He had originally in his service one hundred heroes, of whose exploits there are most extravagant, and indeed incredible relations; and each of them was styled *Samunt*, or *Leader of an Army*. In this battle he was not accompanied by any one of those champions. The following is the sum of the story. Rajah Jychund Rathore, who at that time was supreme monarch of all Hindostan, resided at Kinoje; all the other rajahs paid him homage, and he was of so tolerating a disposition, in regard to religion, that many natives of Persia and Tartary were engaged in his service. He was making preparations for performing the sacrifice called Rajsoo: in which ceremony it was required that every service should be performed by rajahs, even to the duties of the scullery. The supreme monarch also, on this occasion, gave in marriage, to the next most powerful rajah, one of his most beautiful daughters. All the rajahs had repaired to the court of Jychund, in order to assist at the sacrifice, excepting Pithowra, who was making preparations for the journey. But at that instant, somebody happened to remark, that the empire of right belonged to the Chowhan dynasty, and consequently that Jychund was not qualified to preside at such a sacrifice. These words kindled the flames of ambition in the breast of Pithowra, and he put off his journey. Jychund was

 preparing

preparing to lead an army against him; but the courtiers represented, that such an undertaking would require a long time for execution, whilst the hour appointed for the sacrifice was near at hand. Their remonstrances prevailed with Jychund; and in order to make the festival as little incomplete as possible, by the absence of Pithowra, they made an effigy of him in gold, and gave it the office of porter of the gate. Pithowra, enraged at this affront, went to the sacrifice in disguise, accompanied by five hundred men of approved valour; and, after having committed great slaughter, seized the golden effigy and returned with speed. The daughter of Jychund, who was to have been married to another rajah, upon hearing the relations of Pithowra's intrepid valour, became enamoured of him, and refused her consent to the marriage. Jychund, enraged at her conduct, expelled her from his haram, and confined her in a separate palace. When Pithowra received intelligence of this, he was almost distracted with love and rage, and determined to set her at liberty. For this purpose he engaged Chanda, a musician, to go to the court of Jychund, to sing his celebrations; and Pithowra, with a few chosen men, accompanied as his attendants. By this stratagem Pithowra contrived to carry on a correspondence with the princess, whose heart being predisposed in his favour, easily made her escape with him. The before-mentioned hundred Samunts, who had come with him in different disguises, stood one before another, and defeated the troops of Jychund. Gobind Roy Ghelote made the first resistance, and fell, not till he had slain seven thousand of the enemy. There were slain also, in the first day's battle, of these heroes, Nissing Deo, Chand Nundeys, and Sardhool, of the Selunkee tribe; Pelhun Deo, of the Cutchwaheh tribe, and two of his brothers. And the remainder were killed on their way back, after having displayed astonishing feats of bravery. Pithowra and the bride arrived safe at Dehly, attended by Chanda, the musician,

cian. But Pithowra, ſoon after, became the ſport of fortune, for this princeſs ſo engroſſed his attention, that he neglected all public affairs, and gave himſelf up entirely to love and indolence. Shahabeddeen, apprized thereof, formed an alliance with Rajah Jychund, and, having raiſed a large army, came to attack the dominions of Pithowra. He poſſeſſed himſelf of many places, but no one dared to acquaint Pithowra of his misfortunes. At length the nobles aſſembled together and prevailed upon Chanda to diſcover to him the real ſtate of his affairs. Chanda entered the palace, and after having paſſed ſeven gates, arrived at the haram. He then gave the rajah ſome intimation of the condition of the kingdom. The rajah, vain with the remembrance of his former victories, collected together only a ſmall number of troops, and with theſe he marched out to attack the Sultan. But the heroes of Hindoſtan had all periſhed in the manner before deſcribed, beſides Jychund who before had been his ally, and was now in league with his enemy. In the battle which enſued, Rajah Pithowra fell into the hands of the ſultan, and was carried priſoner to Ghuzneen. The faithful Chanda followed his prince to Guzneen, and contrived to gain the favour of the ſultan. Having obtained an interview with the rajah, and adminiſtered comfort to his mind, he told him that he would take an opportunity of praiſing his ſkill with the bow, which would raiſe the Sultan's curioſity to ſee him perform his feats, when he might make a proper uſe of his arrow. In conſequence of Chanda's repreſentation, the ſultan wiſhed to ſee the rajah exerciſe his bow, when he ſeized the opportunity, and ſhot the king dead upon the ſpot. This is according to the Hindoo hiſtorians, but the Perſian authors give quite a different account of the whole tranſaction, and aſſert that the rajah was killed in battle.

This world is a juggler, who is ever exhibiting wonders. We may recollect many events ſimilar to the hiſtory of this prince. But who is happy enough to profit by the example of others?

In Pithowra ended the Chowhan dynaſty of the princes of Dehly; and Sultan Moozeddeen poſſeſſed himſelf of the beſt part of Hindoſtan. He appointed for his viceroy Mullick Kotebeddeen, whom he left at Gehram, and, on his return to Ghuzneen, plundered the northern mountains. The ſame year that the ſultan returned to Ghuzneen, Mullick Kotebeddeen performed wonderful exploits of valour, and poſſeſſed himſelf of Dehly and many of its dependencies.

At the death of Moozeddeen, Ghiaſſeddeen Mahmood, ſon of Ghiaſſeddeen Mahommed, ſent from Feeroz Kouh to Kotebeddeen the umbrella and other inſignia of royalty. Kotebeddeen fixed his reſidence in Lahoor, and was famed for his juſtice, valour, and munificence. He was killed whilſt playing at the game of Chowgong. The nobles elected for his ſucceſſor his ſon, Aram Shah, but a factious party ſet up againſt him Mullick Altumſh, who was firſt purchaſed for a ſlave by Kotebeddeen, and afterwards adopted his ſon. Aram Shah fled, and Altumſh, thus eſtabliſhed, aſſumed the title of Shumſeddeen. It is ſaid that his father was chief of a Turkiſh tribe, and Altumſh, having excited the envy of his brethren and couſins, they ſold him like Joſeph. Through the viciſſitude of fortune, he changed his maſter ſeveral times, and at laſt a merchant brought him to Ghuzneen, where Sultan Moozeddeen Sam wanted to have purchaſed him, but the merchant demanding a moſt exorbitant price, the ſultan was ſo much diſpleaſed, that he forbad any one to buy him. When Kotebeddeen returned to Ghuzneen, from the conqueſt of Gujerat, having obtained permiſſion from the ſultan, he purchaſed Altumſh at a high price, and then adopted him his ſon. Khowjah Kotebeddeen Ouſhy was his cotemporary. When Altumſh died, he was ſucceed-

succeeded in the kingdom by his son; but the whole of his thoughts were turned to the gratification of sensuality and sloth, despising the affection of his subjects; and he committed the affairs of the kingdom to the management of his mother, Shah Turkan. The nobles, enraged at his shameful conduct, rebelled, and raised to the throne, Rezeeah, the daughter of Shumseddeen, and whom he, in his lifetime, had appointed his heir, assigning as his reason for so doing, that "his sons, being drunkards, were unfit to reign."

In the reign of Moozeddeen Bahram Shah, the troops of Chungaze Khan laid waste the territory of Lahoor, and disaffected persons making use of that opportunity seized Moozeddeen, confined him in prison, and there put him to death.

During the reign of Sultan Allaheddeen Massaoud Shah, an army of Moghols entered Bengal, either by the way of Khatai or Tibbet; but they were defeated by the troops of that monarch. At another time Bawuj was leading an army from Turkestan, when the sultan marched out to meet him; but, on the banks of the river Beya, receiving intelligence of the retreat of the Moghols, he returned to Dehly. This prince at last, suffering himself to be corrupted by evil counsellors, was thrown into prison, and there ended his existence.

Nassireddeen Mahommed was a good prince, and gained the hearts of his subjects by his wise administration. The Tebeeat Nassiry is dedicated to this prince. In his reign the Moghols advanced as far as Punjab; but, when they heard of the march of the sultan, retreated. Nassireddeen was a good prince, and reigned happily. He raised to the vizarut Ghiasseddeen Baleen, who had been his slave, and was afterwards his brother-in-law, and upon this elevation he gave him the title of Ulugh Khan. This Ghiasseddeen was

remarkable

remarkable for his wifdom, and gave fplendor to his high office. Sultan Naffireddeen dying without male iffue, this worthy vizier was raifed to the throne, when he embraced every occafion to difcountenance the wicked, and give encouragement to thofe who merited favour. Ghiaffeddeen appointed to the viceroyalty of Punjab his eldeft fon, Mahommed, who was commonly called Khan Sheheed. Through his vigilance and valour, Punjab was reftored to a ftate of tranquillity. Meer Khofru and Meer Haffan were in his fuit. After having paid a vifit to his father, as he was returning to Punjab, with only a few attendants, he was furprifed by an army of Moghols, between Deybalpoor and Lahoor, and flain. Meer Khofru was taken prifoner, but contrived to gain his liberty.

At the death of Ghiaffeddeen, Bughza Khan was his viceroy, in Bengal, and, upon this event, took the title of Naffireddeen. But a party at Dehly raifed to the throne his fon, Kaicobad, to the prejudice of Kai Khofru, whom Ghiaffeddeen had nominated his heir, and who had fucceeded his father, Mahommed, in the government of Multan. Naffireddeen marched toward Dehly, and his fon, Kaicobad, came out with an army to oppofe him. The two armies met on the banks of the river Seroo, near the town of Oud. By the contrivance of evil counfellors, the father returned to Bengal without effecting any thing, leaving Kaicobad in peaceful poffeffion of the empire. It is aftonifhing that Meer Khofru, in his poem entitled *Keran essadain*, fhould celebrate this interview between the father and his rebellious fon. Kaicobad died of hard drinking, and a faction wanted to have fet up his fon, under the title of Shumfeddeen; but he did not fucceed, and his father's corpfe was thrown into the river Jumna. The kingdom was then conferred upon the Khuljian dynafty, Jilaleddeen, who had been paymafter of the imperial forces, being raifed to the throne. Mullick Allaheddeen, his

his nephew, who had been educated under his care, went from Kurrah into the Dekhan, where he amaſſed great wealth, which enabled him to rebel againſt his monarch. The ſultan marched againſt him, and was ſlain by the hands of the traitor, who thereupon aſſumed the title of ſultan, and by the will of heaven obtained the empire. Notwithſtanding the enormity of his crimes to gain the throne, he nevertheleſs inſtituted excellent laws for the government of the empire. He had ſeveral battles with the Moghols, in all of which he proved victorious. Emeer Khoſru dedicated to him his *Kumseh* (or *five Poems.*) But after having reigned well for ſome time, he at length deſerted the paths of wiſdom and virtue, and became enamoured of an eunuch of his palace, whom he made his prime miniſter. This wretch obliged him to put to death Khyzir Khan, and to impriſon his ſons, Shady Khan and Mobarek Khan. At the death of Allaheddeen, this eunuch raiſed to the throne the youngeſt ſon of the late emperor, to whom he gave the title of Shahabeddeen. The other brothers were deprived of their eyeſight, excepting Mobarek Khan, who, through the divine aſſiſtance, eſcaped that misfortune. After a few days the eunuch was murdered, and Mobarek Khan taken out of priſon, and appointed prime miniſter. He ſoon dethroned his brother, and having put him in priſon, aſſumed the title of Kotebeddeen.

He conquered Gujerat and the Dekhan. But he imprudently placed his confidence in Haſan, a man of mean extraction, but remarkable for the beauty of his perſon. To this minion he gave the title of Khaſſah Khan, and regardleſs of the remonſtrances of thoſe who were moſt attached to his intereſt, he delivered himſelf up ſo entirely to the diſpoſal of this man, that at length he cauſed his benefactor to be murdered, mounted the throne under the title of Naſſireddeen, and extirpated the royal family. Upon this Ghazi-ul Mul-

lick,

lick, who had been one of the principal nobles in the court of Allaheddeen, revolted, and, having put to death the usurper, was elevated to the throne by the nobility, under the title of Ghiasseddeen Towghluck Shah. He settled the affairs of Bengal, and then repaired to Dehly. Mahommed Khan, his son, in the course of three days, erected a palace for his reception, within a few cose of Dehly, and, after much entreaty, prevailed upon him to enter it. The roof of the palace fell in, and buried the king in the ruins. Although Zyabirny has pronounced Mahommed Khan to be innocent of the death of his father, yet the circumstance of the haste in which this palace was erected, and the pressing invitation he gave the king to reside in it, contrary to his own inclination, are powerful arguments of the son's turpitude. Sultan Mahommed, in his last testament, appointed for his successor Feeroz, the son of his paternal uncle, Rajeb, and he was a good prince. At his death the affairs of Hindostan fell into some confusion. He was succeeded by his grandson, Towghluck Shah, but a monster of ingratitude soon deprived him of his life. Abubeker succeeded his brother Towghluck Shah. In the reign of Sultan Mahmood, the chief management of affairs was entrusted to Mulloo Khan, who was thereupon dignified with the title of Ekbal Khan; but his administration produced nothing but discontent and strife. A faction of the nobles set up a great grandson of Feeroz Shah, whom they styled Nasserut Shah. The flames of contention were raging at Dehly, when Timur entered Hindostan in A.H. 801. Mahommed then fled to Gujerat, and sedition hid her head. When Timur was leaving Hindostan, Khyzir Khan, who had done him homage, was left in the government of Multan. For two months after this, Dehly was in a state of the utmost anarchy and confusion. Nasserut Shah, who had fled into the Duab, now came to Dehly, and possessed himself of the throne. But Ekbal, a short time after, made himself master of that city, upon which Nasserut Shah

Shah fled to Mewat. Then Sultan Mahmood returned from Gujerat, and the hypocritical Ekbal Khan feigned entering into his ſervice. Sultan Mahmood being in the utmoſt diſtreſs, departed in the night to Sultan Ibraheem Sherky, but meeting with no encouragement, he returned to Dehly. Ekbal Khan commenced hoſtilities, but gained no advantage. Afterwards Ekbal Khan was taken priſoner in battle by Khyzir Khan, when Sultan Mahmood poſſeſſed himſelf again of Dehly, where he ſoon after died a natural death, and in him ended the Khuljian dynaſty.

For ſome days the government was held by Dowlet Khan, an Afghan; but Khyzir Khan haſtened from Multan, and, having made himſelf maſter of the city of Dehly, appointed as viceroy, Mullick Mirdan Dowlet, one of the omrahs of Sultan Feeroz, and whom Soliman, the father of Khyzir, had adopted for his ſon. Khyzir Khan, out of gratitude to his benefactor Timur, did not aſſume the title of ſultan, but continued to have the Khotbah read in the name of that monarch, contenting himſelf with being ſtyled Ayaut Aala, or *the most High in Dignity*.

At the death of Timur, the Khotbah was read in the name of his ſon and ſucceſſor, Shahrokh, concluding with a prayer for the proſperity of Khyzir Khan. At the death of Khyzir, he was ſucceeded by his ſon, Mobarek Shah, conformably to his laſt will and teſtament. This prince, availing himſelf of the diſſentions between Sultan Ibraheem Sherky and Howſheng, attempted to get poſſeſſion of Calpee and its dependencies; but was treacherouſly killed near Dehly, by ſome traitors who had laid in ambuſh for him. Mahommed Shah, who, according to ſome, was the ſon of Fereed, the ſon of Khyzir Khan, whilſt others make him to have been his ſon, was then raiſed to the throne. Sultan Allaheddeen, his ſucceſſor, poſſeſſed not one good quality,

quality, but was continually engaged in unworthy pursuits; upon which Bhelole began to entertain thoughts of greatness. This Bhelole was the nephew of Sultan Sheh Loody, an Afghan of the tribe called Shamoo Khyl. In the reign of Sultan Mahmood, Behram, the father of Bhelole, came with his other sons to Dehly, and there carried on an inconsiderable merchandize. Sultan Shah was an emeer in the court of Khyzir Khan, who gave him the title of Islam Khan, and assigned over to him the revenues of Sirhind for his maintenance. Bhelole, to whom he was great uncle, lived at that time in Sirhind without any employment; Islam Khan was pleased with him, and educated him as his son. Bhelole was born in Multan, and the following circumstances attended his birth. When his mother had nearly gone her full time with him, unfortunately a beam of the house fell upon her and killed her, when Bhelole was cut out of her womb.

Bhelole allowed Allaheddeen to pass his life in retirement, but maintained all the power in his own hands. He reigned happily, and consulted the ease and prosperity of his subjects. He died a natural death in the 80th year of his age. It is said, that before he became rich, he happened to meet with a Derveish, who asked, "who is he who will give me such a sum of money for the kingdom of Dehly?" Bhelole's companions burst into laughter, but he cheerfully gave the Derveish all the money he had, and continued to pay him obedience, and thereby obtained the object of his desire. He carried on several wars with the Sherkyan kings, till at length he conquered Jownpoor, and put an end to that dynasty. He left his son, Barbuck, in Jownpoor, and then returned to Dehly. As he was coming back from the siege of Gualiar, he was seized with a fit of sickness, and died near the town of Sekeyteh. The nobles raised to the throne his son, Nizam Khan, under the title of Sultan Secunder, who made the city of Agra

Agra his capital, and proved a good prince. In the A. H. 911, there happened a dreadful earthquake at that city, a great number of houſes being ſwallowed up by the earth. He was a very handſome man, and was renowned for his juſtice and liberality. When he died, his ſon, Sultan Ibraheem, aſcended the throne of Dehly. The territory of Jownpoor was aſſigned over to his brother, Jilal Khan, but diſputes enſuing between them, Jilal Khan at laſt took refuge with the king of Gualiar, but could obtain no aſſiſtance from him. He then went to Malwah, to Sultan Mahmood, but finding no hopes from that quarter, ſet out for Gowndwaneh, where he fell into the hands of ſome of the troops of Sultan Ibraheem, who carried him to the court of that prince, when he was put to death. In the reign of Sultan Ibraheem ſeveral of the nobles rebelled, amongſt whom were Derya Khan, viceroy of Bahar, and his ſon, Bahadre Khan, who cauſed the Khotbah to be read, and coin to be ſtruck in their own names. Dowlet Khan Loody fled to Kabul, and ſought protection from the Emperor Baber, whom he conducted to the conqueſt of Hindoſtan.

THE SOOBAH OF LAHOOR.

IT is ſituated in the third climate. The length, from the river Seteluj to the Sind, is 180 coſe; the breadth, from Bhembher to Chowkundy, one of the dependencies of Sutgurrah, meaſures 86 coſe. On the eaſt lies Sirhind; on the north Caſhmeer; on the ſouth Beykaneer and Ajmeer; and Multan bounds it on the weſt. This ſoobah has ſix fine rivers, iſſuing from the northern mountains. The Seteluj, formerly called Shetooder, whoſe ſource is in the mountains of Ghahlore; Rooper, Matchwareh, and Lodyaneh, are ſituated upon its bank; after having paſſed by theſe places, it runs on

to

to Bowh Ferry, where it unites with the river Beyah, anciently called Beypaſha. The ſource of the Beyah, called Abyahkoond, is in the mountains of Keloo, in the pergunnah of Sultanpoor. Near it runs the river Ravy, called alſo Iyrawutty, its ſource is in Behdra, and the city of Lahoor is ſituated on its banks. Another river is the Chenab, called alſo Chunderbahka. From the top of the mountains of Kutwar iſſue two ſprings, one called Chunder, and the other Bahka. In the neighbourhood of Khutwar they unite their ſtreams, and are then called Chunderbahka, from thence they flow on to Bhelolepoor, Sooderah, and Hezareh. The Behut, anciently called Beduſta, has its ſource in pergunnah Weer, in Caſhmeer, and having run paſt the city of Sirrynagur, the capital of that ſoobah, it enters Hindoſtan. The town of Behheereh is on its banks. The Sind, according to ſome, riſes between Caſhmeer and Caſhghur, whilſt others place its ſource on Khatai. This river runs through the borders of Sewad, Attock Benaris, Chowparah, and the territory of the Balootchees. His majeſty has given the following names to the duabehs (or countries that are ſituated between two rivers.) All that lies between the Seteluj and the Beyah he has called Beytjalindher. The diſtrict between the Beyah and the Ravy is named Bary. The lands confined by the Ravy and the Chenab, are called Retchna. Thoſe bounded by the Chenab and Behut are named Jenhat. And Sindſagur compriſes all that lies between the Behut and the Sind.

From the Seteluj to the Beyah	50 coſe.
——— Beyah to the Ravy	17 ditto.
——— Ravy to the Chenab	30 ditto.
——— Chenab to the Behut	20 ditto.
——— Behut to the Sind	68 ditto.

This ſoobah is very populous, is highly cultivated, and exceedingly healthy. The cultivated lands are chiefly ſupplied with water from wells. The winter is much feverer here than in any other part of Hindoftan, although confiderably milder than in Perfia and Tartary. Through his majefty's encouragement, here are to be procured the choiceft productions of Turan, Iran, and Hindoftan.

Mufk-melons are procurable here all the year. They are produced in Lahoor during the months of May and June, and fometimes as late as July. When they are almoft out of feafon here, they are brought from Cafhmeer; and laftly, they are imported from Cabul, Badakhfhan, and Turan. Ice is brought from the northern mountains, and fold all the year. Their horfes refemble Irakees, and are very fine. In fome parts, by fifting and wafhing the fands of the rivers, they obtain gold, filver, copper, rowey, tin, brafs, and lead. It is alfo famous for handicraftfmen.

Lahoor is a very large and populous city, fituated in the Duabeh Bary. In ancient aftronomical tables is called Lehawer. Longitude 109° 22′, latitude 31° 50′. The fort and palace are of brick and lime, and when this city was for fome time the feat of government, many other capital buildings were erected, and gardens laid out in tafte and elegance; it became the grand refort of people of all nations, and their manufactures were carried to the higheft pitch of perfection.

Nagerkote is a city fituated upon a mountain, with a fort called Kangerah. In the vicinity of this city, upon a lofty mountain, is a place called Mahama-ey, which they confider as one of the works of the Divinity, and come in pilgrimage to it from great diftances, thereby obtaining the accomplifhment of their wifhes. It is moft wonderful that, in order to effect this, they cut out their tongues, which grow again in the courfe of two or three days, and fometimes in a few hours. Phyficians believe that the tongue, when cut, will grow again; but nothing but a miracle

miracle can effect it so speedily as is here mentioned. According to the Hindoo mythology, Mahama-ey was the wife, but the learned of this religion understand by this word the *power of Mahadeo*, and say that she, upon beholding vice, killed herself, and that different parts of her body fell on four places. That the head, with some of the limbs, alighted on the northern mountains of Cashmeer, near Kamraj, and which place is named Sardha. That some other members fell near Beejapoor in the Dekhan, at a place thence called Tuljabowhwanny. That others dropt in the east, near Kamru, and which place is called Kamtcha. And that the rest remained at Jalindher, on the spot above described. Near this place appear, on the sides of the mountain, lights resembling links and lamps, which people go to visit, and throw different things into the flames, thinking the ceremony to be beneficial to the eyesight. Over those places are erected temples, which are continually thronged with people. Certainly these lights, which the vulgar consider as miraculous, are only the natural effects of a brimstone mine.

In the middle of Sindsagur, near Shumsabad, is the cell of Bulnaut, which they call Tilleh Bulnaut. The devotees have a great veneration for this place, especially the Jowgees, who make pilgrimages to it. Rock-salt is found in this neighbourhood. There is a mountain, twenty cose in length, out of which they dig this salt. Of the quantity excavated three fourths belong to the diggers, and one fourth is allowed to those who carry it out of the mine. The merchants pay for it from half a dam to two dams per maund, and they transport it to great distances. The zemeendar takes from the merchant a duty of ten dams upon every man's load, and he also pays to the state a rupee for every eighteen maunds of salt that he transports. Of this salt they sometimes make dishes, plates and covers, and stands for lamps.

This

This ſoobah contains five duabehs, ſubdivided into 234 pergunnahs. The meaſured lands are 16,155,643 beegahs and 3 biſwahs. Amount of revenue 559,458,423 dams, out of which 9,865,594 dams are Seyurghal. It has 54,480 cavalry and 426,086 infantry.

The SOOBAH of MULTAN.

IT lies in the firſt, ſecond, and third climates. Before that Tatah was compriſed in this ſoobah, it meaſured in length, from Feerozpoor, to Sewiſtan 403 coſe; and was in breadth, from Khutpoor to Jelmeer, 108 coſe. But with the additional length of Tatah it meaſures to Kutch and Mekran 660 coſe. On the eaſt lies ſircar Sirhind; the pergunnah of Shoor joins it on the north; on the ſouth it is bounded by the ſoobah of Ajmeer; and on the weſt are ſituated Kutch and Mekran, both of which are independent territories.

The ſix rivers, which have been deſcribed in Lahoor, paſs alſo through this ſoobah. The river Behut, near the pergunnah of Shoor, unites with the Chenab; and then after running together for 27 coſe, they join the Ravy, near Zufferabad, and thus paſſing on collectively, for the diſtance of 60 coſe, they diſembogue themſelves into the river Sind near Utch. For the diſtance of twelve coſe, near Feerozpoor, the rivers Beyah and Seteluj unite; and then again, as they paſs along, divide into four ſtreams, viz. the Hur, the Haray, Dund, and the Noorny; and near the city of Multan theſe four branches join again. All the rivers that diſembogue themſelves into the Sind take it's name; but in Tatah the Sind is called Mehran.

The mountains of this ſoobah lie on the north ſide. It reſembles Lahoor in many reſpects, excepting that but little

little rain falls here, and the heat is excessive. Multan is one of the most ancient cities of Hindostan, long. 107° 35′ lat. 29° 25′. It has a brick fort, and a beautiful lofty minaret. Sheikh Bahaeddeen Zukria, and many other persons renowned for their piety, are buried here.

Behkur is a good fort. In ancient books it is called Munsoorah. All the six rivers, beforementioned, pass by it in a collective stream, and afterwards dividing into two, one goes to the south, and the other to the north of the fort. Here is very little rain. The fruits are delicious.

Between Seewee and Behkur is a large desert, over which, during three of the summer months, there blows the pernicious hot wind, called in Arabia *Semoom*. The river Sind some years inclines to the north, and sometimes to the south, and the villages change accordingly, on which account the houses are built of wood and stone.

This soobah contains three sircars, subdivided into eight pergunnahs. The measured lands are 3,273,932 beegahs, 4 biswahs. Amount of revenue 151,403,619 dams; out of which 659,948 dams are Seyurghal. It furnishes 13,785 cavalry and 165,650 infantry.

A summary History of the Princes who have reigned in Multan.

THIS soobah was alternately governed by the kings of Dehly, the chiefs of Sind, and the princes of Ghuzneen.

From the conquest of Sultan Moozeddeen Sam, it paid tribute to Dehly, till in A. H. 847, under Allahеddeen, the kingdom falling into confusion, the governors of provinces enriched themselves, and refused obedience

obedience to their ſovereign; and a faction in Multan raiſed to the throne of this ſoobah Sheikh Youſef Coreiſhy, who had been a ſervant in the moſque of Sheikh Bahaeddeen Zukria. They afterwards depoſed him, but he contrived to eſcape their fury, and came to Delhy, where he preſented himſelf before Sultan Bhelole. The kingdom of Multan was then conferred upon a foreigner, with the title of Sultan Mahmood Shah. It is ſaid that this man had given his daughter in marriage to Sheikh Youſef, and, upon account of the relationſhip, frequented his court, till at length he one night contrived means to deprive him of the throne. During the reign of Sultan Kotebeddeen, Sultan Mahmood Khuljy marched from Malwah to have conquered Multan, but he returned without effecting any thing. According to ſome accounts, Sultan Kotebeddeen was the firſt foreigner who reigned in that ſoobah.

Sultan Bhelole, during his reign in Dehly, ſent his ſon, Barbuck Shah, with troops, to the aſſiſtance of Youſef Sheikh, but they returned unſucceſsful. When Sultan Hoſſain became old and infirm, finding himſelf on that account treated with contempt, he abdicated the throne in favour of his ſon Feeroz Khan, afterterwards ſtyled Feeroz Shah, and then went himſelf into retirement. The Vizier Amad ul Mulk put poiſon into the food of Feeroz Shah, and killed him. Upon this occaſion, Sultan Hoſſain reaſcended the throne, but put the whole management of public affairs into the hands of Mahmood Khan, ſon of Sultan Feeroz. When Sultan Hoſſain died, ſome ſay after a reign of 34, whilſt others make it to have been only 30 years, he was ſucceeded by Sultan Mahmood. During his reign, the Mughols made ſeveral incurſions into Hindoſtan, but always returned unſucceſsful. Some artful, wicked people, by propagating a number of falſe reports, created a miſunderſtanding between Sultan Mahmood and his old vizier, Baizeed Jam, till at length he

 was

was obliged to take to flight; and when he arrived in the territory of Shoor, he read the Khotbah in the name of Sultan Secunder Loody. When Sultan Mahmood died, his infant ſon, Sultan Hoſſain, was raiſed to the throne. When Mirza Shah Hoſſain came from Tatah, and conquered Multan, he beſtowed the government upon Luſhker Khan, who was afterwards diſpoſſeſſed by Mirza Kamran for himſelf. Then Multan was ſucceſſively conquered by Sheer Khan, Seleem Khan, and Secunder Khan.

The emperor Hemayun, when he made the conqueſt of Hindoſtan, added alſo this kingdom to his empire; and now, through the royal juſtice, the inhabitants enjoy peace and happineſs.

TABLE

Of the Mahommedan Princes who have reigned in Multan.

	Reigned years.
Youſef Sheikh - - - - - -	2
Sultan Mahommed Shah - - -	17
Sultan Kotebeddeen, his ſon - -	16
Sultan Huſſen, his ſon - - - - -	30
Sultan Feeroz, his ſon - - - - -	1
Sultan Huſſen, a ſecond time - -	
Sultan Mahommed, ſon of Sultan Feeroz	27
Sultan Hoſſain, ſon of Sultan Feeroz -	1
Huſſen Shah	
Mirza Kamran	
Sheer Khan	
Seleem Khan	
Secunder Khan.	

SIRCAR

SIRCAR TATAH.

FORMERLY this was an independent territory, but now it forms a part of the empire. The length, from Bekhur to Kutch and Mekran, is 257 cose; and the breadth, from the town of Budeyan to Bunder Lahry, measures 100 cose; and again, the breadth from Chundu of Bekhur to Beykaneer, is 60 cose. On the east lies Gujerat; on the north Behkur and Seewee; on the south the sea; and on the west Kutch and Mekran. This country is situated in the second climate. The city of Tatah lies in lon. 102° 30′, and lat. 24° 10′.

In ancient times the capital was Brahminabad, which was then a very populous city. The fort had 1400 bastions, a tenab distant from each other; and to this day there are considerable vestiges of this fortification.

Alore is now called Tatah and Debiel. Here the northern mountains form several branches, one of which runs to Kandahar; another branch, commenceing on the sea-coast, goes to the town of Kouhbar, where it is called Ramgur, and from thence proceeds to Sewistan, where it is called Lukhy. Here are a considerable tribe of Belootchees, called Kulmany; they are twenty thousand families, and can raise ten thousand choice cavalry. Camels are bred here. Another chain of mountains runs from Sehwan to Seewee, where it is called Khutter. Here dwell a tribe, named Nomurdy, who can raise three hundred cavalry and seven thousand infantry. At the fort of this territory are another tribe of Belootchees, named Tehzery, who have a thousand choice troops. They breed horses. There is another range, one extremity of which is in Kutch, and the other joins to the territory of the Kulmanies, where it is called Kareh. It is inhabited by four thousand Belootchees.

 In

In this country the winter is ſo temperate, that there is no occaſion for furs; and in ſummer, excepting in Sewiſtan, the heat is very moderate. Here are various fine fruits, and the mangoes are remarkably good. A ſmall kind of melon grows wild. Here are alſo great variety of flowers; their camels are much eſteemed. The inhabitants travel chiefly by water, and they build boats of various conſtructions, and they have not leſs than forty thouſand in number. They hunt the wild aſs, hares, hogs, and the kotehpateheh; and they are fond of fiſhing.

The huſbandman divides his crops with government, and he is allowed to keep two-thirds. Here are iron-mines and ſalt-pits. Rice is fine, and in abundance. At the diſtance of ſix coſe from Tatah, is a mine of yellow ſtone, which is cut in the quarry to any dimenſion, and is uſed in building. The food of the inhabitants is chiefly fiſh and rice. They dry fiſh in the ſun, and make an advantageous trade of it. They alſo extract oil from fiſh, which they uſe in building boats. They have a fiſh, called pulwa, which comes from the ſea into the Indus, and is exceedingly delicious. They have a method of preſerving milk curds for three or four months.

Near Seewee is a lake, two days journey in length, called Munjoor, upon the ſurface of which the fiſhermen have formed artificial iſlands, where they reſide and carry on their occupation.

One of the wonders of this country is the Jiggerkhar, (or *liver-eater*). One of this claſs can ſteal away the liver of another by looks and incantations. Other accounts ſay, that by looking at a perſon, he deprives him of his ſenſes, and then ſteals from him ſomething reſembling the ſeed of a pomegranate, and which he hides in the calf of his leg.

The

The Jiggerkhar throws on the fire the grain before deſcribed, which thereupon ſpreads to the ſize of a diſh, and he diſtributes it amongſt his fellows, to be eaten; which ceremony concludes the life of the faſcinated perſon. A Jiggerkhar is able to communicate his art to another, and which he does by learning him the incantations, and by making him eat a bit of the liver-cake. If any one cut open the calf of the magician's leg, extract the grain, and give it to the afflicted perſon to eat, he immediately recovers. Thoſe Jiggerkhars are moſtly women. It is ſaid, moreover, that they can bring intelligence from a great diſtance, in a ſhort ſpace of time; and if they are thrown into a river, with a ſtone tied to them, they nevertheleſs will not ſink. In order to deprive any one of this wicked power, they brand his temples, and every joint in his body, cram his eyes with ſalt, ſuſpend him for forty days in a ſubterraneous cavern, and repeat over him certain incantations. In this ſtate he is called *Detchereh*. Although, after having undergone this diſcipline, he is not able to deſtroy the liver of any one, yet he retains the power of being able to diſcover another Jiggerkhar, and is uſed for detecting thoſe diſturbers of mankind. They can alſo cure many diſeaſes, by adminiſtering a potion, or by repeating an incantation. Many other marvellous ſtories are told of theſe people.

Tatah is now the fourth ſircar of the ſoobah of Multan. From the northern borders of Tatah to Utch is a range of mountains, of hard black ſtone, inhabited by various tribes of Belootchees; and on the ſouth, from Utch to Gujerat, are ſandy mountains, the reſidence of the Ahſhambehty and other tribes. The country, from Bekhur to Nuſſubpoor and Amerkote, is peopled by the Sowrah, the Jareetcheh, and other tribes.

This ſoobah contains five ſircars, ſubdivided into fifty

fifty-three pergunnahs. Amount of revenue 6,615,293 dams.

A Summary History of the Princes of Tatah.

IN ancient times there lived a rajah, named Sehris, whose capital was Alore, and his dominions extended to the east as far as Cashmeer; on the west they were bounded by Mehran; the sea confined them to the south; and the mountains were the northern extremity. An army from Persia invaded this kingdom; the rajah was killed in battle, and the Persians, after plundering every thing that came in their way, returned home. The rajah was succeeded by his son Roysahy, who reigned with justice, and with the assistance of his vizier, Ram, restored his dominions to a state of prosperity. A Brahmin, named Juj, who had travelled, entered into the service of this vizier, and by exercising flattery and deceit, in a short time obtained an office of consequence, and upon the death of his patron, he succeeded him in the vizarut. He then entered into a criminal connection with the rajah's wife, but notwithstanding the various and repeated representations of the nobles upon this subject, to the rajah, he would not give credit to them. When the rajah was lying upon his death-bed, the abandoned wretch, in confederacy with the ranny, sent for the leaders of the army separately, as if to consult them in private, and then had them destroyed one after another by the hands of their enemies. At the death of the rajah, the Brahmin married his widow, and obtained the throne. Amidst all his vices, he governed well, and added Kutch and Mekran to his dominions by conquest.

During the khalifat of Omar, he sent Megheerah Abul Aas with an army from Bahrain to Debeil, but he met with a powerful opposition, and was at length killed

killed in battle. The khalif, Osman, employed an intelligent person to explore the state of Hindostan, whilst himself was preparing an army. But the messenger reported 'that a large army would perish for want of provisions; whilst a small number of troops could not hope to make any conquest.' One of the generals of the khalif Aly conquered some parts bordering upon Debeil; but, upon receiving intelligence of the khalif's death, the army withdrew to Mekran. Moawiyah twice sent Ameer with an army, but many of his troops were slain without making any conquest. Juj died after a reign of forty years, and was succeeded by his youngest son Dahir. During the khalifat of Waleed, the son of Abdalmalek, Hijaj, governor of Irak, sent to Sind Mahommed Cossim, his cousin and son-in-law, and he fought several battles with Dahir, who was slain in one of them on the 10th of Ramzan, A. H. 99, when Tatah became subject to the Moslems. Mahommed Cossim sent to the khalif, amongst other captives, two of the daughters of Dahir, together with presents of considerable value. The two young princesses, in order to revenge the death of their father, represented falsely to the khalif, that Mahommed Cossim had been connected with them. The khalif hereupon refused to have any thing to say to them, and falling into a rage, gave orders for Mahommed Cossim to be sewed up in a raw hide, and sent in that condition to court. When the khalif's mandate arrived at Tatah, Mahommed Cossim was making preparations for carrying on an expedition against Roy Herchund, rajah of Kinoj; but he paid instant obedience to the khalif's command. When he arrived at court, the khalif showed him to the daughters of Dahir, who expressed great joy upon the occasion, and said they were satisfied at beholding their father's murderer in such a condition. It is astonishing how the khalif could issue such a cruel order, without positive proofs of delinquency. A wise prince never suffers himself to be led away by reports;

reports; but exercises his circumspection, and makes diligent investigation, seeing that truth is scarce and falsehood common; and it behoveth him to be more particularly doubtful of whatever is said to the prejudice of those whom he has distinguished by peculiar marks of his favour, as the world in general bear them enmity even without cause, and the wicked frequently put on the appearance of virtue, to compass the destruction of the innocent.

After the conquest by Mahommed Cossim, this country was for some time governed by the family of Temeem Ansary. Next it was ruled by the family of Soomrah. Then came the dynasty of Seemeh, who esteemed themselves of the stock of Gemsheed, and each took the name of Jam. Jam Banhuttyeh, was thrice attacked by Sultan Feeroz Shah, and defended himself with vigour, till the third invasion, when he was taken prisoner and carried to Dehly. The Sultan at first appointed one of his nobles to the government of Sind, but afterwards discovering the virtue and wisdom of Jam, he took compassion upon him, and made him his viceroy in Tatah. At the death of Jam Towghluck, one Mobarek, his chamberlain, by means of a faction, managed to get himself raised to the throne. Secunder, the son of Jam, was succeeded by Jam, the son of Futteh Khan. In the reign of Jam Nunda, an army, headed by Shah Beg Arghoon, came from Kandahar, and conquered Seeree. The conqueror appointed his brother, Sultan Mahommed, governor, and then returned to Kandahar. Jam sent an army against Mahommed, and he was slain in battle. Shah Beg invaded Tatah a second time, and having possessed himself of Sehwan and other places, appointed governors, and then went back to his own country.

In the reign of Jam Feeroz, one Salaheddeen, his near relation, rebelled, and proving unsuccessful, took refuge

refuge with Sultan Mahmood of Gujerat. The Sultan gave him a ſplendid reception, and ſent him back with an army. Derya Khan, the vizier of Jam Feeroz, betrayed his maſter, and by his management Salaheddeen got poſſeſſion of all Sind, without fighting a ſingle battle. But ſome time afterwards, this ſame Derya Khan returned to the intereſt of Feeroz, recalled him from his retreat, and at length reſtored him to his kingdom. But Salaheddeen applied a ſecond time to the king of Gujerat, and again obtaining ſuccours from that monarch, once more poſſeſſed himſelf of the kingdom of Tatah. Jam Feeroz fled to Kandahar. Shah Beg joined him with troops, and coming to an engagement near Sehwan, Salaheddeen and his two ſons were ſlain. Thus Feeroz became firmly fixed in his kingdom. In A. H. 929, Shah Beg conquered all Sind, and Jam Feeroz fled to Gujerat, where he gave his daughter in marriage to Sultan Bahader, and became one of his nobles. Shah Beg then reigned in Sind without a competitor. He was the ſon of Meer Zulnoon Beg, commander in chief of the army of Sultan Huſſain Mirza, and he held Kandahar by a feudal tenure. Shah Beg was killed fighting the battles of the ſons of Huſſain Mirza againſt Shiebuck Khan Uzbuck. Upon his death, the government of Kandahar was conferred upon his ſon Reſheed, who was not only famed for valour, but alſo renowned for his ſkill in the ſciences. At his death, his ſon Shah Huſſen ſucceeded him; and conquered Multan from Sultan Mahommed. After him, Mirza Iſſa, ſon of Abdul Aly Turkhan, ſucceeded him. Pyindah Mahommed being incapable of governing, on account of inſanity, the reins of government were held by his ſon Mirza Jany Beg, till the troops of our late emperor conquered Tatah, when Mirza Jany Beg became a faithful ſubject of the empire.

Names

Names of the Princes who have reigned in Tatah.

The family of Temeem Anſary, cotemporary with the Khalifs of the houſe of Ommiah.

The Soomrah Family, thirty-six Princes, reigned 500 years.

Of the Seehmeh dynasty.

	Ys.	Ms.
Jam Anvar, reigned - -	3	6
Jam Joona, his brother -	4	0
Jam Banhutteyeh, his ſon -	15	0
Jam Temajee, his brother -	13	& ſome mths.
Jam Salaheddeen - - - -	11	ditto
Jam Nizameddeen, his ſon -	2	& ſome days.
Jam Alyſhere Temajee - -	6	& ſome mths.
Jam Keran, his ſon - -	a day and a half.	
Futteh Khan, ſon of Secunder	11	& ſome mths.
Towghluck, his brother - -	28	0
Mobarek, the chamberlain -	three days.	
Secunder, ſon of Futteh Khan	1	6
Sunjer, commonly called Radmun	8	& ſome mths.
Jam Nizameddeen, commonly called Nunda - - -	60	& ſome mths.
Jam Feeroz, his ſon - -	12	0
Jam Salaheddeen, his ſon-in-law		
Jam Feeroz, a ſecond time.		

THE SOOBAH OF CASHMEER.

IT is ſituated partly in the third and partly in the fourth climate. It is compoſed of Caſhmeer, Pehkely, Bhembher,

Bhembher, Sewad, Bijore, Kandahar, and Zabuliſtan. Formerly it had Ghuzneh, but now it has Cabul for the capital. The length, from Kemberdire to Kiſhengung, is 120 coſe; and the breadth from 10 to 25 coſe. On the eaſt lies Peeriſtan and the river Chenab; on the ſouth-eaſt Bunkul and the mountains of Jummoo; on the north-eaſt great Tibbet; on the weſt Pehkely and Kiſhengung; on the ſouthweſt the territory of Gukher; and on the north-weſt little Tibbet. It is encompaſſed on all ſides with lofty mountains. There are twenty-ſix roads into it from Hindoſtan, but thoſe of Bhembher and Pehkely are the beſt, being paſſable by horſes. The Bhembher road is much the neareſt: it has ſeveral branches, of which the following are very good roads, viz. Huſty and Wutter, through both of which an army may paſs. Peerpunchal, the road by which his majeſty has made three journeys to Caſhmeer. If an ox or a horſe be killed upon theſe mountains, there immediately enſues a tempeſt with ſnow and rain.

The whole of this ſoobah repreſents a garden in perpetual ſpring, and the fortifications with which nature has furniſhed it, are of an aſtoniſhing height, ſo that the grand and romantic appearance cannot fail of delighting thoſe who are fond of variety, as well as they who take pleaſure in retirement. The water is remarkably good, and the cataracts are enchantingly magnificent. It rains and ſnows here at the ſame ſeaſons as in Tartary and Perſia, and during the periodical rains in Hindoſtan, here alſo fall light ſhowers. The ſoil is partly marſhy, and the reſt well watered by rivers and lakes. Violets, roſes, narciſſuſes, and innumerable other flowers grow wild here. The ſpring and autumn diſplay ſcenes delightfully aſtoniſhing. The houſes, which are built of wood, are of four ſtories, and ſome higher, and they are entirely open, without any court yard. The roofs of the houſes are planted with tulips, which produce a wonderful effect in the ſpring. In the

the lower apartments are kept the cattle and lumber; the family live in the ſecond ſtory; and the third and fourth ſtories are uſed for warehouſes. Earthquakes are very frequent here, on which account they do not build their houſes with brick or ſtone, but of wood, with which the country abounds. Here are, however, many ancient idolatrous temples built of brick and ſtone, ſome of which are in perfect preſervation, and others in ruins. Here are various woollen manufactures, particularly of ſhawls, which are carried to all parts of the globe. Although Caſhmeer is populous, and money ſcarce, yet a thief or a beggar is ſcarcely known amongſt them. Excepting cherries and mulberries, they have plenty of excellent fruits, eſpecially melons, apples, peaches, and apricots; grapes, although in abundance, are but of few kinds, and thoſe indifferent. In general they let the vines twiſt round the trunks of mulberry trees. The mulberry trees are cultivated chiefly on account of the leaves for the ſilkworns, little of the fruit being eaten. The ſilkworms eggs are brought from Kelut and little Tibbet, but thoſe of the firſt place are the beſt. The inhabitants chiefly live upon rice, fiſh, freſh and dried, and vegetables; and they drink wine. They boil the rice over night, and ſet it by for uſe for the next day. They dry vegetables to ſerve in the winter. They have rice in plenty, but not remarkably fine. Their wheat, which is black and ſmall, is ſcarce; and mowng, barley, and nakhud, are produced, but in ſmall quantity. They have a ſpecies of ſheep, which they call Hundoo, reſembling thoſe of Perſia, the fleſh of which is exceedingly delicious and wholeſome. The inhabitants wear chiefly woollen cloths, an upper garment of which will laſt ſeveral years. Their horſes are ſmall, but hardy, and ſurefooted, and they are very cheap. They breed neither elephants nor camels. Their cows are black and ugly, but yield plenty of milk, of which is made good butter. Every town in this ſoobah has as many hand-

handicraftſmen as are to be found in the large cities of other countries. They have no fairs, all their goods being ſold at regular ſhops. In their cities and towns there are neither ſnakes, ſcorpions, nor other venomous reptiles. Here is a mountain called Mahadeo, and every place from whence it can be ſeen is free from ſnakes; but the country in general abounds with flies, gnats, bugs, and lice. Sparrows are very ſcarce, on account of the general uſe of Pellet-bows. The inhabitants go upon the lakes, in ſmall boats, to enjoy the diverſion of hawking. They have partridges, the elk is alſo found here, and they train leopards to hunt them. Moſt of the trade of this country is carried on by water, but men alſo tranſport great burdens upon their ſhoulders. Watermen and carpenters are profeſſions in great repute here. Here dwell a great dumber of brahmins.

The Caſhmeerians have a language of their own, but their books are written in the Shanſcrit tongue, although the character be ſometimes Caſhmeerian. They write chiefly upon Tooz, which is the bark of a tree; it eaſily divides into leaves, and remains perfect for many years. All ancient manuſcripts are written upon this bark, and they make uſe of a kind of ink which cannot be waſhed out. Formerly they knew only the Hindoo ſciences; but now they ſtudy thoſe of other nations. They are predictors and aſtrologers, like the Hindoos. The Mahommedans are partly Sunnies, and others are of the ſects of Aly and Noorbukhſhy; and they are frequently engaged in wars againſt each other. Here are many delightful ſingers, but they want variety. The moſt reſpectable people of this country are the Reyſhees, who, although they do not ſuffer themſelves to be fettered by traditions, are doubtleſs true worſhippers of God. They revile not any other ſect, and aſk nothing of any one; they plant the roads with fruit trees, to furniſh the traveller with refreſhment; they

they abſtain from fleſh; and have no intercourſe with the other ſex. There are near two thouſand of this ſect in Caſhmeer.

Of Weights and Coins.——In Caſhmeer the tolah contains ſixteen maſhahs, of ſix rutties each. The gold mohur conſiſts of ſixteen dams, of ſix rutties each. Theſe mohurs are four rutties more in weight than thoſe of Dehly. *Rubsassnu* is a ſmall coin of nine maſhaſhs. *Punchee* is a copper coin, in value one quarter of a dam; it is alſo called *Kusserch.* The *Barahgany* is half of the foregoing. The *Shuckry* is the fourth of the *Barahgany.* Four *Kusseerehs* make one *Hut;* forty *Kusseerehs* make one *Sassnoo*; and one and a half *Sassnoo* make one *Siccah.* One hundred *Sassnoos* make one *Lach,* equivalent to 1000 royal dams.

The Hindoos regard all Caſhmeer as holy land. Forty-five places are dedicated to Mahadeo; ſixty-four to Biſhen; three to Brahma; and twenty-two to Durga. In ſeven hundred places there are carved figures of ſnakes, which they worſhip.

Sirrynagur, the capital of Caſhmeer, is four farſangs in length. The rivers Behut, Mar, and the Lutchmehkul run through it. The one laſt-mentioned is dry during part of the year, and the Mar is ſometimes ſo ſhallow that boats cannot paſs through it. This city has for ages been in a flouriſhing ſtate, and abounding with workmen of every denomination. They manufacture beautiful ſhawls and other fine woollen ſtuffs, amongſt which are thoſe called Doomah and Puttoo*; but, of theſe laſt, the beſt are thoſe brought from Tibbet. Meer Syed Aly Hamadany reſided for ſome time in this city, and founded a monaſtery, which remains a monument of his piety.

* Coarſe kinds of ſhawls.

On the eaſt ſide of this city is a high hill, called Kouh Soliman. Adjoining to the city are two large lakes, which are always full. The water of thoſe lakes will keep good in jars for a long time.

Near the town of Bereng is a long ſtraight, in a mountain, in which there is a reſervoir of water ſeven ells ſquare, which the Hindoos conſider as a place of great ſanctity. This reſervoir is dry eleven months in the year; but, in the month of Ardibeheſht, the water guſhes out from two ſprings. Firſt, the water appears in a hole, which they call Sundahberary, ſituated in one corner of the reſervoir; and, when this is full, the water ſprings up in another corner, called Sut-hrey-ſhy, till at length the reſervoir flows over; after which it immediately begins to decreaſe, and continues doing ſo till it is perfectly dry; and this flux and reflux happens every morning, noon, and evening. When the reſervoir is full of water, people throw into it flowers for the different ſprings, and, to the aſtoniſhment of the beholders, the flowers are afterwards found in the particular ſpring to which they were conſigned. But certainly this is an artifical contrivance of the ancients, to entrap the ignorant. Near it is a ſpring, which is dry for ſix months continuance; but, on a certain day, the huſbandmen of that quarter go thither, and make ſacrifices of ſheep and coats, upon which the water guſhes out, and ſupplies the lands of five villages. If the inundation proves exceſſive, they repeat the ſacrifices till the water ſubſides.

Here is another ſpring, called Kookernag, whoſe water ſatisfies both hunger and thirſt, and it is alſo a remedy for indigeſtion. At a ſmall diſtance from this is another ſpring, in the centre of which is an idol temple of ſtone; a beautiful fabric. Here, in the ſummer, devotees ſurround themſelves with fire, till they are reduced

duced to afhes, and think they are thereby pleafing the deity.

Here is a fpring in which is found touchftone; and to the fouth of it is a very high mountain, where there is an iron mine.

Punjberareh is a town dependent upon Uneej, and which is confidered to be a very holy place: formerly it was a large city. It has feven idol temples, near which is a delightful plain, called Nundymurg.

In Punpoor, dependent upon Vehy, there are ten or twelve thoufand beegahs of land covered with faffron, which, during the end of Firverdeen and the month of Ardibehefht, afford a profpect that would enchant thofe who are the moft difficult to pleafe. They cultivate it after the following manner. After ploughing the ground, they dig it with fpades and form the earth into plats, in which they plant the faffron roots, which refemble onions. In the courfe of a month they fprout. The ftalk is at firft white, and when grown to about a finger's breadth, it begins to flower, and continues doing fo till there are eight in number. In the latter end of the month of Mehr, the plant is in perfection, and then is about a fpan high. The flower has fix petals, of a yellow colour, containing fix threads, three of which are yellow and three of a deep orange, and thefe threads are the faffron. When the plant has done flowering, it bears leaves. It will flower for fix fucceffive years. The firft year it yields but little faffron, but it arrives at perfection in the fecond year, and continues fo till the expiration of the fixth year. At that period they divide the roots, and tranfplant them, for if fuffered to remain any longer in the fame ground, they degenerate.

In the town of Reyvun are a fpring and bafon, which are

are accounted holy; the people believe that the ſaffron ſeed originally came out of this ſpring, and, when they commence planting, they come to worſhip at it, pouring in cows milk which, if it ſinks, is eſteemed a good omen, but if it floats upon the ſurface of the water, they are filled with apprehenſions for the ſucceſs of the ſaffron.

In the village of Kehrow are three hundred and ſixty ſacred fountains; and here is alſo an iron mine.

Mirwardoon adjoins to great Tibbet. Here are bred the ſpecies of ſheep, called Hundoo, which are uſed for carrying burdens. Near this place is a mountain, called Chutterkote, where are ſuch numbers of ſnakes, that nobody can aſcend it. Here is alſo another mountain of difficult aſcent, where is a baſon of water which few people can arrive at, and ſometimes it entirely diſappears. At the foot of the mountain there frequently appear images of Mahadeo, in cryſtal, to the aſtoniſhment of the beholders.

In the vicinity of Ut-cheweel, one of the dependencies of Kuhtar, is a fountain of excellent water, which ſpouts up an ell high. This water is eſteemed a great reſtorative.

In the village of Goonher is a very deep ſpring, ſurrounded with idolatrous temples, built of ſtone; when the water decreaſes, there appears an image of Mahadeo, in ſandal wood.

Near Owler is a very high mountain, which has a ſpring of ſalt water. Here are elks.

Mutten is ſituated upon a raiſed ſpot, where, in ancient times, there was a large idolatrous temple. Here is a ſmall reſervoir, the water of which never decreaſes. Some believe the well of Babal to be at this place, but what is ſhown for it, is only an excavation without wa-

 ter.

ter. At the foot of the eminence is a ſpring, which is formed into a baſon, that is full of large fiſh, but out of reſpect for the place, no one meddles with them. On one ſide of the reſervoir is a cave, of unfathomable depth.

In Kahwerparah is a ſpring, the water of which flows over obliquely, with a tremendous noiſe.

At the village of Uſh, in the middle of a mountain, is the retreat of Baba Zeineddeen Reeſhy. It is ſaid that, till this recluſe came hither, there was not any water to be found in this mountain; but, that a ſtream iſſued out immediately, upon his taking up his reſidence here. After dwelling here twelve years, he entered the cave, cloſed the mouth thereof with a large ſtone, and has never ſince been ſeen by any one.

The town of Dutchenpareh is ſituated at the foot of a mountain, on the ſide of great Tibbet, and the ſtream abovementioned paſſes by it. Between great Tibbet and this pergunnah is a cave, in which is ſometimes to be ſeen an image, in ice, called Amernaut, and which is held in great veneration. The image makes its appearance after the following manner: two days before the new moon, there appears, in the cave, a bubble of ice, which increaſes in ſize every day till the fifteenth day, at which time it is an ell or more in height; then, as the moon decreaſes, the image alſo gradually diminiſhes, till at laſt no veſtige of it remains. This congealment the Hindoos regard as the image of Mahadeo, and believe that, by worſhipping it, their deſires will be accompliſhed. Near this cave is a rivulet, called Amrowty, the clay of whoſe bed is perfectly white; this they eſteem holy, and rub it over their bodies. The ſnow on the mountains of this country never decreaſes, ſo that what with cold, the narrowneſs of the roads, and the extreme heights, they cannot be paſſed but with the utmoſt difficulty.

In

In the village of Dakhamoon is a ſpring: whenever the water thereof becomes turbid, and filth floats upon the ſurface, ſome calamity befals the country. Near it is a quarry of Solomon's ſtone, of which are made plates and diſhes.

The pergunnah of Phak abounds with flowers and odoriferous plants. Adjoining to it is a large lake, called Dull, one ſide of which is cloſe to the town. On the ſurface of this lake are artificial iſlands, made for the purpoſe of cultivation, and ſometimes robbers will cut off pieces of theſe floating lands, and convey them away to another part of the lake. Sultan Zeinulabeddeen conſtructed a dam, of ſtone and clay, a coſe in length, which extended from the city of Sirrynagur to the pergunnah of Phak. Near this lake is a ſpring, which is a remedy for many diſorders. In the village of T-hed is a moſt delightful ſpot, where is to be ſeen the junction of ſeven ſtreams; and here are many ancient buildings of ſtone. Here is alſo a ſpring, which in winter is very hot and in ſummer very cold.

In the village of Bazwal is a cataract, called Shalamar, which falls from the mountain of Shahkote, in a ſurpriſing manner. Here fiſh are caught, in great abundance, in wicker baſkets.

In Aiſhahbalary is a ſacred ſpring, called Soorysir, on the ſides of which are idolatrous temples of ſtone. The fountain of Shukernag is dry all the year, excepting that, when the ninth day of the month falls on a Friday, the water ſprings up in the morning, and continues flowing till the evening: and multitudes of people flock together to partake of the bleſſing.

In the village of Zinabul is a ſpring and baſon, into which people throw walnuts, to know what will be the iſſue of any affair; the walnuts floating is a good omen,

 and

and on the contrary, if they ſink, it is a ſign of bad luck.

At Banhal is a temple, called Durgah. When any one wants to know what ſucceſs his enemy will have againſt him, he fills two veſſels with rice, one of which is for himſelf, and the other for his enemy. Theſe are left all night in the temple, the doors of which are ſhut. The next day he brings them out with great ceremony, and opens them. The veſſel in which are found flowers and ſaffron denotes ſucceſs to its owner; and that which is full of ſtraw and rubbiſh portends ill luck to the perſon to whom it belongs. But the following ceremony is more ſurpriſing. If any parties have a diſpute upon a point of right, which is difficult to determine, they ſend two perſons to the temple, each carrying two fowls and two goats. They then give poiſon to the fowls and goats, after which they rub them with their hands, when the animals, of him whoſe claim is juſt, recover; and thoſe of the other expire.

At Weerſir is the ſource of the river Behut, with a baſon, meaſuring a jereeb, from whence the water ruſhes out with an aſtoniſhing noiſe, and it is unfathomable. This ſpring is called Weernag; it has a ſtone border, and on the eaſt ſide are temples.

In Kumber is a fountain, called Bewunſindh, which flows during two months in the ſpring, increaſing its ſtream daily.

In Deoſirberbala is a baſon, called Pehloonag, the water from which ruſhes out in a column, meaſuring twenty ſquare ells. If any one wiſhes to know whether or not it will be a plentiful ſeaſon, or to diſcover any circumſtance reſpecting his own fortune, he fills an earthen veſſel with rice, writes his name upon one ſide of it, and after cloſing the mouth, throws the veſſel into the

the bason. The vessel soon rises of itself to the surface of the water, and if, upon opening it, the rice is hot, and has a fragrant flavour, it is an omen of good luck; but if it appears mixed with straw and rubbish, it is a bad omen. Here is also a delightful rivulet, called Wissy, issuing from a mountain, from the height of two hundred ells, making an astonishing noise in its descent. Frequently devout Hindoos precipitate themselves down this cataract, and think that, by thus ending their lives, they ensure to themselves reward in the next world.

In Kotehar is a fountain, which continues dry for eleven years, and, when the planet Jupiter enters the sign Leo, the water springs out on every Friday, but is dry all the rest of the week during that year.

Near the village of Mettelhameh is found the bird called Okar, whose feathers are plucked, to be worn in the turbans of the nobility. A certain allowance is made by government for the maintenance of those birds in these forests.

Near Shookroah is a fountain, which plays incessantly, and is a place of great religious resort. It never snows upon this mountain.

In Nagama is a stream, called Neelahnag, the bason of which measures forty beegahs, and the water is delightfully clear. This is also held sacred; and many fanatics consume themselves with fire on its border. They likewise try their fortunes by it in the following manner. A walnut, divided into four parts, is thrown into the spring; if an odd number floats, it is accounted a good omen, and an even number is deemed unlucky. They also throw milk into the spring, which sinking indicates good luck, but if it floats the omen is bad. In ancient times there was found, in this spring,

a book

a book, entitled Neelmut, containing a particular description of Cashmeer, with the history of this place of worship. It is asserted that, at the bottom of this spring, there is a large inhabited city, and that Burreo Shah, a Brahmin, went and remained there two or three days, and, on his return, gave a wonderful description of it.

In the town of Parwa is a spring, in which lepers bathe themselves every Sunday morning, and are thereby cleansed. Adjoining to this is a plain, remarkable for fattening the cattle that graze upon it.

In the pergunnah of Lytch, in the village of Hulthul, is a tree, of which if the smallest twig be shaken, it agitates the whole tree from the very root.

Lar adjoins to the mountains of great Tibbet; to the north of it is the loftiest mountain in Cashmeer, and which is of very difficult ascent. At the foot of it are two springs, two ells distant from each other, the water of one of which is cold, and of the other hot. They are both held sacred, and the Hindoos sometimes devote their lives here. On the middle of the mountain is a very large lake, into which the Hindoos throw the ashes of their dead, considering it the surest way of approaching the deity. If the flesh of any animal fall into the lake, there immediately arises a storm of snow and rain. In this vicinity is a rivulet, called the Sind, which has its source in great Tibbet: the water is so clear that the fish are visible, and they strike them with iron spears.

Shahebeddeenpoor is situated on the Behut, whose banks are planted with plane trees. At this town the rivers Behut and Sind unite their streams. In Teelahmoolah is a spot of ground, about one hundred beegahs in extent, which, during the time of the rains, is inundated: when the water subsides, and the mud is almost dry, the inhabitants take sticks, about an ell in length, which

which they work about in the mud, and find large fiſh and great quantities of little fry.

In Sutpoor is a baſon of water that is unfathomable, and to which the Hindoos pay adoration. There is another place of worſhip, called Bhooteeſir, dedicated to Mahadeo; thoſe, who come to this place to worſhip, hear ſtrange noiſes, without being able to diſcover from whence they ariſe.

At Ghoyahhamoo, adjoining to little Tibbet, is a large lake, called Ouller, meaſuring twenty-eight coſe in circumference, and into which the river Behut empties itſelf.

In the middle of this lake Sultan Zeinulabeddeen built a magnificent palace, which is called Zienlunk. They ſink, in the lake, boats filled with ſtones and branches of trees, and, after letting them remain under water for three or four months, draw them up with ropes, and by this means take great quantities of fiſh. Wild fowl are alſo caught on this lake.

Near the village of Ahſen are hunted great numbers of elks, that come to the lake.

Adjoining to Matchamoo is an iſland, covered with trees, and whenever the trees are ſhaken by the wind, the iſland is alſo agitated.

At Purriſpoor are fields of ſaffron. Here ſtood a lofty idolatrous temple, which was deſtroyed by Secunder, the father of Zeinulabeddeen. In the ruins was found a plate of copper, with an inſcription in the Hindovy language, purporting that, after the expiration of 1100 years, the temple ſhould be deſtroyed by a perſon named Secunder.

Turrehgong,

Turrehgong, in the pergunnah of Kamraj, was the residence of the princes of the Chuck tribe. Here is a spring, called Chetternag, the water of which is very wholesome, and in the centre of the spring is a very ancient stone building. In this spring are very large fish, but whoever catches them suffers some misfortune.

Adjoining to Gurgong is a pass, called Sowyum, at the extremity of which is a spot of ground measuring ten Jereebs. When the planet Jupiter enters the sign Leo, for a month's continuance, the soil of this place is so intensely hot, that it destroys the trees; and if a kettle be set upon the ground, it will boil. Belonging to it is a well-inhabited town; the pass to which, coming from Kamraj, joins on one side to Cashghur. On the west lies Puckely, where gold is found after the following manner. In the stream of the river they spread goat skins with long hair, fastening them down with stones, so that the water cannot move them. After two or three days, they take up the skins, and expose them to the sun. When they are perfectly dry, they shake them, and obtain grains of gold, some of which will weigh three tolahs. Another pass, called Goolkut, joins to Puckely, and leads to Cashghur. Here gold is obtained by washing the earth.

At the distance of twelve cose from Hahyhamoo, is a river called Pudmutty, which comes from the territory of Dawurd. Gold is found in the sands of this river. On its banks is an idolatrous temple of stone, dedicated to Durga. On the eight ti-h of Shuckulputch * the temple shakes in an astonishing manner.

The revenues of this soobah are collected by estimate, and the crops divided with government, it not being customary in any part of this country to demand,

* Vide Vol. I.

by

by meaſurement, or to receive money, excepting for a ſmall part of the Syerjehat*.

Every coin, and even manufactures, are eſtimated in kherwars of rice. Although, formerly, government was ſaid to take only a third of the produce of the ſoil, yet in fact the huſbandman was not left in the enjoyment of near one half; but his majeſty has now commanded, that the crops ſhall be equally divided between the huſbandman and the ſtate.

Cazy Aly fixed the revenues at 3,063,050 kherwars, and 11 tureks; the kherwar being eſtimated at 3 maunds and 8 ſeers of Akberſhah.

They have a weight of two dams, called pul, and they alſo make uſe of the half and the fourth of this weight. Seven and a half of theſe puls make a ſeer; four ſeers are a mun; four muns are a turek; royal ſeers. Having taken the medium prices for ſeveral years, the kherwar turned out 29 dams, and this rate was fixed for the receipt of the revenues in grain; and the money kherwar was left at 13½ dams. By this mode of calculation the amount revenue came to 746,700,411 dams, out of which 901,663 kherwars, 8 tureks, were paid in money, and were equivalent to 12,022,183 dams. The revenue fixed by Aſof Khan is 3,079,543 kherwars, out of which 1,015,330½ kherwars are in money. His majeſty granted a general remiſſion of all baj and tumghat†, which deductions amounted to 67,824¼ kherwars, or 898,400 dams; and for the farther eaſe of the huſbandman, the kherwar was increaſed in value five dams. Although Aſof Khan's ſettlement exceeds that of Cazy Aly 16,392 kherwars 5 tureks, yet, by calculating at the preſent rate, the amount to be collected is actually leſs 86,034½ dams, becauſe the Cazy overrated the money kherwar.

* Vide vol. I. † Ibid.

According

According to the rental depoſited in the royal archives by Cazy Aly, Caſhmeer contains forty-one pergunnahs, whilſt Aſof Khan's ſtatement makes out only thirty-eight. This difference proceeds from Cazy Aly having made two diviſions of pergunnah Kamraj, under the names of Kerna and Derow; and alſo by forming into two parcels the pergunnah commonly called Syer Mowaza. The Cazy gave the name of Pergunnah Havelly to forty villages on the ſide of Meraj. and eight villages in the Kamraj quarter he left without any denomination.

The ancients divided Caſhmeer into two parts only, calling the eaſtern diviſion Meraj, and the weſtern diviſion Kamraj.

There are now but few troops in Caſhmeer, the native ſtanding army being only 4892 cavalry and 92,400 infantry.

KINGS OF CASHMEER.

TABLE I.

Fifty-three Princes reigned 1266 years.

Owgnund. Damuder. Bal.

After these reigned thirty-five Princes, whose Names are forgotten.

Loo.
Kiſhen.
Kehgunder.
Serendir.
Gowdher.
Suren.
Jennek.
Teyjeenir.

Aſhowg.
Jewlowk.
Damuder.
Beyſhek.
Zeſhek. } three brothers.
Kenſhek.
Abehmun.

TABLE

TABLE II.

Twenty-one Princes reigned 1015 *years and* 29 *days.*

	Ys.	Ms.	Ds.		Ys.	Ms.	Ds.
Rajah Kenund	35	0	0	Ebiſkeh -	60	0	0
Bikhun	53	0	0	Merhkul -	70	0	0
Inderjeet	35	6	0	Bek -	63	0	13
Rawen	30	0	0	Kutnund -	30	0	0
Beebeekhun	35	6	0	Viſſnund -	52	2	0
Nerkh, called alſo Kher	39	9	0	Nir -	60	0	0
				Uj - -	60	0	0
Sideh -	60	0	0	Kubaret -	60	0	6
Adutbeelabeh	30	6	0	Kurren -	57	0	11
Hirnya -	37	7	0	Nurundrawut	36	3	10
Hirenkul -	60	0	0	Jewdiſhter	48	0	10

TABLE III.

Six Princes reigned 192 *years.*

	Ys.		Ys.
Pertaubadut, ſaid by ſome to be a deſcendant of Bickermadut	32	Bunjir - -	36
		Bejeery - -	8
		Chunder - -	37
Juggook - -	32	Ariraj - -	47

TABLE IV.

Ten Princes reigned 592 *years,* 10 *months, and* 1 *day.*

	Ys.	Ms.	Ds.		Ys.	Ms.	Ds.
Megdahen, grandſon of Jewdiſhter	34	0	0	Materkunt, Brahmin	4	9	1
				Pirwirſein -	63	0	0
Sereſhſain -	30	0	0	Jewdiſhter	0	39	3
Heren -	30	2	0				

Lekhmen,

	Ys.	Ms.	Ds.		Ys.	Ms.	Ds.
Lekhmen, called alſo Runadut	0	13	0	Kernadut -	0	300	0
				Beckermadut	0	42	0
				Baladut -	0	0	36

TABLE V.

Seventeen Princes reigned 257 *years,* 5 *months, and* 20 *days.*

	Ys.	Ms.	Ds.		Ys.	Ms.	Ds.
Dirleyir Dirwun, ſon-in-law of Baladut	36	0	0	Pertoohanund	4	1	0
				Sungranund	7	0	0
				Jeyanund -	31	0	0
				Jujnund	ſome months		
Pertaubadut	50	0	0	Lultanund	12	0	0
Chundranund	8	8	0	Sungramanund	37	0	0
Taranund -	4	0	24	Briſput -	12	0	0
Lultadut -	36	7	11	Ajeyanund	36	0	0
Kulyanund -	1	0	15	Anunkanund	3	0	0
Bijradut -	7	0	0	Atbalanund	2	0	0

TABLE VI.

Fifteen Princes reigned 89 *years,* 1 *month, and* 17 *days.*

	Ys.	Ms.	Ds.		Ys.	Ms.	Ds.
Aduntderma	28	3	3	Barteh, a ſecond time	1	4	0
Sunkerderma	18	8	19				
Gopaulderma	2	0	0	Jikkerderma, a ſecond time	0	6	0
Sungut - -	0	0	10				
Ranny Sogundrah, mother of Gopaul	2	0	0	Sunkerderma	3	0	0
				Jikkerderma, a third time	3	0	0
Barteh ..	15	0	10	Unmuntderma	2	2	0
Nerjetderma	1	1	0	Soorderma, a ſecond time	0	6	0
Jikkerderma	10	0	15				
Soorderma	1	0	0				

TABLE

TABLE VII.

Ten Princes reigned 64 years, 3 months, and 14 days.

	Ys.	Ms.	Ds.
Jeſſgeerdeo, who was originally a peaſant	9	0	0
Poorunt -	0	0	1
Sungramdeo	6	6	7
Birdkunt, who was originally a peaſant -	1	4	0
Khimkunt, his ſon	8	6	0
Abhemun -	14	0	0
Nundkunt -	1	1	9
Tirbhown -	2	0	6
Bhimkunt -	4	3	20
Dudda Ranny, mother of Abhemun -	23	6	0

TABLE VIII.

Twenty-seven Princes reigned 351 years, 6 months, and 17 days.

	Ys.	Ms.	Ds.
Sungram, nephew of Dudda Ranny	0	2	0
Hurray -	0	0	22
Anunt -	5	5	0
Kuluſſder -	26	0	0
Ungruſs -	0	0	22
Hurruſs -	12	0	0
Utchul -	10	4	2
Ruddeh, one of the murderers of Utchul	one night and three hours.		
Sulhen, Utchul's brother -	0	3	27
Seetel -	7	10	0
Behkyajir -	0	6	12
Seetel, a ſecond time -	2	3	0
Jyſingh -	27	0	0
Hermanek -	9	6	10
Dunjiey -	7	2	0
Behtydeo -	9	4	17
Buſſdeo -	18	13	0
Jugdeo -	14	2	0
Rajdeo -	23	3	7
Sungramdeo -	16	0	10
Ramdeo -	21	1	13
Letchmendeo	13	3	12
Seemehdeo	14	5	27
Seenehdeo	9	3	26
Runjun Tibbety, a native of Tibbet	10 years and ſome months.		
Adundeo -	15	2	10
Ranny Kotadevy wife of Adundeo	0	6	15

Mahommedan

Mahommedan Princes, who have reigned in Cashmeer.

TABLE IX.

Thirty-two Princes reigned 282 *years,* 5 *months, and* 1 *day.*

	Ys.	Ms.	Ds.
Sultan Shumſeddeen, who was in the ſervice of Senehdeo - - - - -	2	11	25
Sultan Jemſheer, his ſon - - -	1	10	0
Allaheddeen, ſon of Shumſeddeen -	12	8	13
Sultan Shahabeddeen, ſon of Shumſeddeen	20	0	0
Sultan Kotebeddeen, ſon of Shumſeddeen	15	5	2
Sultan Secunder, ſurnamed Sunkar, ſon of Kotebeddeen - - - - -	22	9	6
Aly Shah, ſon of Secunder - -	6	9	0
Sultan Zeinulabeddeen, ſon of Secunder	52	0	0
Sultan Hajy Hyder Shah, ſon of Zeinulabeddeen - - - - - - -	1	2	0
Sultan Haſan Khan, ſon of Hyder Shah	12	0	5
Sultan Mahommed Shah, ſon of Sultan Haſan	2	7	0
Futteh Shah, grandſon of Zeinulabeddeen	9	1	0
Sultan Mahommed Shah, a ſecond time	0	9	9
Sultan Futteh Shah, a ſecond time -	1	1	0
Sultan Mahommed Shah, a third time	11	11	11
Sultan Ibrahim, ſon of Mahommed Shah	0	8	25
Sultan Nazek Shah, ſon of Futteh Shah	1	0	0
Sultan Mahommed Shah, a fourth time	34	8	10
Sultan Shumſeddeen, ſon of Mahommed Shah	0	10	0
Iſmail Shah, ſon of Sultan Mahommed -	2	9	0
Bazek Shah, a ſecond time - -	13	9	0
Iſmail Shah, a ſecond time - - -	1	5	0
Mirza Hyder Gurgan - - -	10	0	0
Nazek Shah, a third time - -	1	0	0
Ghazi Khan, ſon of Kajee Chuck -	10	6	0
Huſſain Chuck, brother of Ghazi Khan	6	10	0
Aly Chuck, brother of Ghazi Khan -	8	0	9

Youſef

	Ys.	Ms.	Ds.
Youfef Shah, fon of Aly Chuck - -	1	0	8
Syed Mobarek Shah, who was one of the nobles of Youfef Shah - - -	0	0	25
Luker Chuck, grandfon of Kajee Chuck	1	2	0
Youfef Shah, a fecond time - -	5	3	0
Yacoub Khan, fon of Youfef Shah -	1	11	0

Altogether one hundred and ninety-one princes; reigned 4109 years, 11 months, and 9 days.

A summary History of the Kings of Cashmeer.

THE firft time that his majefty led his victorious ftandards into this region of perpetual fpring, the natives prefented him with a book, called Raj Turungee, written in the Shanfcrit language, and containing the hiftory of the princes of Cafhmeer, for upwards of four thoufand years back. His majefty, who is ever the patron of learning, commanded fome proficients in the Shanfcrit tongue to tranflate this hiftory into the Perfian language. In this hiftory it is faid, that in the early ages of the world all Cafhmeer, excepting the mountains, was covered with water, and was then called Suttyfir. Sutty is the wife of Mahadeo, and Sir fignifies a refervoir. The fpace of one of the days of Brahma confifts of fourteen munounters, each of which comprifes feventy kulps; and feventy quadruple jowgs are equal to one kulp. Down to this prefent time, which is the fortieth year of his majefty's reign, there have elapfed from the period at which Cafhmeer became inhabited, twenty-feven kulps of the feventh munounter, three jowgs of the twenty-eighth kulp, and of the fourth jowg, four thoufand feven hundred and one folar years.

When the water had fubfided, Kufhup, renowned

for the austerity of his manners, first brought the Brahmins to inhabit this country. Afterwards, when the number of the people had greatly increased, it became necessary for them to have a ruler; and having called a general assembly for determining upon this point, they then elected for their king one famous for his virtues; and from that period monarchy became established amongst them, and continued in force till the commencement of the reign of Owgnund, which is placed 4444 years prior to this day. This Owgnund was killed by the hands of Bulbehder, Kishen's elder brother, in a battle that was fought at Mehtra between Kishen and Jerasindeh, rajah of Bahar. In consequence thereof, as some of the relations of Kishen were going to a marriage feast at Kandahar, Damooder, the son of Owgnund, in order to revenge the death of his father, attacked them with an army on the banks of the Sind, and lost his life in the action. His wife had been foretold by the astrologers, that the child, with whom she was then pregnant, would be a son. Upon him Kishen bestowed the kingdom of Cashmeer. After him reigned in succession thirty-five tyrannic princes, whose names are entirely forgotten.

Loo was a just prince. He founded in Kamraj the city of Looloo, vestiges of which are to be seen at this day. It is said that the buildings in this city were eighty crore in number.

Ashowg, the nephew of Rajah Jenneh, established, during his reign, the Brahminy rites, and substituted in their stead those of Jyen. This prince ruled with equity. He was succeeded by his son Rajah Jelowk, who carried his conquests to the sea-shore. On his return to Cashmeer, he brought with him from Kinoje (at that time the capital of Hindostan), many learned and wise men, out of which number he selected seven to preside over the following departments: 1. The administration

miniſtration of juſtice. 2. The revenues. 3. The treaſury. 4. The army. 5. Commerce. 6. Controul of the houſehold. 7. Aſtrology and alchymy. It is ſaid, that this aſtrologer had at his command a large ſnake, upon whoſe back he travelled great diſtances by water. He ſometimes appeared as an old man, and at other times he ſeemed to be a youth. Many other wonderful ſtories are told of him. During the reign of Jelowk the doctrine of Bowdh was tolerated.

Damooder (the ſecond) is ſaid by ſome to have been the deſcendant of Aſhowg; and others make him of another family. He was a pious prince; but having offended a devotee, he was, at his curſe, transformed into a ſnake.

In the reign of Rajah Nerkh, the Brahmins got the better of the followers of Bowdh, and burnt down their temples.

Mehrkul was a ſhameleſs tyrant; but heaven permitted him to make conſiderable conqueſts. As he was deſcending an eminence, which is known by the name of Huſtywutter, an elephant having ſlipt and fallen down, uttered doleful cries. He delighted with beholding the diſtreſs of the poor animal, and commanded a hundred others to be precipitated and deſtroyed in like manner. From this circumſtance the height obtained it's preſent name; *Husty* ſignifying an *elephant*, and *Wutter* meaning *injury*. During his reign, a large ſtone appeared in one of the rivers of Caſhmeer, and entirely blocked it up; and whatever was cut away from it in the day-time grew again in the courſe of the night. The workmen gave over in deſpair. Then a voice was heard proclaiming, that if a virtuous woman would lay her hand upon the ſtone, it would diſappear. Orders were iſſued accordingly, and they brought woman after woman, who touched it with-

 out

out producing any effect. The rajah put to death the women for their incontinency, their children for being bastards, and the husbands for permitting the wickedness, till at length three millions of persons were massacred. At length the miracle was performed by the hand of a woman who was a potter. At last Rajah Mehrkul was seized with a fit of sickness, when he threw himself into a fire, and was burnt to death.

Rajah Kubaret governed with wisdom and justice, and made considerable conquests. Throughout his dominions no one was suffered to take away the life of any animal, all ranks of people being commanded to abstain from eating flesh. The temple which is now standing upon Solomon's mountain, was founded by this monarch's vizier.

Rajah Jewdishter commenced his reign with justice; but shortly after gave himself up to sensual gratifications, and following evil advice, became such an insufferable tyrant, that the kings of Hindostan and Tibbet formed an alliance against him, and the chiefs of Cashmeer, encouraged thereby, threw him into prison.

In the reign of Rajah Bunjir, whilst the sun was in Leo, there was a fall of snow which totally destroyed the harvest, and occasioned a terrible famine.

Rajah Chunder was blest with a vizier, endowed with wisdom and fidelity; but the wicked envying bis virtues, propagated unfavourable reports regarding him. On these occasions the great are generally staggered in their opinions, and make no use of their reason, forgetting every thing which they have read in history, on the direful effects of envy. Thus Rajah Burjin gave ear to the stories fabricated against his vizier, and dismissed him from his office. The faithful vizier bore his disgrace with the utmost submission; but his enemies,

enemies, not ſatisfied with what they had compaſſed againſt him, repreſented to the rajah, that he was plotting to raiſe himſelf to the throne; and the deluded prince ordered him to be crucified. A ſhort time after the execution, the vizier's peer* paſſed the corps, and read it decreed in his forehead as follows: "That he ſhould be diſmiſſed from his office, be ſent to priſon, and then crucified; but that after all, he ſhould be reſtored to life, and obtain the kingdom." Aſtoniſhed at what he beheld, he took down the body from the croſs, and carried it to a ſecret place. Here he was inceſſantly offering up prayers to heaven for the reſtoration of his life, till one night the aerial ſpirits aſſembled together, and reſtored the body to life, by repeating incantations. He ſhortly after mounted the throne, but deſpiſing worldly pomp, ſoon abdicated it.

Megdahen was renowned for his virtues; and conquered Hindoſtan as far as the ſea-ſhore.

Rajah Heren died without iſſue; when the nobles of Caſhmeer ſubmitted themſelves to the government of Bickermajeet, rajah of Hindoſtan.

Rajah Materkunt was originally a Caſhmeerian Brahmin, in a private ſtation. Rajah Bickermajeet, charmed with his wiſdom and virtue, gave him a ſum of money to enable him to travel to his own country, with a a letter addreſſed to the nobles there; and he was commanded to go without any companion. The Brahmin, with a heavy heart, repaired to Caſhmeer, and delivered the rajah's letter. In it was written, "I am indebted to the bearer of this for many ſervices, and he has experienced a variety of cares and diſappointments. On receipt of this letter, commit to his charge

* Spiritual guide.

the government of Cashmeer; and, as you dread our royal displeasure, yield him obedience." The nobles of Cashmeer called a council to deliberate upon the occasion, when it was resolved to obey the mandate.

Rajah Perwersein was a private person in Hindostan, till a religious person foretold that he would be a monarch. Upon which he went to Nuggerkote, and possessed himself of that place.

Materkunt abdicated the throne of Cashmeer in favour of Perwersein, and came to Benaris, where he led a private life.

Rajah Perwersein was a good prince. He built Sirrynagur, the capital of Cashmeer, which is said to have then contained three millions six hundred thousand houses. He possessed unbounded liberality; as an instance of which, he sent to Materkunt eleven years revenue of Cashmeer, to be distributed by him amongst the needy.

Rajah Runadut ruled with justice, and made considerable conquests. Near Cushtwar, on the river Chenab, he went into a cave, accompanied by many of his relations and courtiers, and they were never heard of more. Many wonderful stories are related of this adventure.

Rajah Baladut reigned over Hindostan, and extended his dominions to the sea-shore.

In the reign of Rajah Chundranund, a Brahminy woman came to sue for justice, against the unknown murderer of her husband. The rajah demanded, whether she had reason to suspect any one of the deed. She replied, that her husband was a man of a very fair character, and that she had never known any one bear him

him ill-will, excepting one man, with whom he was continually difputing upon points of philofophy. This perfon being brought before the rajah, denied the charge; and the wife was not fatisfied with the caufe being determined by the ordeal trial, from the dread that he might efcape by the means of witchcraft. The rajah was fo much perplexed how to decide upon the cafe, that he could neither eat nor fleep. At length he faw in a dream, a fage, who taught him an incantation, which he fhould utter over a heap of rice flour, and then fcatter the meal upon the ground, and direct the fufpected perfon to walk over it: that if there appeared upon the meal the impreffion of the feet of two perfons, then the accufed was certainly the murderer. When the rajah awoke, he did as the vifion had commanded him; and the Brahmin was proved guilty. But fince it is not lawful to take away the life of a Brahmin, even for murder, an image was made in iron, refembling a man without a head, with which he was branded on the forehead.

Rajah Lultadut was a glorious prince, and gave great attention to the profperity of his kingdom; and, with the divine affiftance, he conquered Iran, Turan, Fars, Hindoftan, Khatai, and almoft all the reft of the habitable world. He died in the northern mountains. It is faid, that, at the curfe of a holy man, he was tranfformed into ftone. There are other marvellous ftories of him, too tedious for relation.

Rajah Ageyanund extended his dominions by conqueft, and was fo exceedingly bountiful, that he beftowed in charity, at Benaris, ninety-nine thoufand nine hundred and ninety-nine horfes, together with neceffaries of every kind for the needy. One day the rajah afked an old man, whether his own armies, or thofe of Rajah Lultadut, were moft numerous? The old man replied, "In your army there are only 80,000 fukpals, ſukpals*, and in that of your grandfather were 125,000 of theſe carriages; from whence the complete ſtrength of each may be calculated." Rajah Ajeyanund having carried his victorious arms to a great diſtance from his capital, Juj, his wife's brother, erected the ſtandard of rebellion; and the Omrahs of Caſhmeer, from the dread of what might otherwiſe befal their wives and children, eſpouſed his cauſe. The rajah, when informed of this, repaired immediately to Bengal, and, with the aſſiſtance of the troops of that country, repoſſeſſed himſelf of his throne, Juj being ſlain in battle.

Rajah Lultanund delighted in the company of mean people and idle jeſters, whereby he gave great offence to the wiſe and experienced nobility. His vizier continually gave him good advice; but finding at length that it availed nothing, went into retirement.

Rajah Sunkerderma conquered Gujerat, Sind, and afterwards the Dekhan; but reſtored the latter to it's former monarch. In the commencement of his reign he governed equitably; but in the end proved a tyrant.

In the reign of Jeſſgeerdeo, a Brahmin, who had loſt a purſe, containing a hundred gold mohurs, was ſo overcome with grief at the misfortune, that he was going to kill himſelf. The thief hearing this, went to him, and ſaid, "If I find the purſe, how much of the money will you be ſatisfied with?" He anſwered, "Whatever you pleaſe." The thief brought him ten gold mohurs. The Brahmin enraged hereat, ran to demand juſtice from the rajah, relating to him what had happened. The rajah ſummoned the thief, and ordered him to return ninety mohurs, ſaying, that he was only entitled to ten mohurs, the reward for finding the purſe.

* Sukpal is a kind of palkee.

Seenchdeo

Seenehdeo had in his ſervice one Shahmeer, a Mahomeddan, who carried his genealogy up to Arjunpandu. During the reign of this prince, Zuljoo, the paymaſter of the troops of the king of Kandahar, rebelled; and, after plundering the whole of that kingdom, betook himſelf to the narrow paſſes in the mountains, from whence he made frequent inroads upon the peaſants, extorted money from them; and, in order to ingratiate himſelf with the rajah, ſent him conſiderable preſents. At length the rajah marched to join Zuljoo, who came out of his retreat, and returned to Kandahar. Many of the rajah's troops were buried in the ſnow in the mountains. Alſo, during the reign of Seenehdeo, Runjun, ſon of the king of Tibbet, invaded Caſhmeer, and committed great depredations. Upon the death of Seenehdeo, he eſtabliſhed himſelf on the throne, and ruled with wiſdom and juſtice. He appointed Shahmeer, abovementioned, his vizier; and was by him converted to the Mahommedan faith.

Rajah Adundeo dying, Shahmeer married his widow; and in A. H. 742, cauſed the Khotbah to be read, and the coin to be ſtruck in his own name, aſſuming the title of Sultan Shumſeddeen. He exacted from the huſbandman only a fourth of the produce of the ſoil. Before he came to Caſhmeer, it was revealed to him in a dream, that he ſhould obtain the kingdom.

Sultan Allaheddeen, during his reign, made it a law, that a widow, convicted of want of chaſtity, ſhould not enjoy her deceaſed huſband's eſtate.

Sultan Shahabeddeen, a wiſe and upright prince, conquered Tibbet, Nuggerkote, and other countries.

In the reign of Sultan Kotebeddeen, Meer Syed Aly Hamadany came to Caſheer, and was treated with great reſpect by the Sultan.

 Sultan

Sultan Secunder was a rigid Mahommedan, putting to death thoſe who refuſed to become converts to the faith, and he deſtroyed all the conſiderable idolatrous temples. Timur, when he conquered Hindoſtan, ſent him ten elephants. The Sultan wiſhed to have had an interview with Timur, and ſet out from Caſhmeer for that purpoſe; but hearing on the way, that it had been reported to Timur, that he was bringing with him thirty thouſand horſes for a preſent, he made an excuſe and went back again.

Aly Shah abdicated the kingdom in favour of Zeinulabeddeen, and ſet out upon a pilgrimage to Mecca; but loſing his reſolution, and following ill advice, returned to Caſhmeer without viſiting Mecca, and with the aſſiſtance of the king of Jummoo, again poſſeſſed himſelf of the kingdom. Zeinulabeddeen returned to Punjab, where he formed an alliance with Jefferut Gowhker. Hereupon Aly Shah collected together a large army, marched to Punjab, where a great battle was fought, in which Aly Shah was put to flight, and Zeinulabeddeen regained the kingdom of Caſhmeer. Jefferut then took leave of Zeinulabeddeen, and marched to Dehly, where, being defeated in battle by Sultan Bhelole, he returned to Caſhmeer; but with the ſultan's army, he conquered all Punjab. The ſultan ſubdued Tibbet and Sind. He was a very wiſe prince, and never perſecuted any on account of religion. He was honoured and reſpected by all ranks of his ſubjects, who unanimouſly beſtowed upon him the title of Wullee *(or Saint.)* He is alſo ſaid to have poſſeſſed the power of tranſmigrating his ſoul into any body he pleaſed; and he predicted, that during the reign of one of the princes of the Chuck tribe, the kingdom ſhould be transferred from the hands of the natives to the monarchs of Hindoſtan; and this prediction, after a long period, was accompliſhed. Such was his beneficence and love of his ſubjects, that he aboliſhed the poll-tax, which

which was used to be levied from the Hindoos, forbade oxen being slain, and entirely abolished all taxes, together with the custom of offerings and presents of every kind. He enlarged the Jereeb, in favour of the husbandmen: and supported his expences by the produce of certain copper mines. He always presided in person in the courts of justice, and resolved difficult points. Robbers he put in chains, and employed them upon public works. His humanity made him prohibit hunting; and he himself never ate any flesh. He translated many books from the Arabic, Persian, Cashmeerian, and Shanscrit languages. Under his reign, musicians came to Cashmeer, from Iran and Turan, amongst whom were from Khorasan Oudee, the scholar of the well-known Khajeh Abdulcader of Khorasan, and Mulla Jemmeel, who was inimitable both in music and painting. Sultan Abuseyed Mirza sent to Zeinulabeddeen, from Khorasan, presents of Arabian horses, and Bokhty camels. Sultan Bhelole Loody, monarch of Dehly, and Sultan Mahmood, king of Gujerat, also formed alliances with him.

When Sultan Hussen came to the kingdom, he led an army into Punjab, fought several battles against Tatar Khan, and plundered and laid waste the country.

When Futteh Shah sat upon the throne, Meer Shums, one of the disciples of Shah Cossim Anwar, came from Irak to Cashmeer, and taught the tenets of Noor-Buckhshy; the first introduction there of the doctrine of the *Sheis*.

At the time that Mahommed Shah regained the kingdom a third time by the help of Secunder, the emperor Baber undertook the conquest of Hindostan.

In the reign of Sultan Ibraheim Abdal, it was represented to Baber, that Cashmeer would be an easy conquest.

queſt. Baber ſent thither Aly Beg, Mahommed Khan, and Mahmood Khan. They were at firſt victorious; but the inſurrections of the natives would not allow them to eſtabliſh themſelves there: they therefore accepted of a contribution in money, and left the country. Nazek Shah hereupon obtained the kingdom.

When Mahommed Shah was reſtored to his kingdom the fourth time, the emperor Hemayun was upon the throne. Mirza Kamran commanded at that time in Lahoor; and thoſe who were well acquainted with Caſhmeer, aſſured him it would prove an eaſy conqueſt. He, guided by their advice, ſent thither Mehrum Kowkeh, who, with the aſſiſtance of ſome of the natives, ſubdued Caſhmeer. This Kowkeh exerciſing great tyranny, the people roſe againſt him, and the Moghul chiefs were obliged to ſue for quarter, and return to their own country.

In A. H. 930, Sultan Syed Khan, king of Caſhghur, ſent his ſon, Secunder Khan, and one Mirza Hyder, with an army of ten thouſand men, who entered Caſhmeer by the way of Tibbet and Lar. They committed great depredations, but returned in a ſhort time upon terms of compromiſe.

In A. H. 948, Mirza Hyder was ſent again into Caſhmeer, by the emperor Hemayun, and, by the help of ſome natives, conquered the whole of that country; and alſo a part of Great Tibbet. Khajee Chuck came into Hindoſtan, and obtained aſſiſtance from Sheer Khan. He afterwards fought Mirza Hyder, but was defeated; and Mirza eaſily prevailed upon the Caſhmeerians to read the Kotbah, and ſtrike the coin in the name of the emperor Hemayun, inſtead of that of Nazek Shah.

SIRCAR

SIRCAR PUCKELY

Meaſures in length 35, and in breadth 25 coſe. On the eaſt lies Caſhmeer; on the eaſt Kinore; on the ſouth the territory of the Gehker tribe; and on the weſt is Attock Benaris. Timoor left a ſmall number of troops to keep poſſeſſion of this quarter, and ſome of their deſcendants are there to this day.

Snow is continually falling in the mountains of this diſtrict, and ſometimes in the plains. The winter is very ſevere, but the ſummer heat moderate. Like Hindoſtan, Puckely has periodical rains.

Here are three rivers, viz. Kiſhengung, Behut, and Sind. The language of the inhabitants has no affinity with thoſe of Caſhmeer, Zabuliſtan, or Hindoſtan. Nakhud and barley are the moſt plentiful grain here. Apricots, peaches, and walnuts, grow wild; no pains being taken here with fruit trees. Their game, horſes, mules, oxen, and buffaloes, are but indifferent.

Formerly the rajah of this country was tributary to Caſhmeer.

SIRCAR SEWAD.

IT compriſes three territories, viz. Bembher, Sewad, and Bijore. The length of Bembher is 16, and the breadth 12 coſe. On the caſt lies Puckley; on the north, Kenore and Caſhghur; on the ſouth, Attock Benaris; and Sewad is the weſtern extremity. There are two roads to it from Hindoſtan, one by the heights of Surkhaby, and the other by the Molondery hills.

Neither

Neither of these roads are good, but the first is the most difficult to pass.

Sewad measures in length 40, and in breadth from 5 to 15 cose. On the east lies Bembher; on the north, Kenore and Cashghur; on the south, Bickram; and on the west, Bijore. In the mountains of this country are several passes. Near the pass of Dumghar, adjoining to Cashghur, is the city of Munglore, the residence of the governor of the province. There are two routes to it from Hindostan; one by the height of Mulkund, and the other by the pass of Sheer Khan. The summer and winter are very temperate. The mountains are always covered with snow, but in the plains it melts in three or four days after the fall. Here are spring and autumn*, and periodical rains, as in Hindostan. Both their spring and autumn harvests are very plentiful. Here are all the flowers of Tartary and Hindostan; violets, narcissuses, and a variety of fruits, grow wild. The apricots and pears are remarkably fine. The hawks are good. Here is an iron-mine.

Bijore is in length 25, and in breadth from from 5 to 10 cose. On the east lies Sewad; on the north, Kenore and Cashghur; on the south, Bickram; and on the west, Guznoorgul. It has an old fortress, of some strength, where the governor resides; and there are several passes on the side of Cabul. Emeer Syed Aly Hamadany is said to have died here, but that, in compliance with his last testament, his body was conveyed to Khotlan.

The air of this district resembles that of Sewad, excepting that the heat and cold are felt rather more severely here. It has only three roads, one leading to Hindostan, called Danishkote, and two that go to Cabul,

* In Hindostan the trees are in perpetual verdure.

one

one of which is named Summej, and the other Guznoorgul. Danishkote is the best road. Adjoining to Bijore, and confined by the mountains and the rivers of Cabul and Sind, is a desart, measuring in length 30, and in breadth from 20 to 25 cose.

The whole of this sircar consists of hills and-wilds; and is inhabited by the tribe of Yousef-Zy. In the time of Mirza Ulugh Beg, the tribe of Sultan, who assert themselves to be the descendants of the daughter of Sultan Secunder Zulkermain, came from Cabul, and possessed themselves of this country. They say that Secunder left treasure in Cabul under the care of some of his relations; and some of their descendants, who carry their genealogical table in their hands, now dwell in the mountainous parts.

During this immortal reign, many of the turbulent inhabitants of this country have been destroyed, others taken prisoners, and others have betaken themselves to the wilds.

SIRCAR DERUNEYUN AND ISSA KHYL.

THIS is a territory situated to the south east of Cabul. The inhabitants are Afghans, mostly of the tribes of Sirany, Gurany, and Zeery.

SIRCAR KANDAHAR

IS situated in the third climate. The length, from Kelat Bunjareh to Ghurgistan, is 300 cose; and it measures in breadth, from Sind to Furreh, 260 cose. On the east lies Sind; on the north Ghour and Ghurgistan;

giſtan; on the ſouth Sewee; and on the weſt Furreh of Cabul. On the northweſt it is bounded by Ghuzneen.

It ſnows but ſeldom near the city of Cabul, but in the mountains it falls almoſt inceſſantly.

Of Coins. 18 dinars are a tuman, each tuman being equivalent to 800 dams. The tuman of Khoraſan is 30, and the tuman of Irak 40 rupees.

Moſt kinds of grain are computed in kherwars. The kherwar is equal to 40 Kandahary, or 10 Hindoſtany maunds.

Kandahar is the capital of this ſircar, and is ſituated in longitude 170° 40′, and latitude 33°. It has two forts. The heat is very ſevere, and the cold temperate, except, in the months of December and January, when water freezes. Snow does not fall here above once in three or four years. Here are flowers and fruits in abundance. The wheat of Kandahar is very white, and is ſent togreat diſtances as a rarity.

At the diſtance of five coſe from Kandar is a mountain, called Azderkouh, in which is a remarkable cave, known by the name of Ghar Gemſhied *(Ghemshied's Cave.)* You enter it with lights, but from there being no circulation of air, the lights are extinguiſhed before you can reach the bottom of the cave.

At the diſtance of eight coſe from Kelat is a large mountain, in the centre of which is alſo a wonderful cave, called Ghar Shah, *(the King's Cave.)* In the middle of it are two natural pillars, one of which unites with the roof of the cave, being 30 ells high, and from its top iſſues a ſtream of water, which flows into a baſon that is near it. The other pillar is only 11 ells in height, and from its baſe iſſues a rapid ſtream. The ſources of of theſe two ſtreams are between Balkh and Cabul, and are called Hirmund and Birkutmund. Mollana Moiyeneddeen, in his hiſtory of Khoraſan, ſays, that a thouſand ſtreams iſſue from theſe ſprings. At the diſtance of 16 coſe from Kelat, at the foot of a large mountain, is a ſpot, called Bumbul, where were formerly many aqueducts; now it is cultivated with melons. In this mountain are many ſprings. At the foot of the mountain is a furnace for ſmelting iron, an ancient work.

In a long tract of country, between Dawurd and Seiſtan, ſnow never falls. The river Hirmund runs through it; the whole is in high cultivation, and well defended by forts.

In the vicinity of Kandahar are the ruins of a large city, the native place of the Ghaurian ſultans; of whoſe grandeur many monuments remain.

Between Hirmund and Kandahar is ſituated the well-known city of Meymund, mentioned in old aſtronomical tables.

Wheat and barley, in the dialect of Kandahar, is called Sefeidtery *(white vegetable ;)* and the lands cultivated therewith are meaſured by the jereeb, of 60 ſquare guz of Cabul, equal to 54 guz of Kandahar. In the calculations for the royal exchequer, out of every ten kherwars of the produce of the ſoil, there is taken one fifth for the revenue and charges.

Rates

Rates of Collection of Revenue from a Jereeb, according to the Degrees of excellence of the Soil.

Kinds of Lands.	Medium Produce in Kherwars.	Revenue in Maunds.
1	3	24
2	$2\frac{1}{2}$	20
3	2	16
4	$1\frac{1}{2}$	12
5	1	8
6	30 maunds.	6
7	8 ditto.	$1\frac{1}{2}$

If the husbandman does not approve of measurement, then the produce is made into three heaps, two of which are for himself; and the other being divided into three parts, two are taken by the state, and one third goes for Jehat *.

On grapes, the revenue is collected either by measurement, or by agreeing to pay a certain sum. For measurement, some experienced persons estimate the produce of the vineyard, and the state exacts four baberies from every kherwar. In the reign of Hemayun the rate was two baberies and four tungahs. A babery is one miskal; two and a half baberies are equivalent to one rupee. Besides these three kinds (barley, wheat, and grapes,) which are called *Sefeidtery*, there are taken upon the following articles, which are styled *Subzting* (or greens), seven and a half baberies for every jereeb, viz. rice, melons, cucumbers, onions, turnips, carrots, poppies, and lettuce. Formerly they were rated at five baberies. Upon other vegetables they formerly exacted two baberies per jereeb, but now three are taken.

In the tract, between Dawurd and Seistan, described above, if the crops are made into three heaps, the same

* Vide Vol. I.

as

as in Kandahar, then for *Sefeidtery*; out of every meafured jereeb the ftate takes twenty maunds. The kherwar of this diftrict confifts of 100 maunds, which are equivalent to ten maunds of Hindoftan. Upon grapes the duty is the fame as at Kandahar; and the articles of Subztery pay two baberies per jereeb.

The fame equitable practice alfo obtains in Dawurd upon Sefeidtery.

SIRCAR CABUL

IS fituated in the third and fourth climates. The length, from Attock Benaris, on the banks of the Sind, to Hindookouh, is 150 cofe; and the breadth, from Carabagh to Chaghanferai, 100 cofe. On the eaft lies Hindoftan; on the weft, inclining to the north, are mountains, between which is fituated Ghour; on the north is Inderab of Badakhfhan, and Hindookouh; on the fouth Firmel and Nughz. It is impoffible to give in writing an adequate idea of the excellence of the air and water of this country. Although the winter is rather fevere, yet it never does any injury. The parts in which fnow falls, and thofe which are entirely free from it, are fo near to each other, that you may pafs from heat to cold in the courfe of a day, which is not to be experienced in any other inhabited country of the whole globe. The fnow begins to fall in the mountains in September, but not in the plains till November. Baber, in his Commentaries, remarks, that fnow never falls, on the fide of Hindoftan, nearer than the hills of Badam Chefhmeh. This certainly might have been the cafe in his time; but now it comes even to the edge of the Niemlah hills, and indeed to the Khyber heights.

 This

This country abounds with delicious fruits; the melons, however, are an exception, being but indifferent; and the harvefts are not very flourifhing. The furrounding mountains and wilds defend Cabul from fudden invafions. Hindookouh lies in the centre, between Cabul, Badakhfhan, and Balkh. There are feven roads from Turan to Cabul. Thofe from the fide of Bunjeer are Hawak, Tool, and Bajaruck. Tool is the beft road, but rather long, as its name implies*. The ftraighteft is that by the Bazaruck height. In the middle of the road is a large mountain, around which are feven hills, called Huft Butch (the feven children). The fourth road, in coming from Inderab, divides into two branches, which unite at the foot of the hill. The fifth road is by the hill of Kipchack; and this is alfo fomewhat eafy to pafs. The fixth is by the hill of Sheertoo; but, in the fummer, when the waters are out, as foon as you defcend the mountain, you muft go by the route of Bamian and Talakan. The feventh is by the way of Abdereh. In winter travellers make ufe of this road, it being the only one paffable in the depth of that feafon.

There is alfo a road by the way of Khorafan and Kandahar, which is without any winding, and free from hills. From Hindoftan to Cabul, there are fix roads: 1. Kurpeh, on which road, after paffing two hills, you come to Jilalpoor. Baber has not taken any notice of this road; we muft therefore conclude, that in his time it was not ufed. 2. Khybir, which was formerly a little difficult, but his majefty has had it levelled in fuch a manner that carriages now pafs with eafe. The people of Turan and Hindoftan come and go by this road. 3. Bungifh. In order to go this way you pafs the river Sind, at Dunkhote Ferry. 4. Nughz. 5. Fermel, to which you pafs over the Sind at Chowporah Ferry.

* Tool, in the Perfian, fignifies long.

No

No leſs than eleven languages are in uſe in the ſoobah of Cabul, each nation ſpeaking its own; viz. Turkiſh, Mughooly, Perſian, Hindy, Afghany, Puſhtowey, Purratchee, Gubree, Burkee, Lumghanee, and Arabic.

The natives are chiefly of the tribes of Hezareh and Afghan, and they poſſeſs all the paſturage. The tribe of Hezareh are the remains of the Chaghtai army, which Mangu Khan ſent into theſe parts to the aſſiſtance of Holaku Khan, under the command of his ſon Nikodar Oghlan; and they inhabit the country from Ghuzneen to Kandahar and Mydan, to the borders of Balkh. They are upwards of 100,oco families, a third of whom are cavalry. They all breed horſes, ſheep, and goats. Their pride and ſelf-conceit frequently occaſion parties amongſt them, which end in ſtrife and bloodſhed.

The Afghans ſay that they are deſcended from the children of Iſrael. They aſſert that, their grand progenitor, Afghan, had three ſons: 1. Surreen, from whom the tribe of Surreenee are deſcended. 2. Ghurghuſt, the founder of the Ghurguſty tribe. 3. Tubben, the progenitor of the Tubnee tribe. From thoſe three ſtocks have ſprung various tribes, diſtinguiſhed by the names of their founders. Amongſt this number are Turreen, Purreetch, Myaneh, Gheen, Khurgheen, Shiranee, Owzmur, Kaſſy, Jummond, Kheiſhky, Kuttany, Kheleel, Mahmoundzie, Daoudzie, Youſefzie, Gilyanee, Birkalany; all deſcended originally from Surreen. Again the Soorawhy, Jylum, Wurekzie, Afreedee, Juktanee, Khutkee, Keranee, Bawur, Munnoob, Kakerna, Ghurbanee, Muſſwanee, Bunny, and Tarun, who all carry their pedigree up to Ghurghuſt. Together with the Ghilzie, Loody, Neyazee, Noohanie, Soory, Sorwany, and Kuckboor, of the ſtock of Tubben.

They ſay that Muth Aly Ghowry, whom the Afghans

 call

call Muttee, had criminal connection with one of the daughters of Tubben; and that, when the days of her pregnancy were nearly accomplished, he married her, and thereby preserved her character. Of this marriage were born three sons: 1. Ghilzee. 2. Loody. 3. Seewany.

Some Afghans consider themselves to be of Egyptian extraction, asserting that, when the children of Israel returned from Jerusalem to Egypt, this tribe emigrated to Hindostan. The history of this event is of too great length for insertion here.

There are other unsettled tribes, viz. those of Kajah Khyzree, Kakshal, Mydany, Uzbek, Kolunjee, Beranjee, Teelboorjee, Nuckdurree, Beksoodel, Seedeebaiy, Tofukundaz, Arub, Gulaban, Tookbaiy, &c. These are numerous, but do not equal the multitude of Afghans. At present many of these tribes acknowledge a dependence upon the Jageerdars.

The CITY of CABUL.

IT is situated in longitude 104° 40′, and latitude 34° 30′. It is a very ancient and beautiful city. Pusheng is said to have been the founder. There are double walls of mud, of considerable strength. On the south-east quarter is a small hill, named Shah Cabul *. One of their ancient kings must have built upon it, from which circumstance it obtained its name.

Aruck is the city now standing upon the abovementioned small hill. At the foot of it are rich plains, decorated with delightful gardens. The most famous of

* The King of Cabul.

these

these is that called Sherara, in which are two pleasant rivulets. One of them, the rivulet of Kheteeben, comes from Lelunder, and, after passing through this garden, goes on to the city of Cabul. The other takes its rise in the village of Yaconb, and passes the city of Cabul before the Dehly gate. This last is called the rivulet of Pul Musten, and its water is better than that of the other. In the neighbourhood of this place is a delightful spot, called Gulgooneh. From the hill Shah Cabul issue three rivulets, which run towards the city. At the head of one of them is the shrine of Khajah Hummoo. Another is said to have been visited by the prophet Khyzir; and the third springs up opposite to the tomb of Khajah Abdulsumud, who is also called Khajah Rosheny.

From early antiquity Cabul and Kandahar have been accounted the gates of Hindostan; one affording entrance from Turan, and the other from Iran; and if both places are properly guarded, the extensive empire of Hindostan is safe from the irruptions of foreigners.

In Cabul, as well as in Samarcand and Bokhara, a pergunnah, which is composed of villages and hamlets, is called Tooman.

Tooman Bekram, commonly called Peishore, enjoys a delightful spring season. Here is a temple, called Gorekehtery, a place of religious resort, particularly for Jowgies.

Tooman Neyknebar. Formerly the governor of the province resided at Adeenehpoor; now Jilalabad is his place of residence. Snow falls here; but the winter is not severe. In this province grows the seedless pomegranate. This Tooman has nine rivulets, which secure success to the harvests. In Jilalabad is the garden called Suffa, a monument of the Emperor Baber. Near Adeeneh-

Adeenehpoor is a garden, called Wuſſa, another monument of the ſame monarch. On the ſouth ſide of Jilalabad is a mountain, of a wonderful appearance, it being perpetually covered with ſnow; and, on this account, it is called the *White Mountain.* Whenever ſnow falls in Cabul, it does the ſame upon a hill in this quarter.

Tooman Munderar abounds with monkeys. Here the rivers Alyſhung and Alunka unite their ſtreams, and diſembogue themſelves into the river Baran. The river of Chughanſerai, after paſſing through the north-eaſt quarter, enters Kuttore.

Tooman Alyſhung is ſurrounded with large mountains, covered with ſnow, in which is the ſource of the river bearing the ſame name. The inhabitants are called Kafurs (infidels). Here is a tomb in which, according to ſome people, lies interred Lamek, the father of Noah. The natives of this country change the letter *Kaf* ک into *Ghain* غ, calling this place, inſtead of Lumekan, Lumeghan.

Tooman Bekhrad is alſo full of infidels. Inſtead of lamps they burn green fir, which gives a very good light. Here is an animal, called the *Flying-Fox,* which flies up about an ell from the ground. Here are alſo mice that have a fine muſky ſcent.

Cherkh, one of the dependencies of Tooman Lahooker, gives names to Mollani Yacoub Cherkhy. Sijawund is alſo one of the well-known villages of this Tooman.

The mountains of Tooman Budrow are inveſted with infidels, and wild Hezareh and Afghan tribes.

Tooman

Tooman Ulſaiy has ſnow on one ſide, whilſt the other ſide is a warm climate. Here are plenty of game in the ſpring.

Tooman Bungiſh has 7000 cavalry and 87,800 infantry, viz. Of the Mehmund tribe, 500 cavalry and the like number of infantry. The Kheleel tribe 500 cavalry and 65,000 infantry. The Daoudziey, 9000 cavalry and 97,000 infantry. Kakjany, 500 cavalry and 4000 infantry. Sany, 100 cavalry and 1400 infantry. Iman Khyel, 50 cavalry and 850 infantry. Uljee, 100 cavalry and 2900 infantry. Khyzir Khyel, 20 cavalry and 550 infantry. Sheerger, 20 cavalry and 1400 infantry. Khurgoony, 10 cavalry and 200 infantry. Khutky, 200 cavalry and 4000 infantry. Abdulrahmany, 100 cavalry and 2500 infantry. Afreedy, 500 cavalry and 2500 infantry. Dirwuck, 500 cavalry and 5500 infantry.

Tooman Gurdeyz has a ſtrong fort, and moſt of the houſes are four ſtories high.

Tooman Ghuzneen is in the ſecond climate. It is alſo called Zabul, and was the capital of Sultan Mahmood, Sultan Shahabeddeen, and ſeveral other monarchs. Formerly this country was called Zabuliſtan, and Kandahar reckoned a part of it. Here are the tombs of Hakheem Sunnaiy, and many other holy men. The winter here is the ſame as in Samarcand and Tebriz. A river runs from north to ſouth, and fertilizes all the cultivated lands; but the huſbandman undergoes great labour, from being obliged to bring freſh mould, from Cabul, every year, the natural ſoil of the country being too poor for cultivation. In the time of Baber here was a tomb which ſhook whenever bleſſings were implored for the prophet; but, upon inveſtigating the cauſe, it was diſcovered to be a trick. If any filth is thrown into a certain ſpring near this place, there

there immediately enſues a dreadful tempeſt, with rain and ſnow.

Tooman Damenkouh is incomparable for abundance of flowers, and for the beauty of its ſpring and autumn.

Tooman Gharbund. It has an inconceivable variety of fragrant ſhrubs and flowers. There are thirty ſpecies of tulips, one of which has the fragrance of the roſe, and is called the *roſe-ſcented tulip.* Here are mines of ſilver and lapis lazuli. Near the mountains is a ſandy deſart, called *Khajah regrevan.* In the ſummer ſeaſon there is heard, in this deſart, the noiſe of drums and kettledrums.

In Tooman Zohac Bamyan, the caſtle of Zohac, a monument of great antiquity, is in good condition, whilſt the fortreſs of Bamyan lies in ruins.

In the midſt of theſe mountains are twelve thouſand receſſes cut out of the rock, and ornamented with carving and plaiſter-work. Theſe places are called Summij; and, in ancient times, were the winter retreat of the natives. Here are three aſtoniſhing idols; one repreſenting a man eighty ells high; another, of a woman, fifty; and the third, which is the figure of a child, meaſuring fifteen ells in height. In one of theſe Summijes is a tomb, where is a coffin, containing a corpſe, concerning which the oldeſt man can give no account; but it is held in great veneration. The ancients certainly were poſſeſſed of ſome medical preparations, with which, if they anointed dead bodies, and afterwards buried them in a dry ſoil, they ſuffered no injury from time; and there can be no doubt but this corpſe muſt have been preſerved after that manner, although the ignorant ſuppoſe it ſomething miraculous.

The whole of Cabul, which has been deſcribed, contains twenty Toomans. The Emperor Baber, in his Commentaries, reckons the revenue and tumgha * at eight lacks of Shahrokhees, which are equivalent to three lacks and twenty thousand rupees of Akbershahy, or one crore twenty-eight lacks of dams. Now, through the blessing of his majesty's immortal glory, although a variety of taxes have been remitted, the revenue is increased to six crore, seventy-three lacks, six thousand nine hundred and eighty-three dams. This increase has arisen from the improved state of the country; besides that Pershawer, Ashtughar, and some other places have been since added: and it is, moreover, to be considered, that the officers of government were not at that time under such good management as they are at present.

In A. H. 77, Abdulmullick, son of Merwan, removed Ommiah, the son of Abdullah, from the government of Khorasan, and conferred it upon Yousef, the son of Hejaj. At the same time he appointed, to the government of Seistan, Abdullah, the son of Abubeker. The latter levied an army, and marched against Runtehl, Rajah of Cabul. Runtehl, finding himself unable to cope with him, retreated to the heights; and Abdullah, ill advised, pursued him. The country people seized the opportunity of revenging themselves, blocked up all the passes with stones, and, thereby cutting off his retreat, reduced his army to such distress, for want of provisions, that he was obliged to purchase a peace at the price of seven lacks of dirhems, equivalent to three lacks of rupees of the present time. When Shureeh, the son of Hany, heard what had befallen Abdullah's army, he was greatly troubled, and, notwithstanding his extreme old age, hastened to renew the war, and died fighting gallantly. As soon as the tidings of those disasters were brought to Hejaj, he reprimanded Abdullah,

* Vide Vol. I.

and

and deprived him of the command. In the year 80 Hejaj appointed Abdulrahman, the fon of Mahommed Afhufs, governor of the province of Seiftan and its dependencies, and gave him the conduct of the war againft the Runtchl. Abdulrahman, when he arrived on the borders of Cabul, prudently took care to poft chofen troops in all the paffes. He performed great feats of valour, and obtained confiderable plunder; but, from the nature of the country, he could not maintain his conqueft. When he returned to Seiftan, Hejaj fent him a letter, couched in the following terms: "Your fervices of this year amount to nothing; immediately on the receipt of this letter return to Cabul, and poffefs yourfelf of that country. Should you prove in the leaft difobedient, by extending your delay till next year, I fhall difmifs you from your government, and in fuch cafe the whole army are hereby required to obey Ifhac, the fon of Mahommed, as their general." Upon the receipt of the letter, Abdulrahman entered into a confederacy with his officers, concluded a treaty with the Rajah of Cabul, and marched to attack Hejaj. In the treaty, with the Rajah of Cabul, it was agreed, that if the Mahommedans proved victorious, they would not, in any fhape, moleft the rajah's dominions; but that, if they fuffered a defeat, he fhould afford them protection. Hejaj, enraged, marched out to meet them, and a battle was fought near Tufter, in which Abdulrahman proving victorious, Hejaj returned to Bafrah. In a fecond engagement he defeated Abdulrahman, who retreated to Boft, which was in the hands of one of his agents. But the bafe wretch, in order to ingratiate himfelf with Hejaj, feized Abdulrahman, and intended to have fent him to his enemy, when, at that inftant, the Rajah of Cabul flew to his relief, and carried him to Cabul. This prince enabled him to profecute the war againft Hejaj, but he never gained any advantage in any battle that he fought. At laft Runtchl, gained over by the feducing promifes of Hejaj, fent prifoner prisoner to him Abdulrahman, who, in a fit of despair, on the road, threw himself headlong from a precipice, and thus ended his life. In the year 107, under the Khalifat of Heshan, the son of Abdulmullick, his governor of Khorasan, Ameen, the son of Abdallah Casheery, conquered Ghour, Ghurghistan, and Neemroz of Cabul. From that time, under the khalifs of the houses of Ommiah and Abbas, these provinces continued to be dependent upon Khorasan, till the government of the Sammanians, when Aleptigheen, a slave belonging to that family, rebelled, and possessed himself of Ghuzneen and Cabul, where he ruled with absolute sway. When he died, Sebucktegheen, the father of Sultan Mahmood, obtained the kingdom, and it continued in the possession of the Ghuzneen princes.

This kingdom at first belonged to the Ghaurian princes; next it was possessed by their slaves, one of whom was Ilduz. After the slaves, it was held by the Khovarezmians. Then the army of the great Khan Chungaze conquered it. From him it descended to Timur and his posterity.

Of the CROUH, or COSE.

THE measurement of roads, for the ascertaining of distances, being an object of public utility, his majesty has given great attention to it, and has caused the distances to be measured in crouhs, each consisting of 100 tenabs of 50 Alaiy guz*: or 400 bamboos of $12\frac{1}{2}$ guz each. By either of these methods, a crouh contains 5000 guz.

Whenever his majesty marches at the head of his ar-

* Vide Vol. I.

mies,

mics, or performs a journey, the road is carefully meaſured with the above-mentioned bamboos, by perſons appointed for that purpoſe, whoſe accounts are checked by a Darogha and Muſhriff.

Sheer Khan fixed the crouh at ſixty jereebs, each containing ſixty Secundery guz; and this is the rule ſtill obſerved in the ſoobah of Dehly.

In Gujerat, a crouh is the greateſt diſtance at which may be heard the ordinary lowing of an ox; and this is eſtimated to be fifty jereebs.

In Bengal they uſe the *Depeyeh Crouh*, which is the diſtance that a man can go at a quick pace, without being out of breath. According to others, a man is to pluck a green leaf, and, placing it upon his head, is to walk with it till it is dry, which diſtance they ſay is a crouh.

Others make use of the following rule of Calculation.

6 hairs of a mule's tail	make one	Barleycorn.
6 barleycorns	make one	Inch.
24 inches	make one	Guz.
4 guz	make one	Bagh.
12,000 baghs	make one	Meel (or mile).
3 miles	make one	Furſukh.
3 furſukhs	make one	Bereed.

According to Hindoo Philosophers.

8 barleycorns ſtripped of the huſk, when laid in breadth,	make one	Inch.
24 inches	make one	Duſt (or cubit).
4 duſts	make one	Dund (or Dehnuck).
2000 dehnucks	make one	Crouh, or, as they call it, coſe.
4 coſe	make one	Jowjun.

Some

Some Hindoos reckon the cofe to confift of 1000 fteps made by a woman, carrying a jar of water on her head and a child in her arms.

Praife be unto God, that, by the affiftance of his divine grace, I have completed the Inftitutes, and the Hiftory of the Soobahs.

The accounts of the zemeendary troops coft me a great deal of trouble collecting; and I found fuch difficulty in afcertaining dates, and in reconciling the contradictions in the feveral hiftories of the princes of Hindoftan, that I had nearly refolved to relinquifh the tafk altogether. But who can avoid the decrees of Fate?

Whatever appeared moft confonant with my own knowledge, I admitted in preference to relations of which I was entirely ignorant. I truft that thofe who have been able to obtain better information, will not dwell upon my errors; but that, upon the whole, I may meet with approbation.

TUKSEEM JUMMA;

OR THE

ASSESSMENT OF THE LANDS

OF

HINDOSTAN.

TUKSEEM JUMMA

OF THE

SOOBAH OF BENGAL.

SIRCAR OUDUMBER,

COMMONLY CALLED

T A N D E H,

Containing 52 Mahls, 24,079,399½ Dams.

	Dams.
Ak Mahl,	133,017
Achelah, Durſparah, Aſhriſſthal,	404,277½
Ibrahimpoor	369,357
Owjial Ghatty,	231,057
Ungatchy,	369,657½
Berkenkel,	666,200
Bhatall,	415,170
Bahadrepoor,	314,780
Bahurroy,	206,155
Phoolwary,	193,025
Bahadre Shahy,	138,102
Tandeh, with its dependencies	4,326,102
Tajepoor	201,997
Talook Birmahgoor,	11,925
Tenowly,	196,380
Chunghatty,	589,467
Chandpoor,	190,027
Naſeeby,	120,205
Chownknudya,	145,305
Hajepoor,	106,255
Huſſainabad,	226,545
Khanpoor,	31,410
Dahdah,	250,597
Davyapoor,	559,557
Davud Shahy,	240,802
Durgatchy,	225,745
Rampoor,	115,532
Rupeſſpoor,	138,122
Seroopſing,	1,368,877
Sultanpoor Owjeal,	456,394
Soliman Shahy,	198,742

	Dams.
Solimanabad,	197,960
Solimanpoor,	187,097
Sumbela,	174,550
Sheer Shahy,	178,230
Shumſkkany,	321,952
Sheerpoor,	163,097
Firozepoor,	347,787½
Koonwerpertab,	1,607,200
Gungjook,	1,589,332
Cattahgurh,	1,265,632
Kengerch,	894,027
Coſſypoor,	350,760
Kuchla,	36,240
Kafoordya,	1,440
Mulyſir,	1,503,352
Mungelpoor,	226,770
Petty Talookdars,	145,637
Nawanagur,	825,985
Neſybpoor,	37,750

SIRCAR JENNETABAD.

Containing 66 Mahls, 1,573,196 Dams.

Jennetabad, commonly called Gour,	7,869,292
Jawaragra, including 14 pergunnahs, viz.	1,573,196
Ajore,	138,925
Bazghogera,	192,508
Belyr,	127,300
Havelly Agra,	215,260
Dehnpoor,	140,340
Derſerruk,	112,208
Seernoor,	70,000
Shaballa,	98,000
Shalelſery,	8,000
Ghagteer,	50,200
Mudnowty,	151,890
Moodyhaut,	6,980
Nahet,	242,710
Huſtgujpoor,	27,515
Jewarderſurg, 16 mahls, viz.	2,009,944
Owjareekaneh,	7,800
Bhetya,	826,430
Bhelbary,	91,560
Eſtabliſhed Markets,	37,600
Derſerrug,	628,035
Raggamatty,	1,200
Syer Duties on Exports and Imports,	170,800
Skeerpoor and Kengalpoor, 2 mahls,	2,000
Shabazpoor within the city,	400
Ghiaſſpoor,	41,920
Kemelah,	163,077
Gatkachappa,	12,000

	Dams.
Moody Mahl,	13,000
Mineh Mahl,	360
Duties from the new Market,	11,760
Jewardihykote, 7 mahls, viz.	869,000
Berarypinjer,	698,600
Tagore,	37,720
Dihykote,	316,240
Dehlgong,	130,720
Shahzadehpoor	84,360
Malygong,	141,460
Moodypoor,	61,880
The Environs of Ramowty, 7 mahls,	749,795
Badhtehly,	207,500
Ramowty,	194,767
Sebelgehrya,	103,000
Sengkekerah,	93,320
Sultanpoor,	29,210
Singdewar,	14,447
Mahynagur,	107,550
The Environs of Serſabad, 10 mahls,	3,192,377
Akbarpoor,	97,360
Pardyar,	8,528
Khyzirpoor,	306,100
Serſabad,	553,080
Cutwally,	788,427
Giramend,	3,034,380
Gerhy,	200,000
Mekrayin,	106,480
Hentenda and Manickpore, 2 mahls,	630,770
The Environs of Maldah, 11 mahls, viz.	
Barbuckpoor,	
Yuſef Bazar,	
Havelly Maldah,	
Dheerpoor,	
Sujapoor,	
Sermadhelpoor,	
Sengoodya,	
Saleeſery,	
Shahhindoovy,	
Tettahpoor,	
Moezzeddunpoor.	

In this sircar there is a brick fort. It furnishes 500 *cavalry, and* 17,000 *infantry.*

SIRCAR FUTTAHABAD.

Containing 31 Mahls, 7,969,567 Dams.

Jyſir Acharej,	34,304
Phoolbail,	384,452
Belon,	124,872
Bhagelpore,	6,115
Badhadya,	1,442
Taylhatty,	377,290

Chernluckhy,

	Dams.
Chernluckhy,	35,645
Churha-ey,	30,200
Havelly Futtahabad, including the city,	902,662
Haffil Nimuck (falt duties)	277,758
Hazerutpoor,	11,640
Market duties,	11,467
Ruffoolpoor,	103,767
Soondeep,	1,182,450
Sirhargorl,	788,430
Sirryfany,	173,227
Serowya,	53,882
Sudhewah,	37,167
Sewamil, commonly called Jilalpoor,	1,857,230
Shahbazpoor,	732,172
Kherregpoor,	118,135
Kuffodya,	102,405
Kowfa,	68,350
Mukewrgunge,	3,157
Mufnedgoor,	55,312
Miranpoor,	22,172
Petty Talookdars,	123,365
Nukutleyfir,	49,422
Nyametpoor,	20,960
Hezarhatty,	21,597
Yufefpoor,	258,125

This sircar furnishes 900 *cavalry and* 50,700 *infantry.*

SIRCAR MAHMOODABAD.

Containing 88 Mahls, 11,610,256 Dams.

Adenya,	76,113
Anootumpoor,	43,365
Owjealpoor,	37,307
Indercolly,	11,250
Aindeh,	192
Bazooraft,	652,507
Bazoochup,	271,240
Eerary,	604,122
Eyfy,	25,247
Pereenjumlah,	102,202
Peethurya,	96,317
Batnaun,	85,447
Banka,	41,317
Balewary,	29,395
Tebdewall,	26,155
Paty Kamara,	22,710
Bahben Kerla,	14,695
Prawnpoor,	12,577
Bernapoor,	6,717
Putkabary,	3,567
Pepubarya,	2,045
Bagotya,	217
Buleguffy,	123,387
Turakeyna,	675,790
Teeyaghatty,	92
Taraowjeal,	391,365

Chadya,

	Dams.
Chadya,	9,325
Jeyaruky,	11,505
Jugnautpoor,	762
Jeedyburrya,	447
Jeedya,	44,700
Chytun Bazoo,	952,950
Huſſain Owjeal,	345,135
Havelly,	91,575
Khaliſſpoor,	56,805
Kheezerkhany,	1,092
Korempoor,	265
Dekary,	51,750
Doorlubpoor,	13,775
Dhooly,	13,665
Dewra,	107
Dehkut Jilalpoor,	12,300
Dooſhynya,	1,052
Dhumerhaut,	42,505
Sudkychalkota,	8,205
Serootya,	6,530
Sirſirrya,	72,947
Sunkerdeyh,	10,212
Selimpoor,	33,637
Gocma, commonly called Sultara Owjeal,	789,220
Serooppoor,	7,482
Salyberrya,	6,760
Satore,	290,727
Shahowjeal,	344,687
Sheerpoorberry,	9,402
Sheerpoorutaſhaly,	2,797
Azmetpoor,	14,422
Gheznypoor,	12,367
Ferketpoor,	301,790

	Dams.
Futtahpoor Noſyka,	102,525
Kotebpoor,	23,352
Cazypoor,	2,352
Kundalya,	20,417
Khelpharty,	19,940
Kundynewy,	8,487
Koolberya,	6,517
Gowda,	6,535
Kulyanpoor,	26,232
Kuly Mahl,	26,717
Lanyan,	313,286
Loongohal,	15,425
Mehman Shahy,	575,727
Mukhya,	514,505
Mahmoodſhahy,	226,552
Meerpoor,	2,307
Meheſirpoor,	42,652
Mudhooduma,	695
Maaroofdeeyeh,	2,302
Nuldy,	804,440
Neſſaret Shahy,	289,450
Neekerehal Kootya,	61,935
Neeker Banka,	33,182
Naſhypoor, called alſo Owjain,	91,080
Humtunpoor,	477,360
Hulda,	122,566
Hawallghatty,	66,217
Hettapawn,	3,665
Hooſypoor,	17,425

This sircar furnishes 200 *cavalry and* 10,100 *infantry.*

SIR-

SIRCAR KHALIFETABAD,

Containing 35 Mahls, 5, 402,140 Dams.

	Dams.
Bahl, with its Kusbahs,	475,102
Bhalga,	203,515
Polah,	130,215
Poonga,	104,205
Baghmara,	81,807
Phanda,	25,300
Bhadeys,	11,225
Bhalyanah,	9,527
Phoolnagur,	6,660
Talook Cossinaut,	297,720
Talla,	174,376
Talook Serysing,	26,427
Talook Mahays Mundel,	23,727
Talook Nermoder Bhattacharej,	13,860
Talook Seryput Kubraj,	8,675
Jessore, commonly called Russoolpoor,	1,723,650
Cherowla,	99,553
Chebrah,	20,920
Havelly Khalifetabad,	31,442
Khalisspoor,	32,770
Danya,	522,885
Ranekdya,	129,910
Sahesspoor,	260,340
Solimanabad,	168,504
Sahess,	91,500
Sohbnaut,	51,662
Saleesery,	11,484
Amudpoor,	97,110
Ghograll,	105,520
Kunkeesh Talook Permanund,	166,327
Moondehgatch,	126,360
Mullikpoor,	61,327
Mudehrya,	45,007
Mangoreghaut,	18,842
Mehrysa,	11,170

This sircar furnishes 100 *cavalry and* 15,150 *infantry.*

SIRCAR BOKLA,

Containing 4 Mahls, 7,130,645 Dams.

Ismailpoor, commonly called Bokla,	4,347,960
Sirryrampoor	252,000
Shahzadehpoor,	977,245
Adelpoor,	1,553,440

This sircar furnishes 320 *cavalry and* 15,000 *infantry.*

SIR-

SIRCAR POORENEAH,

Containing 9 Mahls, 6,408,793 Dams.

	Dams.		Dams.
Affownja,	734,225	Syer Hafil Feelan (duties on ele-phants,)	85,000
Jyrampoor,	467,385	Kuttyary,	590,100
Havelly Poore-neah,	2,686,995	Gudwan,	280,592
Dulmallpoor,	671,530		
Sultanpoor,	502,206		
Sirrypoor,	390,200		

This sircar furnishes 100 cavalry and 5000 infantry.

SIRCAR TAJEPOOR,

Containing 29 Mahls, 6,483,857 Dams.

Pungut,	3,307,385	Delawerpoor,	944,055
Budekher,	238,855	Deyhut,	124,196
Phooly,	60,860	Sayfehra,	372,760
Bundole,	190,830	Sajapoor,	244,507
Bowbyra,	23,192	Shahpoor,	126,235
Bhownfyra,	118,295	Gowrapoor,	406,000
Bergong,	9330	Kuffargong,	258,742
Baffygong,	104,492	Gopaulnagur,	233,160
Bungong,	111,990	Gogehra,	147,392
Bahadrepoor,	96,012	Mhafoon,	194,475
Bahanagur,	91,303	Neelnagur,	267,612
Budulya,	71,564	Neeloon,	147,510
Talldewar,	218,540	Yufefpoor,	146,240
Chupertall,	243,255	Zekaut,	78,487
Havelly Taje-poor, with the city,	854,286		

This sircar furnishes 100 cavalry and 5000 infantry.

SIRCAR GHORAHGHAUT,

Containing 84 Mahls, 8,383,072½ Dams.

	Dams.
Adhweh,	91,292
Amdeher,	75,010
Undelgong,	154,337
Anwerban,	31,022
Allgong,	171,695
Embethura,	25,326
Ahmedabad,	18,517
Ambylagatchy,	9,200
Anwermullick,	8,020
Allhaut,	7,508
Alhadadpoor	2,192
Bazoo and Zafer Shahy, two mahls,	735,835
Bazoofolad Shahy,	711,412
Takdewar,	102,440
Phoolwary,	6,580
Barbuckpoor,	84,952
Bamunpoor,	49,070
The city of Naſſeretabad,	336,445
Berſylla,	233,680
Berry Jamokballa,	146,767
Berry Ghorahghaut,	165,827
Baizeedpoor,	144,227
Pataldeehey,	41,365
Balka,	30,335
Bhooly,	12,040
Bajeputtary,	7,900
Bunwarkatcher,	4,452
Bhaleghautty,	3,245
Bazar Chetaghaut,	387

	Dams.
Balasſbary,	7,000
Banje Matka,	5,340
Toolſyghaut,	164,340
Talook Huſſein,	35,410
Talook Balnaut,	27,962
Talook Seewan,	15,490
Talook Keſſay,	15,267
Tachel,	8,290
Talook Ahmed Khan,	238,475
Hamela,	6,580
Khyerabady,	5,610
Khasſbary,	2,734
Rokenpoor,	10,950
Sultanpoor,	108,377
Seekſheher,	93,071
Sanhypoor,	49,570
Serhutta,	344,497
Subdee,	206,224
Seetpoor,	128,775
Seryakundy,	24,622
Saghaut,	16,412
Sheerpoor Goweybary,	15,675
Futtahpoor,	353,355
Kuttyary,	1,344,280
Gyapoor,	107,005
Kabulpoor,	98,465
Gunge Sawkhmala,	98,465
Cundkehdy,	81,565
Gocul,	56,865
Coothy and Tary, two mahls,	47,807

Khulſy,

	Dams.		Dams.
Khulfy,	264,322	Mukufhpoor,	124,005
Gurrybary,	125,797	Mohubetpoor,	46,512
Cooly Bazar, commonly called Jorpoory,	115,680	Musjid Huffein Shahy,	28,945
Gobindpoorakhend,	40,675	Musjid Underkhany,	3,447
Gautnall,	40,367	Mullyer,	24,800
Kanikfookher,	28,065	Nundehra,	61,050
Ghautnagur,	27,922	Nopara,	19,202
Kowahgatchy,	25,600	Nihyehjown Batore.	49,010
Katybary,	24,847	Vakerehhazer,	30,346
Gowrah (a custom-houfe)	18,000	Wutchy,	16,830
Gowgran,	13,120	Wahreeb,	4,230
Kabul,	11,690		
Gurhya,	10,980		
Gocunpara,	9,[illegible]50		

This sircar furnishes 900 cavalry, 50 elephants, and 32,600 infantry.

SIRCAR PINJERAH.

Containing 21 Mahls, 5,803,275 Dams.

Apole,	1,058,725	Digha,	149,637
Ambary,	86,525	Dewra,	107,727
Ungotcha,	101,822	Sidherbary,	276,045
Barengpoor,	635,390	Suckta,	251,410
Bijanagur,	719,107	Sultanpoor,	203,292
Baizeedpoor,	255,445	Sasfbeer,	165,180
Behernagur,	119,720	Solimanabad,	42,532
Baryghecr,	84,277	Khetta,	777,255
Badookher,	55,205	Keedabary,	213,383
Takaffy,	374,490		
Haloon,	82,142		
Havelly Pinjerah,	93,967		

This sircar furnishes 50 cavalry and 7000 infantry.

SIRCAR BARBUCKABAD,

Containing 38 Mahls, 17,451:532 Dams.

	Dams.
Omrole,	560,382
The city of Barbuckabad,	315,340
Baſſdole,	190,885
Polabar,	136,712
Buſſtole,	652,367
Burburrya,	64,335
Bungong,	319,000
Baltapoor,	179,840
Jayrya Bazoo,	755,522
Chowrah,	159,832
Jaſſnud Chowgong 2 mahls,	477,640
Chandloy,	289,640
Haynaſoo,	85,787
Havelly Seekſheher,	1,629,175
Dhermen,	350,895
Daoudpoor,	80,910
Sunkardel, commonly called Nizampoor,	389,985
Shikarpoor,	327,342
Sheerpoor and Behrampoor, 2 mahls,	391,625
Tahyrpoor,	505,825
Cazyhutty,	620,477
Kerdcha,	1,390,572
Goozerhaut,	1,296,240
Khaſs,	881,080
Chuckdul, a well-known grain market,	694,655
Gobendpoor,	410,535
Kallygygohetya,	341,057
Kheral,	210,132
Godanagur,	129,550
Kallygy,	196,932
Luſhkerpoor,	255,090
Maltchypoor,	925,680
Muſſdha,	689,712
Munſemaly,	594,792
Mahmoodpoor,	124,532
Vizierpoor,	169,190

This sircar furnishes 50 *cavalry and* 7000 *infantry.*

SIRCAR

SIRCAR BAZOOHA,

Containing 32 Mahls, 39,516,871 Dams.

	Dams.
Allap Shahy,	760,667
Burbazoo Nuſ-ſeetſhahy, & Mehrowneh, Kharana, He-ranah, and Serally, 5 mahls,	4,178,140
BehſoryaBazoo,	2,820,740
Behwal Bazoo,	1,935,160
Pertaub Bazoo,	1,881,265
PokereahBazoo,	1,715,170
Huſſain Shahy,	1,827,540
Duſkehona,	1,645,610
Dukha Bazoo,	1,902,022
Selim Partaub Bazoo, Sultan Per-taub Bazoo Chaund Per-taub Bazoo	4,625,475
Soonaghutty Ba-zoo,	1,910,440
Sona Bazoo,	1,705,290
Silbers,	1,484,320
Syer Jelkur,	261,280
Shahowjeal Ba-zoo,	405,120

	Dams.
Zufferowjeal Bazoo,	650,047
Kuttermul Ba-zoo,	2,804,390
Kutta Bazoo,	123,720
Mehmaun Sha-hy,commonly called Seer-poor Moor-cheh,	2,207,715
Senghude-men, Meer Huſ-ſain, Nuſſeret Shahy, Sing Neſſeret Owjeal,	1,867,715
Mobarek Ow-jeal,	468,780
Hurryall Bazoo,	344,140
Yuſef Shahy,	1,670,900

This sircar furnishes 1700 *cavalry*, 10 *ele-phants, and* 45,300 *infan-try.*

SIRCAR

SIRCAR SUNARGONG,

Containing 52 Mahls, 10,331,333 Dams.

	Dams.
Ovter Shapoor,	388,442
Allchap,	53,090
Ovter Oſmanpoor,	24 880
Bikrampoor,	3,335,052
Bhelwajewar,	1,331,480
Buldakhal,	694,090
Bowalya,	237,320
Perchandy,	120,100
Bat-hkurra,	4,080
Palaſſghauty, &c.	43,205
Berdya,	36,312
Phoolry,	19,000
Panhutty,	7,367
Towra,	104,902
Tajpoor,	60,000
Terkee,	18,270
Jowgydya,	512,080
Jewar Bunder,	72,632
Chokendy,	17,827
Chundyaher,	30,322
Chaundpoor,	120,000
Havelly Sunargong, with the city,	459,532
Khyzirpoor,	40,308
Dowhar,	458,524
Dandera,	421,380
Decan Shapoor,	239,910
Delawerpoor, Haſſil Zekat,	127,207
Decan Aſmanpoor,	8,740
Roypoor,	4,535
Sukhergong,	320,365
Sukery,	184 780
Selimpoor,	91,090
Salvſerry, with the Syer Jelker,	40,725
Sukwa,	308,000
Sukadeyh,	28,000
Seberchaul,	13,000
Shumſpoor,	22,000
Kurrapoor,	293,402
Gurdy,	89,590
Katikpoor,	80,000
Khandy,	40,140
Kowlhurry,	34,160
Ghattydunaiy,	20,000
Mherkole,	1,039,470
Mazempoor,	236,830
Mehar,	90,800
Menowherpoor,	53,301
Mehyjaul,	25,000
Narainpoor, and the Syer Zekat,	943,760
Nulwakote,	16,080
Himta Bazoo,	281,280
Hautghautty,	10,285

This sircar furnishes 1500 cavalry, 200 elephants, and 46,000 infantry.

SIRCAR

SIRCAR SILHET,

Containing 8 Mahls, 6,681,620 Dams.

	Dams.
Pertaubghur,	372,000
Byan Khung,	1,672,080
Bahoowaſabir,	2,094,080
Chyntar,	272,200
Havelly Silhet,	1,029,717
Sirkundel,	392,472
Lawed,	246,202
Hernagur,	1,002,852

This sircar furnishes 1100 cavalry, 190 elephants, and 42,920 infantry.

SIRCAR CHATGONG,

Containing 7 Mahls, 11,424,310 Dams.

Chatgong,	6,649,402
Malgong,	506,000
Dewgong,	775,540
Solimanpoor, commonly called Sheikhpoor,	1,572,400
Syeraz Nimuckſar, duties from the ſalt works,	737,520
Sahwā,	479,840
Nowapara,	703,600

This sircar furnishes 100 cavalry and 1500 infantry.

SIRCAR SHEREEFABAD,

Containing 26 Mahls, 22,488,750 Dams.

Burdwan,	1,876,142
Behrore,	1,736,795
Bareek Seel,	1,540,695
Bhergodah and Akbar Shahy, commonly called Sandel, 2 mahls,	1,276,195
Bagha,	509,840
Bhatſeela,	307,340
Bazar Ibraheempoor,	15,740
Jungy,	937,705
Kotemakund,	2,311
Dahnyan,	1,508,850
Soliman Shahy,	721,635

Soneya,

	Dams.		Dams.
Soneya,	92,370	Kodela,	63,125
Havelly Sheerpoor Attaey,	816,068	Mhalend,	1,731,890
Azmet Shahy,	1,660,045	Menowher Shahy,	1,709,920
Futtah Sing,	2,096,463	Mozuffer Shahy,	1,552,175
Hussain Owjeal,	393,345	Neffung,	782,517
Kurgong,	348,260	Nubran,	203,560
Keertpoor,	225,775		
Khund,	196,380		
Khunga,	184,360		

This sircar furnishes 200 cavalry and 5000 infantry.

SIRCAR SOLIMANABAD,

Containing 31 Mahls, 17,629,964 Dams.

Inderayin,	592,120	Sahuffpoor,	314,842
Ismailpoor,	184,540	Sunghowly,	72,747
Unnelya,	124,577	Sultanpoor,	44,572
Owla,	89,277	Omarpoor,	223,320
Buffundhurry,	2,266,280	Alumpoor,	28,280
Bhowst,	1,968,990	Kabuzpoor,	747,200
Purrduwah,	1,823,292	Gobinda,	357,942
Bajemore,	601,495	Petty Talookdars,	232,067
Baly Chunga,	417,185	Mahommedpoor,	48,515
Chootypoor,	554,950	Moolkher,	792,107
Joomha,	405,901	Muckeen,	910,990
Jaypoor,	44,250	Nayera,	872,945
Hussein poor,	352,090	Neffung,	500,765
Dharsah,	95,250	Neepa,	77,017
Raysak,	68,257		
Havelly Solimanabad,	2,051,090		
Saatfunga,	757,111		

This sircar furnishes 100 cavalry and 5000 infantry.

SIRCAR SATGONG,

Containing 53 Mahls, 16,724,720 Dams.

	Dams.
Benwa, Cutwally, and Ferasfetghur, 3 mahls,	1,541,770
Owkera,	726,360
Anwerpoor,	246,950
Erfaad Towaly and Satgong, 2 mahls,	234,890
Akbarpoor,	115,502
Bowdhen,	956,457
Bewan and Selimpoor, 2 mahls,	952,505
Poorah,	652,470
Bermaheerah and Manickhutty,	383,803
Beelgong,	230,602
Balinda,	125,250
Bagwan and Bungabary, 2 mahls,	100,000
Baleya,	94,725
Pehlga,	38,245
Bermudhutty,	25,027
Toorterya,	36,604
Havelly Shehr,	502,330
Huffainpoor,	324,322
Hajeepoor and Barbuckpoor, 2 mahls,	142,590
Dhalyapoor,	78,815
Rannyhaut,	1,358,815
Sadghatty,	1,358,510

	Dams.
Sakota,	204,072
Sirunrajepoor,	125,792
Duties collected from the Bunder and other markets,	1,200,000
Saghaut and Katfal, 2 mahls,	45,757
Futtahpoor,	80,702
Calcutta, Mekooma, and Barbuckpoor, 3 mahls,	936,215
Kharer,	365,275
Khundalya,	242,160
Cillarawa,	197,522
Mukowra,	801,302
Meetary,	307,845
Midnymull,	186,242
Mozufferpoor,	108,332
Mooudagatcha,	98,565
Mahyhatty,	49,935
Nuddya and Satenpoor, 2 mahls,	1,508,820
Sellky,	90,042
Hattykundeh,	55,702
Hyagurh,	781,360

This sircar furnishes 50 cavalry and 6000 infantry.

SIRCAR

SIRCAR MADARUN,

Containing 16 Mahls, 9,403,400 Dams.

	Dams.
Unhutty,	122,655
Balgurry,	937,077
Beerbhoom,	541,245
Bhewalbhoom,	495,220
Chitwa,	806,542
Chunpanuggry,	412,250
Havelly Madarun,	1,727,077
Saynbhoom,	615,805
Summerſanhuſs,	274,461
Sheergurh, commonly called Sukerbhoom,	915,237
Shahpoor,	634,460
Keytt,	46,447
Mundelghaut,	906,775
Nagore,	4,025,608
Meena Baag,	279,322
Huſſowly,	263,207

This sircar furnishes 150 *cavalry and* 7000 *infantry.*

SIRCAR JELASIR,

Belonging to ORISAH,

Containing 28 Mahls, 50,052,737 Dams.

Banſud, commonly called Hufthoor, (here are five ſtrong forts,)	4,211,430
Belly,	1,011,430
Paly Shahy,	963,430
Balkhohy,	756,220
Perbudah, has 3 forts,	640,000
Bhoguroy, has a very ſtrong fort,	497,140
Bugdy, has alſo a good fort,	394,280
Bazar,	125,720
Bahbehnbhoom,	114,208
The town of Jelaſir, here is a brick fort,	12,007,110
Tumlook has a ſtone fort,	2,571,430
Terkole, here is a fort in the wilds,	720,570
Tarah, commonly called Dawerſoorbhoom,	1,342,860
Khumna, (here are five forts,)	5,062,360

Rayn,

	Dams.
Rayn on the borders of Orisah, here are three forts,	2,182,860
Roypoor is a large town, & has a very strong fort,	986,970
Sumbuk, has a very strong fort in the wilds,	1,257,140
Sayary,	108,570
Cossyjurah,	893,160
Kurrugsore, has a very strong fort in the hills,	528,570
Keydarkend, has three forts,	468,570
Keerry,	285,720
Kuknapoor,	85,720
Kerowly,	68,570
Maljeekta,	9,318,310
Midnapoor is a large city, where where there are two forts, one old and the other new,	212,930
Mahakaunghaut, commonly called Kotebpoor, has a very strong stone fort,	240,000
Narainpoor, commonly called Khundhar, here is a very strong fort upon a hill,	2,182,860

This sircar furnishes 3470 *cavalry*, 2 *elephants, and* 43,810 *infantry*.

SIRCAR BUDERUCK,

Belonging to ORISAH,

Containing 7 Mahls, 18,687,770 Dams.

Berwa, has two strong forts,	3,240,000
Jowkutchery,	57,140
Havelly Buderuck (here is a fort called Dhamnagur,)	9,542,760
Sehensoo, here are two strong forts,	3,504,280
Gyman, (here is a stone fort of great strength)	1,515,840
Gursoo,	731,430

	Dams.
Petty Talookdars (three forts,)	85,720

This circar furnishes 750 cavalry and 3700 infantry.

SIRCAR CUTTEK,

Belonging to ORISAH.

Containing 21 Mahls, 91,432,730 Dams.

All,	6,429,130
Uſkek,	3,186,680
Atgurh (here is a fort of great ſtrength,)	1,174,680
Poorubdigh, (here are four forts,)	22,881,580
Petchimdigh,	6,662,490
Bahar,	5,129,620
Buſſaiy Dewarpoor,	2,746,650
Berrung (here nine forts amongſt the hills & wilds)	2,133,940
Bhijnegur, has a ſtrong fort,	860,390
Bunhoo,	766,206
Perſotim,	691,530
Jowiſkite, here are 4 ſtrong forts,	2,398,970
Hubbeſh, commonly called Hajypoor, has a fort,	2,073,780
Decandigh (here are 4 forts)	22,065,770
Seeran,	2,978,030
Sheergurh,	1,403,580
Kotedeys has 3 forts,	4,708,980
The city of Cuttek Benaris, (has a ſtone fort of great ſtrength)	2,605,600
Kehterra has a ſtrong fort,	1,120,230
Manikdeytun is a large bunder, where ſalt duties are collected,	600,000

This sircar furnishes 1920 cavalry & *108,160 infantry.*

SIRCAR

SIRCAR KULLENGDUNDPAUT,

Belonging to ORISAH,

Containing 27 Mahls, 5,560,000 Dams.

This sircar furnishes 500 *cavalry and* 3000 *infantry.*

SIRCAR RAJE MAHINDRAH,

Belonging to ORISAH,

Containing 16 Mahls, 5,000,000 Dams.

This sircar furnishes 1000 *cavalry and* 500 *infantry.*

TUKSEEM JUMMA

OF THE

SOOBAH OF BAHAR.

SIRCAR BAHAR,

Containing 46 Mahls.

Meaſurement, 952,598 Beegahs,

Revenue, 83,196,390 Dams,

Seyurghal, 2,270,147 Dams.

	Dams.
Arwel,	4,260,780
Owkehry gohkery,	3,747,504
Eykel,	3,035,260
Amreetu,	1,821,333
Imbelee,	847,908
Unhja,	6,700,000
Unterry,	147,980
Bahar and its dependencies, (has a fort of brick and ſtone,	5,534,151
Behlawer,	3,651,640
Beeſook,	2,706,539
Peletch,	2,270,438
Belya,	2,056,502
Patnah has two forts, one of brick and the other of mud,	1,922,430
Phoolwary,	1,585,420
Pahra,	941,160
Bheempoor,	824,584
Punderuck,	727,640
Telladch,	2,920,363
Jedder,	979,363
Chergong,	904,440
Jaeychempa,	620,000
Dawer,	262,500
Dhiker,	215,680
Rowh,	250,100
Rampoor,	363,820
Rajgurh,	288,228
Sunnote,	2,824,180
Semaey,	2,537,080
Sehreh,	2,079,000
Sandeh,	1,889,957
Seyur,	1,250,591
Ghiaſſpoor,	5,657,290
Gundhore,	1,452,500
Katybehra,	737,447
Kaber,	560,375
Kouh,	374,880

Kurrenpoor,

	Dams.
Ghautlyſehar,	360,820
Kurrenpoor,	363,820
Giya,	74,270
Mynerwa,	7,049,179
Moodeh,	4,631,080
Maldah,	2,151,575
Menerwa,	585,500
Mekeir,	1,776,540
Nerhut,	2,380,309

This sircar furnishes 2115 *cavalry and* 67,350 *infantry.*

SIRCAR MUNGEER,

Containing 31 Mahls, 109,625,981½ Dams.

Abhypoor,	200,000
Ooſela,	189,760
Ungu,	147,800
Utbelu,	50,000
Bhagelpoor,	4,696,110
Bellya,	3,287,320
Bhurkyeh,	3,000,000
Puhtrareh,	140,920
Buſſee,	132,000
Tunoor,	88,408
Chihy,	928,000
Chundowey,	360,000
Dehrempoor,	4,000,000
Dandſukhwar,	136,000
Rowhenny,	95,360
Serowhy,	1,783,000
Sukdehra,	690,240
Sakhowly,	360,000
Soorejgurh,	299,445
Sunghraſany,	160,000
Sutyaree,	58,730
Khelgong,	2,800,000
Kehrhy,	689,044
Kowzreh,	260,200
Kehtky,	160,000
Lekhenpoor,	633,280
Musjidpoor,	1,259,750
Mungeer and its dependencies,	808,907½
Muſſdy,	29,725
Hendowy,	108,000
Hurarungy,	9,179

This sircar furnishes 2150 *cavalry and* 50,000 *infantry.*

SIRCAR

SIRCAR CHUMPARUN,

Containing 3 Mahls,

Meafurement, 85,711 Beegahs, 5 Bifwahs.

Revenue, 5,513,420 Dams.

	Dams.
Sumroon,	590,095
Mahfy,	3,518,435
Mujhowreh,	1,404,890

This sircar furnishes 700 cavalry and 3000 infantry.

SIRCAR HAJYPOOR,

Containing 11 Mahls,

Meafurement, 436,952 Beegahs, 15 Bifwahs,

Revenue, 27,331,030 Dams.

Akbarpoor,	195,040
Bofawy,	624,791
Befarra,	6,380,000
Ballagatcheh,	913,660
Taykehra,	3,518,354
Hajypoor and its dependencies,	3,833,460
Rutty,	1,824,980
Serreyfa,	6,704,300
Amadpoor,	795,870
Gurhfunneh,	876,200
Nypoor,	1,663,980

SIRCAR SARUN,

Containing 17 Mahls,

Meafurement, 229,052 Beegahs, 15 Bifwahs,

Revenue, 16,172,004½ Dams.

Inder,	534,990
Berracy,	533,820
Pall,	4,893,378
Bara,	983,797½
Berhen,	654,508
Petchlekheh,	437,997

Cheranend,

	Dams.		Dams.
Cheranend,	633,270	Kusmeer,	1,314,539
Chowpara,	400,000	Mangeah,	611,813
Jewenyeh,	309,285	Mundhel,	998,140
Digsy,	277,630	Mucker,	811,095
Sepah,	290,596		
Kewreh,	2,012,950		
Kellyanpoor,	774,496		

This sircar furnishes 1000 cavalry and 50,000 infantry.

SIRCAR TERHOOT,

Containing 74 Mahls,

Measurement, 266,464 Beegahs, 6 Biswahs,

Revenue, 19,179,777½ Dams.

Ahesspoor,	310,550	Bhedwar,	130,471½
Ooterkhend,	128,412	Purharpoor,	121,067½
Ahelwar,	62,212	Bahaderpoor,	119,305
Owbehy,	60,000	Peypera,	112,591
Owkehra,	53,980	Berhey,	90,369½
Uthayis,	34,356	Purharraghow,	81,605
Bessery, &c. 4 mahls,	1,125,000	Behowra,	69,608
Behrwareh,	942,000	Pulwareh,	65,328
Banpoor,	894,792	Bowra,	55,757
Bereil,	789,858	Bunwa,	40,539
Peddery,	554,258	Purharpoor,	37,736
Bussowtera,	546,627	Buggy,	31,550
Butchty,	361,920	Bujhawar,	12,675
Bhennore,	289,773½	Purasary,	12,695
Butchnore,	275,185	Turrany,	443,242
Putchembhegu,	275,826	Telookjawend,	149,896
Bukda,	267,862½	Tajpoor,	85,434
Poorebbhegu,	222,280	Tandeh,	63,768
Pundrajah,	195,837½	Terfown,	61,180
Badybhusady,	175,585	Terhoot and its dependencies,	1,307,706
Bhalla,	145,437	Jakher,	268,020

Jerrayil,

	Dams.
Jerrayil,	515,732
Jugmenny,	321,326
Jukhel,	196,020
Jubdy,	54,025
Dehrore,	202,818
Derbhunga,	159,052
Ramjownd,	470,005½
Serreeſta,	941,010
Selimpoor,	29,094
Selimabad,	4,184
Sejoolymudera,	150,843½
Allawelpoor,	442,466
Fuckeerabad,	72,355
Khenowly,	408,804
Kherchawend,	349,480
Godokhund,	243,377

	Dams.
Korady,	90,000
Khunda,	21,443
Gurdawery,	142,495
Mehla,	946,048
Mowrowh,	515,485
Mundeh,	66,393
Murga,	39,022
Mulhemy,	9,728
Noorem,	288,140
Nowten,	209,153
Hathy,	159,790½
Herny,	50,342
Halee,	230,700

This sircar furnishes 700 *cavalry and* 80,000 *infantry.*

SIRCAR RHOTAS,

Containing 18 Mahls,

Meaſurement, 473,340 Beegahs, 12 Biſwahs.

Revenue, 40,819,493 Dams.

Abreh,	4,028,100
Bhowjpoor,	4,903,310
Beyrn,	3,407,840
Punwar,	1,677,000
Budgong,	842,400
Chowndeh,	4,440,360
Jeydra,	1,634,110
Denwarch,	2,076,520
Dunyar,	350,000
Rhotas, and its dependencies,	2,258,620
Ruttenpoor, has a ſtrong fort,	783,425½
Sirſy,	2,769,466
Sahſarong,	2,370,790
Futtahpoor Bihya,	3,736,040
Kotera,	1,829,300
Kote has a ſtone fort,	847,920
Mungrore,	925,000
Nunnore,	2,000,000

This sircar furnishes 4550 *cavalry and* 162,000 *infantry.*

TUK-

TUKSEEM JUMMA

OF THE

SOOBAH OF ILLAHABASS,

COMMONLY CALLED

ALLAHABAD.

SIRCAR ALLAHABAD,

Containing 11 Mahls,

Meaſurement, 573,611 Beegahs, 4 Biſwahs.
Revenue, 28,833,374 Dams,
Scyurghal, 740,071½ Dams.

	Dams.
Allahabad, &c. 2 mahls, has a ſtone fort,	6,297,359
Behdowhy, has a brick fort on the banks of the Ganges,	3,660,918
Jilalabad, &c. 4 mahls,	737,220
Serong,	3,247,127
Singrore has a brick fort,	1,885,666
Secunderpoor,	1,867,704
Kentet, has a ſtone fort,	856,555
Kewary,	721,115
Kheeragurh,	400,000
Meh has a ſtrong fort upon a mountain,	1,139,981
Hadyabaſs,	2,018,014

This sircar furnishes 580 *cavalry and* 7100 *infantry.*

SIRCAR GHAZIPOOR,

Containing 19 Mahls,

Meaſurement, 288,770 Beegahs, 7 Biſwahs.

Revenue, 13,431,300 Dams.

Seyurghal, 131,825 Dams.

	Dams.
Belya,	1,250,000
Pechowler,	698,204
Belyabaſs,	655,769
Behryabad,	355,340
Behlayej	112,461
Chowſa,	791,853
Deehba,	128,811
Syedpoor Nemedy,	1,250,280
Zeheerabad,	657,920
Havelly Ghazipoor, and the city, (has a brick fort on the banks of the Ganges,)	572,350
Keryat Belly,	75,467
Goopajeet has a brick fort,	942,191
Gundeha,	500,000
Kerendeh,	293,515
Lukkneyr,	126,636
Mudden Benaris,	2,760,130
Mahommedabad and Purharbary, two mahls,	2,260,707

This sircar furnishes 310 *cavalry and* 16,650 *infantry.*

SIRCAR BENARIS,

Containing 8 Mahls,

Meaſurement, 136,663 Beegahs, 12 Biſwahs.

Revenue, 8,869,318 Dams.

Seyurghal, 338,184 Dams.

Afrad,	853,226
The city and Havelly of Benaris,	1,734,721
Byalſee,	547,634
Penderhah,	844,221
Kuſſora,	2,290,160
Cuthyr has a	

brick

	Dams.
brick fort,	1,874,230
Herhowa,	713,426

This sircar furnishes 830 cavalry and 8400 infantry.

SIRCAR JOWNPOOR,

Containing 41 Mahls,

Meaſurement, 870,265 Beegahs, 4 Biſwahs.

Revenue, 56,394,127 Dams.

Seyurghal, 4,717,654 Dams,

Aldeemow,	3,099,990
Anglee,	2,713,551
Beehtery,	844,357
Behdang,	229,514
Telkunnee,	654,363
Jownpoor with the Havelly, has a ſtone fort,	4,247,043
Chandypoor,	1,467,221
Chandeh,	989,286
Cheryakowt,	870,848
Jugeyſir,	286,586
Khereed has a brick fort,	1,445,743
Kaſſpoor Tandeh,	986,953
Khanpoor,	306,020
Dewgong,	2,583,205
Rary,	1,326,229
Sinjholy,	2,938,209
Sicunderpoor has a brick fort,	1,706,417
Suckdee,	1,274,721
Serherpoor,	1,164,095
Shadyabad,	1,700,742
Zufferabad,	156,926
Keryat Muttew,	551,410
Keryat Doſtpoor,	481,524
Keryat Mundeh,	394,870
Keryat Sownhah,	206,753
Kowleh,	1,363,332
Kehweh,	1,241,291
Ghewſy,	1,037,934
Gudawareh,	513,942
Gowdyah,	341,890
Gopaulpoor,	180,403
Keraket,	2,302,748
Mendyahoo has a brick fort,	5,289,465
Mehommedabad,	3,229,063
Mowngra,	529,730
Mehjowra,	420,164
Mow,	209,067
Nezamabad,	6,020,592
Naikwan,	758,796
Nehtupoor,	273,472

This sircar furnishes 915 cavalry and 36,000 infantry.

SIRCAR MANICKPOOR,

Containing 14 Mahls,

Meaſurement, 666,222 Beegahs, 5 Biſwahs.

Revenue, 33,916,527 Dams.

Seyurghal, 2,446,173 Dams.

	Dams.
Arwel has a brick fort,	2,957,077
Behlool,	1,832,283
Telhendy,	383,251
Jilalpoor Bilkher has a brick fort,	3,913,017
Jayiſs has a brick fort,	1,424,737
Dulmow has a brick fort on the banks of the Ganges,	3,626,067
Roybereyly has a brick fort,	3,650,984
Saloon has a brick fort,	2,717,391
Keryat Kerareh,	2,461,077
Keryat Paygah,	1,117,926
Kehtoot has a brick fort,	514,909
Manickpoor, with the Havelly, has a brick fort on the banks of the Ganges,	6,737,729
Neſſeerabad,	2,582,079

This sircar furniſhes 2040 cavalry and 42,900 infantry.

SIRCAR CHUNADEH, commonly called CHUNAR,

Containing 13 Mahls,*

Meaſurement, 106,270 Beegahs, 8 Biſwahs,

Revenue, 5,810,654 Dams.

Seyurghal, 109,065 Dams.

Aheerwareh,	109,073
Bhooly,	1,112,656
Bedhool,	361,364
Tandeh,	488,010
Chunar with the Havelly (here is a ſtone fort,)	833,098
Dhowſs,	235,644

Raghu-

	Dams.
Raghupoor,	451,962
Villages near the river,	845,371
Mujwarch,	549,817
Mehayej,	390,609
Mehwary,	227,067
Mehowy,	206,283

This sircar furnishes 500 cavalry and 18,000 infantry.

SIRCAR BUHTGORAH,

Containing 39 Mahls,

Revenue, 7,262,880 Dams.

This sircar furnishes 4304 cavalry, 200 elephants, and 57,000 infantry.

SIRCAR KALINJER,

Containing 11 Mahls,

Meafurement, 508,273 Beegahs, 12 Bifwahs.

Revenue, 23,839,474 Dams.

Seyurghal, 614,580 Dams.

Akwafy has a brick fort,	2,502,893
Ajeygurh has a ftone fort,	200,000
Senehda has a ftone fort,	6,262,333½
Sehmoony has a brick fort,	2,247,346
Shadypoor,	2,798,329½
Ruffen,	512,026
Kalinjer with the fuburbs,	970,259
Kehreleh has a brick fort,	1,275,325
Mehoba has a ftone fort,	5,242,014
Mohdha has a ftone fort,	2,998,062

This sircar furnishes 1210 cavalry, 12 elephants, and 18,100 infantry.

SIRCAR

SIRCAR KORAH,

Containing 9 Mahls,

Meaſurement, 341,170 Beegahs, 10 Biſwahs.

Revenue, 17,397,567 Dams.

Seyurghal, 469,350 Dams.

	Dams.
Jaymow has a fort on the banks of the Ganges,	3,106,346
Korah, with the Havelly, 2 mahls, here is a brick fort,	6,771,891
Kahtempoor,	3,667,564
Mehjawen,	1,323,339
Cotyeh,	584,274
Kenyr,	513,497
Kerenpoorkenar,	830,070
Mohſenpoor,	600,586

This sircar furniſhes 500 cavalry, 10 elephants, and 15,000 infantry.

SIRCAR KURRAH,

Containing 12 Mahls,

Meaſurement, 447,556 Beegahs, 19 Biſwahs.

Revenue, 22,682,048 Dams.

Seyurghal, 1,498,862 Dams.

Jyjhee,	1,624,034½
Ahterben,	894,036½
Jyaſa,	845,766
HavellyKurrah,	5,121,970
Rary,	2,707,034
The city of Kurrah has a fort,	236,868
Kerary has a brick fort,	141,753
Kulela,	909,234
Kutera commonly called Kurſoon has a brick fort,	693,487½
Futtahpoor Kunſweh,	2,892,705
Hutgong,	2,723,508½
Heſheweh,	2,123,661½

This sircar furniſhes 390 cavalry and 8700 infantry.

TUKSEEM JUMMA

OF THE

SOOBAH OF OWDH.

SIRCAR OWDH,

Containing 21 Mahls,

Meaſurement, 2,796,206 Beegahs, 19 Biſwahs.

Revenue, 40,956,343 Dams.

Seyurghal, 1,680,249 Dams.

	Dams.
Owdh with the Havelly,	2,008,366
Ambodeh has a brick fort,	1,298,724
Ibraheemabad,	445,417
Anhoneh, has a brick fort,	1,268,470
Petchemrateh,	4,207,104
Belhery has a brick fort,	815,831
Beſowly,	505,473
Tanneh Bedhong,	427,509
Bektha,	385,008
Deryabad has a brick fort,	5,369,528
Rudowly has a brick fort,	3,248,380
Seelek, ditto	4,723,299
Sultanpoor, do.	5,832,530
Satenpoor, ditto	1,660,741
Subeeheh,	1,609,293
Sirwapaly,	1,201,335
Seterkeh,	1,126,295
Gowarejh,	3,773,417
Keſhny has a brick fort,	1,339,286
Mungelly,	1,360,753
Nypoor,	308,788

This sircar furnishes 1340 *cavalry,* 23 *elephants, and* 31,900 *infantry.*

SIRCAR

SIRCAR GOWRECKPOOR,

Containing 24 Mahls,

Meaſurement, 244,283 Beegahs, 13 Biſwahs.

Revenue, 11,926,790 Dams.

Seyurghal, 51,235 Dams.

	Dams.
Atrowlah has a brick fort,	1,397,367
Anhowla,	201,120
Benyekpoor has a brick fort,	600,000
Banbhenparah,	414,194
Bhunwaparah,	155,900
Tilpoor has a brick fort,	400,000
Cheeluparah has a brick fort,	289,302
Deryaparah, do.	1,517,708
Dewaparah and Kotela, two mahls,	717,640
Rehly,	1,618,074
Ruſſoolpoor and Ghooſy, two mahls,	622,030
Ramgurh & Koory, 2 mahls,	485,943
Goreckpoor with the Havelly has a brick fort on the banks of the river Rabety,	568,385
Kethela has a brick fort,	40,000
Kehlapara, do.	425,845
Mehowly, do.	618,206
Mundewh,	452,321
Mendeleh,	51,100
Mengher and Ruttenpoor, two mahls. Here is a brick fort,	1,352,585

This sircar furniſhes 1010 *cavalry and* 22,000 *infantry.*

SIRCAR

SIRCAR BERAYITCH,

Containing 11 Mahls,

Meafurement, 1,823,435 Beegahs, 8 Bifwahs,

Revenue, 24,120,525 Dams.

Seyurghal, 466,482 Dams.

	Dams.
Berayitch with the Havelly, two mahls, here is a fort on the banks of the river Sowd,	9,139,141
Behreh,	37,135
Heffampoor has a brick fort,	4,707,035
Dangdoon,	404,562
Rejhet,	166,780
Senjholy,	877,007
Sultanpoor,	166,001
Fukherpoor has a brick fort,	3,157,376
Firozabad has a brick fort,	1,933,079
The fort of Nowagurh,	2,140,858
Gehrownfa has a brick fort,	1,315,051

This sircar furnishes 1170 cavalry and 14,300 infantry.

SIRCAR KHYERABAD.

Containing 22 Mahls,

Meafurement, 1,987,700 Beegahs, 60 Bifwahs.

Revenue, 43,644,381 Dams.

Seyurghal, 1,713,342 Dams.

Birduranjeh,	4,325,237
Bifwah has a brick fort,	8,545,643
Paly,	1,849,270
Bawen,	1,161,235
Befreh,	60,063
Behrwareh has a brick fort,	435,430
Biffara,	276,066
Peela,	48,022
Chetyapoor,	1,765,641
Khyerabad with the Havelly, 2 mahls, here is a brick fort,	2,161,884

	Dams.
Sandy has a brick fort,	3,055,339
Sirrah,	2,091,983
Seedderpoor,	831,185
Goopamow has a brick fort,	5,620,466
Ghuny has a brick fort,	3,250,522
Ghunygurh has six forts, which are not perceptible till you are close upon them,	1,829,328
Ghurghella,	483,727
Gungkhutmow,	235,656
Laherpoor,	3,023,479
Mutcherhuttch,	2,112,176
Neemkhar has a brick fort,	3,566,055
Hurgrown,	1,000,000

This sircar furnishes 1160 *cavalry and* 27,800 *infantry.*

SIRCAR LUKHNOW,

Containing 55 Mahls,

Measurement, 3,307,426 Beegahs, 10 Biswahs.

Revenue, 80,716,120 Dams.

Seyurghal, 4,572,566 Dams.

Embehty has a brick fort,	376,480
Anam has a brick fort,	2,012,372
Asowly, do.	1,697,238
Aleyun,	830,625
Asewha,	509,901
Oontchehgong,	417,958
Belgrowng has a brick fort,	5,124,113
Bengermow, do.	3,802,122
Bijlowr,	2,506,047
Bary,	1,284,799
Behrymow,	591,405
Punkewan,	420,732
Bit-howly,	340,191
Punhun,	267,809
Peersunden,	238,537
Patten,	214,255
Burashkore,	163,534
Jehlooter,	1,123,176
Deyree has a brick fort,	1,933,837
Dewrekeh,	689,536
Dowreh,	73,737
Kunbunpoor has a brick fort,	2,425,885
Ramkote has a brick fort,	268,099
Sendylh, do.	10,623,901

Sacypoor

	Dams.
Saeypoor,	2,625,388
Seroofy,	1,239,767
Satenpoor,	1,028,800
Sehaly,	694,707
Seedhore,	1,692,281
Seedhopoor,	505,018
Sendy,	392,313
Seroon,	210,316
Kettahpoor has a brick fort,	3,161,449
Kettahpoor Chowraffy,	909,176
Gurhembehty has a brick fort,	1,800,000
Koorfy, do.	1,693,844
Gakowry, do.	1,134,432
Kehnjer,	818,472
Gahtempoor,	552,561
Kutchundow,	430,596
Kerendeh,	334,769
Khombhy,	267,809
Lukhnow with the Havelly,	1,746,771
Lufhker,	168,529
Meleehabad has a brick fort,	4,479,250
Melaweh,	3,598,713
Mohan has a brick fort,	1,996,673
Mowrong,	1,098,444
Madeegong,	1,136,313
Mehooneh,	977,860
Munwee has a brick fort,	771,372
Mekrayed,	576,200
Kedheh has a brick fort,	2,450,522
Kerdowry,	359,748
Henhar,	329,735

TUKSEEM JUMMA

OF THE

SOOBAH OF AGRA.

SIRCAR AGRA.

Containing 33 Mahls,

Meaſurement, 9,107,622 Beegahs, 4 Biſwahs.

Revenue, 191,719,265 Dams.

Seyurghal, 14,566,818 Dams.

	Dams.
Agra, with the Havelly,	44,956,458
Etaweh, has a brick fort,	10,739,365
Owl,	5,509,542
Owdhy,	2,884,365
Owed,	1,003,848
Bejwareh,	10,966,568
Byaneh,	7,110,104
Bary,	5,866,158
Behſawer,	5,505,460
Benawer,	155,360
Bheem Toodeh,	3,733,075
Bheeker,	289,102
Jeleyſer, has a brick fort,	6,835,400
Chunour,	11,442,250
Chowſeeheh,	4,182,248
Khanweh,	2,922,495
Dhoolpoor has a brick fort,	9,729,715
Rapery, do.	13,508,035
Rutchoher,	1,694,203
Soonagur Soonegurry,	985,700
Futtahpoor has a ſtone fort,	8,494,005
Koonmer,	745,955
Mehawen has a brick fort,	6,784,787
Mehtra, do.	1,155,807
Mehooly,	1,502,246
Mungooteleh,	1,148,035
Mundawer,	132,500
Vezeerpoor,	2,009,255
Hindoon,	9,249,331
Hutkant has a brick fort,	5,693,307
Heelek,	2,789,494

This sircar furniſhes 11,560 *cavalry and* 100,800 *infantry.*

SIRCAR

SIRCAR CALPEE,

Containing 16 Mahls,

Measurement, 300,029 Beegahs, 9 Biswahs.

Revenue, 49,456,730 Dams.

Seyurghal, 1,078,292½ Dams.

	Dams.
Owley,	1,297,379
Balasspoor,	3,714,547
Bedheteh,	1,260,199
Deerapoor,	1,760,750
Dewgully,	1,466,955
Rateh has a brick fort,	9,270,894
Roypoor,	1,200,000
Seekenpoor,	1,507,887
Shahpoor,	8,843,420
Calpee with the Havelly, 2 mahls,	4,871,053
Kenar,	4,971,053
Khundowt,	3,027,917
Kendchleh,	671,733
Mahommedabad,	1,617,257
Hemynpoor,	4,803,828

This sircar furnishes 1540 *cavalry*, 30 *elephants and* 34,000 *infantry*.

SIRCAR KINOJE,

Containing 30 Mahls.

Measurement, 2,776,673 Beegahs, 16 Biswahs.

Revenue, 52,584,607½ Dams.

Bhoogong has 3 forts and a reservoir of water,	4,578,010
Bhowjpoor,	3,446,738
Belgrong,	3,387,076
Behtur,	2,921,389
Belhoror,	2,828,349
Puttyaly,	1,877,600
Puttyalypoor,	1,153,636
Puttynaghut,	566,997
Burneh,	450,000
Bara,	400,000
Phephong,	5,432,391
Sukeeteh,	3,230,752
Sownj,	3,230,752
Schawer,	1,200,000
Sewly,	623,473

Suckutpoor,

	Dams.
Suckutpoor,	623,441
Sugrong,	539,050
Sehar,	486,550
Sewburgeh,	465,328
Secunderpoor Adhoo,	276,918½
Serwer,	447,563
Secunderpoor Aterchhy,	269,622
Shumſabad has a fort on the banks of the Ganges,	7,138,453
Clupramow,	1,522,128
Dewha,	483,171
Kinoje with the Havelly has a brick fort,	2,470,743
Kunpul,	1,651,586
Kerawely,	1,409,988
Mulkowſeh,	1,500,000
Nanamow,	136,921

This sircar furnishes 3765 *cavalry and* 88,350 *infantry.*

SIRCAR COWL,

Containing 21 Mahls,

Meaſurement, 2,461,731 Beegahs.

Revenue, 54,992,943 Dams.

Seyurghal, 2,094,840 Dams.

Atrowly,	5,434,459
Akberabad,	3,003,409
Ahar has a brick fort,	2,106,554
Bahſoo,	2,502,562
Bulram,	2,131,765
Bejlana,	624,825
Tuppel has a brick fort,	1,802,571
Tanneh Tereeda,	212,750
Jilally,	2,957,910
Jendoſe,	1,749,238
Khoorjeh,	3,703,020
Debenhoy has a brick fort,	2,169,933
Secundarow has a brick fort,	4,412,631
Sowroon has a brick fort,	805,016
Sidhoopoor,	989,458
Shekarpoor,	1,984,828
Cowl has a brick fort,	10,412,305
Gungeyree,	372,050
Marhereh,	3,679,582
Mullickpoor,	1,446,132
Nouh has a brick fort,	1,311,955

This sircar furnishes 4035 *cavalry and* 78,950 *infantry.*

SIRCAR GUALIAR,

Containing 12 Mahls.

Meafurement, 1,146,465 Beegahs, 6 Bifwahs.

Revenue, 29,683,749 Dams.

Seyurghal, 240,350 Dams.

	Dams.
Anhown has a brick fort,	2,277,747
Budruhteh, do.	696,800
Chentower, do.	1,051,341
Jelhowda, do.	290,306
Dundrowly,	1,807,207
Roypoor,	1,017,721
Sirfeenny,	832,128
Semawely,	801,344
Sirbundeh has a brick fort,	267,497
Allapoor has a brick fort,	5,123,866
Gualiar with the Havelly,	12,483,072
Kehtowly,	3,105,319

This sircar furnishes 2490 *cavalry and* 43,000 *infantry.*

SIRCAR IREJ,

Containing 16 Mahls.

Meafurement, 2,202,124 Beegahs, 18 Bifwahs,

Revenue, 37,785,421 Dams.

Seyurghal, 456,493 Dams.

Irej,	2,922,436
Perhar has a brick fort,	5,237,096
Pehandeer,	2,533,449
Beejpoor,	1,241,097
Pondore,	464,111
Jehtereh has a brick fort,	11,787,804
Ryabaneh has a fort,	500,000
Shahzadpoor,	450,781
Kutchoweh, &c. has a fort,	3,000,000
Kejhodeh,	755,200
Kydar,	120,000
Kownj has a fort,	1,851,802
Gungeys has a fort,	1,343,073

Kanty,

	Dams.
Kanty,	240,000
Kehayereh has a brick fort,	4,776,357
Mehowly,	502,102

This sircar furnishes 6160 cavalry, 190 elephants, and 68,500 infantry.

SIRCAR SANWAN,

Containing 27 Mahls.

Measurement, 762,014 Beegahs.

Revenue, 8,459,296 Dams.

Seyurghal, 82,662 Dams.

Untry is famous for its beetle-nuttrees, which yield a large revenue,	906,140
Umwary,	223,000
Jytewan,	165,165
Oeteyleh,	32,455
Beyong,	801,285
Punwar,	417,439
Perantcheh,	396,193
Budnoon,	275,000
Bhasinda,	169,040
Chitore,	548,331
Jirhely,	144,055
Jugtan,	123,680
Dahmeleh,	17,306
Ruchadeh,	472,839
Ruttengurh has a fort,	355,955
Rowhcereh,	1,017,682
Sowhindy has a brick fort,	896,959
Kenowleh,	364,368
Kerhereh,	277,000
Kisjud (here is a pass in the mountains)	196,304
Kundha,	162,661
Kundeejreh the great,	112,079
Kundeejreh the little,	68,470
Kehtery haul,	112,079
Gujhareh has a stone fort,	82,291
Kudwaheh,	43,296
Mow has a fort,	850,429

This sircar furnishes 1105 cavalry and 18,000 infantry.

SIRCAR

SIRCAR NURWER,

Containing 5 Mahls,

Measurement, 394,350 Beegahs,

Revenue, 4,233,322 Dams.

Seyurghal, 95,994 Dams.

	Dams.
Berowey has a fort,	638,700
Bowly has a fort on the banks of the river Sekla,	141,915
Sewpoory has a stone fort,	1,250,000
Kowlarus has 2 forts,	764,380
Nurwer with the Havelly has several old stone forts,	438,025

This sircar furnishes 500 cavalry and 20,000 infantry.

SIRCAR MUNDLAYER,

Containing 14 Mahls,

Measurement, 65,646 Beegahs.

Revenue, 3,703,884 Dams.

Ooontgurreh has a stone fort on the banks of the river Chembel,	493,978
Bijheepoor,	359,706
Belawely,	324,091
Bakher,	261,746
Bagrownd,	* *
Jugwar,	38,498
Dang Bughowry,	493,978
Doongery,	64,126
Rutten ballaher,	82,098
Sumertehleh,	526,330
Kumukehreh,	116,163
Kehrnoon,	54,074
Kehlowny,	51,944
Mundlayer has a fort upon a mountain on the north side of the river Chembel,	697,794

This sircar furnishes 4000 cavalry and 50,000 infantry.

SIRCAR ALOWR,

Containing 43 Mahls,

Meaſurement, 1,662,012 Beegahs,

Revenue, 39,832,234 Dams.

Seyurghal, 699,212 Dams.

	Dams.
Alowr has a ſtone fort upon a mountain,	2,679,820
Antehlehhabroo,	850,731
Amren,	642,453
Iſmailpoor,	503,840
Beerat has a ſtone fort,	7,201,791
Behrozpoor,	2,621,958
Bahaderpoor,	1,951,000
Behrkowl,	678,733
Bulhar,	443,612
Beroodeh Futtah Khan,	201,059
Penayen,	195,680
Beroodeh Mow,	153,045
Bodehtehl,	146,000
Bheewan,	122,088
Beſaneh,	100,656
Bijeereh,	104,890
Balhettch,	133,507
Jilalpoor,	393,499
Haſſanpoor Bedoher,	947,871
Haſſanpoor Kowry,	1,259,659
Hajypoor has a ſtone fort,	456,779
Dewty Jagary,	1,600,000
Dedeker,	695,262
Dehra,	512,613
Sukhen,	804,262
Rateh,	229,741
Khowhery Rana,	4,359,282
Kehlooher,	1,459,048
Kowldehwar,	627,100
Kyarch,	600,000
Kehrtehly,	465,640
Ghaut Seyvur has a fort,	357,110
Kowhrana, do.	166,666
Mendawer has a brick fort,	1,889,097
Mowjpoor,	639,858
Mobarekpoor,	514,193
Munghoona has a ſtone fort,	475,260
Mundawereh,	27,051
Nowgong,	856,512
Nahergurh,	604,194
Hurſewry,	227,096
Hurpoor,	686,605
Hurſana,	208,281

This sircar furnishes 6514 *cavalry and* 42,020 *infantry.*

SIRCAR

SIRCAR TEJAREH.

Containing 18 Mahls.

Meaſurement, 740,001 Beegahs, 5 Biſwahs.

Revenue, 1,770,061 Dams.

Seyurghal, 701,761½ Dams.

	Dams.
Indore has a fort upon a mountain,	1,995,216
Owjyeneh,	428,347
Omrahomry,	307,037
Beyroo,	215,800
Poor,	545,345
Bungwan,	1,323,350
Bunbohra has a ſtone fort,	1,416,7[illegible]5
Tejareh has a fort,	3,603,569
Jumrawut has a ſtone fort upon a mountain,	496,202½
Khanpoor,	195,620
Sakerus,	406,088
Santhawary,	406,115
Feerozpoor,	3,042,642
Futtapoor Mewngowneh,	1,135,140
Koteleh has a brick fort,	1,552,196
Gurheyreh,	330,076
Kehwarka Tanneh,	168,719
Nekynan,	377,357

This sircar furniſhes 1227 cavalry and 9,650 infantry.

SIRCAR NARNOWL.

Containing 17 Mahls,

Meaſurement, 2,080,046 Beegahs,

Revenue, 50,046,711 Dams,

Seyurghal, 775,103 Dams.

Barheh,	2,060,662
Baboy has a ſtone fort, and in its mountains are ſeveral copper mines,	921,170
Beroodeh Rana,	592,995

Chalk-

	Dams.
Chalklaneh,	7,844,027
Jehojeyur has a ftone fort,	2,329,069
Senghaneh has a copper mine, and a mint for coining that metal,	11,881,629
Kanodeh,	4,356,128
Kowtpootely has a ftone fort; and in the village of Bedhawer is a copper mine,	4,266,837
Kanoory has 3 forts,	2,721,126
Khendeyla,	1,300,000
Kohdaneh,	808,109
Lahooty,	1,512,470
Three villages at the foot of the mountains, have copper mines, and a mint,	274,674
Narnowl has a ftone fort,	5,913,218
Nerher,	4,262,837

This sircar furnishes 7520 cavalry and 37,220 infantry.

SIRCAR SEHAR.

Containing 6 Mahls,

Meafurement, 763,474 Beegahs,

Revenue, 5,917,569 Dams.

Seyurghal, 109,447 Dams.

Pehary,	1,228,999
Behdoly,	441,840
Sehar has a fort,	2,489,816
Kameh,	505,724
Kowhmejahed,	170,365
Noonhureh,	618,115
Howdel,	462,710

This sircar furnishes 265 cavalry and 1000 infantry.

TUKSEEM

TUKSEEM JUMMA

OF THE

SOOBAH OF MALWAH.

SIRCAR OWJAIN,

Containing 10 Mahls.

Meaſurement, 925,622 Beegahs,

Revenue, 43,827,960 Dams,

Seyurghal, 281,816 Dams.

	Dams.
Owjain with the Havelly has a ſtone and brick fort,	13,882,035
Unhul,	2,712,972
Bedhnawer has a ſtone fort,	3,056,195
Panbahar,	1,937,596
Deibalpoor,	6,000,000
Ruttam,	4,421,540
Sanweer,	2,418,375
Kehnayl has a a ſtone and brick fort,	2,907,817
Kehjrowr,	2,651,044
Newlahy has a brick fort on the banks of the river Chembel,	3,851,886

This sircar furniſhes 3250 *cavalry and* 11,170 *infantry.*

SIRCAR ROYSAYN,

Containing 32 Mahls,

Aſſapoory, &c. 6 mahls,	173,064
Bhilſeh,	6,094,970
Bhoory,	316,017

Bhowj-

	Dams.
Bhowjpoor,	220,592
Balabhet,	215,122
Tanneh Meer Khan,	735,315
Jajewy,	215,122
Jitanewy,	184,757
Jelodeh,	13,290
Khulijypoor,	41,060
Dahmowty,	788,389
Dekhwareh,	292,313
Dewrood,	144,000
Dahnyeh,	21,502
Royſayn with the Havelly has a ſtone fort upon a mountain,	934,739
Seywany,	580,828
Sirſyeh,	279,346
Shahpoor,	89,067
Ghoomlaſeh,	645,665
Gheyreh,	560,037
Kyſureh,	473,267
Khamgurh,	378,460
Kergurh,	365,707
Kooroy,	145,566
Laherpoor,	32,268
Mahſummund,	43,024

SIRCAR GURREH,

Containing 57 Mahls,

Revenue, 11,877,080 Dams.

Amowdgurh has a ſtone fort on a mountain,	1,039,485
Bary and Benker 2 mahls,	485,000
Bunger,	400,025
Bhutgong, &c. 3 mahls,	395,000
Penar and Nejehly, 2 mahls,	300,000
Bakhereh,	238,000
Benaker and Amreyl, 2 mahls. A ſtone fort,	140,000
Beey,	82,000
Beeragurh has a ſtrong fort,	45,000
Chandpoor and Chandery, 2 mahls,	39,000
Jeytgurh, Buhkdavy, and Havelly, 3 mahls,	12,000
Cheyta,	12,000
Demowdeh,	1,355,000
Dehmra and Duhmree 2 mahls,	49,000
Dowgong,	25,000
Dowhar and Hoorbehiſht 2 mahls,	18,000
Dergurh,	18,000
Ruttenpoor and Purhar 2 mahls,	613,000

Ran-

	Dams.
Rangurh,	400,000
Ramgurh and Sarunpoor, 2 mahls,	1,055,000
Ruſſoolya,	12,000
Seetelpoor,	85,000
Shahpoor and Juragh 2 mahls. A ſtone fort,	350,000
Gurreh, with the Havelly. A ſtone fort,	1,857,000
Kehtowleh,	121,000
Keydarpoor, &c. 12 mahls,	1,626,000
Lalljee, Kerowleh, and Dornkrowleh, three mahls,	1,000,000
Mendella,	352,000
Hererya & Dowgurh 2 mahls,	909,000

This sircar furnishes 5495 cavalry and 54,000 infantry.

SIRCAR CHENDARY,

Containing 61 Mahls,

Meaſurement, 554,277 Beegahs, 17 Biſwahs.

Revenue, 31,037,783 Dams.

Seyurghal, 26,931 Dams.

Owdypoor has a ſtone fort,	832,086
Azdur,	1,016,000
Eyren,	101,953
Itaweh,	80,000
Bhowraſeh has a ſtone fort,	755,000
Bunder Jehleh,	720,000
Bareh, &c. 5 mahls, have five ſtone forts and one of brick,	635,500
Bederwaſs and Akeh, 2 mahls,	304,800
Bechahr, has a brick fort with a reſervoir of water, on a ſmall hill,	174,000
Bayly,	70,000
Talberudeh,	1,092,000
Tumoon,	312,504
Tahtaberyar,	22,500
Tehnwareh, Leletpoor, &c. 3 mahls, a ſtone fort,	619,997
Chundary with the Havelly, 2 mahls,	1,186,388

Jan-

	Dams.
Janjown and Dewhorry the little, 2 mahls,	387,480
Jewrſinkar, &c. 5 mahls,	447,000
Jehrkoon has a fort,	200,000
Jewaſeh,	144,000
Dowharry the Great,	857,998
Doobjaker has a ſtone fort,	580,500
Dudaneh, &c. 4 mahls,	147,282
Renood has a ſtone fort with a large reſervoir of water, which is a place of Hindoo worſhip,	364,000
Rowdy, &c. 5 mahls, has a ſtone fort, near to which is a pagoda,	206,653
Rakh has a ſtone fort,	84,000

	Dams.
Sironje,	11,065,765
Sehjen, &c. 3 mahls,	3,956,700
Sadhewreh,	334,290
Kenah has a brick fort,	1,092,162
Kerejeeyreh has ſtone fort,	468,000
Kowrwy,	252,000
Kangreh has a ſtone fort,	239,990
Kudrowleh has a ſtone fort,	168,000
Kolakote has a ſtone fort on a mountain,	156,450
Kojan,	69,152
Kerwaleh,	168,000
Moongowty has a brick fort,	1,440,000
Mayaneh,	688,000
Mehedpoor,	144,000

This sircar furniſhes 5970 *cavalry,* 90 *elephants, and* 60,685 *infantry.*

SIRCAR SARENGPOOR,

Containing 24 Mahls,

Meaſurement, 706,202 Beegahs,

Revenue, 32,994,880 Dams.

Seyurghal, 324,462 Dams.

	Dams.
Aſhteh,	3,000,790
Akberpoor,	170,610
Agra,	472,363
Bajilpoor,	647,544
Beyloon,	610,544
Bhuraſeh,	259,777
Bejon,	65,820
Banyan,	40,841
Bayawer,	156,740
Teleen,	1,800,700
Khuljypoor,	6,027
Zeerapoor,	387,352
Sarengpoor, with the Havelly, 2 mahls, has a brick fort,	1,294,321
Saharbabahajy,	1,093,049
Sunderſy,	434,389
Suſember,	54,376
Shujapoor,	8,017,184
Kerhely,	7,447,906
Kateyeh,	1,193,396
Kanher,	297,047
Kerherry,	17,252
Mahommedpoor,	1,981,133
Nowgong,	2,755,433

This sircar furniſhes 3125 cavalry and 21,719 infantry.

SIRCAR BEEJAGURH,

Containing 32 Mahls,

Meaſurement, 283,278 Beegahs, 13 Biſwahs.

Revenue, 12,249,121 Dams.

Seyurghal, 3574 Dams.

Unjery,	707,093
Anown and Sengwer,	298,648
Ablahutteh,	226,677
Banhungong,	781,014
Belgowareh,	407,014
Berowdreh,	369,898

	Dams.
Bekengong has a ftone fort, and is famous for its horfes,	369,125
Budkhel, fituated near the river Nerbudeh,	223,615
Banfyeh,	85,000
Budrya,	84,293
Benheleh has a wild where elephants are hunted,	52,939
Byrore,	391,333
Teykery,	645,245
Jilalabad with the Havelly. A ftone fort,	414,268
Chemary has a ftone fort,	543,994
Dewlagheeta,	392,080
Dewlanerher,	98,569
Sewraneh,	627,207
Sedhowa,	353,819
Seelwareh has a ftone fort,	325,544
Sangorey,	179,202
Kefrawed,	1,150,569
Kherghone,	753,194
Kanehpoor,	126,846
Ghowrgong,	85,082
Leherpoor commonly called Mahommedpoor,	205,743
Lewarykouh,	50,000
Mendawerah has a famous pagoda,	777,381
Mehowy near the river Nerbudeh,	395,206
Mowraneh has a ftone fort,	355,902
Nawory, ditto.	408,164
Nenkelwary,	370,208

This sircar furnishes 1773 *cavalry and* 19,480 *infantry.*

SIRCAR MENDOW,

Containing 16 Mahls,

Meafurement, 229,969 Beegahs, 11 Bifwahs.

Revenue, 13,788,994 Dams,

Seyurghal, 127,732 Dams.

Amchereh,	395,400
Berowdeh,	1,307,765
Puhnman,	656,556
Jowly Mehyr,	968,370

Haffel-

	Dams.
Hassełpoor,	210,000
Dehar,	279,306
Dekhtan,	958,986
Dheremgong,	116,442
Sangore,	683,384
Sonassy,	3,097,192
Kotereh,	2,393,871
Mendow with the Havelly, two mahls,	48,698
Menawereh,	102,164
Nalcheh,	545,952
Nowaly,	224,608

This sircar furnishes 1180 *cavalry and* 10,625 *infantry.*

SIRCAR HINDYEH,

Containing 23 Mahls,

Measurement, 89,573 Beegahs, 17 Biswahs,

Revenue, 11,610,969 Dams.

Seyurghal, 157,054 Dams.

Ownchowd,	2,037,877
Awelgong,	42,294
Amowndeh,	21,864
Bijnowla,	44,418
Bayasheh,	25,251
Balhassy,	825
Chukhowda,	158,876
Chumpaneer,	20,653
Deywass,	6,718,000
Rajowr,	25,641
Sutwass,	89,080
Sumerny,	52,115
Syamgurh,	8,494
Seyowly,	2,250
Kenduha Islampoor,	1,298,571
Mowdy,	19,443
Merdanpoor,	450
Nemawer,	94,346
Nowgong,	79,264
Neymen,	75,152
Handeh,	146,044
Hendyeh with the Havelly has a stone fort on the banks of the Nerbudeh,	350,051

This sircar furnishes 1296 *cavalry and* 5921 *infantry.*

SIRCAR

SIRCAR NUZERBAR,

Containing 7 Mahls,

Meaſurement, 859,604 Beegahs,

Revenue, 50,162,250 Dams.

Seyurghal, 198,478 Dams.

	Dams.
Bhanbeereh,	6,924,355
Sultanpoor,	28,119,749
Kehayer,	53,310
Nuzerbar with the Havelly, two mahls,	14,252,199
Neyr,	722,760
Nemowry,	89,585

This sircar furnishes 500 *cavalry and* 6000 *infantry.*

SIRCAR MERUSOOR,

Containing 17 Mahls,

Revenue, 6,861,396 Dams.

Seyurghal, 23,387 Dams.

Eyknood,	716,353
Owjenwaſs,	170,953
Biſahereh,	511,400
Boodeh,	255,062
Behtore,	109,220
Burleet,	106,703
Berowdeh,	95,970
Bhutpoor,	63,104
Tall,	1,600,000
Teerood,	500,000.
Jemyawareh,	619,759
Sewkereh,	46,090
Ghiaſſpoor,	138,890
Kyumpoor,	175,304
Kowry,	303
Meruſoor with the Havelly,	1,651,920

This sircar furnishes 1194 *cavalry and* 4280 *infantry.*

SIRCAR

SIRCAR GAGROON,

Containing 12 Mahls,

Meaſurement, 63,529 Beegahs,

Revenue, 4,535,794 Dams.

	Dams.
Owrmal,	502,774
Akberpoor,	62,500
Beetchbahar,	1,573,560
Jeyhet,	225,640
Khyerabad,	646,000
Roypoor,	287,805
Sewthel,	281,909
Sendar,	81,929
Ghatty,	600,046
Gagroon with the Havelly,	19,781
Neemtohore,	608,834

SIRCAR KOWTRYBERANEH,

Containing 10 Mahls,

Meaſurement, 190,039 Beegahs,

Revenue, 8,031,925 Dams.

Aſowp,	1,733,927
Ajygurh,	855,612
Ahore,	532,056
Berowdeh,	923,667
Dak Doodharlya,	458,144
Sohet,	693,585
Kowtryberaneh, &c. 2 mahls,	1,856,566
Gungrar,	1,066,683
Ghoſey,	116,380

This sircar furnishes 2245 cavalry and 6500 infantry.

TUKSEÊM JUMMA

OF THE

SOOBAH OF DANDEES.

Containing 32 Mahls,

Revenue, 12,647,062 Tungehs.

	Tungehs.		Tungehs.
Asseer,	1,060,221	Jelood,	317,205
Atral,	264,249	Jewereh,	730,965
Arundowel,	543,328	Dankery,	915,325
Unmeleysra,	2,406,180	Damry,	352,300
Punetgong,	215,504	Ranweer,	2,083,855
Banjureh,	206,728	Ruttenpoor,	820,971
Poormal to the west of Burhanpoor,	162,830	Sadwa,	430,008
Poormal to the south-east of do. &c.	183,540	Mahil,	290,311
* * *	58,111	Suckudgeng,	256,931
* * *	26,112	Nebadu,	308,782
Baneyr,	594,239	Nasseershumshad,	595,608
Jamood,	175,844	* * *	316,338
Jaseer,	470,042	Lelung,	352,644
Chandsseer,	198,900	Sunderty,	104,754
		Adelabed,	527,223
		Lohara,	247,965
		Manjrord,	104,925
		Nasseerabad,	824,925

TUKSEEM

TUKSEEM JUMMA

OF THE

SOOBAH OF BERAR.

SIRCAR KAWEEL,

Containing 46 Mahls,

Revenue, 134,666,140 Dams,

Seyurghal, 12,874,048 Dams.

	Dams.
Eletchpoor has a ſtone fort,	14,000,000
Aſhty,	4,800,000
Arown,	3,200,000
Aujy,	1,600,000
Anjengong,	3,200,000
Babeel,	640,000
Bary,	114,368
Baharkully,	3,200,000
Beeyaweda,	1,280,000
Biſrowly,	700,000
Bilſeyker,	960,000
Balla,	800,000
Berore,	1,280,000
Belgong,	817,350
Booſnah,	914,460
Bubheranty,	4,825,300
Betuſeh,	2,000,000
Thoogong,	5,600,000
Jughucky,	2,400,000

	Dams.
Deryapoor,	6,400,000
Dhamoory,	2,718,540
Reedhore,	6,400,000
Kehrygurrum,	2,400,000
Sereſſgong,	5,200,096
Serrala,	1,835,390
Sirſoon,	4,800,000
Salore,	340,000
Sheerpoor,	48,000
Kholapoor,	4,870,014
Karenja & Budhola, 2 mahls,	4,800,000
Kurenjgong and Keheyreh, 2 mahls,	5,232,000
Kummergong,	640,000
Karenjaſly,	4,200,000
Koozha,	4,800,000
Maneh,	1,800,000
Myna,	800,000

Manjhergheer.

	Dams.
Manjhergheer,	640,000
Malkhyr,	480,000
Mungalore,	2,800,000
Moorjhy,	4,800,000
Tuppeh Nundgong,	6,633,826
Nundgong,	3,200,000
Neer,	3,200,000
Hatgong,	1,600,000

SIRCAR PUNAR,

Containing 5 Mahls.

Revenue, 13,440,000 Dams.

Havelly Punar, has a ſtone fort,	4,000,000
Sewenbarah and Kantbarah,	640,000
Seelu,	1,600,000
Kylchery,	2,400,000
Mandgong Kerer,	4,800,000

SIRCAR KEHRLEH,

Containing 35 Mahls,

Revenue, 17,600,000 Dams.

Umneer,	3,200,000
Aſhteh,	160,000
Putten,	1,200,000
Beleſſdehy,	1,600,000
Berwer,	2,800,000
Baſed,	480,000
Powny,	400,000
Havelly Kehrleh,	3,200,000
Sater Umbeer, 2 mahls,	1,600,000
Sahenkhereh,	2,000,000
Kuſbeh Jerore,	480,000
Mundowry,	480,000
Multany,	* *
Durgeh,	* *
Manikdary,	
Malabiel,	* *
Malwy,	* *
Munga,	* *
Waldeh,	* *
Dicygong,	* *
Deotahna,	* *
Boory,	* *

1 Salowy,

	Dams.
Salowy,	* *
Ramjowg,	* *
Henayeh,	* *
Chopar,	* *
Hameyanpoor,	* *

This sircar furnishes 100 cavalry and 2000 infantry.

SIRCAR NERNALEH,

Containing 34 Mahls,

Revenue, 130,954,476 Dams,

Seyurghal, 11,038,422 Dams.

Amkote,	6,470,066
Adgong,	8,000,000
Umneer, &c. 2 mahls,	4,800,000
Angoleh,	11,200,000
Ballapoor,	22,000,000
Punjer,	2,000,000
Partahkulſy,	2,864,000
Bulbulgong,	2,400,000
Babooſhiekh,	3,700,000
Barygong,	1,600,000
Paterreh,	3,342,500
Banbher,	1,568,000
Budcera bhownjy,	2,764,452
Budcera Kanka,	4,813,700
Jelgong,	10,000,000
Jypoor,	400,000
Chandore,	4,887,000
Deharwer,	1,200,000
Dhinda,	5,600,000
Dhengeer, has a ſtone fort,	2,000,000
Rajore,	1,000,000
Sewla,	640,000
Sheerpoor,	48,000
Kerundkheer,	2,400,000
Kothel,	1,409,000
Kotehly,	640,000
Mungong,	4,800,000
Meheer,	600,000
Mulkapoor,	11,200,000
Meelgurh,	94,360
The villages of Rajore,	400,000
Madroodreh,	1,200,000
Huſtgong,	1,500,000

This sircar furnishes 50 cavalry and 3000 infantry.

SIRCAR KULLEM,

Containing 31 Mahls, eight of which are dependent upon Chanda,

Revenue, 32,828,000 Dams.

	Dams.
Indorey,	* *
Amrawuty,	1,200,000
Iyny,	1,600,000
Poonah,	360,000
Boory,	1,200,000
Beyleh,	2,700,000
Belygong,	100,000
Telygong and Dygong,	4,800,000
Doongur,	1,600,000
Ranygong,	200,000
Salowr,	3,200,000

	Dams.
Kowrhar,	960,000
Kullem,	500,000
Geelapoor,	1,200,000
Ladkheer,	1,600,000
Nygong,	960,000
Najengong,	640,000
Nonitlowhara,	128,000
Berkehond,	* * *

The remaining pergunnahs are in the possession of the Zemindars.

SIRCAR BASSUM,

Containing 8 Mahls,

Revenue, 32,625,250 Dams,

Seyurghal, 1,825,250 Dams.

Owndeh,	4,864,000
Baſſum,	8,161,250
Banhy,	2,400,000
Chartalhnah,	4,800,000
Kelſchpoory,	3,200,000
Kerory Dehmny,	1,200,000
Mangolore,	3,200,000
Nirſee,	4,800,000

SIRCAR

SIRCAR MAHORE,

Containing 20 Mahls,

Revenue, 42,885,444 Dams,

Seyurghal, 97,844 Dams.

	Dams.		Dams.
Unſungeh,	960,000	Deharweh,	2,400,000
Amerkhur,	6,400,000	Dhangy,	320,000
Booſeh,	4,000,000	Seewala,	2,400,000
Tamſa,	2,177,844	Soorety,	64,000
Jughely,	3,200,000	Keroly,	32,000
Hejoly,	2,400,000	Khenowl,	1,200,000
Havelly Mahore, with the Kusſbahs of Dehſore and Sooreh, 3 mahls,	3,680,000	Koreh,	480,000
		Mehenteh,	2,400,000
		Mehgong,	1,600,000
		Nadapoor,	2,000,000
		Huldhotā,	* * *

SIRCAR MANIK DURG,

Containing 8 Mahls,

Revenue, 14,400,000 Dams.

Bhawel,	2,400,000	Rajore,	2,400,000
Bhan,	2,000,000	Koret,	2,000,000
Chandore,	2,400,000	Neer,	1,600,000
Jayir,	1,600,000		

SIRCAR PAHTERY,

Containing 18 Mahls,

Revenue, 80,705,954 Dams,

Seyurghal, 11,580,954 Dams.

	Dams.		Dams.
Ardhapoor,	1,600,000	Seyool,	3,600,000
Pahtehry,	25,114,740	Kofery,	3,200,000
Burree,	8,000,000	Loohgong,	4,800,000
Banjelgong,	2,000,000	Muckutbedeh-geer,	2,400,000
Balhore,	2,400,000	Matergong,	480,000
Biſtnet,	11,200,000	Mandeer,	6,871,203
Baar,	1,600,000	Vaſa,	400,000
Bungully,	640,000	Hata,	1,200,000
Chitore,	3,600,000		
Jehry,	1,600,000		

SIRCAR TELINGANEH,

Containing 19 Mahls,

Revenue, 71,904,000 Dams,

Seyurghal, 6,600,000 Dams.

Indore has a ſmall ſtone fort,	4,800,000	Keryat Kodavend Khan,	640,000
Owleh,	800,000	Dhekwar,	96
Boden,	8,000,000	Rajore,	1,600,000
Bhancer,	1,600,000	Gurkote,	2,200,000
Bhilſa,	6,400,000	Kherka,	6,400,000
Balkunda,	6,400,000	Koſumpulteh,	664,000
Peemgul,	2,400,000	Mudmool,	6,400,000
Panoora,	3,200,000	Loohgong,	11,200,000
Bhooker,	1,600,000	Neermul,	6,400,000
Tamoorny,	160,000		

SIRCAR

SIRCAR RAMGUR,

Containing 5 Mahls,

Revenue, 9,600,000 Dams.

	Dams.		Dams.
Belarab,	800,000	Havelly Ram-gur,	2,560,000
Chitore,	3,200,000	Kundhad,	2,240,000
		Murgmool,	800,000

SIRCAR BHEKER,

Containing 4 Mahls,

Revenue, 45,122,900 Dams,

Seyurghal, 376,000 Dams.

Havelly Bhe-ker,	25,600,000	Dewelgong,	5,600,000
Summerny,	7,200,000	Suckerkherleh,	6,776,000

SIRCAR PUTTYALEH,

Containing 9 Mahls,

Revenue, 19,120,000 Dams,

Seyurghal, 4,800,000 Dams.

Owdungong,	400,000	Deha,	4,800,000
Atawan,	2,400,000	Dhaweer,	2,600,000
Pattyalehbary,	1,200,000	Sewna,	640,000
Chandore,	1,280,000	Sownlapara,	1,600,000
Junghully,	2,000,000		

TUKSEEM

TUKSEEM JUMMA

OF THE

SOOBAH OF GUJERAT.

SIRCAR AHMEDABAD,

Containing 28 Mahls,
Meaſurement, 8,024,153 Beegahs,
Revenue, 208,306,994 Dams,
Seyurghal, 6,511,441 Dams.

	Dams.
The city of Ahmedabad,	15,000,073
Havelly Ahmedabad,	23,999,371
Arhermatra,	9,669,754
Ahmednager has a ſtone fort,	1,770,912
Iyder,	1,616,000
Bheel,	6,088,920
Barahſewah,	2,814,124
Beerpoor has a ſtone fort,	1,778,300
Beelowd,	1,493,249
Beeranty,	2,076,574
Bunder Soleh,	600,000
Putlad,	771,960
Thameneh,	600,000
Chalabarha has a brick fort,	34,908,220
Chalawarah has a ſtone fort,	4,825,390
Dhulkeh,	1,650,000
Dhundhookh has a ſtone fort,	11,307,704
Sirnal,	10,188,105
Kurry,	30,125,987
Khambayit,	20,147,986
Kerneej has a ſtone fort,	30,125,778
Mundeh,	22,147,973
Muraſeh has a brick fort,	4,235,119
Mahmoodabad,	1,747,080
Maſſaudabad has a brick fort,	1,400,000
Mungeritch has a ſtone fort,	121,762
Neryad,	8,103,098
Hirſoor,	752,212

This sircar furnishes 4120 cavalry and 20,500 infantry.

SIRCAR

SIRCAR PUTTEN,

Containing 16 Mahls,

Meafurement, 3,750,015 Beegahs,

Revenue, 600,325,099 Dams,

Seyurghal, 210,327 Dams.

	Dams.
Putten has two forts,	957,462
Beejapoor,	6,001,832
Palhunpoor,	3,600,000
Burnagur has a ftone fort,	1,844,324
Beelnagur,	674,348
Tehrar has a brick fort,	4,000,000
Teerwareh has a brick fort,	2,130,000
Havelly Putten,	254,045
Radhun has a brick fort,	4,000,000
Summy,	1,266,998
Satilpoor,	287,340
Kherang,	4,000,000
Kakreejy,	1,312,590
Mownjpoor,	909,630
Moorwarch,	320,030
Weyfeh,	1,600,000

This sircar furnishes 715 cavalry and 6000 infantry.

SIRCAR NADOWT,

Containing 12 Mahls,

Meafurement, 541,817 Beegahs, 16 Bifwahs,

Revenue, 8,797,596 Dams,

Seyurghal, 11,328 Dams.

Amroly,	143,620
Awdha,	17,076
Befroy,	2,061,368
Bedal,	272,645
Tilkowareh,	1,595,525
Tehwa,	165,500
Jemoogong,	412,093
Kyar,	80,308
Murghedereh,	62,328
Manden,	16,000
Nadowt with the Havelly,	3,929,330
Nutrung,	165,500

SIRCAR BERODEH,

Containing 4 Mahls,

Meafurement, 922,212 Beegahs,

Revenue, 41,145,895 Dams,

Seyurghal, 388,358 Dams.

	Dams.
Berodeh, with the Havelly, has a ftone fort,	20,403,485
Bahaderpoor, has a ftone fort,	6,243,280
Dubhowey, has a ftone fort,	6,252,550
Senoor,	5,746,580

This sircar furnishes 900 *cavalry and* 5800 *infantry.*

SIRCAR BEHROATCH,

Containing 14 Mahls,

Meafurement, 349,771 Beegahs,

Revenue, 21,845,663 Dams,

Seyurghal, 141,820 Dams.

Owrparah,	1,655,877
Akleyfir,	558,010
Aneer,	307,737
Behroatch, has a brick fort,	456,230
Turkyeh,	5 651
Jehrmundowey,	122,795
Havelly Behroatch,	7,022,690
Deetchparah,	1,174,540
Kady,	4,275,000
Kulleh,	353,670
Kundhar,	244,000
Noorek,	1,277,250
Mukboolabad,	2,912,040
Hanfooh,	2,439,158

This sircar furnishes 990 *cavalry and* 20,800 *infantry.*

SIRCAR

SIRCAR CHANPANEER,

Containing 9 Mahls,

Meaſurement, 800,337 Beegahs, 11 Biſwahs,

Revenue, 10,109,884 Dams.

Seyurghal, 173,730 Dams.

	Dams.
Arawereh,	48,209
Chanpaneer with the Havelly, 2 ſtone forts,	1,429,649
Chundwareh,	21,530
Chowraſy,	2,215,275
Dhowd, has a ſtone fort,	1,283,300
Dhowl,	172,992
Dilawereh,	48,628
Sownkhereh,	2,999,796
Sanvees, has a ſtone fort,	2,300,000

This sircar furniſhes 550 cavalry and 1600 infantry.

SIRCAR SOORET,

Containing 31 Mahls,

Meaſurement, 1,312,315 Beegahs, 16 Biſwahs.

Revenue, 19,035,177 Dams,

Seyurghal, 182,370 Dams.

Anawel has a ſtone fort,	424,355
Purchowl,	1,508,000
Bullyar,	1,281,420
Beleyſir,	1,016,045
Beyawereh, has a ſtone fort,	554,320
Belwareh, has a ſtone fort,	478,620
Bhyſroot,	425,055
Parneer,	1,277,475
Bhoolſir,	146,230
Balowreh,	592,180
Tellary,	917,890
Timba,	236,390
Jugehlee,	383,320
Dehmoory,	860,520
Raneer,	63,690
Sooret, with the Havelly, has a	

	Dams.
ſtone fort,	5,530,145
Supa,	7,331,510
Sirbhoon,	601,275
Khublury,	26,760
Khundbowey,	735,330
Khirka,	629,310
Kerodeh,	383,240
Camreetch,	328,205
Kows has a ſtone fort,	228,390
Loohary,	85,280
Merawely,	370,410
Mehweh,	190,200
Narnoly,	65,220
Nowſary,	297,720
Neryad,	130,900

This sircar furnishes 2000 *cavalry and* 5500 *infantry.*

SIRCAR KODEHRA,

Containing 12 Mahls,

Meaſurement, 535,255 Beegahs,

Revenue, 3,418,324 Dams.

Owdha,	184,935
Atladera,	34,660
Beyra,	257,202
Jednagur,	120,660
Jhalood,	794,654
Dhamnood,	* * *
Sehra,	146,392
Kodehra, with the Havelly, 2 Mahls,	785,660
Kohaneh,	785,669
Meeral,	525,975
Mehdwara,	18,026

This sircar furnishes 1000 *cavalry and* 5000 *infantry.*

SIRCAR SORET,

Containing 73 Mahls,

Out of which number, 13 Mahls are on account of Port Duties.

Revenue, 63,437,366 Dams.

Adeneh,	7,630,388
Artchja,	780,500
Amrely,	1,784,160
Apletch,	1,214,592

Puttendco,

	Dams.
Puttendeo,	4,453,990
Banwareh,	4,809,640
Bilkha,	140,000
Bulsar,	509,760
Beyry,	14,560
Birwa,	50,664
Bundeh,	84,960
Bandowr,	14,060
Bheemradeh,	28,320
Palytahneh,	240,592
Beksera,	56,340
Berer,	734,792
Berwara,	74,792
Bhadeyly,	14,160
Telaja,	2,435,520
Jowgh,	453,120
Jennetpoor,	12,832
Jugget,	803,200
Jowrwar,	936,970
Chowra,	97,288
Jeytehry,	1,071,360
Jirhoon,	98,560
Havelly Soret,	932,000
Dank,	41,410
Doongur,	760,400
Dowletabad,	357,424
Dherwar,	59,792
Dhentroor,	252,048
Dhary,	644,272
Ranpoor,	16,128
Ralkun,	113,280
Ramoot,	28,320
Siyoor,	42,480
Sirsy,	4536
Sultanpoor,	424,800
Karbadhar,	623,040
Gowrynar,	4,538,360
Khookeh, exclusive of the port,	666,560
Ghatasayera,	42,480
Kunker,	598,704
Kurrydehry,	127,480
Gowndel,	56,640
Kotyara,	1,797,256
Gundowlna,	198,432
Loolyaneh,	1,423,080
Simurabanwa,	487,576
Lat-hy,	296,152
Mulkapoor,	995,048
Meheweh,	2,051,136
Mundowy,	2,107,440
Mangalore,	16,680,472
Meydereh,	2,208,160
Moorly,	2,603,336
Meyaneh,	14,160
Naguny,	755,376
Hulteny,	9,121,025

PORT DUTIES.

	Mahmudi.
Bunder Mangalore,	27,000
Bunder Putten Deo,	25,000
Bunder Gowrynar,	1000
Bunder Nagserry,	10,000
Bunder Poor,	27,628
Bunder Meheweh,	14,000
Bunder Mylkore,	3000
Bunder Doorgur,	1000
Bunder Telaja, 2 mahls,	7000
Bunder Adeneh,	15,000

This sircar furnishes 17,000 *cavalry and* 36,500 *infantry.*

TUKSEEM JUMMA

OF THE

SOOBAH OF AJMEER.

SIRCAR AJMEER,

Containing 28 Mahls,

Meaſurement, 5,605,487 Beegahs,

Revenue, 62,153,390 Dams.

Seyurghal, 1,475,714 Dams.

	Dams.
Ajmeer, with the Havelly, has a fort on a mountain,	6,214,731
Embeer, has a ſtone fort on a mountain,	12,256,297
Arayin,	1,755,960
Pereet,	2,200,000
Baghorvy,	486,161
Pehnoy,	1,400,000
Behnaey,	271,256
Bowal,	749,773
Bahel,	600,000
Bandhen Soondery,	435,664
Behrdundeh,	200,072
Tuſyna,	2,330,090
Jowneereh,	214,442
Jagh,	501,844
Dowgong,	1,200,000
Roſhenpoor,	692,512
Sembher, has a ſtone fort,	9,649,947
Serwar, has a brick fort,	1,616,825
Sehteela,	1,270,009
Solimanabad,	1,860,016
Keykery,	1,880,000
Kehrweh,	7,020,347
Mahroot,	5,756,402
Muneverabad,	1,452,577
Muſſaudabad,	1,587,991
Neranyeh,	2,660,159
Herſoor, has a brick fort,	1,200,926

This sircar furnishes 16,000 *cavalry and* 80,000 *infantry.*

SIRCAR

SIRCAR CHITORE,

Containing 26 Mahls,

Meaſurement, 1,678,802 Beegahs, 17 Biſwahs,

Revenue, 30,047,649 Dams,

Seyurghal, 360,737 Dams.

	Dams.
Iſlampoor, commonly called Rampoor,	7,000,000
Owdypoor,	1,120,000
Apermal,	280,000
Arlood,	200,000
Iſlampoor, commonly called Mohen,	108,600
Boodhnore, has a ſtone fort,	4,311,551
Phoolya, has a ſtone fort,	2,843,470
Punehra,	3,296,290
Poor,	2,601,041
Bheenſeroor has a ſtone fort,	1,200,000
Bagore,	395,550
Beygoon,	1,175,729
Beyſee Hajypoor has a ſtone fort,	1,375,000
Chitore, with the Havelly, two mahls, a ſtone fort,	800,000
Jyren,	1,985,250
Sanwerghaty,	470,294
Sandery, has a ſtone fort,	400,020
Semeel,	100,000
Kowſyaneh,	263,812
Mandelgurh, has a ſtone fort upon a mountain,	3,384,750
Mandel, has a brick fort,	447,090
Medarye,	160,000
Neemij, &c. 3 mahls,	719,202

This sircar furnishes 22,000 cavalry and 82,000 infantry.

SIRCAR

SIRCAR RHINTENPOOR,

Containing 83 Mahls,

Meaſurement, 6,024,196 Beegahs, 11 Biſwahs,

Revenue, 89,864,576 Dams,

Seyurghal, 181,834 Dams.

	Dams.
Alhenpoor,	1,562,239
Ownyara,	1,237,169
Itada,	770,525
Atwan,	600,000
Iſlampoor,	77,500
Unghoreh,	160,000
Untoorweh,	1,500,000
Ivanbooſameer,	1,200,000
Boondy, has a ſtone fort upon a mountain,	1,620,000
Booly has a ſtone fort,	2,622,747
Beroodeh,	4,571,000
Burdareh,	1,969,776
Paten,	2,800,000
Bhudlown,	2,686,389
Pucklant,	1,200,000
Pelatyeh,	1,400,000
Bhoſoor,	600,000
Benehta,	542,356
Beylooneh,	456,479
Beyjery,	334,890
Balaghetery,	300,000
Bhoorybhary,	110,000
Baran,	880,000
Toonek,	75,000
Tooda,	5,859,060
Toodry,	5,456,340
Telad,	423,288
Jeetpoor,	928,500
Chatſoo,	7,536,829
Cheldweh,	500,000
Jahyen,	475,000
Khuljypoor,	1,209,386
Dehry,	1,800,000
Deehlwareh, &c.	409,260
Dylaneh,	739,400
Rhinterpoor, with the Havelly,	156,895
Reevandhneh,	430,354
Sewyſoper,	5,041,306
Sarſoop,	258,876
Sehnſary,	300,000
Kowta has a ſtone fort upon a mountain near the river Chembel,	3,000,000
Khunder, has a ſtone fort on a mountain,	400,000
Khunkehreh,	1,511,994
Kehrny,	528,177
Khownly,	200,000
Gudawed,	188,095
Kerore, has a	

ſtone

	Dams.
ſtone fort upon a mountain,	200,000
Lahkery, has a ſtone fort upon a mountain,	800,000
Loherwareh,	250,000
Lowndeh,	250,000
Lehawed,	125,000
Moomydaneh, &c. 16 mahls,	4,100,000
Mellerneh,	3,299,241
Mangore,	204,348
Nowahy,	930,000
Nugger,	1,000,000

This sircar furnishes 9000 *cavalry and* 25,000 *infantry.*

SIRCAR JEWDEHPOOR,

Containing 22 Mahls,

Revenue, 14,528,750 Dams.

Aſoop, has a brick fort,	600,000
Arundrowty,	8000
Phooly, has a brick fort,	640,000
Pelparah,	1,463,000
Belara,	314,000
Paly, &c. 3 mahls, a ſtone fort,	250,000
Baheleh,	189,000
Poodeh, has a ſtone fort,	46,000
Bhadrajoon, has a ſtone fort,	800,000
Jewdehpoor, with the Havelly, has a ſtone fort upon a mountain,	280,000
Jeytaren, has a ſtone fort,	3,000,000
Dootara, has a ſtone fort,	100,000
Suhet, has a ſtone fort,	2,812,750
Satelmeer, has a ſtone fort on a mountain,	560,000
Saywana, has a ſtone fort on a mountain,	1,200,000
Kherwa,	220,000
Kheyconſir, has ſtone fort,	170,000
Ghoondej, has a ſtone fort,	90,000
Meheweh,	960,000

This sircar furnishes 15,000 *cavalry and* 50,000 *infantry.*

SIRCAR

SIRCAR SIROWHY,

Containing 6 Mahls,

Revenue, 42,077,437 Dams.

	Dams.
Anergurh and Sirowhy, two mahls, the latter has a ftone fort,	12,000,000
Banfwareh, has a ftone fort,	8,000,000
Jalore and Senjore, 2 mahls, a very ftrong ftone fort,	14,077,437
Doongurpoor,	8,000,000

This sircar furnishes 8000 *cavalry and* 38,000 *infantry.*

SIRCAR NAGORE,

Containing 31 Mahls,

Meafurement, 837,450 Beegahs, 16 Bifwahs,

Revenue, 40,389,830 Dams,

Seyurghal, 308,051 Dams.

Amerfernagin,	7,029,370
Indaneh,	1,313,006
Bhedaneh,	1,271,960
Buldoo,	570,000
Batoodeh,	322,816
Beroodeh,	220,663
Barehgayin,	58,000
Chagil,	955,273
Jaroodeh,	974,285
Jakehreh,	137,757
Kharijkehtoo, has a ftone fort,	348,814
Deendwaneh, has a brick fort,	4,586,828
Dewnpoor,	7,080,085
Rejwafa,	1,995.824
Roon,	913,261
Ruffoolpoor,	704,606
Rehoot,	189,137
Sadeyleh,	1,266,930
Futtahpoor Jehenjown, has a ftone fort,	1,233,222
Kaffely,	1,587,154
Khayeleh,	558,560
Gojewreh,	466,890

	Dams.
Goleyweh,	352,305
Kombary,	435,604
Geyren,	57,160
Ladoon,	780,342
Meeret, has a ſtone fort,	7,701,522
Menohernagur,	2,903,386
Nokha,	380,756
Nagore, with the Havelly, a brick fort,	313,581

This sircar furnishes 4500 *cavalry and* 22,000 *infantry.*

SIRCAR BEYKANEER,

Containing 11 Mahls,

Revenue, 4,750,000 Dams.

Bickumpoor,	* *
Beerſelpoor,	* *
Bahermeel,	* *
Pokul,	* *
Parkul,	* *
Pokhrun,	* *
Beykaneer and Jeleelmeer,	* *
Johtur,	* *
Kotera,	* *
Dewader,	* *

This sircar furnishes 1200 *cavalry and* 50,000 *infantry.*

TUKSEEM JUMMA

OF THE

SOOBAH OF DEHLY.

SIRCAR DEHLY,

Containing 48 Mahls,

Meaſurement, 7,126,107 Beegahs, 17 Biſwahs.

Revenue, 123,012,590 Dams,

Seyurghal, 10,990,260 Dams.

	Dams.
Iſlamabad Pakel has a ſtone fort upon a mountain,	1,779,407
Adeheh,	513,081
Panyput has a brick fort,	10,756,647
Palem,	5,726,788
Beren has a brick fort,	3,907,928
Baghput,	3,532,368
Pulwel has a brick fort on a hill,	1,769,493
Bernadeh,	1,379,125
Pooteh has a brick fort,	621,749
Beryduyeldehn,	1,404,225
Tilput has a brick fort,	3,077,913
Tandehbahgwar,	1,289,306
Tilbegumpoor,	370,374
Jehjehr,	1,422,451
Jharſeh has a ſtone fort in the village of Dahneh,	3,605,228
Jeyore,	1,878,378
Jehnjeneh,	1,700,250
Jehrowly,	1,138,759
Jillalabad,	1,333,711
Jillalpoor Seroot has a wild,	1,001,875
The old Havelly,	1,422,451
The new Havelly,	3,635,311
The city of Dehly,	736,460
Daſneh,	4,933,302
Daderytaha,	4,326,059
Dunkoor,	1,016,682
Rohtek has a brick fort,	8,599,270

	Dams.
Soonput has a brick fort,	7,727,323
Sefeedoon has a brick fort,	1,975,596
Secunderabad,	1,259,199
Seraweh,	1,583,899
Sunyeet,	854,191
Syaneh,	2,049,090
Shukerpoor,	2,111,996
Kernal,	5,678,242
Kenore has a brick fort,	1,718,792
Gurhmuktesir has a brick fort on the banks of the Ganges and a pagoda,	1,591,492
Ketaneh,	1,423,779
Kadeleh,	1,374,403
Kasneh,	1,522,315
Kherkodeh,	1,505,856
Kenkeerkehreh has a brick fort situated between two rivers,	316,405
Lowny has a brick fort situated between two rivers,	3,274,878
Meeret has a brick fort situated between two rivers,	4,391,996
Mendohty,	2,858,223
Massaoudabad has an old brick fort,	2,809,478
Hustnapoor, an ancient place of Hindoo worship on the banks of the Ganges,	4,466,904
Hapoor,	2,103,589

This sircar furnishes 2000 *cavalry and* 32,980 *infantry.*

SIRCAR BUDAYOON,

Containing 13 Mahls,

Measurement, 8,093,850 Beegahs, 10 Biswahs,

Revenue, 34,717,063 Dams.

Seyurghal, 457,181 Dams.

Ajong,	1,362,867
Ownleh,	690,620
Budayoon with the Havelly,	7,357,571
Bereyly,	12,507,434
Birsir,	2,147,324

Pownd

	Dams.
Pownd,	260,340
Tulhy,	1,077,811
Sehsowan,	2,493,398
Sonnassmundyeh,	795,315
Sunya,	1,315,722
Kant,	2,439,369

	Dams.
Kotesalbahen has a fort,	1,229,165
Goleh,	1,136,631

This sircar furnishes 2850 cavalry and 26,700 infantry.

SIRCAR KEMAUN,

Containing 21 Mahls,

Revenue, 40,437,700 Dams.

Adown,	400,000
Bhooksyand Bhagsa, two mahls,	400,000
Basweh,	200,000
Pachowter,	400,000
Bheekunde var,	200,000
Bhagty,	11,000,000
Bhoory,	* *
Beteela,	10,025,000
Jhungy,	400,000
Jugram,	5,000,000
Jurryeh,	3,000,000
Javun,	2,500,000
Chawly,	* *
Sehujgur,	* *
Guzirboor,	* *
Kote Dewareh,	* *
Mulwareh,	2,500,000
Malakore, Setakhoor, and Kymoos, three mahls,	5,037,700

No account is made of the other five pergunnahs.

This sircar furnishes 3000 cavalry and 50,000 infantry.

SIRCAR

SICAR SEMBHEL,

Containing 47 Mahls,

Meafurement, 4,047,193 Beegahs, 2 Bifwahs,

Revenue, 66,341,431 Dams,

Seyurghal, 2,892,394 Dams.

	Dams.
Amrowheh,	6,342,000
Azempoor,	2,389,478
Iflampoor Behrow,	1,330,640
Owjahry,	697,609
Akberabad,	640,264
Iflampoor Derkow,	429,675
Iflampoor Durgoo,	346,348
Bijnore,	3,355,425
Bejhrong,	828,322
Perowhy,	150,000
Befara,	200,000
Chandpoor,	4,131,071
Jilalabad,	1,470,072
Chowmaleh,	1,340,312
Chaloo,	237,809
Judwar,	828,348
Havelly Sembhel,	3,322,448
Deoreh,	1,924,837
Dehkeh,	670,364
Deyhary,	1,080,306
Dudeyleh,	210,000
Rajpoor,	700,000
Rejebpoor,	612,978
Sembhel, has a brick fort,	850,953
Sewhareh,	1,333,732
Siry,	958,769
Sehenfpoor,	644,804
Sirfaweh,	308,065
Sheerkote,	4,921,051
Shahy,	900.496
Kunderky,	674,936
Keeretpoor,	2,410,609
Cutch,	1,248,995
Gindore,	751,520
Kaber,	566,539
Kenore,	267,919
Kahnkery,	200,000
Lukhnore,	2,499,208
Leefweh,	100,000
Moghoolpoor,	3,580,300
Munjoleh,	737,556
Mundawer,	1,256,995
Nudeeneh,	2,647,242
Nehtore,	1,738,160
Niyoodeneh,	304,675
Nerowly,	1,408,093
Humteneh,	250,000

This sircar furnishes 4375 cavalry, 50 elephants, and 31,550 infantry.

SIRCAR

SIRCAR SEHARUNPOOR,

Containing 36 Mahls,

Meafurement, 3,530,370 Beegahs, 3 Bifwahs,

Revenue, 87,839,359 Dams,

Seyurghal, 4,991,485 Dams.

	Dams.
Indery, has a brick fort,	7,078,326
Uneefteh,	324,560
Budhonah,	3,698,041
Beydowly,	3,115,125
Bhutghunjyawer,	2,676,407
Bhowgpoor,	2,338,120
Pooretchpar,	2,191,460
Bhooneh,	2,135,496
Bughra,	1,913,196
Bhut,	1,321,440
Tanneh Bheem,	3,578,540
Talookpoor,	222,277
Chowraffy,	2,471,277
Jowly,	1,310,057
Jertahwel,	1,668,882
Havelly Seharunpoor, has a brick fort,	6,951,540
Deobund, has a brick fort,	641,977
Rampoor,	1,778,997
Roorky,	1,628,360
Roypoortatar,	369,080
Seekrybhokerhurry,	3,003,311
Sirfaweh, has a brick fort,	2,516,165
Seeroot,	2,208,779
Sirowhneh,	1,590,606
Sumbeltera,	1,011,078
Serenbulry,	574,320
Ghatowly,	3,624,588
Ghody,	2,514,673
Geeraneh,	2,025,238
Gungweh,	2,029,032
Lukhnowty,	1,796,058
Mozufferabad,	4,074,460
Mangolore has a brick fort,	2,350,311
Mulhypoor,	2,244,070
Nagore,	1,337,070
Nanuteh,	724,153

This sircar furnishes 3955 *cavalry and* 22,280 *infantry.*

SIRCAR REYWARY,

Containing 12 Mahls,

Meaſurement, 1,155,011 Beegahs, 10 Biſwahs,

Revenue, * * *

Seyurghal, 739,268 Dams.

	Dams.
Padel,	4,114,753
Patoodehy,	2,270,080
Bhoohereh,	755,543
Tawerd, has a brick fort,	986,228
Reywary, with the Havelly, a brick fort,	11,956,847
Remaïy Chenaïy,	228,603
Kote Coſſim Aly,	3,357,930
Ghylote,	656,688
Gohaneh,	421,440
Soheneh, has a ſtone fort upon a mountain, and a hot well, which is an object of Hindoo worſhip,	3,928,364
Himraneh, has a ſtone fort upon a mountain,	682,159

This sircar furnishes 2175 cavalry and 14,600 infantry.

SIRCAR HISSAR FEEROZEH,

Containing 27 Mahls,

Meaſurement, 3,114,497 Beegahs,

Revenue, 55,004,905 Dams,

Seyurghal, 1,406,519 Dams.

Agrowdeh,	1,743,970
Ahrowhy,	857,357
Unghereh, has a brick fort and a place of Hindoo worſhip called Kowres,	1,576,200

Bhun-

	Dams.
Bhungeedal,	1,800,000
Poonyan,	1,200,000
Bharengy,	880,832
Perwaleh,	1,097,807
Bhetu,	440,280
Burwa,	64,680
Tahneer, has a brick fort,	933,042
Toohaneh, has a brick fort,	4,694,354
Toosam,	1,068,548
Jeneed,	5,004,749
Jimalpoor,	4,277,461
Hissar with the Havelly, two forts, one of stone and the other of brick,	4,039,895
Dhateret, has a brick fort,	977,028
Sirsa, has a brick fort,	4,361,368
Seyuran,	400,000
Sudhemkeh,	171,372
Sutwany,	76,750
Shanzdekeryat,	960,111
Futtahabad, has a brick fort,	1,184,392
Gohaneh,	2,876,115
Khandeh,	1,119,364
Mehem, has a brick fort,	4,958,613
Hansy, has a brick fort,	5,434,438

This sircar furnishes 6875 *cavalry and* 55,700 *infantry.*

SIRCAR SIRHIND,

Containing 33 Mahls,

Measurement, 7,729,466 Beegahs, 7 Biswahs,

Revenue, 160,790,594 Dams,

Seyurghal, 11,697,330 Dams.

Embaleh,	4,198,094
Benore,	12,549,953
Payil, has a brick fort,	7,362,262
Bhooder,	3,103,269
Bhetundeh,	3,125,000
Powndereе,	686,870
Tehareh, has a brick fort, on the banks of the river Setlej,	7,850,809
Tahnesr, has a brick fort,	7,850,803
Jhut,	7,509,094
Jerk,	1,538,090

Khzyer-

	Dams.
Khyzerabad, has a brick fort,	12,059,918
Dowraleh,	2,188,443
Dewtch,	1,601,346
Deoraneh,	580,985
Rooper, has a brick fort,	5,005,549
Sirhind with the Havelly, two mahls, a brick fort,	12,082,630
Semaneh,	10,822,280
Senam, has a brick fort,	7,007,696
Sadhooreh, has a brick fort,	4,298,064
Sultanpoor bareh,	427,035
Shahabad,	6,751,468
Futtahpoor,	684,370
Keryat Roysemu,	1,220,090
Keythel, has a brick fort, and a place of Hindoo worship,	10,638,630
Gheram, has a brick fort,	6,138,630
Lodyaneh, has a brick fort on the banks of the river Setlej,	2,291,633
Mustofyabad,	7,476,691
Mussunker,	7,053,259
Munoorpoor,	1,830,025
Malneer,	1,060,580
Matchwareh, has a brick fort,	653,552
Hapery,	1,145,118

This sircar furnishes 9225 cavalry and 55,700 infantry.

TUKSEEM JUMMA

OF THE

SOOBAH OF LAHOOR.

SIRCAR DOOABEH BEYT JALENDHER,

Containing 60 Mahls,

Meaſurement, 3,279,302 Beegahs, 17 Biſwahs,

Revenue, 124,365,212 Dams,

Seyurghal, 2,651,788 Dams.

	Dams.
Aſleemabad,	458,122
Putty Dheneyat,	3,601,678
Bhoonga,	2,760,530
Bejwareh,	2,425,813
Bheloon, has a ſtone fort,	1,305,006
Birweh,	668,000
Palekwah,	200,000
Betchrytu,	160,000
Beyſaly and Khutteh two mahls,	566,366
Telown,	6,780,337
Talarpoor, has a ſtone fort,	170,388
Jalendehr, has a brick fort,	14,751,626
Chowraſy,	5,463,913
Jewra,	2,474,854
Jaſown Balakotee, has a ſtone fort,	600,000
Chitore,	313,000
Hajypoor Saryaneh,	2,693,874
Dardek,	9,707,993
Deyſooheh, has a brick fort,	4,474,950
Dedeyal, has a ſtone fort,	1,650,000
Dadeh, has a ſtone fort,	1,200,000
Derperreh,	900,000
Durdhy,	600,000
Doonnagore,	455,870
Dhenkely,	72,000
Rehcemabad,	2,480,639
Rajpoor Putten,	

has

	Dams.
has a ftone fort,	1,800,000
Sultanpoor, has a brick fort,	2,418,232
Suckhut Mundowy, has fome iron and copper mines,	1,680,000
Soper,	1,000,000
Seebeh, has a ftone fort,	800,000
Suren,	213,333
Sheikhupoor,	4,722,604
Sheergurh,	194,294
Iffapoor,	316,867
Kothey,	5,546,661
Gurh Dumbaleh,	2,670,087
Koteleh,	1,680,000
Kotelehr, has a ftone fort,	1,310,867
Kehrekdehar,	480,000
Gheyoonkhera, has a ftone fort,	240,000
Kunkote, has a ftone fort,	240,000
Khereh,	240,000
Ghewafs,	586,906
Lohydehry,	563,414
Lalfinghy,	236,850
Myany Noorneh,	2,106,156
Meylfy,	1,823,559
Mahommedpoor,	1,802,558
Manfewal,	286,667
Melote,	460,620
Mudhoteh,	426,367
Nekowder,	3,710,796
Nuckrowh,	1,300,061
Nunkel,	2,315,368
Nundown,	5,300,000
Hirbanch and Akberabad, 2 mahls,	6,032,032
Hadyabad,	519,467

This sircar furnishes 4155 *cavalry and* 79,536 *infantry.*

SIRCAR DOOABEH BARY,

Containing 52 Mahls,

Meafurement, 4,580,002 Beegahs, 18 Bifwahs,

Revenue, 142,820,183 Dams,

Seyurghal, 3,923,922 Dams.

Unchereh,	500,000
Undowreh,	1,193,739
Abhypoor,	168,000
Owder,	9600

The

	Dams.
The city of Lahoor,	2,912,600
Phulwary,	452,694
Phulra,	2,413,268
Punjgramy,	1,461,630
Bhirly,	4,060,507
Bhelwal,	3,181,699
Putty Hybetpoor,	28,395,380
Buttaleh,	16,820,998
Bythan, has a brick fort,	7,297,015
Punyal,	4,266,091
Beyah,	3,822,255
Bahaderpoor,	447,750
Telwarch,	514,666
Tehndowt,	610,064
Chundrow,	263,568
Charbagh Berhy,	58,502
Jemary,	8,813,140
Jilalabad,	5,163,119
Jeht and Umbaleh, 2 mahls,	2,300,000
Jutker,	45,600
Khanpoor,	280,038
Debhawaleh,	6,280,139
Dehmehry,	1,600,000
Durweh,	240,000
Derweh Deegur,	24,000

	Dams.
Sungha Arwel,	544,145
Sundhewan,	5,854,649
The ſuburbs of Lahoor,	674,053
Shaphoor,	2,382,235
Sherpoor,	480,000
Ghorbutravun,	411,985
Kuſſoor,	3,915,506
Kelanoor,	8,329,111
Kanoonvahen,	3,511,499
Ghoghowal,	3,475,510
Gualiar,	2,643,000
Kangereh, has a ſtone fort,	2,400,000
Koteleh,	182,518
Gurgerong,	16,000
Mullickſhah,	1,475,562
Mowd and Bunneh, 2 mahls,	2,400,000
Mehrore,	24,000
Hoſhyar Kernaleh,	489,372
Palem,	These four pergunnahs are deſolated.
Puttyar,	
Behty,	
Jirjur,	

This sircar furnishes 31,055 *cavalry and* 129,600 *infantry.*

SIRCAR

SIRCAR DOOABEH RETCHNABAD,

Containing 57 Mahls,

Meafurement, 4,253,148 Beegahs, 3 Bifwahs,

Revenue, 172,047,691 Dams,

Seyurghal, 2,684,134 Dams.

	Dams.
Amraky Behty,	1,942,606
The lands of Bagh Roy Boocheh,	52,837
Umnabad, has a brick fort,	24,853,006
Beejnagur,	1,181,622
Birferore,	27,978,583
Budoobhundel,	1,611,822
Putty Zuffrawal, has a fort,	3,697,338
Putty Birhely,	525,953
Bhelote,	818,182
Bhedan,	240,000
Belawereh,	240,000
Bhootyal,	96,000
Bun,	48,000
Tarel,	2,144,945
Talowndy,	1,518,227
Jeemehcheteh,	5,878,698
Chendenwerek,	6,128,631
Chotadehr,	1,391,692
Jeodehry,	815,587
Jenyoot, has a brick fort,	2,806,369
Jemmu, has a ftone fort,	3,956,000
Jeffroteh,	* * *
Cheryjeena,	240,000
Hafezabad,	4,548,000
Khanpoor,	28,028
Dowletpoor,	115,050
Dooudbhendal,	1,725,079
Dowletabad,	241,740
Roopnagur,	410,513
Reehna,	275,550
Retchna,	8,680,742
Sahoomooly,	5,574,764
Sidehpoor,	3,127,212
Syalkote, has a brick fort,	22,090,702
Sejhrow,	362,326
Sedherah, has a high brick minaret, fituated on the banks of a river,	7,096,710
Shanzdez Sinjrow,	1,556,480
Shoor,	2,278,940
Berhy Fettubhendal,	613,917
Fuzelabad,	136,528
Gobindal,	1,253,957
Kat-hooha,	5,888,254
Berhy Goojran,	670,936
Kalayuns,	203,964
Karnry, commonly called	

Sanyar,

	Dams.
Sanyar,	1,500,000
Kherlyterly,	768,000
Lukknore,	681,818
Mungutwaleh,	3,890,690
Berby Mahommed Dookroow,	1,127,903
Mehrore,	5,005,602
Meengree,	1,475,225
Mankote, has 4 ftone forts,	85,119
Vun,	3,711,553
Hummeenagur,	8,391,087
Huntyal,	240,000

This sircar furnishes 6795 *cavalry and* 99,652 *infantry.*

SIRCAR DOOABEH JENHET,

Containing 21 Mahls,

Meafurement, 2,633,202 Beegahs, 5 Bifwahs,

Revenue, 64,502,394 Dams,

Seyurghal, 511,070 Dams.

Inderhul,	485,418
Aghundore Umbaran,	392,000
Beheereh,	19,910,000
Bhelolepoor,	3,830,575
Booleit,	400,080
Bhinber,	1,200,000
Bhedoo,	192,000
Bohety,	57,222
Sayila and Doodyal, 2 mahls,	735,741
Shoorpoor,	3,121,546
Shukerpoor,	1,050,819
Gujerat,	8,266,150
Keryaly,	2,643,270
Ghoghar, has a brick fort,	2,320,594
Ghurry,	1,505,241
Lalore,	3,746,166
Mengely,	432,000
Metole Roy Kedary,	370,549
Heryu,	9,150,878
Hezareh, has a brick fort,	4,689,136

This sircar furnishes 3730 *cavalry and* 44,200 *infantry.*

SIRCAR

SIRCAR SINDH SAGER,

Containing 42 Mahls,

Meafurement, 1,409,979 Beegahs,

Revenue, 51,912,201 Dams,

Seyurghal, 4680 Dams.

	Dams.
Akberabad Terkhery,	5,491,738
Attock Benaris,	3,202,216
Awan,	415,970
Phurhaleh, has a ftone fort,	5,158,109
Bil Ghazi Khan,	720,000
Balagehter,	1,000,040
Byrogehter,	48,000
Beloky Dhen,	1,316,801
Terchuckdamy,	250,575
Havelly Rhotas, has 2 forts,	6,043,140
Khufhab,	2,702,509
Dangurry,	3,301,201
Dhenkote, here is a falt pit,	480,000
Derbend,	100,000
Dherab,	96,000
Dowdvut,	96,000
Reyfhan,	92,496
Shumfabad,	7,034,503
Shembala,	624,000
Futtahpoor Kalowry,	4,263,831
Gulbehlek,	2,883,253
Khiyefs,	934,161
Kharderwazeh,	24,541
Kerchak,	961,755
Cutchakote,	340,000
Kahwan, has a ftone fort,	192,000
Kanput,	96,000
Lunkahuffyar,	96,000
Makhyaleh, here is a falt pit, and a ftone fort,	384,000
Meraly,	240,000
Melote, has a ftone fort,	133,233
Mundunpoor, has a brick fort,	24,110
Neelab,	481,305
Narmy,	38,091
Nokooferalkehteh,	38,092
Hezareh Fereek,	1,805,342
Huttyarlunek,	300,000
Hezareh, Goojran,	

	Dams.	
ran,	270,896	*This sircar furnishes* 8553 *cavalry and* 69,700 *infantry.*
Himmut Khan Kermoon,	48,000	

SEPARATE PERGUNNAHS.

Beylote,	322,740	Dams.
Sėhlore,	1,700,000	do.
Kahlore,	1,800,000	do.

TUKSEEM JUMMA

OF THE

SOOBAH OF MULTAN.

SIRCAR MULTAN,

Containing 47 Mahls,

Meaſurement, 558,649 Beegahs, 4 Biſwahs,

Revenue, 53,916,317 Dams,

Seyurghal, 5,494,236 Dams.

This sircar furnishes 8965 *cavalry and* 90,650 *infantry.*

DOOABEH BEYT JALENDHER,

Containing 9 Mahls,

Meaſurement, 52,090 Beegahs,

Revenue, 17,240,147 Dams,

Seyurghal, 108,884 Dams.

	Dams.
Adam Damen,	369,445
Jilalabad,	299,798
Deenapoor,	1,876,862
Rajpoor,	92,397
Sheergurh,	5,741,200
Futtahpoor,	4,020,661
Kherdher,	3,058,456
Kaheeyooldy,	594,233
Khelookhareb,	1,201,086

This division furnishes 1410 *cavalry and* 17,100 *infantry.*

DOOABEH BARY,

Containing 11 Mahls,

Meafurement, 137,629 Beegahs, 13 Bifwahs,

Revenue, 9,863,341 Dams,

Seyurghal, 207,382 Dams.

	Dams.
Iflampoor, has a brick fort,	1,550,896
Ifmailpoor,	49,932
The city of Multan, has a brick fort,	1,719,168
Telembeh,	1,200,778
Chowkhendy,	191,054
The fuburbs of the city of Multan,	2,288,354
Khutpoor,	149,578
Degrawy,	50,146
Shah-Alumpoor,	1,555,563
Kaheebooldy,	490,654
Metylch,	608,418

This division furnishes 775 cavalry and 14,550 infantry.

DOOABEH RETCHNAD,

Containing 6 Mahls,

Meafurement, 83,229 Beegahs, 18 Bifwahs,

Revenue, 5,113,883 Dams.

Irejpoor and Degrawy,	2,377,300
Chowkhendy,	215,830
Khutpoor,	505,398
Delybehty,	256,569
Kulbeh,	958,786

This division furnishes 77 cavalry and 9500 infantry.

DOOABEH

DOOABEH SINDH SAGER,

Containing 4 Mahls,

Meaſurement, 34,812 Beegahs,

Revenue, 2,178,192 Dams,

Seyurghal, 13,399 Dams.

	Dams.
Iſlampoor,	373,357
Rungpoor,	1,410,737
Roypoor,	356,068
Detached villages,	38,030

This division furnishes 220 cavalry and 2000 infantry.

PERGUNNAHS SEPARATE,

Containing 17 Mahls,

Meaſurement, 205,893 Beegahs, 13 Biſwahs,

Revenue, 18,820,255 Dams,

Seyurghal, 38,688 Dams.

Obadereh,	915,256
Owj,	1,910,140
Bhoortydamen,	1,336,029
Jumſheer,	348,037
Dudaiy, has a brick fort,	2,400,000
Dewarawel,	140,000
Doodkhan,	1,440,000
Rajpoor,	29,854
Repery,	1,080,000
Seetpoor,	4,608,000
Sewrohy,	28,800
Futtehpoor,	330,779
Kherore,	87,289
Meloot Ghazipoor,	2,400,000
Mowh, has a brick fort,	707,069
Meroot, has a brick fort,	204,000
Mehend,	8,014,000

This division furnishes 5800 cavalry and 57,600 infantry.

SIRCAR

SIRCAR DEYBALPOOR,

Containing 29 Mahls,

Meaſurement, 1,433,767 Beegahs, 8 Biſwahs,

Revenue, 129,334,153 Dams,

Seyurghal, 2,079,170 Dams.

This sircar furnishes 5210 *cavalry and* 53,300 *infantry.*

DOOABEH BEYT JALENDHER,

Containing 10 Mahls,

Meaſurement, 710,946 Beegahs, 2 Biſwahs,

Revenue, 88,808,755 Dams,

Seyurghal, 1,481,564 Dams.

	Dams.
Putten, has a brick fort,	2,628,928
Deybalpoor Luckhy, has a brick fort,	13,514,059
Dhunſhah, has a brick fort,	3,484,375
Deotur,	2,489,850
Rehmutabad,	1,825,009
Luckhy Keboo-leh, has a brick fort,	4,803,817
Luckhy Kyam-poor, has a fort,	2,008,274
Luckhy Kulna-ky,	2,985,969
Luckhy Go-grayin,	1,011,715
Luckhy Yuſka-ny,	3,156,759

This division furnishes 2400 *cavalry and* 20,400 *infantry.*

DOOABEH BARY,

Containing 6 Mahls,

Meafurement, 193,495 Beegahs, 9 Bifwahs,

Revenue, 1,175,393 Dams.

	Dams.
Bherahpal,	1,175,393
Bababhowj, has a fort,	2,020,256
Cheny,	1,200,600
Reheemabad,	1,186,714
Sedkheereh,	3,551,630
Mundhaly,	2,703,429

This division furnishes 1100 *cavalry and* 14,000 *infantry.*

DOOABEH RETCHNAD,

Containing 7 Mahls,

Meafurement, 142,856 Beegahs, 2 Bifwahs.

Revenue, 8,534,915 Dams,

Seyurghal, 5,808 Dams.

Khanpoor,	1,285,740
Dulchychundher,	605,557
Shahzadeh Belootch,	789,742
Abidyabad,	343,932
Fereedabad,	1,098,694
Kherel,	1,907,069
Mees,	2,504,182

This division furnishes 710 *cavalry and* 6300 *infantry.*

SEPARATE

SEPARATE PERGUNNAHS,

Containing 6 Mahls,

Meafurement, 386,470 Beegahs, 7 Bifwahs,

Revenue, 20,580,771 Dams,

Seyurghal, 549,970 Dams.

	Dams.
Jilalabad,	1,739,289
Jungel,	653,516
Alumpoor,	1,579,558
Feerozepoor,	11,479,404
Lucky Keboo-leh,	1,636,550
Mahommedote, has a brick fort,	3,492,454

This division furnishes 1000 *cavalry and* 12,300 *infantry.*

DOOABEH BEHKER,

Containing 12 Mahls,

Meafurement, 282,013 Beegahs,

Revenue, 18,424,947 Dams,

Seyurghal, 60,419 Dams.

Alore, has a fort,	1,132,150
Behker, has a ftrong fort,	74,362
Jandoleh,	3,102,709
Jetowey,	2,346,873
Durbeyleh,	1,262,761
Sunker,	1,808,628
Seywee,	1,381,930
Futtahpoor,	477,859
Ghurjaneh,	645,205
Kehreh Kakun,	2,732,331
Kakehry,	2,106,431
Manheleh,	1,353,713

This sircar furnishes 4690 *cavalry and* 11,100 *infantry.*

TUKSEEM

TUKSEEM JUMMA

OF THE

SOOBAH OF TATAH.

SIRCAR TATAH,

Containing 18 Mahls,

Revenue, 25,999,991 Dams.

	Dams.
Bunder Lahery,	5,521,419
Butwar,	4,932,386
Bahrampoor,	1,311,612
Bowry,	434,305
Jeker,	348,462
Jara,	82,390
Durg,	2,970,441
Denkery,	315,921
Reteneh,	842,144
Sankoreh,	2,120,097
Sirfyjam,	142,641
Kerker,	3,328,476
Lekenkeyreh,	535,795
Mujeh,	1,105,606
Manjir,	1,221,752
Nezampoor,	352,724

SIRCAR HAJYKAN,

Containing 11 Mahls,

Revenue, 11,784,586 Dams.

Bagh Futteh,	340,173
Beyleh,	656,317
Hajykan,	566,699
Jown,	3,165,418
Rahban,	742,973
Villages dependent upon Kahban,	346,783
Kerorey,	529,937
Lownda,	1,119,973
Mundery,	3,094,269
Medowy,	2,552,605
Nopyar,	1,280,439

SIRCAR

SIRCAR SEWISTAN,

Containing 9 Mahls,

Revenue, 15,546,808 Dams,

	Dams.		Dams.
Paler,	2,020,884	Khut,	1,329,923
Baghbanan,	1,948,152	Sewiſtan with the Havelly,	1,669,732
Butten,	1,902,033	Kahan,	1,640,764
Booſtkan,	1,825,191	Lakhawet,	1,231,776
Junjeh,	1,978,953		

SIRCAR NUSSEERPOOR,

Containing 7 Mahls,

Revenue, 7,834,600 Dams.

Amerkote,	1,057,802	Kaſar,	401,738
Telſereh,	326,104	Nuſſeerpoor,	1,878,126
Semadany,	3,031,530	Markundun,	623,696
Kydal,	515,904		

SIRCAR CHUCKERHALEH,

Containing 8 Mahls,

Revenue, 5,085,408 Dams.

Arpoor,	731,190	Tewary,	571,073
Chuckerhaleh,	747,175	Kehryjooneh,	508,152
Seyar,	719,207	Kekhmenawely,	491,368
Ghazipoor,	983,655	Birhee,	333,588

TUKSEEM JUMMA

OF THE

SOOBAH OF CABUL.

SIRCAR CASHMEER,

Containing 38 Mahls,

Revenue, 311,318 Kherwars, 12 Tureks of Grain, being equivalent to 62,113,040½ Dams; out of which is paid in money the value of 943,506 Kherwars, 14 Tureks, amounting to 1,251,880 Dams.

This sircar furnishes 3210 *cavalry and* 27,765 *infantry.*

TUREF MERATCH,

Containing 22 Mahls,

Revenue, 1,792,819 Kherwars, being equivalent to 35,796,122½ Dams; out of which is paid in money the value of 670,551 Kherwars, 12 Tureks, amounting to 8,875,248 Dams.

It furnishes 1620 *cavalry and* 14,600 *infantry.*

THE CITY OF SIRYNAGUR.

PERGUNNAHS situated to the east of Sirynagur,
Containing 3 Mahls,
Uneej, Bereng, and Vehy.

PERGUNNAHS ſituated to the north-eaſt of Sirynagur.

Containing 7 Mahls.

Owler,
Phak,
Dutchenpareh,
Khawerpareh,
Kut-har,
Merwadun,
Mutten.

PERGUNNAHS ſituated to the ſouth-eaſt of Sirynagur,

Containing 11 Mahls.

Adeon,
Iytch,
Banhal,
Batu,
Deoſir,
Zeenehpoor,
Sooperſumen,
Shawereh,
Shekerweh,
Nagam,
Weer,

TUREF KUMRAY,

Containing 11 Mahls,

Revenue, 1,218,799 Kherwars, 12 Tureks, being equivalent to 26,316,918 Dams; out of which is paid in money the value of 272,954½ Kherwars, amounting to 3,616,632 Dams.

It furnishes 1590 *cavalry and* 18,165 *infantry.*

PERGUNNAHS to the north-weſt of Sirynagur,

Containing 2 Mahls,

Zeenehgur and Geyehamoon.

PERGUNNAHS

PERGUNNAHS to the south-west of Sirynagur,

Containing 12 Mahls.

Inderkole,
Purrispoor,
Butten,
Banekul,
Berowey,
Teelgong,
Denesoo,
Dutchenkhawer,
Duties,
Koher,
Kumraj,
Kerohun,

SIRCAR PUCKELY,

* * *

SIRCAR SEWAD,

Divided into Beneer, Sewad, and Bijore.

SIRCAR DERUNEYUN AND ISSA KHYL,

Is a Territory situated to the south-east of Cabul, now inhabited by Afghans; formerly it belonged to the tribes of Soorany, Kerany, and Zeery.

SIRCAR KANDAHAR,

Containing 24 Mahls,

Revenue, 8114½ Toomans and 29,600 Dinars in money; 45,775 Sheep; 45 Balootchy Horses; 3,762,977 Kherwars of Barley; 420 Kherwars of Rice; 2 Kherwars of Wheat-flour; and 20 Maunds of Ghee.

This sircar furnishes 13,775 *cavalry and* 65,260 *infantry.*

THE CITY OF KANDAHAR,
50,270 Toomans in money and 35,120 Kherwars of Grain.

DEPENDENCIES of Kandahar to the east.

The territory of Dooky has a brick fort.
9 Toomans in money; 1900 Kherwars of Grain; 12,000 Sheep; and 15 Belootchy Horses.

The territory of Pusheng has a mud fort.
33 Toomans in money; 3200 Sheep; and 500 Kherwars of Grain.

The territory of Shal has a mud fort.
4½ Toomans in money; 940 Sheep; and 770 Kherwars of Grain.

The territory of Mustung has a mud fort.
10 Toomans in money; and 8000 Dinars; and 470 Kherwars of Grain.

The territory of Chelguzzy.
12 Toomans in money; and 415 Kherwars of Rice.

Ulous Punney, 60 Sheep;

Ulous Abdally
Formerly paid 1000 Sheep; but the Kuzzlebash fixed it to 100 Toomans.

Ulous Abdall,
2800 Sheep, 5 Kherwars of Rice, and 1 Kherwar of Ghee.

Ulous Jemundy, 11 Toomans and 4000 Dinars.

Rabat Beloochan, included in the city of Kandahar.

DEPENDENCIES to the ſouth of Kandahar.

Kelat Bunjareh has a mud fort.
30 Belootchy Horſes, and 30 Camels.

Shurabek, 1200 Sheep.

Ulous Beyſkee, 225 Sheep.

Ulous Meerkany, 9 Toomans in money; and 3350 Sheep.

Ulous Muſtewany, 200 Sheep and 7 Maunds of Ghee.

To the north of Kandahar.

The territory of Kelat Berlook has a ſtrong mud fort.
520 Toomans and 9060 Dinars in money; 4346 Sheep; 1270 Kherwars of Grain; 1 Maund of Ghee; and 1 Maund of Rice.

Hezareh Dehleh, 1454 Sheep and 20 Kherwars of Grain.

Hezareh Dehjirbenjy, 160 Sheep.

The territory of Terreen has a ſtrong fort.
15,000 Sheep and 1000 Kherwars of Grain.

To the weſt of Kandahar.

The territory of Gurrumſeer.
602 Toomans and 8000 Dinars in money; 1219 Kherwars of Grain.

The territory of Zemeendawer. * * *

Ulous Syeh Khaneh, 42 Toomans.

The caſtle of Kſhe knekhood, included in the city of Kandahar.

SIRCAR

SIRCAR CABUL,

Containing 22 Mahls,

Revenue, 80,507,465 Dams,

Seyurghal, 137,178 Dams.

This sircar furnishes 28,187 *cavalry and* 212,700 *infantry.*

THE CITY OF CABUL.

12,758,410 Dams.

To the east of Cabul.

	Dams.
Tooman Bekram,	9,692,410
Tooman Neyknehar,	11,894,003
Belook Kameh,	* * *

To the north of Cabul.

	Dams.
Tooman Munderar,	2,684,880
Tooman Alysheng,	3,701,150
Tooman Alengar,	1,544,677
Pooluk Bekhrad,	2,045,451
Tooman Lehooker,	3,193,214
Tooman Budrow,	413,885
Tooman Ulsaiy,	600,000
Tooman Punjmeer,	461,940

To

To the ſouth of Cabul.

	Dams.
Tooman Bungiſh,	3,332,348
Tooman Kohuſt,	701,620
Tooman Nughz,	854,000
Tooman Gurdeiz,	2,030,032
Tooman Meydan,	1,606,799
Tooman Ghuzneen,	3,868,642

To the weſt of Cabul.

	Dams.
Tooman Firmul,	325,716
Tooman Damenkouh,	16,461,785
Tooman Ghaurband,	1,574,760
Tooman Zohak Bamiyan,	861,750

A

DESCRIPTION

OF

HINDOSTAN.

THE tranflator is indebted to Mr. Reuben Burrow, for the notes on the aftronomical part of this volume. This gentleman, whofe mathematical reputation has been long eftablifhed in England, has applied with great diligence to the ftudy of the Sanfcrit language, and has acquired a perfect knowledge of the Hindoo aftronomy, which it is hoped he will be induced to make publick.

Extract of a General Letter from the Governor General and Council, to the Honourable the Court of Directors, dated 31ft *December*, 1785.

In the 187th paragraph of our letter of the 23d October, 1783, by the Nurbudda, we informed you of a propofal made to us by Mr. Francis Gladwin, for the publication of a complete tranflation from the Perfian language, of a book entitled the *Ayeen Akbery*; and we then acquainted you, that we confented to fubfcribe for 150 fets of this work, on account of the Company; but fome objections arifing afterwards againft the payment of fo large a fum from our treafury at that time, Mr. Gladwin voluntarily waved his claim to the fubfcription money, until your pleafure fhould be known.

Mr. Gladwin has lately addreffed a letter to us, recapitulating the circumftances which attended his firft propofal, fetting forth that he is far advanced in this laborious and expenfive undertaking, the firft and fecond volumes of the work being already publifhed, and fome part of the third*; and requefting that, in confi-

* This work was originally publifhed in three volumes.

deration of the expence and trouble he has been ſubjected to, we would repeat our recommendation of the undertaking, and intercede with your honourable court for your acquieſcence in our promiſed ſubſcription.

Senſible as we are of the merit of Mr. Gladwin's labours, the encouragement that is due to every undertaking which has for its end the promotion and extenſion of eaſtern literature, as well in regard to the uſe its advancement may be of to the perſons employed in your ſervice, as the knowledge it may afford to the European quarter of the globe, we cannot but repeat our earneſt ſolicitation that your honourable court will permit us to confirm the ſubſcription for 150 ſets, which we formerly promiſed to take, as we conſider our former recommendation, and the known liberality which your honourable court have ever ſhewn towards the encouragement of works of this nature, to have been the inducements which led Mr. Gladwin to commence ſo arduous a work, and thereby ſubject himſelf to a great expence, from which he could only expect to be relieved through the liberality of his employers.

A true extract,

(Signed) W. BRUERE, Sec.

INTRODUCTION.

INTRODUCTION.

I HAD long ſet my heart upon writing ſomething of the Hiſtory of Hindoſtan, together with an account of the religious opinions of the Hindoos. I know not if my anxiety herein proceeds from the love of my native country, or whether I am impelled by the deſire of ſearching after truth, and relating matter of fact.

At firſt my head was filled with the idle tales of Benagutty, Haſez Abroo, and other ancient authors, who have written ſtories of things that never exiſted but in their own imaginations. But at length becoming ſenſible of the ignorance of mankind, and of their evil diſpoſition towards one another, I reſolved to endeavour to eſtabliſh peace and amity. However, multiplicity of buſineſs occaſioned delay, until I undertook to write this book, which has run out to great length; and having finiſhed the Hiſtory of the Soobahs, (including a good part of the Hiſtory of Hindoſtan), I thought this a fit time for carrying into execution my long concealed intention.

Before this period, I had acquired ſome knowledge of the ſubject, but deeming that inſuf-

insufficient, I had again recourse to those who were capable of instructing me, and renewed my former studies.—From my ignorance of the signification of Hindoo terms, and the want of an able interpreter, my researches became painful, as I was obliged to make repeated inquiries after the same thing. At length, by the will of heaven, unremitted assiduity has obtained the object of my wishes.

It has now come to light, that the general received opinion of the Hindoos, being polytheists, has no foundation in truth; for although their tenets admit positions that are difficult to be defended, yet that they are worshippers of God, and only one God, are incontrovertible points.

In order to establish what I have here advanced, I shall set forth the various faiths and ceremonies of this immense multitude, that the necessary proofs may be found collected together, and strife and animosity be thereby moderated.

Although there have never been wanting in the world men of upright and honest intentions, yet from the following causes there have always been dissensions regarding this religion.

FIRST.

The difference of language, which has prevented the Hindoos, and those of other nations,

tions, from comprehending the meaning of each other, and occasioned much strife.

SECOND.

The remoteness of situation, which has prevented the Hindoos from having any intercourse with the learned of other countries.

Or if it happened that one of each met together, no communication of ideas could be effected, for want of an intermediate person; it being very difficult to find an interpreter so well acquainted with the depths of science, and the various philosophical doctrines, as to be able to explain himself thereon in a satisfactory manner. Even now, notwithstanding his majesty has taken such pains to assemble the learned of all nations, who aid and assist each other in their researches after truth, the inconvenience still remains unremedied. Where then is a person to be found possessed of the qualifications requisite for this task?

Supposing the throne to be filled by a monarch resembling Noorsheervan, who, amidst the splendor of royalty, sought after the jewel of wisdom, still there is required a Vizier like Buzerchemehr, who, divesting himself of envy, found out Poozruyah the philosopher, and sent him into Hindostan under the disguise of a merchant; and he, as industrious when absent as if he had been present, did, after various researches and laborious investigations, acquire possession of the stores of knowledge.

Or

Or a taſk like this, demands an indefatigable perſon like Tumtum the Indian, who, in order to ſtudy under Plato, travelled from Hindoſtan into Greece, regardleſs of the dangers of the ſeas and deſarts; and having obtained the grand panacea, regulated the temperament of the mind as well as that of the body.

Or a man ſuch as Abul Maaſhar of Balkh, who, becoming enamoured of knowledge, preferred a foreign ſoil to his native country, and relinquiſhing eaſe for toil, travelled from Khoraſan into Hindoſtan, and acquired a variety of knowledge at Benaris, and carried back rare preſents to the ſtudious of his own country.

THIRD.

The ſubjection of mankind to their corporeal ſenſes, inſomuch that they will not allow any thing to exiſt, which they themſelves have not felt; and are ſo governed by prejudice, that they will not liſten to the relation of any thing foreign, even though it ſhould be told as a fable calculated for mere amuſement. When this is the caſe, what judgment can they form?

FOURTH.

The indolence of mankind, which induces them to prefer the little they actually poſſeſs to the proſpect of increaſing it by the fatigues of commerce, which inclines them to adopt eaſe

eaſe and reject labour, and to forego the pains required in ſearching after knowledge; contenting themſelves with diſputes about appearances only, regardleſs how far they are conſonant with truth and reality.

FIFTH.

The habit of imitation, which people of all nations fall into, without aſking why or wherefore. Whatever they have received from their father, tutor, acquaintance, or neighbour, they conſider as the rule of conduct moſt acceptable to the Deity, and ſtamp thoſe who differ from them with the name of INFIDEL OR ZENDEK.

SIXTH.

The reſerve which prevents a candid communication between perſons of different perſuaſions, and to this it is owing that no inſtance can be produced of two or three perſons meeting for the purpoſe of diſcuſſing the tenets of their reſpective creeds, and of aſcertaining the principles on which they are founded. If this communication had taken place among men of learning and candour, a rule of conduct might ere this have been fixed, by the upright deciſions of impartial juſtice.

Even monarchs, deeming the inveſtigation unimportant, have either treated it with indifference, or actuated by the pride and ſelf-conceit of ſectaries, have prohibited free discussion and enquiry. A regard for self-preservation, therefore, induces men either to be silent; or to express themselves in obscure language; or compels them to conform to the temper of the times. But if princes had evinced a disposition to promote the search after truth, many illustrious men, having no grounds for fear or apprehension, would have published to the world, with freedom, their sentiments and opinions. The monarch's example is a law to all; and thus every sect becomes infatuated with its particular doctrines: animosity and dissention prevail, and each man deeming the tenets of his sect to be the dictates of truth itself, aims at the destruction of all others, vilifies reputation, stains the earth with blood, and has the vanity to imagine he is performing meritorious actions. If the voice of reason was attended to, mankind would be sensible of their error, and lament the weakness which misled them to interfere in the concerns of each other. Persecution, after all, defeats its own ends; it obliges men to conceal their opinions, but produces no change in them.

Seventh.

The success which too often attends the wicked and ill disposed, from the facility with which the professions of virtue and rectitude gain belief. Hence a variety of evils are derived, and truth lies buried under a load of errors. Enough, Abul Fazel, enough: the various forms of divine vengeance

geance are inexplicable; the hiſtory of them is long and intricate; proceed to execute your original deſign of attempting to eſtabliſh peace and unanimity.

Although ſome will be diſturbed with the information they receive, others will embrace it with ſatisfaction.

Thanks be unto God, who hath no equal, I am neither of the number of thoſe who are ready to condemn the ignorant, nor averſe to praiſe thoſe who know better.

A

DESCRIPTION

OF

HINDOSTAN.

HINDOSTAN is washed by the ocean on the east, the west, and the south; to the eastward lies Malacca, together with Sumatra, the Moluccas, and many other islands. On the north are high mountains, part of which forms the boundary of Hindostan on that quarter, and the rest belong to Turan and Iran. Beyond these mountains, as far as Chinese-Tartary, are several fertile territories, particularly Cashmeer, the two Tibbets and Kushtwar. The north side of Hindostan is plentifully supplied with rivers, so that it may be said to have water on all quarters.

The whole extent of this vast empire is unequalled for the excellency of its waters, salubrity of air, mildness of climate, and the temperate constitutions of the natives. Every part is cultivated and full of inhabitants, so that you cannot travel the distance of a cose without seeing towns, and villages, and meeting with good water. Even in the depth of winter, the earth and trees are covered with verdure; and in the rainy season, which in many parts of Hindostan commences

in

in June, and continues till September, the air is ſo delightfully pleaſant, that it gives youthful vigour to old age.

Summarily, the Hindoos are religious, affable, courteous to ſtrangers, cheerful, enamoured of knowledge, fond of inflicting auſterities upon themſelves, lovers of juſtice, given to retirement, able in buſineſs, grateful, admirers of truth, and of unbounded fidelity in all their dealings. Their character ſhines brighteſt in adverſity. Their ſoldiers know not what it is to fly from the field of battle; but when the ſucceſs of the combat becomes doubtful, they diſmount from their horſes, and throw away their lives in payment of the debt of valour. Frequently they hamſtring their horſes, to deprive themſelves of the means of flight; and thus rendered deſperate, ſoon bring the battle to a ſucceſsful iſſue. They have great reſpect for their tutors; and make no account of their lives, when they can devote them to the ſervice of God.

They one and all believe in the unity of the Godhead; and although they hold images in high veneration, yet they are by no means idolaters, as the ignorant ſuppoſe. I have myſelf frequently diſcourſed upon the ſubject with many learned and upright men of this religion, and comprehend their doctrine, which is, that the images are only repreſentations of celeſtial beings, to whom they turn themſelves whilſt at prayer, to prevent their thoughts from wandering; and they think it an indiſpenſable duty to addreſs the Deity after that manner.

In all their prayers, they implore bleſſings from the ſun.

They conſider the Supreme Being to be above all labour, believing Brahma to be the creator of the world;

world; Bishen its providence and preserver; and Roodre (who is also called Mahadeo) its destroyer.

One sect believes that God, who hath no equal, appeared on earth under the three above mentioned forms, without having been thereby polluted in the smallest degree; in the same manner as the Christians speak of the Messiah.

Others hold, that all three were only human beings, who, on account of their sanctity and righteousness, were raised to these high dignities.

Without compliment, there are to be found in this religion, men who have not their equal in any other for their godliness, and their abstinence from sensual gratifications.

They reckon the universe to have had no beginning; but some of them believe that it will have an end, as will be spoken of hereafter.

It is astonishing, that if any man of another cast wants to become a Brahmin, he is not allowed; neither may a Brahmin change his cast.

They have no slaves among them.

When they go to war, or are attacked by an enemy, they put all their women together in one place, which they surround with wood, straw, and oil; and some stony-hearted men are left with them, who, when those engaged in battle have no hopes of preserving their lives, set fire to the pile, and reduce the women to ashes.

If any person in distress flies to them for protection, although he be a stranger, they take him by the hand,

and will defend him at the expence of their property, reputation, and life.

Formerly it was the cuſtom to decide the fate of battle by ſingle combat; but now this method is not followed.

The greateſt part of this empire is arable land; and in ſome places the ſoil has ſuch ſtrength that they always cultivate the ſame ſpot, without there being any difference in the crops. In many places they have three crops of rice in a year, and in ſome even more. The vine bears fruit in the firſt year.

In Hindoſtan are many mines of diamonds, rubies, gold, ſilver, copper, lead, and iron. It abounds in odoriferous plants, and has great variety of fruit trees. They manufacture various kinds of cloths and ſtuffs. their elephants are the beſt in the world; in many parts they breed horſes equal to Arabs; and their oxen are exceedingly fine.

But they were notorious for the want of cold water; the intolerable heat of their climate; the ſcarcity of grapes and melons; and that they had not any manufactures of carpets; neither did they breed camels. His majeſty remedied all theſe evils and defects. He taught them how to cool water by the help of ſaltpetre, and had ſnow and ice brought from the northern mountains. He ordered mats to be woven of a cold odoriferous root called *Khuss*, of which are formed convenient apartments, and when wetted with water on the outſide, thoſe within enjoy a pleaſant cool air in the height of ſummer Gardeners were brought from Iran and Turan, who cultivated the vine, and various kinds of melons. The manufactures of ſilk and woollen carpets were introduced, together with that of brocades; and now the breed

breed of camels is ſuch, that they excel the Arabian Bokhtu.

Having now ſpoken in a ſummary way of Hindoſtan and the Hindoos, I ſhall proceed to treat of ſome particulars in a fuller manner; but ſtill this muſt be conſidered as only a little of much, one out of a thouſand.

OF THE CREATION.

Of the various changes which the univerſe has undergone, there are no leſs than eighteen different opinions; but it will be ſufficient to ſpeak of three of them.

THE FIRST OPINION.

God, who hath no equal, took upon himſelf the form of man, who is Brahma. He by his will created four ſons, Singh, Sunden, Suntoakomar, and Sunnatun. And Brahma commanded thoſe four ſons to employ themſelves in acts of creation. But they being ſtrongly attached to the preſence of Brahma, did not execute this command. At which Brahma was wroth, and cauſed another form to iſſue from his forehead, whom he called Mahadeo. But neither was he found fit for the taſks of creation. Then Brahma of his will created ten other ſons; beſides whom there iſſued from his own body two forms, one male and the other female. The name of the man is Munnoo, and of the woman Sutrooka, and theſe are the progenitors of the human race.

THE SECOND OPINION.

God manifeſted himſelf under the form of a woman, who is called Mahaletchmeen. From the eſſence of Mahaletchmeen proceeded three attributes, the firſt called Sut, the ſecond Ruj, and the third Tum. And when Mahaletchmeen willed that the world ſhould be created,

created, ſhe united herſelf with Tum, and produced another form, called Mahakalee, and who is alſo named Mahamya. And by joining herſelf with Sut, another form appeared, called Sirſootee. After this Brahma iſſued from Mahaletchmeen, under the form of a man, and Sree under the form of a woman, who is alſo called Sawuteree. Then from Mahakalee iſſued Mahadeo, under the form of a man, and Teeree under the form of a woman. This latter is alſo called Mahabedya, and likewiſe Kamdheen. From Sirſootee iſſued Biſhen, under the form of a man, and Gowree under the form of a woman. Then Mahaletchmeen willed that the luſts of the fleſh ſhould operate. Teeree united with Brahma; Gowree with Mahadeo; and Sree with Biſhen. The conjunction of Brahma and Teeree produced an egg, which Mahadeo divided into two parts. Of one half are formed the Dewtah, Diyit, and others who are celeſtial beings; and of the other half are formed mankind, and all other living creatures, together with plants and inanimate bodies.

The Third Opinion.

And this is the one moſt generally received.

In the book called Soorej Sudhant, which was complied ſome hundred thouſand years ſince; it is thus related:

Towards the end of the Sut Jowg, lived Mydeyit, who, from the contemplation of the various parts of the univerſe, became filled with wonder and amazement; and, in order to learn all the realities of the creation, inceſſantly ſupplicated the ſun for that purpoſe, for the ſpace of a thouſand years. After ſuffering great anxiety, the illuminator of heaven and earth appeared to him under a beautiful form, and aſked him what was his deſire. Mydeyit anſwering, ſaid, "Draw back the veil that conceals the wonders of the ſtars and

of

of the heavens; difcover to me the things that are hidden; inftruct me in the divine myfteries; and beftow upon the ignorant the light of knowledge." The celeftial form replied, "Employ yourfelf in a certain place in worfhipping me, when quickly a form fhall appear, who will inftruct you regarding thefe things."

Mydeyit, in the manner commanded, was praying in the appointed place near the clofe of the Sut Jowg, when the promifed figure appeared to him. Mydeyit made enquiries from him regarding the upper and the lower regions, and other truths; and received fatisfactory information upon all thefe points. A collection was made of the queftions and anfwers, which form the book called Soorej Sudhant. To this day all the aftronomers of Hindoftan rely entirely upon this book.

In this book it is faid that the creation commenced from the fun, this luminary being confidered as a reprefentation of God.—They fay that God formed a hollow fphere of gold, compofed of two parts, to which he imparted a ray of his own light, and it became the fun. The fun produced the twelve celeftial figns, and the figns produced the four Bedes. Then were created the moon, the akafs, air, fire, water, and earth, in the order here mentioned. Then from the akafs was produced the planet Jupiter; air produced Saturn; fire, Mars; water, Venus; the earth, Mercury; and from the ten human doors proceeded the other parts of the creation. By the ten doors are meant the two eyes, the two ears, the nofe, the mouth, the navel, the fore-end, the hind vent, and the aperture in the crown of the head, which in holy men, opens at the time of their death. His majefty has added to the above the two apertures of the breafts, increafing the number to twelve. After a length of time the human race became of four kinds, in the manner that fhall hereafter be related.

ASTRO-

ASTRONOMY.

OF THE UPPER AND THE LOWER REGIONS.

THE Hindoo philosophers maintain that the elements are of a circular form, and they add a fifth, to which they give the name of *Akass*. The *Akass*, they say, encompasses the universe, and pervades all nature. They do not reckon any number of heavens, but like Ptolemy in his Almagestum, say that they are formed of circles.

They divide the Zodiac into twelve equal parts, and call each division *Rass*.

SIGNS OF THE ZODIAC.

1 Meykh,	Aries.
2 Brikh,	Taurus.
3 Mit-hun,	Gemini.
4 Kirkh,	Cancer.
5 Singh,	Leo.
6 Kunnyan,	Virgo.
7 Tola,	Libra.
8 Britchuck,	Scorpio.
9 Dhun,	Sagittarius.
10 Mucker,	Capricornus.
11 Koomb,	Aquarius.
12 Meen,	Pisces.

The Persian, the Egyptian, and the Grecian philosophers say, that the heavens are beings, that they are formed of a transparent substance, which is neither subject to inrcease nor decrease, whose constituent particles can neither separate nor coalesce, nor are liable to decay or alteration; that they are neither pliant nor hard, that they cannot be recreated, and that they are not compounded, but simple. They possess not heat, cold, moisture, nor dryness, neither have they gravity nor

nor levity. They have not only life, but are alſo endowed with reaſon, and are not ſubject to anger, or any kind of deſire. The number of the heavens, according to ſome of theſe philoſophers, is eight, others ſay nine, whilſt others increaſe them to eleven.

The Hindoo philoſophers ſay, that the fixed ſtars and the planets are beings, that they are formed of water, congealed like hail, and borrow their light from the ſun. Some indeed aſſert that they derive their light from the moon, and believe each to be under the influence of a celeſtial ſpirit. Others think that the ſtars are the ſouls of men departed this life, and raiſed to this high dignity in reward for their virtues and auſterities.

Names of the Planets, and Days of the Week.

1 Addittee,	*Sunday*,	The ſun.
2 Soom,	*Monday*,	The moon.
3 Mungul,	*Tuesday*,	Mars.
4 Boodh,	*Wednesday*,	Mercury.
5 Beerhuſput,	*Thursday*,	Jupiter.
6 Shookur,	*Friday*,	Venus.
7 Shenceſcher,	*Saturday*,	Saturn.

Each day of the week is named after the planet that rules it, with the addition of *war* (day.) Thus Sunday, which begins their week, is called Adittwar, and Monday Soomwar, &c.

Of the Use of the Ghurryal.

The Ghurryal is an inſtrument made of Huſt Joaſh, reſembling a frying-pan, only ſomewhat thicker, and is ſuſpended by a ſtring, but no one may have it rung without the royal permiſſion. When his majeſty travels, or any of the nobility who have obtained permiſſion, the ghurryal makes part of the equipage.

The

The Hindoos divide the day and night into four parts, each of which they call pehr. In many countries the pehr never exceeds nine ghurries, nor is less than six; and this ghurry is the sixtieth part of a day and night. The ghurry is divided into 60 pul, and the pul is subdivided into 60 beepul.

The method of measuring a ghurry. They make a vessel of brass, or any other metal, 100 tanks in weight. It is in the shape of a cup, narrow downwards, and perforated at the bottom, so as just to admit a golden pin, that weighs one mashah, and is in length the breadth of five fingers. The vessel is twelve fingers in diameter. It is put into a bason of pure water, in a place where it cannot be affected by the wind, or shaken by any accident. When the vessel is full of water, one ghurry is elapsed; and in order to give information thereof to those who are far or near, one stroke is given upon the ghurryal; for two ghurries two strokes, and so on. When a pehr is past, they first ring the number of ghurries in that pehr, slowly, and then reiterate them quicker. The emperor Baber, in his commentaries, says as follows: "formerly at the end of every pehr, they rang only the number of ghurries, so that the pehr was not known. I commanded that in future, after striking the ghurry, they should also ring the number of the pehr."

The Hindoos say, that a man of temperate habit, in full health, respires 360 times in the space of a ghurry, or 21,600 in the course of a day and night.

The Order of the Elements.

First is earth, over which is placed water, but not so as to cover all parts of it; over this is fire, and over that air, but its concave is not spherical.

The Hindoos divide the air into eight kinds: 1. Bohoobaiy

hoobaiy, which is the air to the diſtance of forty-eight coſe from the ſurface of the earth, and it produces clouds, rain, and lightning. 2. Abeh, which is the air extending from that laſt-mentioned to the body of the moon. 3. Pheh, that which reaches from the laſt-mentioned to Venus. 4. Sooneyeh, that which extends from Venus to the Sun. 5. Sobeh, that which reaches from the Sun to Mars. 6. Purrehbeh, from Mars to Jupiter. 7. Purrehbeh, from Jupiter to Saturn. 8. Purbhanib is the air which lies betwixt Saturn and the fixed ſtars, and it is the revolution of the Purhanib from eaſt to weſt that occaſions day and night. The other ſeven winds have a diurnal motion from weſt to eaſt. But the moſt intelligent ſay that theſe ſeven, alſo, revolve from eaſt to weſt; they however agree as to the height of each.

The Akaſs is ſituated above all theſe, and has no limits.

The mean motions, which the Hindoos call Mudhum, they make to differ from the Greeks, in the ſeconds and thirds. According to the Soorej Sedhant, which makes the day and night to commence from midnight, the following are the calculations of the mean motions.

	Degrees.	*Minutes.*	*Seconds.*	*Thirds.*
The Moon, - -	13	10	34	53
Mercury, - - - } Venus, - - - - } Sun, - - - - - }	0	59	8	10
Mars, - - - -	0	31	26	28
Jupiter, - - -	0	4	59	9
Saturn, - - - -	0	2	0	23

According

According to the Greeks.	Degrees.	Minutes.	Seconds.	Thirds.
Moon - - - - -	13	0	35	2
Mercury - - - } Venus, - - - - } Sun, - - - - }	0	0	0	19
Mars, - - - - -	0	0	27	40
Jupiter, - - -	0	0	0	16
Saturn, - - - - -	0	0	0	35

The Hindoos in general maintain, that the motion of the planets is voluntary; and they confider them all to have equal velocity. Their motion, in the courfe of a night and day, is 11,858 jowjens and 3 cofe, their progrefs being from weft to eaft. Their periods differ according to the extent of their orbits. Their paths lie one above each other.

Some of the Hindoos confider the progreffive motion of the fixed ftars to be the fame as that of the planets, but, contrary to the Greeks, they fay that the ftars in the zodiac advance in one year 54 feconds, or one degree in the courfe of 66 years and 8 months. Thofe which are not included in the zodiac, when they have moved from the 10th of Aries to the 27th, or according to others, to the 24th degree, have a retrograde motion till they return to the 28th degree of Pifces, after which they come again to Aries; and this is invariable. The conftellation of the great bear, in the Hindoovy language *Supputrigh*, has a preceffion in one year from weft to eaft, of 17 feconds and 47 thirds, or one degree in the courfe of 206 years and 6 months*.

A par-

* The author here talks, as if he was not well acquainted with this particular part of aftronomy: the motion of 54 feconds annually, fuppofed by the Hindoos, is a motion in longitude common to all

A particular ſect believe all the phenomena to depend ſolely upon the power of the Almighty.

The ancient Greek philoſophers were ignorant of the progreſſion of the fixed ſtars, excepting Ariſtotle and Hipparchus, who knew ſomething of the preceſſion of ſome of the ſtars near the zodiac, but were not able to calculate the time. Ptolemy made the fixed ſtars to advance a degree in the ſpace of one hundred ſolar years. Ebn Aalum, and ſome others, reckoned 60 ſolar years. Naſſereddeen Touſſy agrees with the laſt; but Mohyeddeen Meghreby, at the ſame obſervatory, found that Aldebaran, the Scorpion's heart, and ſome other ſtars, advanced a degree in 66 years. In the tables of Ulugh Beg, it is made to be 70 Yedzigird year, which year is 365 days exactly.

all the ſtars, except ſome few that have particular motions of their own, whoſe cauſes are yet undiſcovered; but the retrograde motion, he mentions, is the variation of right aſcenſion; and this is different at different times in the ſame ſtar, and likewiſe variable on account of the latitude in different ſtars; but it is not true that ſuch ſtars as are out of the zodiac have the retrograde motion he ſpeaks of, for none are ſubject to it, but thoſe that are included within a circle deſcribed about the pole of the ecliptic, at the diſtance of the obliquity for that particular time; and of ſuch ſtars, though the longitude may be any quantity at pleaſure, the extreme points of right aſcenſion will always be within certain limits, depending on the latitude of the ſtar, which can never be greater than a ſemicircle, but may be leſs than any quantity aſſigned: In ſhort, if two circles be drawn through the poles of the equator to touch the ſtar's parallel of latitude on oppoſite parts, they will determine the limits of right aſcenſion; and if they are drawn through two ſucceſſive places of a given ſtar, the ratio of the motion in longitude to the motion in right aſcenſion, is alſo aſſignable: and hence it is alſo obſervable, that the "*Supputrigh*" cannot be "*Conſtellation*," but muſt be a particular ſtar; and though it may have the velocity the author mentions, at one time, at others its motion muſt be different: however, it is evident that the ſtar being known, its ſituation is determinable from its velocity, and thence alſo the time when the ſtar had that particular ſituation, with other curious matters, &c. &c. B.

The Orbits of the Planets, according to the Hindoos.

	Jowjens.	*Cose.*
Moon, - -	324,000	0
Mercury, -	1,043,207	3
Venus, - -	2,664,636	2 and a fraction.
Sun, - -	4,331,500	and a fraction.
Mars, - -	8,146,960	3
Jupiter, -	11,375,764	1
Saturn, -	127,668,255	1 and a fraction.
A fixed star,	259,890,012	0

	make one
3 Mustard seeds	Barley corn.
8 Barley corns	Inch.
24 Inches	Cubit.
4 Cubits	Duddun.
2000 Duddun	Cose.
4 Cose	Jowjen.

The Mansions of the Moon.

The Hindoos call the moon's mansions Nekihter, and they are 27 in number, each contains 13 degrees 20 minutes.

Mansions.	*Number of Stars.*	*Mansions.*	*Number of Stars.*
1 Oshoonee, - - -	3	11 Poorbapahluggonee,	2
2 Bhirnee, - - -	3	12 Ooterapahluggonee,	2
3 Kirteka, - - -	6	13 Hust, - - - -	5
4 Rokeenny, - - -	5	14 Chittera, - - -	1
5 Mirgussir, - - -	3	15 Sowatee, - - -	1
6 Ardera, - - -	1	16 Beeshakha, - -	4
7 Poonerbuss, - -	4	17 Unnooradha, - -	4
8 Powkh, - - -	3	18 Jeyshdha, - - -	3
9 Ashleekha, - -	5	19 Mool, - - -	11
10 Mugha, - - -	5	20 Poorbakahdha,	4

3 21 Oote-

Manſions.	*Number of Stars.*
21 Ooterakahdha,	3
22 Sherrown, - - -	3
23 Dhunſhittah, - -	4
24 Shutbehkha, -	100
25 Poorbahbhaderpud,	2
26 Ooterabhaderpud,	2
27 Rewtee, - - -	32

Altogether 221 ſtars, which the moon paſſes through in the courſe of a month.

The moon never remains longer than $65\frac{1}{2}$ ghurries, nor leſs than $54\frac{1}{4}$ ghurries, in any one nekihter.

For ſome particular purpoſes, 3 degrees and 20 minutes of the 21ſt nekihter to the 48th minute of the 22d nekihter, are formed into a manſion, and which is called Abehjit.

The Greeks reckoned 28 manſions, making each to contain 12 degrees 51 minutes and 26 ſeconds.

Table of the Moon's Mansions, according to the Greeks.

Manſions.		*Number of Stars.*	*Magnitudes.*
1	Shirteen, - -	2	3
2	Buteen, - - -	3	5
3	Althuraiya, - -	6	5
4	Dubberan, - -	1	1
5	Huckaah, - -	3	0
6	Sehabeehuckaah, -	4	6
7	Zoraa, - - -	2	4
8	Nufferah, - -	2	4
9	Turfah, - - -	2	4
10	Zubhah, - - -	4	0
11	Zoberah, - - -	2	2 & 3
12	Surfeh, - - -	1	1
13	Awa, - - -	5	3

Mansions.		Number of Stars.	Magnitudes.
14	Sumack, - - -	1	1
15	Akur, - - -	3	4
16	Zubana, - - -	2	2
17	Ekleel, - - -	3	4
18	Kulub, - - -	1	2
19	Sowlek, - - -	2	2
20	Naaim, - - -	4	3
21	Buldeh, which is a round ſpot of the ſky.		
22	Saadzabeh, - -	2	3
23	Saadbulaw, - -	2	3 & 4
24	Soaoud, - -	2 or 3	3 & 5
25	Ajyneh, - - -	4	3
26	Mukudum, - -	2	2
27	Mowucker, - -	2	2
28	Raſha, - - -	1	3
		66	

Or altogether 67 ſtars.

The Magnitudes of the fixed Stars.

The Hindoo philoſophers divide the ſtars into ſeven magnitudes, meaſuring as follows:

DIAMETERS.

Magnitudes.	Minutes.	Seconds, or Jowjens.	Coſe.	Dudduns.	Cubits.	Inch.
1	7	3 or 900,239	2	700	0	0
2	6	15 or 750,199	2	1250	0	0
3	5	30 or 660,175	2	1580	0	0
4	4	0 or 480,127	3	238	2	2
5	3	0 or 360,095	0	678	3	13
6	2	0 or 240,063	3	1119	1	1
7	1	0 or 120,031	3	1559	2	12

According to ſome of the Greeks, the diameter of one of

of the largeſt ſtars is ſix times that of one of the ſmalleſt degree. But herein they were greatly miſtaken, it being well known to thoſe who are acquainted with the dimenſions of the ſtars, and their diſtances from each other, that a ſtar of the 2d degree of the 1ſt magnitude is ſix times larger than one of the 3d degree of the 2d magnitude. And Euclid, in the laſt propoſition of the twelfth book of his Elements, ſays, "If the diameter of one circle be equal to the half of that of another, the leſſer circle will be $\frac{1}{2}$ of $\frac{1}{2}$ of $\frac{1}{2}$ or $\frac{1}{8}$. Or if the diameter of one be only a third of the other, then will it be $\frac{1}{3}$ of $\frac{1}{3}$ of $\frac{1}{3}$ or $\frac{1}{27}$, and ſo on."

Therefore, if it be as thoſe have conjectured, the body of a ſtar of the firſt degree will be more than ſix times bigger than a ſtar of the ſixth degree, ſo that this calculation is very wide of the truth.

The largeſt ſtars which have been obſerved, are, according to the Greeks, two hundred and twenty-two times as big as the earth; and the ſmalleſt, twenty-three times as big as the earth. The fixed ſtars are ſo numerous, that they have not all been numbered; but 1022 have been obſerved.

Magnitude.			*Number.*
1	-	-	15
2	-	-	45
3	-	-	208
4	-	-	474
5	-	-	49

Beſides 14 whoſe degrees have not been aſcertained; five of which are dim, and nine almoſt dark. This is taken from Ptolomy.

But according to Abdalrahman Ben Omar al Soofee, they are as follows:

Magnitude.

Magnitude.			*Number.*
2	-	-	37
3	-	-	200
4	-	-	421
5	-	-	267
6	-	-	70

Besides four dim stars.

Of the Deeps, or Islands.

The Hindoo philosophers say, that the terrestrial globe contains seven deeps or islands, encompassed by seven seas. The whole land and water measuring 7,957,752 jowjens.

The island of Jummoodeep is encompassed by the ocean. It is the habitation of the human race, and the greatest part of the brute creation. Half of the ocean they consider as belonging to Jummoodeep. The breadth of the ocean is 130 jowjens, and of the land 1265 jowjens, including 65 jowjens of water. The superficial contents of this island, including the water, is 3,978,875 jowjens, of which 417,360 jowjens are water, and the rest land. They say also, that in the centre of this deep is a golden mountain, of a cylindrical form. That part of the mountain which appears above the surface of Jummoodeep, and which measures 84,000 jowjens, they call Sommeir; and they believe that the different degrees of paradise are on the sides and summit of this mountain. This is the account given by those who believe in fables; but the learned among them believe, with the Greeks, that the highest mountain does not exceed $2\frac{1}{3}$ pharsangs. The Hindoos believe, that it descends as far beneath as it rises above the surface of the earth. The lower part they call Budwanel, and tell strange stories concerning it.

Shakdeep; one side of which is bounded by half of the ocean. It measures, including its sea, 427,424 jowjens.

jowjens. Beyond this deep is a ſea of milk, the contents of which are 810,097 jowjens.

Shalmuldeep meaſures 320,120 jowjens. The ſea which lies next beyond it is of milk-curds, and meaſures 633,553 jowjens.

Kuſhedeep meaſures 286,749 jowjens. The ſea that lies beyond it is of ghee, and meaſures 459,792 jowjens.

Karownchehdeep meaſures 181,684 jowjens. The ſea beyond it is of the juice of ſugar-cane, and meaſures 250,504 jowjens.

Goomieduckdeep meaſures 86,580 jowjens. Beyond it lies the ſea of wine, meaſuring 81,648 jowjens.

Phowkerdeep meaſures 14,204 jowjens. Beyond it is the river of freſh water, meaſuring 28,160 jowjens.

Each ſea meaſures in breadth 103 jowjens, and each of the iſlands, beyond Jummoodeep, is in breadth 70 jowjens. In theſe laſt ſix deeps they place the different degrees of hell.

They ſay that the earth is not inhabited beyond the 52d degree of latitude, being 728 jowjens.

A particular Deſcription of Jummoodeep.

A number of fables being related of the other ſix deeps, which cannot poſſibly be reconciled to reaſon, I ſhall confine myſelf to a few particulars concerning Jummoodeep.

On the four quarters of the earth, at the extremities of the equinoctial lines, where it is bounded by the ocean, they place four cities encompaſſed with walls, built

built of bricks of gold, viz. Jumkote, Lunka, Siddahpore, and Roomuck.

Jumkote is that from whence they begin to reckon the earth's longitude, in the ſame manner as the Greeks begin from Gungdudj; but I am ignorant for what reaſon they do ſo*.

Theſe four places are ſituated at the diſtance of 90 degrees from each other; thoſe that are oppoſite to each other being diſtant 180 degrees.

The mountain of Sommeir is centrical to the four, being 90 degrees from each.

The north ſides of theſe four cities lie under the equator, which in the Hindovee language is called *Nickwutbirt*. This is an arch which paſſes over the zenith of the inhabitants of thoſe four cities, and the ſun, twice in the year, culminates in this point; and the day and night throughout the year are nearly equal. The ſun's greateſt altitude is 90 degrees. He goes from Lunka to Roomuck, from thence to Siddahpore, then to Jumkote, and returns to Lunka. When the ſun is on the meridian at Jumkote, he begins to riſe at Lunka, ſets at Siddahpore, and it is midnight at Roomuck; and ſo on. There being 15 ghurries diſtance between each of thoſe cities.

In the northern direction, from Lunka to Sommeir, are three mountains, Heemachel†, Heemakote, and

* The reaſon is very evident; for the time at Lunka was reckoned from ſunriſe, and by taking Jumkote for the beginning of longitude, the time of the day at Lunka always ſhewed the longitude of the place that had the ſun then upon the meridian. B.

† Heemachel ſeems to be the Rhymmicis mountains, &c. of Ptolomy: Heemakote ſeems to be the part of the Imaus and the Emodi mountains; and Nekh the Deenis, &c. of Ptolomy. B.

Nekh,

Nekh, and each of these mountains extend to the ocean on the east, and on the west.

In the direction from Siddahpore to Sommeir are three other mountains, Sirungwunt, Sokul, and Neel.

Between Jumkote and Sommeir is a mountain called Malwunt, which unites with Nekh and Neel.

There is also a mountain between Roomuck and Sommeir, called Gundahmadun, and which likewise unites with Nekh and Neel.

Many wonderful stories are told of these mountains, too long to be contained in this volume. But something shall be said of what lies between Lunka and Heemachel; which tract is called Behrutkhund.

Behrut was a great monarch, and gave name to this country. From Lunka to Heemachel, being 52 degrees, is inhabited, but to the 48th degree, more so than the last four, on account of the extreme coldness of the climate beyond this degree.

According to the belief of these people, one celestial degree is equal to fourteen jowjens, by which rule of calculation these 52 degrees make 728 jowjens; the latitudinal extent of the habitable world.

The tract between Heemachel and Heemakote, comprising 12 degrees of latitude, they call Kinnerkhund.

The tract between Heemakote and Nekh, comprising 12 degrees, they call Hurrykhund.

The tract between Siddahpore and Serungwunt, comprising 52 degrees of latitude, they call Koorkhund.

The

The tract between Serungwunt and Sookul, comprising 12 degrees of latitude, they call Hurrunmeekhund. And the whole of this country is of gold.

The tract between Sookul and Neel, comprising 12 degrees of latitude, they call Rummeekhund.

The tract between Jumkote and Malwunt, comprising 76 degrees of longitude, they call Budrasookhund.

The tract between Gundahmadun and Roomuck, comprising 76 degrees of longitude, they call Kietmal.

The tract bounded by Malwunt, Gundahmadun, Nekh, and Neel, each side measuring 14 degrees from Sommeir, they call Illawurtkhund.

The square measurement of each of these nine khunds are equal, although some are narrower than others.

Four other mountains surround Sommeir, viz. Mindu on the east, Suhgundah on the south, Beepul on the west, Sooparss on the north. The height of each is 18,000 jowjens.

Having spoken of the nine divisions of Jummoodeep, something more shall be said of the first, or Bherutkhund.

Between Lunka to Heemachel, they place seven ranges of mountains, extending from east to west, but smaller than those already described. The names of these mountains are Mehinder, Sookole, Moolee, Redheck, Perjatter, Sheshej, and Binder.

The tract between Lunka and Mehinder, they call Indrekhund. What lies between Mehinder and Sookole,

kole, is Kooſeirkhund. Sookole and Moolee, include Taniebcrpurrunkhund. The country between Moolee and Redheck, is Gobhiſtmuntkhund. Between Redheck and Perjatter, is Nagkhund. Between Perjatter and Sheſhej, lies Soomkhund. The country between Sheſhej and Binder they divide into two equal parts, the eaſtern called Komarkhund, and the weſtern Barenkhund.

Other Divisions.

The Hindoos alſo divide the world into three regions. The uppermoſt region they call Soorglogue, and believe it to be a place where men receive the reward of their good actions in this world. The middle region is Bhologue, being the part inhabited by mankind. The inferior region they call Patall, and make it to be the place of puniſhment, for bad actions in this life.

The learned among them ſay, that the univerſe is made up of ſuperficies, which they divide into fourteen regions.

The Seven Superior Regions. 1. Bhoologue. 2. Bhowurlogue. 3. Songlogue, 4. Mahrlogue. 5. Junnoologue. 6. Tuppoologue. 7. Sutlogue.

The Seven Inferior. 1. Atul. 2. Bitul. 3. Sootul. 4. Tullatul. 5. Mehatul. 6. Reſatul. 7. Pattall.

Wonderful ſables are told of the inhabitants of each region, too long for inſertion here.

They alſo divide the world into ſeven ſeas and ſeven iſlands. Of Jummoodeep they all give nine ſubdiviſions, but differ very much in their arrangement and extent, inſomuch that ſome increaſe the height of the mountain Sommeir to 84,000 jowjens, and the breadth to 16,000 jowjens. It is the general belief that this mountain descends as far below the surface of the earth as it rises above it.

They in general believe Behrutkhund to be the only part of Jummoodeep that is inhabited by the human race. But some say; that beyond the ocean, there is a land of gold inhabited by mortals, who invariably live to the age of one thousand years, and never suffer sickness nor sorrow, neither are they subject to fear, avarice, or ignorance. They never speak ill of, nor envy any one, and they are all men of integrity and truth, affectionately attached to, and striving to prevent the wishes of one another. They know not old age, but continue in the vigour of youth all their lives. They are all of one religion. Many other wonderful stories are told of this island, to which those who judge from common appearances refuse to listen, but they who worship God, and know his almighty power, are not astonished at the relation.

They also divide Koomarkhund into two parts. The first, where the antelope is not to be found, they call Muleetchdeys, and consider it as a place not fit to be inhabited. The part where the antelope lives, is called Jugdeys. This they again subdivide into four parts. 1. Arjawurt, bounded on the east and west by the ocean, and on the north and south by a long chain of mountains of Hindostan, 2. Mudehdeys, bounded on the east by Allahabad, on the west by the river Benassa, (at the distance of 25 cose from Tahnesir,) and on the north and south by the above-mentioned mountains. 3. Berchmekdeys contains the following places: 1. Tahnesir and its dependencies, Beerat, Cumpalah, Mehtrah, and Kenoje, 4. Brihmawurt lies between the rivers Sirsooty and Roodrakussy.

GENERAL

General DESCRIPTION of the EARTH.

Some of the Hindoos believe the earth to be ſpherical, and that its centre is the centre of the univerſe; and they ſay that all inequalities of its ſurface, occaſioned by accidental violence of winds or waters, are ſo inconſiderable as not to make any material alteration in its form. They reckon the circumference of the earth 5059 jowjens, 2 coſe, and 1154 dunds.

The ancient Greeks computed the circumference of the earth to be 8000 pharſangs, and the diameter 2545$\frac{1}{7}$ pharſangs. The modern Greeks make the circumference 6700 pharſangs and a fraction. In both calculations the pharſang is reckoned to be three miles.

The Hindoo Proportion between the Diameter and the Circumference of a Circle.

The diameter being multiplied by 3927, the product is to be divided by 1250, when the quotient will be the circumference of the circle. *To find the diameter of any given circle,* they multiply the circumference by 1250, and divide the product by 3927; when the quotient will be the diameter.

Hindoo Terms.

Circumference,	*Chucker.*	Diviſor,	*Bhag.*
Diameter,	*Beeyass.*	Quotient,	*Lubdeh.*
Multiplier,	*Goont.*		

The Hindoos are not ignorant of the rule, which has been handed down among the Greeks from Archimedes; which is, that the circumference is to the diameter as ſeven to twenty two, or about thrice the diameter and one-ſeventh. They multiply any given diameter by twenty two, and dividing the product by ſeven, the quotient is the circumference. And in order to learn the diameter, they multiply the circumfe-

rence

rence by ſeven, and dividing the product by twenty-two, the quotient is the diameter. But in fact, the fraction is ſomewhat leſs than $\frac{1}{7}$, being nearer to $\frac{10}{71}$.

It is evident the Greeks were ignorant of the Hindoo rule, for if they had poſſeſſed it, they would not have failed to have mentioned it. It is wonderful that theſe ſhould be the only people acquainted with the exact proportion between the diameter and the circumference.

What is ſaid above, is confined to the meaſurement of lines. The earth is meaſured after the following manner.

On an even ſpot of ground, they take the elevation of the north pole, and then go either north or ſouth, till they have raiſed or depreſſed the pole one degree by the Aſtrolabe, or ſome ſuch inſtrument; and the diſtance meaſured between the two ſtations is the length of a degree. By this method they calculate the circumference of the earth. The ancient Greeks, by this operation, reckoned the degree to be twenty-two pharſangs and two tiſſwas, or $66\frac{2}{3}$ miles.

At the command of the khalif Mamoon, the plains of Senjar were choſen for the purpoſe of meaſuring a degree. Khaled Ben Abdulmullick Mazoory, with ſome other learned men, went towards the north, and Aly Ben Iſſa Aſtrolaby, with ſome others, went ſouthward. Thoſe who went to the north, found the degree longer than thoſe who went to the ſouth; for when they meaſured their reſpective diſtances, thoſe who had gone to the north found it $18\frac{1}{8}$ pharſangs, or $56\frac{2}{3}$ miles, and the ſouthern obſervers had $\frac{2}{3}$ of a mile leſs than that ſum*. Mamoon, by way of experiment, required to be

* From the ſpheroidity of the earth the degrees ought to increaſe towards the north; but this difference is much greater than it ought to be according to theory. B.

be informed, by both parties, the distance between Mecca and Baghdad, and they agreed in computing it to be twelve degrees forty-four minutes. The degree of 56⅔ miles, multiplied by 12 degrees 44 minutes, makes about 720 cose*. Afterwards Mamoon caused an actual measurement to be made upon the straightest and nearest road between those two cities, when the difference between the computed and the measured distance was found to be but very inconsiderable.

It is surprising that the accurate Nassereddeen Tousee, in his Tuzkerah, should ascribe to the ancient philosophers this measurement of a degree of the meridian, which was made in the reign of Mamoon. And on the contrary, Kotebeddeen Shirazy, in his Tofah, and other works, gives credit to the astronomers of Mamoon's time, for what was discovered by the ancients. They are certainly both reprehensible for their inadvertency.

The Hindoo astronomers make the degree 14 jowjens, 436 dunds, 2 cubits and 4 inches; and explain it in the same manner as the Greeks. They use also the following method for measuring a degree. On a level spot of ground, they observe the exact time of sunrise with a sektajunter, an instrument resembling an hour glass, but which runs sixty ghurries. Then with this in their hands, they walk towards the east, and after going 84 jowjens, and something more, one ghurry is elapsed, and the day is so much advanced. This distance being multiplied by 60, gives the circumference of the earth†.

* As the true length of a degree is between 69 and 70 miles, and there is reason to believe that the measures could not be far wrong, it follows that we have not the proper length of their measures; for if we had, there can be little doubt but the result would agree with ours. B.

† The author in this, and in some other instances, seems to have been rather defective in his description of the practices of the Hindoos.

This the Hindoos call *Lumbun*, and, like the Greeks, make it to consist of 180 degrees. But they commence

doos. Their intent, in the present case, was evidently to measure a degree of longitude in a parallel circle. The principle of the method was exactly the same as that of our modern longitude watches; and the general practice was to adjust their sektajunter to the time of the meridian they set out from; and to go eastward till the difference of the times shewn by it, and by observation, appeared to be one ghurry. For if the instrument was exact, whatever meridian it was carried under, it would still continue to show the time under the meridian of the first place; and if the place arrived at was one degree more to the east, the time found at that place (whether by the sun's rising, or any other method) would be one ghurry more; and so in proportion: and this is what is meant by the *day being so much advanced*. The Hindoos must doubtless have observed the necessity of allowing for the change of declination in the time of sunrise; but according to the mode prescribed by the author, it would be requisite to restrict the time of making the experiment to that of the solstice.

The moderns have often made proposals for measuring degrees of longitude, but have not yet put them in practice; the readiest method both for that, and extensive surveys, seems to be by employing air-balloons.

On account of the affinity of the subjects, it will not be improper to subjoin an explication of a passage in the first volume, which at present seems very obscure—it is at page 261, where it is asserted that the day is computed in Roomuck from sunset to sunset; in Delhi and Lunka from midnight to midnight, and in Jumkote from sunrise to sunrise. The obvious sense is totally different from the true, which implies that at the time when it is midnight at Lunka and Delhi, it is sunset at Roomuck, and sunrise at Jumkote; from hence a very curious and useful conclusion follows; namely, that Lunka is not the island of Ceylon, as is generally supposed, but a place determined by the intersection of the equator and the meridian of Delhi; which answers to the southern extremity of the Maldivy islands. Indeed there are many reasons for concluding Lunka to have been a part of the Taprobane of the ancients, and that Taprobane (or more properly *Tapoban*, which in Shanscrit signifies the wilderness of prayer), was a very large island, including the whole, or greatest part of the Maldivy islands, which may have since been destroyed by inundations. This agrees very well with Ptolomy's description; and his islands of monkeys seem to relate to those in the Ramaion.

From hence it also appears, that the Hindoo map of Jummoodeep, is a sort of orthographic projection of the northern hemisphere their reckoning from *Jumkote*, the eastern extremity of the earth, according to their system. They believe the sun's motion to be the cause of day and night, and suppose that he rises in their neighbourhood.

The Greeks commence their reckoning of the longitude from the Khalidat*, which are six islands in the Western Ocean, which in ancient times were inhabited, but now they are inundated†. On account of the mildness of the climate, the beauty of their flowers, the excellence of their fruits, and the delightful verdure of the soil, navigators named these islands *Khalidat*, or *Paradises;* and *Saadat*, or *Fortunate.* Others make the *Saadat* to be twenty four islands situated between the Khalidat islands and the western continent.

Some of the Greeks commenced their longitude from the shore of the western sea, which they called *Oceanus* (ocean); and which is ten degrees east of the Khalidat islands. These ten degrees, according to the ancient mode of measurement, are equal to 222 pharsangs and 2 tissaws; or 188$\frac{3}{4}$ pharsangs, according to the modern calculation.

They both perfectly agree regarding the longitudinal distances of places.

The longitude of places, is their distance from the commencement of the habitable earth; and is measured upon the equator, of which it is an arch.

phere upon the plane of the equator; only instead of placing the parallels of latitude in concentric circles, they have done them very improperly in right lines: however, there can be no dependence on this particular map, as there are others very different. Sommeir is the north pole of the earth. B.

* The Fortunate, or Canary Islands.

† This seems to be the Atlanta of the ancients.

 The

The Method to discover the Longitude of a Place.

At the firſt place, or the place whoſe longitude is known, obſerve of a lunar eclipſe, either its commencement, middle, or duration; marking the hour at which it happens; and let the ſame be done at the place whoſe longitude is required. If the hour was the ſame at both places, their longitude will be the ſame. If the obſervation happens later at the place whoſe longitude is ſought, it is more to the eaſtward. And if it is earlier, the place ſought is more weſterly.

Four minutes of time are equal to one degree, or fifteen degrees to an hour, or ſix degrees to a ghurry.

As the Hindoo philoſophers commence their reckoning of the longitude from the eaſt, ſo their calculation is juſt the reverſe of what has been given above from the Greeks.

Of the Latitude of the Earth.

The Hindoos call it *Atcheh*, and reckon it from Lunka to the 54th degree of latitude. This ſpace they divide into populous territories. To 14 degrees farther, they ſay it is but thinly inhabited, on account of the ſeverity of the cold; and that all beyond 66 degrees is not habitable.

The Greeks reckon their latitude from the equator; and as that line paſſes through Lunka, there is not any difference in fact, both coming to the ſame end.

The Latitude of Places.

This is an arch extending from the equator to the zenith of the place. In ſhort it is the diſtance of the place from the equator, and is meaſured by the elevation of the pole.

TABLES

TABLES

OF

LONGITUDES AND LATITUDES OF PLACES.

The LONGITUDE *calculated from the* FORTUNATE ISLANDS

THE FIRST CLIMATE.

	Longitude. D. M.	Latitude D. M.
جزيره طروقاي The Island of Terufaiy *(one of the Cape de Verds),* - -	12 15.	. 17 15
ساحلي بحراوقيانوس The Shore of the Western Ocean,	11 18.	. 18 18
جزيره تنبله The Island of Combeleh *(probably Prince's Island),* -	21 0.	. 3 0

		Longitude. D.	M.	Latitude. D.	M.
خليج اوانيطس	The Gulf of Awanites,	12	30..	8	25
عانه معدن الذهب	Aneh Maadin al Zheb, a city to the south of the equator,	19	0..	10	0
كوكوه	Kukueh, south of the equator, - -	14	11..	10	0
سقاله	Sekaleh, south of the line, - -	60	0..	2	30
وسطبحره كوزي	The middle of the sea of Kuzy *(the Western Ocean)*, -	68	0..	4	0
حسيمي	Hesimy, on the Nile,	63	15..	9	0
سحرتا	Sihrta, on the Nile,	65	0..	6	0
جرمي	Jermi, the capital of Ethiopia, - -	65	0..	9	30
زغاوه	Zeghaweh, - -	66	0..	1	10
ههيه	Hehiah, - -	66	0..	2	0
نريلغ	Nereelegh, - -	71	0..	8	0
مقدشو	Mekedshoo, -	72	0..	2	0
عدن	Aden, - - -	76	0..	11	0
بربره	Berbereh, Barbary,	78	0..	4	30
خليج ازانيطيفتوس	The Gulph of Azanetuftoos, -	12	35..	12	30

		Longitude. D.	Longitude. M.	Latitude. D.	Latitude. M.
شبام	Shebam, a town of Hussenmout, -	81	55..	12	30
مرباط	Merbat, - -	82	0..	12	0
جزيره سرانديپ	The Island of Serendeep *(Ceylon)*, -	130	0..	12	0
جزيره سقوطره	The Island of Secotora,	——	..	12	0
جبال قامرون	Gebal Kamarun, *(Cape Komorin)* famous for Lignum Aloes,	130	0..	10	0
خزيره لامري	The Island of Lamery, famous for a wood called Bacam, (resembling logwood,)	135	0..	9	0
جزيره كله	The Island of Keleh,	140	11..	8	0
جزيره مهراج	The Island of Mahraj,	150	0..	1	0
جمكوت	Jumkote, *(in China,)*	176	0..	5	0
سنلي	Sunlee, - -	180	0..	5	0
كنكدر	Gungdej, on the borders of the Eastern Ocean, - -	180	0..	——	
ارم	Irem, - - -	——	..	——	
كناره بحراوقيانوس	The confines of the ocean, - -	20	0..	36	0

		Longitude. D.	M.	Latitude. D.	M.
جزيره بادونه	The Island of Baduna,	38	0. .	36	21
برنيسا	Bernisa, *the city of Berenice,* - -	32	0. .	20	35
جزيره سولي	The Island of Suly,	38	30. .	23	0
جزيره سواکن	The Island of Sewaken,	48	30. .	18	0
طره	Tireh, - - -	49	20. .	39	0
دبقله	Dubkeleh, - -	68	0. .	44	30
درقله	Derkeleh, - -	58	40. .	14	30
بجه	Bejeh, - -	65	0. .	14	0
بلدره	Beldereh, - -	68	0. .	17	0
جزيره دهلک	The Island of Dehlek,	71	0. .	14	0
مارب	Mareb, - -	78	0.	14	0
مهجم	Mahjem, - -	74	45. .	17	15
زبيد	Zebeed, - -	74	20. .	14	10
حصن دلموه	Hysn Dulmooh, -	74	40. .	14	5
شرجه	Shirjeh, - -	74	40. .	17	15
جند	Jend, - - -	75	30. -	14	30
جبله	Jebeleh, - -	74	0. .	——	
حصن بعدان	Hasan Badan, -	75	30. .	18	40
بخران	Bokhran, - -	76	30. .	19	15
صغار	Safar, - - -	77	0. .	14	30
ذمار	Zamar, - -	77	15. .	18	30
سرين	Serrin, - -	77	15. .	20	0
حالي بن يعقوب	Hully Ben Yacoub,	77	20. .	18	30

		Longitude. D.	M.	Latitude. D.	M
صعده	Saadah, - -	77	20. .	17	15
خيوان	Khaiwan, - -	77	20. .	15	20
ظفار	Zefar, - -	77	35. .	13	20
حرش	Jeresh, near the sea coast, - -	77	5. .	17	15
صخار	Sekhar, - -	84	15. .	19	20
مهره	Mehrah, - -	85	0. .	16	0
جزيره زبيح	The Island of Zich, in the Red Sea, -	95	0. .	15	0
تاسند	Tasend, on the coast of the Indian Ocean,	82	0. .	19	20
معبر	Mabir, - -	82	0. .	17	30
كوبم كوكم	Kobemkokem, where there are pepper and bacam in great abundance, -	120	0. .	15	0
زيتون	Zytun *(in China)*,	154	0. .	17	15
سوفاره	Sufarah, - -	154	15. .	19	30
سندان	Sindan, - -	155	20. .	19	15
خانقو	Khankou, - -	150	0. .	14	0
خانجو	Khanjoo, - -	162	30. .	14	0
سندابل	Sandabel, - -	——	. .	——	
سمندان	Semendan, - -	——	. .	——	

		Longitude. D. M.	Latitude. D. M.
علاقي	Allaky, some place it in the second Climate,	—— ..	——
شقاله	Shekaleh, where is a bird that talks better than a parrot, -	—— ..	——
شهنج	Shahnej, - -	—— ..	——
قاع	Ka-i, betwixt Oman and Hussenmout, -	—— ..	——
لنجويه	Lenjuyeh, is a large Island near Zenj, and its vines bear thrice in a year, -	—— ..	——
النجه	Alenjeh, has a mine of emeralds, -	—— ..	——
شيلا	Sheela, - -	—— ..	——
قلزم	Kulzum, in Egypt,	—— ..	——
بكبل	Bukbel, where grows a tree from which they gather poison,	—— ..	——
قعاره	Kaareh *(vul Cairo)*	—— ..	——
تكرور	Tekrore, - -	—— ..	——
رامني	Ramni, - -	—— ..	——
قلهات	Felhat, - -	—— ..	——

		Longitude. D. M.	Latitude. D. M.
معلا	Maalla, - -	—— ..	——
مدينه الطيب	Medinet'l Tiyet, -	—— ..	——
سهر	Sehir, - - -	—— ..	——

THE SECOND CLIMATE.

سوس اقصى	Sus Aksa, - -	15 30. .	22 0
ملطه	Multeh, - -	17 30. .	27 0
درغه	Durgheh, - -	28 4. .	25 4
اودغشت	Oudeghshet, -	25 15. .	27 0
تخمايه	Tekhmyeh, - -	32 15. .	25 5
قوص	Kows, - -	61 30. .	24 35
اخميم	Akhmim, - -	61 30. .	27 15
اقصر	Aksir, - -	61 40. .	24 15
اسنا	Isna, - - -	62 0. .	23 30
انصبا	Inseba, - -	68 0. .	23 0
اسوان	Iswan, - -	66 15. .	22 30
معدن زمرد	Maaden Zemrud, the mine of emeralds; the same place is Allenjeh in the first Climate,	66 15. .	21 0

		Longitude. D.	M.	Latitude. D.	M.
تیما	Taima, - -	67	15..	25	40
معدن ذهب	Maaden Zheb, -	67	35..	21	15
اعیذاب	Iyzab, - -	68	40..	21	40
علانی	Allany, - -	68	40..	27	15
قصیر	Kesir, - - -	69	0..	27	0
قطیف	Katif, - -	74	0..	25	0
الینبغ	Alinbegh, - -	74	0..	24	0
جحفه	Jehfeh, - -	74	0..	24	0
مدینه طیبه	Medina Tiyebeh, -	75	20..	25	0
خیبر	Khiber, - -	75	20..	25	20
جده	Jiddeh, - -	77	10..	21	0
مکه معظمه	Mecca Moazzemeh,	77	0..	21	40
طایف	Taif, - - -	77	30..	21	20
فرع	Fera, - - -	77	30..	25	15
فند	Funed, - -	78	10..	27	0
حجر	Hejir, - - -	81	10..	25	15
جزیره طاقا البسو	The Island of Tukalabus, - -	68	15..	27	12
جزیره سولي	The Island of Suly,	38	30..	23	0
اسافل دریاي مصر	The extremity of the Sea of Egypt,	14	0..	30	22
یمامه	Yemameh, - -	81	10..	24	15
هجر بحرین	Hejer Bahrain, -	83	15..	25	15

		Longitude. D. M.	Latitude. D. M
جساوجس	Jesawejes,	88 30. .	24 15
اخرالبحرين	The extremity of Bahrain, - -	84 20. .	27 15
جزیره اوال	The Island of Awal,	86 15. .	22 0
جزیره سیلاب	The Island of Sylab,	83 30. .	25 0
هرموز	Hormuz, - -	92 0 .	25 0
جیرفت	Jereft, - -	93 0. .	27 30
دبیل	Debeil, *(Sind)* -	102 30. .	24 10
تیز	Teiz, on the sea coast,	83 0. .	24 15
بیرون	Beroon, - -	104 30. .	24 15
منصوره	Mansurah, - -	104 0. .	26 40
صنم سومنات	Senem Sumnat, -	107 10. .	22 15
احمداباد کجرات	Ahmedabad in Gujerat, - -	—— . .	23 15
نهرواله	Nehrwaleh in Gujerat,	—— . .	23 30
امرکوت	Amerkote, his Majesty's birth place, -	—— . .	24 40
منداو	Mendow, - -	—— . .	22 15
اجین	Owjain, - -	—— . .	22 30
بهروچ	Berootch, - -	—— . .	21 20
کنبایت	Kembayet, - -	109 20. .	26 20
کنوج	Kenoj, - -	154 50. .	26 35
کره	Kereh, - -	154 0. .	26 35

		Longitude. D. M.	Latitude. D. M.
سورت	Suret, - - -	——	21 0
چروج	Cheroj, - -	——	22 30
اجمیر	Ajmeer, - -	——	24 0
بنارس	Benaris, - -	117 20	26 15
ماهوره	Mahooreh, - -	117 20	24 40
اکره	Agra, - -	——	24 23
فتح‌پور	Futtehpoor, -	——	26 41
گوالیار	Gualiar, - -	——	27 0
مانکپور	Manikpoor, - -	——	27 16
جیونپور	Jawenpoor, - -	——	26 36
سنارکام	Sonargong, - -	——	27 0
پندوا	Pendewa, in Bengal,	——	27 0
لکهنوتي	Lukhnowty, in Bengal,	——	26 30
قلعہ کالنجر	The Foot of Kalinger,	——	24 25
اجوده	Ajewda, - -	——	25 50
شیرکیر	Sheergeer, - -	——	——
منیر	Meneer, - -	——	——
الهاباس	Ilhabas vul Allahabad,	——	——
بهلسه	Bhilseh, - -	——	25 0
غازي‌پور	Ghazipoor, - -	——	——
حاجي‌پور پتنه	Hajypoor Patna, -	——	——
لکهنو	Lukhnow, - -	——	——
دوکم	Dukem, - -	——	——

			Longitude. D.	M.	Latitude. D.	M.
دولت آباد	Dowletabad,	-	——	..	——	
اتاوا	Itaweh,	- -	——	..	——	
اوده	Owedh,	- -	——	..	——	
ديوكر	Deogur,	- -	——	..	——	
دلهو	Dulmow,	- -	——	..	——	
كالم‌پور	Galimpoor,	- -	——	..	——	
كورره	Kowrreh,	- -	——	..	——	
اسبوط	Asboot,	- -	——	..	——	
بسكره	Bisgurreh,	- -	——	..	——	
بحرم	Behrem,	- -	——	..	——	
بخد	Bekhed,	- -	——	..	——	
مابة	Mayeh,	- -	——	..	——	
خلسه	Khelseh,	- -	——	..	10	15
پنجو	Penju *(capital city of China)*,	- -	127	0 ..	22	0
مانجو	Manju,	- -	127	0 ..	19	0
نرور	Nerwer,	- -	——	..	——	
چيناپتن	Chinaputten,	-	——	..	——	
هلداره	Heldareh,	- -	——	..	——	
بارام	Baram,	- -	——	..	——	
تبت	Tibbet,	- -	——	..	——	
تكتاباد	Tektabad,	- -	——	..	——	
سلامته	Selameteh,	- -	——	..	——	

		Longitude. D. M.		Latitude D. M.
كشمير	Cashmeer, - -	——	..	——
كليا	Kelya, - -	——	..	——
مليبار	Mulleybar, vul Malabar,	——	..	——
مغروقين	Mekrukeen, -	——	..	——
ندهمه	Nedehmeh, - -	——	..	——
اعينبع	Aiyinba, - -	——	..	——
بطن مره	Baten Mereh, -	——	..	——
فقط	Feket, - -	——	..	——
ارمنت	Arment, - -	——	..	——
قيس	Kais, - - -	——	..	——
سلار	Salar, - - -	——	..	——
لحسا	Lahsa, - -	——	..	——

THE THIRD CLIMATE.

		Longitude D. M.		Latitude D. M.
اسفي	Asfi, - - -	2 15	..	35 15
فاس	Fas, Fez, - -	18 15	..	32 0
جزيره جون	The Island of Juna, *(Maderia,)* -	19 15	..	32 15

		Longitude. D.	M.	Latitude. D.	M.
سجلماسه	Sejel Masah, -	20	0..	31	30
مراكش	Merakesh, *(Morocco,)*	21	15..	29	15
تادلاستادلا	Tadelasitadela, -	22	0..	30	15
تلمسان	Telmesan, - -	24	0..	33	40
كناره بحر ر	Kenareh Behr Rum, the coast of the Mediterranean sea, -	25	0..	32	0
بسكره	Buskereh, - -	32	40..	30	15
تاهرت عليا	Upper Tahart, -	35	30..	29	0
تاهرت سفلى	Lower Tahart, -	35	30..	31	30
شطيف	Shetif, - -	37	15..	31	0
مشيله	Meshileh, - -	38	40..	30	20
باحر	Bahir, - -	39	15..	31	15
قيروان	Keirwan, - -	41	15..	31	15
مهديه	Mahadyeh, - -	42	15..	32	30
تونس	Tunis, - -	42	30..	35	31
اسافل درياي مص	The northern extremity of the sea of Egypt, - -	40	0..	30	22
وسطبلاد شام	The middle of Syria,	44	15..	33	38
جزيره رودس	The Island of Roodus, *Rhodes*, - -	44	30..	36	0
سوس سيه	Sus Syah, *Suez*, -	44	15..	32	30

		Longitude. D.	M.	Latitude. D.	M.
اطرابلس مغرب	Atrabolus Magreb, Tripoly in Syria, -	44	15..	32	30
تورز	Turez, - -	47	30..	29	30
زويله	Zuweeleh, - -	49	40..	30	15
قصر احمد	Kesir Ahmed, -	41	25..	33	30
برقه	Berkeh, - -	12	15..	30	15
ظلميشا	Zelmeesha, - -	14	0..	33	10
مدينه سرت	The city of Sirt, -	17	15..	21	15
عقبه اول ديار مصر	The northern extremity of Egypt,	19	0..	30	0
بهنا	Behena, - -	68	33..	28	15
اسكندريه	Iskenderyah, *Alexandria*, - -	61	54..	30	58
رشيد	Resheed, - -	62	20..	31	30
مصر	Mesr, *Egypt*, -	63	0..	30	20
دمياط	Demyat, *Demiata*,	63	30..	31	35
قيوم	Kiyoom, - -	63	15..	29	15
قلزم	Kulzum, - -	64	15..	28	30
نينس	Nynes, - -	64	30..	30	40
غره	Ghoreh, - -	36	10..	32	40
اربله	Areeleh, - -	66	15..	29	15
بيت المقدس	Beitulmekeddes, *Jerusalem*,	66	30..	31	50

		Longitude. D.	M.	Latitude. D.	M.
رمله	Ramlah, - -	66	50..	32	0
قيساريه	Kysaryeh, *Cæsarea,*	66	30..	32	50
عمان	Oman, - -	66	30..	31	30
عسقلان	Askelan, *Ascalon,*	66	30..	32	0
ياقا	Yeaca, *Acca,* -	66	15..	32	20
كرك	Kirk, - - -	68	30..	34	30
طبريه	Teberyah, *Tiberias,*	68	15..	32	0
بيستان	Bystan, - -	68	15..	32	50
غسكا	Aska, - - -	68	20..	33	20
صور	Sur, *Tyre,* - -	68	30..	33	0
صيدا	Syda, *Sidon,* -	68	30..	33	15
بعلبك	Baalbek, - -	70	15..	33	15
دمشق	Demeshk, *Damascus,*	70	0..	33	20
هيث	Heyis, - -	78	20..	33	0
حله	Hulleh, - -	79	15..	32	15
كوفه	Cufah, - -	79	30..	31	30
انبار	Ambar, - -	79	30..	33	15
عسكرا	Askera, - -	79	0..	33	30
بردان	Berdan, - -	79	15..	33	30
بغداد	Baghdad, - -	80	55..	33	20
مداين كسري	Medain Kisera, one of Khosru's palaces,	80	20..	33	0
هجر	Hajir, - - -	70	30..	38	30

		Longitude. D.	M.	Latitude. D.	M.
بابل	Babel, - -	80	55. .	32	15
نعمانيه	Naamanyeh, -	80	20. .	33	15
قصر هبيره	Kyser Hebireh, -	80	30. .	32	15
جرجرايا	Jirherya, - -	80	30. .	33	15
فم الصلح	Femalselch, - -	80	15. .	32	15
نهر الملك	Nehr al Malek, -	80	50. .	33	52
جلولا	Jelula, - -	81	10. .	33	30
واسط	Wasit, - -	81	30. .	32	20
حلوان	Holwan, - -	82	15. .	33	0
بصره	Basrah, - -	84	0. .	30	0
ابله	Ebleh, - -	84	0. .	30	20
اهواز	Ahwaz, - -	84	0. .	31	0
تستر	Tuster, - -	84	30. .	31	30
ارجان	Arjan, - -	84	30. .	32	30
عسکر مکرم	Asker Mekerrem, -	84	30. .	32	15
جزیره سقطر	The Island of Secotora,	84	30. .	33	0
حصن مهدي	Hasen Mahady, -	84	15. .	30	15
سينسر	Sinsir, on the Persian Gulph, - -	84	30. .	32	0
عبادان	Abadan, - -	84	30. .	30	0
رامهرمز	Ramhormez, -	84	15. .	31	0
اصفهان	Isfahan, - -	106	40. .	32	25
کازرون	Gazeroon, - -	87	0. .	29	15

		Longitude. D.	M.	Latitude. D.	M.
شوشتر	Shushter, - -	86	20..	31	30
شاپور	Shapoor, - -	86	55..	30	0
عمان	Oman, - -	67	20..	31	0
نوبندجان	Nubendjan, -	87	55..	30	10
جنبابه	Jembabeh, *commonly called Kenahneh,*	87	20..	30	15
ابرقوه	Aberkuh, - -	87	20..	31	30
فيروزاباد	Firozabad, - -	87	30..	31	30
شيراز	Shiraz, - -	88	0..	29	36
سراف و بقال سلاب	Seraf and Bokal Selab, - -	89	15..	29	0
شبانكاره	Shebankareh, -	79	0..	28	28
اصطخر	Istekher, *Persepolis,*	88	30..	30	0
يزد	Yezd, - - -	89	0..	32	0
حصن ابن عماره	Hisn Ebn Amareh,	95	0..	30	20
داراجرد	Darajird, - -	90	15..	28	15
باقد	Baked, - -	90	15..	29	15
سيرجان	Sirjan, - -	90	20..	29	30
كرمان	Kerman, - -	91	30..	30	5
طبس كيلي	Tebs Kili, - -	92	0..	33	0
زرند	Zerend, - -	92	15..	30	15
بردشير	Birdshir, - -	92	30..	30	15
جنيس	Jenys, - -	93	0..	31	0

		Longitude. D.	M.	Latitude. D.	M.
بم	Bum, - - -	94	0.	. 24	30
طبس مسينا	Tebs Mesyna, -	94	19.	. 33	15
خواش	Khewash, - -	94	40.	. 33	0
زرنج	Zerenj, an ancient city,	97	40.	. 32	30
کچ	Kutch, - -	99	0.	. 28	30
حالق	Halik, - -	99	0.	. 30	0
خالتان	Khaltan, - -	99	0.	. 33	35
رزم	Rezem, - -	99	0.	. 28	30
بست	Bost, - - -	100	0.	. 33	0
تکنیاباد	Teknyabad, - -	101	15.	. 33	0
رحج	Rehej, - -	103	15.	. 28	15
سيروين	Sirween, - -	105	15.	. 28	15
ميمند	Mimend, now dependent on Kandahar,	81	55.	. 33	0
غزنه	Ghezneh, - -	104	20.	. 33	25
رباط امير	Rabat Emir, -	105	0.	. 34	0
قندهار	Kandahar, - -	107	40.	. 33	0
تهلواره	Tehlwareh, - -	108	20.	. 33	30
مولتان	Multan, - -	106	25.	. 29	40
لهاور	Lehawer, commonly Lahoor, - -	109	20.	. 31	50
دهلي	Dehly, - -	154	38.	. 28	15
تاهنيسر	Tahniser, - -	——		. 30	10

		Longitude. D. M.	Latitude. D. M.
شاه آباد	Shahabad, - -	—— ..	30 12
سنبل	Sembel, - -	—— ..	28 4
امروهه	Amruheh, - -	—— ..	——
پاني پت	Panypet, - -	—— ..	28 12
برن	Beren, - -	—— ..	28 48
باغ بهت	Baghbehut, vul. Baghput, - -	—— ..	28 32
كول	Koal, - - -	—— ..	28 20
كردهماله	Kerdehmaleh, -	—— ..	31 10
كوت كرور	Kowtkerore, -	—— ..	31 0
سيالكوت	Syalkote, - -	—— ..	33 0
سلطان كوت	Sultankote, - -	—— ..	28 30
جيلم	Jeylum, - -	—— ..	33 15
رهتاس	Rhotas, - -	—— ..	33 15
قلعه بندنه	The fort of Bundneh,	—— ..	33 10
پرشاور	Pirshawur, commonly Peishore, - -	—— ..	33 25
فرمل	Firmel, - -	—— ..	32 15
سنام	Senam, - -	—— ..	30 30
سرهند	Sirhind, - -	—— ..	——
روپر	Ruper, - - -	—— ..	——
ماچهي واره	Macheewareh, -	—— ..	——
پايل	Payil, - - -	—— ..	——

		Longitude. D. M.	Latitude. D. M.
لودهیانه	Ludehyaneh, -	—— ..	——
سلطانپور	Sultanpoor, - -	—— ..	——
کلانور	Kalanore, - -	—— ..	——
دیسوهه	Deysoheh, - -	—— ..	——
پرسرور	Purserore, - -	—— ..	——
امناباد	Amnabad, - -	—— ..	——
سودره	Sudereh, - -	—— ..	——
دیفهه	Dyfeheh, - -	—— ..	——
بهیره	Behireh, - -	—— ..	——
خوشاب	Khushab, - -	—— ..	——
هزاره	Hezareh, - -	—— ..	——
جندنوب	Jendnoob, - -	—— ..	——
اتک بنارس.	Attok Benaris, built in the reign of his Majesty, - -	—— ..	——
هردوار وملکو و قلعه کلیر	Hirdewar, and Melku and the fort of Kelyr, ancient cities which are now thinly inhabited	—— ..	——
جوتاول	Jutawel, - -	—— ..	——
کیرانه	Keraneh, - -	—— ..	——
جهنجانه	Jehnjaneh, - -	—— ..	——

		Longitude. D. M.	Latitude. D. M.
بکهر	Bukher, - -	—— ..	——
جهت	Jeht, - - -	—— ..	——
بنکش	Bungish, - -	—— ..	——
رودراله	Rudraleh, - -	—— ..	——
نهتور	Nehtore, - -	—— ..	——
کیتهل	Keytehl, - -	—— ..	——
رهتک	Rohtek, - -	—— ..	——
ججهر	Jejher, - -	—— ..	——
ماهم	Mahem, - -	—— ..	——
پتي هيبتپور	Putty Hybetpoor, -	—— ..	——
خضرآباد	Khyzirabad, -	—— ..	——
سادهوره	Sadhoreh, - -	—— ..	——
سفیدن	Sefeden, - -	—— ..	——
جنید	Jenyd, - -	—— ..	——
کرنال	Kernal, - -	—— ..	——
هانسي حصار	Hansy Hissar, -	—— ..	29 15
سهارنپور	Saharenpoor, -	—— ..	——
دیوبن	Deobun, - -	—— ..	——
انباله	Embaleh, - -	—— ..	——
بهومه	Bhumeh, - -	—— ..	——
هستناور	Histnawer, - -	—— ..	——
سنپت	Sunpet, - -	—— ..	——
صنجر	Sinjir, - - -	—— ..	——

		Longitude. D. M.	Latitude. D. M.
اعبات	Amat, - -	—— ..	——
هيدان	Heydan, - -	—— ..	——
رعه	Raah, - - -	—— ..	——
رياسه	Ryaseh, - -	—— ..	——
منقلوت	Munkelote, - -	—— ..	——
فسطاط	Festat, - -	—— ..	——
بوطنج	Bootunj, - -	—— ..	——
اشهشويين	Ashmeshuieen, -	—— ..	——
منسيه	Munseeah, - -	—— ..	——
قابس	Kabis, - -	—— ..	——
سيوسه	Seyuseh, - -	—— ..	——
صغاقش	Sefakish, - -	—— ..	——
غزامش	Ghezamish, - -	—— ..	——
قابلس	Kabelis, - -	—— ..	——
صلت	Sult, - - -	—— ..	——
ازرعات	Azeraat, - -	—— ..	——
بصري	Busry, - -	—— ..	——
سرخد	Sirkhud, - -	—— ..	——
حل	Hul, - - -	—— ..	——
قادسيه	Kadesiah, - -	—— ..	——
صرصر	Sirsir, - - -	—— ..	——
جيره	Jeereh, - -	—— ..	——
بسا	Bessa, - - -	—— ..	——

		Longitude. D. M.	Latitude. D. M.
داراجون	Darajoon, - -	—— ..	——
عزنه	Uzneh, - -	—— ..	——
طيب	Teib, - - -	—— ..	——
ترفوب	Kerkoob, - -	—— ..	——
جسي	Jussee, - -	—— ..	——
ختا	Kheta, *in China*, -	165 15. .	28 30
حصن اردستان	Hasen Ardestan,	—— ..	——
سيو	Siyu, - - -	—— ..	——
صلا	Sela, - - -	—— ..	——
سهيرم	Simerem, - -	—— ..	——
بسم	Bisem, - -	—— ..	——
بلنان	Belnan, - -	—— ..	——
بلزم	Belzum, - -	—— ..	——
بيصا	Bisa, - - -	—— ..	——
جوسين	Jowseen, - -	—— ..	——
كنيسه	Keneeseh, - -	—— ..	——
جوز	Jowz, - -	—— ..	——
دمندان	Demendan, - -	—— ..	——
سبقه	Subkeh, - -	—— ..	——
صعالبيه	Salebeyeh, - -	—— ..	——
عين الشمس	Ain al Shems, -	—— ..	——
عين حاره	Ain Hareh, - -	—— ..	——
كدوال	Kedwal, - -	—— ..	——

		Longitude. D. M.	Latitude. D. M.
كفر طانه	Kuffer Taneh, -	——	——
كفر	Kuffer, - -	——	——
نجده	Nejdeh, - -	——	——
كوار	Kowar, - -	——	——
مربوط	Mirboot, - -	——	——
دها	Deha, - - -	——	——
وسكره	Weskereh - -	——	——
منيف	Menif, *Memphis*, -	——	——
مورجان	Murjan, - -	——	——
ناصره	Nasareh, *Nazareth in Palestine* -	——	——
مغراره	Meghrarreh, -	——	——

THE FOURTH CLIMATE.

		Longitude. D. M.	Latitude. D. M.
طنجه	Tanjah, *Tangur*, -	18 15	35 0
قصر عبدالكريم	Kesr Abdul Kereem,	18 30	37 40
قرطبه	Kortubeh, *Cordaua in Spain*, - -	18 40	35 40
اشبيله	Ashbileh, *Seville*,	18 50	36 50

		Longitude. D.	M.	Latitude. D.	M.
سبته	Sebteh, *Xativa in Valencia,* - -	19	15..	35	30
جزيره خضرا	The island of Khizra, *one of the Cape de Verd Islands,* -	19	15..	35	50
مارده	Mardeh, *Madrid,* -	20	15..	38	15
طليطه	Telyteh, *Toledo,* -	20	40..	35	30
غرناطه	Ghernateh, *Granada,*	21	40..	37	30
حنان	Henan, - -	21	0..	31	15
المريه	Almiryeh, *Almera,*	24	40..	35	15
مدينه الفرح	Medinah al Fireh,	24	15..	36	40
مانقه	Manakah, *the Island of Minorca,* - -	26	0..	37	40
ملته	Maltah, *the Island of Malta,* - -	30	18..	38	30
جزيره يابسه	The Island of Yabeseh, *Yvica,* - -	30	15..	38	30
جزيره مابرقه	The Island of Mabirkeh, *Majorca,* -	35	30..	38	30
بونه	Booneh, - -	38	0..	38	15
جزيره بردانيه	The Island of Berdaneeah, *Corsica,*	41	15..	38	15

		Longitude. D.	M.	Latitude. D.	M.
قاعده جزيره صقلبيه	The Metropolis of the Island of Sakel-biyeh, *Sardinia,*	41	15..	38	10
بلرغدامس	Bilraghdamis, -	44	10..	39	10
جزيره ناس	The Island of Nas, *Nasia,*	52	40..	38	10
جزيره اقريطس	The Island of Akerites, *Crete or Candia,*	55	40..	36	30
جزيره قبوس	The Island of Kebus, *Cyprus,* - -	62	15..	35	35
جزيره رودس	The Island of Rudes, *Rhodes,* - -	61	40..	36	15
جزيره همريا	The Island of Hemerya, *Amorgo,* - -	54	15..	38	35
سقليه	Sekulyah, *the Island of Sicily,* -	65	0..	36	0
مدينة الحكما	Atinyeh, Medinet ul Hukema, Athens, the city of Philosophers,	65	40..	37	20
جيرون	Jyroon, - -	66	30..	35	15
طرسوس	Tersoos, *Tarsus,* -	68	40..	36	50
بيروت	Beirut, - -	69	30..	34	0
اياس	Iyas, *Issus,* - -	69	15..	36	15
اونه	Uneh, - -	69	15..	36	50
مصيصه	Mesyseh, - -	69	15..	36	45

		Longitude. D.	M.	Latitude. D.	M.
برسبرت	Birsbirt, - -	69	20..	37	15
اطرابلس	Atrabolus, *Tripoly*,	69	40..	34	15
بغراس	Baghras, - -	70	15..	35	43
باسكندريه	Bascunderyeh, -	70	15..	36	10
الدقيه	Ladkyeh, *Laodicea*,	70	40..	35	15
حمص	Hems, *Emessa*, -	70	45..	34	0
شعرنكاس	Sharunkas, - -	71	0..	35	0
سويديه	Sewedyeh, - -	71	0..	36	0
مليطيه	Melityeh, *Milete*,	71	0..	37	0
شيرر	Shirir, - -	71	10..	37	50
انطاكيه	Anhtakyah, *Antioch*,	71	20..	35	40
سرمين	Sirmin, - -	71	50..	35	15
قنسرين	Kennasrin, - -	72	0..	35	30
حلب	Heleb, *Aleppo*, -	72	10..	35	50
شمشاط	Shumshat, - -	72	35..	37	30
حصن منصور	Hasn Mansur, -	72	24..	34	0
سروج	Sirooj, - -	72	0..	34	0
منبج	Membej, - -	72	50..	36	30
رقه	Rakah, - -	73	0..	36	15
حران	Harran, - -	73	15..	37	50
قاليقلا	Kalikala, - -	73	15..	34	0
ماردين	Mardeen, - -	74	15..	37	50
ميافارقين	Mya Farkeen, -	74	15..	38	0

		Longitude. D.	M.	Latitude. D.	M.
متاح	Metah, - -	74	30. .	37	45
قرقيسيا	Kerkisya, - -	74	40. .	36	40
جزيره ابن عمر	The Island of Ebn Omar,	75	30. .	37	30
نسيبين	Nasebin, *Nisibis*, -	75	20. .	37	40
تدليس	Tedlis, - -	75	30. .	35	45
سنجار	Sinjar, - -	76	0. .	36	0
معرة النعمان	Maretul Naaman,	71	45. .	35	0
اربل	Erbel, *Erbela*, -	77	20. .	35	0
عانه	Aneh, - - -	76	30. .	36	0
مدينة بلد	The City of Beled,	76	40. .	37	40
موصل	Mosul, - -	76	0. .	34	50
ارجيس	Arjis, - - -	76	0. .	38	30
حديثه	Hadyseh, on the Euphrates, - -	77	20. .	36	15
آبد	Abid, - - -	77	20. .	36	12
حديثه	Hadyseh, on the Dejileh,	77	30. .	96	15
نوشهر	Nowshehr, - -	78	20. .	38	10
تكريت	Tekreet, - -	78	25. .	34	0
سامرا	Samra, - -	79	15. .	37	40
سلماس	Sulmas, - -	79	5. .	37	40
خوي	Khowey, - -	79	40. .	37	40
اروميه	Aroomiyeh, -	79	15. .	37	0
اربيل	Arbil, - - -	79	15. .	37	20

		Longitude. D.	M.	Latitude. D.	M.
مرند	Marend, - -	80	43..	37	59
شهرزور	Shehrzur, - -	80	20..	35	30
اردبيل	Ardebil, - -	80	30..	37	0
اوجان	Awjan, - -	81	30..	37	20
نخجوان	Nekhjowan, -	81	15..	37	40
قصر شيرين	Kesr Shirin, -	81	40..	38	45
مراغه	Maraghah, - -	82	0..	37	20
تبريز	Tebriz, - -	82	0..	37	0
ميانه	Meyaneh, - -	82	20..	37	0
قرماسين	Kermasin, - -	83	0..	34	32
دينور	Dinore, - -	83	0..	35	0
همدان	Hamadan, - -	83	0..	35	10
زنجان	Zenjan, - -	83	0..	36	30
موقان	Mukan, - -	83	0..	38	0
سهرورد	Sohirwird, - -	83	20..	36	0
نهاوند	Nehawend, - -	83	15..	34	20
همان شهر	Hemanshehr, -	84	33..	37	30
يزدجرد	Yezdijird, dependent on Hamadan, -	84	30..	34	20
ابهر	Abher, - -	84	30..	36	45
كويم	Koyem, - -	84	40..	37	20
كرج	Kurj, - - -	84	45..	34	0
ساوه	Saweh, - -	85	0..	36	15

		Longitude. D.	M.	Latitude. D.	M.
قزوين	Cazvin, - -	85	0. .	37	15
سلطانيه	Sultanyeh, - -	84	0. .	36	30
آبه	Abeh, - - -	85	10. .	34	40
قم	Kom, - - -	84	40. .	34	45
جرباذخان	Jerbadkhan, -	85	35. .	34	15
كاشان	Kashan, - -	86	0. .	36	15
دماوند	Demawend, -	86	20. .	36	15
ري	Rei, - - -	86	20. .	36	0
كجور و كلار	Kajur and Kalar, -	86	15. .	36	25
خوار	Khowar, - -	87	10. .	35	40
الموت	Almowt, - -	85	37. .	36	21
طالقان	Talakan, - -	85	45. .	36	10
هوسم	Husem, - -	85	10. .	37	10
ديلمان	Dileman, - -	——	. .	——	
دشت	Desht, - -	——	. .	——	
لاهجان	Lahjan, - -	——	. .	36	10
ديمت	Dymet, *a town of Damawend,* -	87	20. .	37	10
آمل	Amol, - -	87	20. .	36	30
دامغان	Dameghan, - -	88	55. .	36	20
سمنان	Simnan, - -	87	20. .	36	40
بيار	Biyar, - -	82	50. .	35	45
ساري	Saree, - -	88	0. .	37	0

			Longitude. D.	Longitude. M.	Latitude. D.	Latitude. M.
بسطام	Bostam,	- -	89	30. .	36	10
استراباد	Asterabad,	- -	89	35. .	36	50
جرجان	Jerjan,	- -	95	0. .	36	50
فراوه	Forawch,	- -	90	0. .	39	0
سبزوار	Sebzwar,	- -	91	30. .	36	15
اسفراين	Esfarayin,	- -	91	40. .	37	15
آبكون	Abgoon,	- -	89	30. .	37	15
مزنيان	Muznyan,	- -	90	30. .	37	0
ترشيز	Tershez,	- -	92	0. .	35	0
نيشاپور	Nishapoor,	- -	92	30. .	36	21
طوس	Toos,	- - -	92	30. .	34	30
مشهد رضا	Meshed Reza,	-	92	33. .	34	29
تون	Toon,	- - -	92	30. .	34	30
نوقان	Nukan,	- -	92	15. .	38	40
قاين	Kayin,	- -	93	20. .	36	30
زوزن	Zozun,	- -	93	30. .	35	39
نورجان	Nurjan,	- -	94	0. .	37	0
مرو شاهجهان	Maru Shahjehan,	-	97	0. .	37	40
هرات	Herat,	- -	94	20. .	34	30
سرخس	Serekhs,	- -	94	30. .	36	0
بادغيس	Badghis,	- -	94	30. .	35	20
مرو الرود	Maru al Rud, *called also Merghab,*		97	0. .	36	30

			Longitude. D.	M.	Latitude. D.	M.
مالين	Maleen,	- -	95	30..	34	30
پوشنک	Pusheng,	- -	94	0..	37	50
بعشور	Bashur,	- -	96	25..	36	0
ترنين	Caznin,	- -	97	55..	37	15
رنديقان	Rendyekan,	-	97	30..	34	45
اشبورقان	Ashburkan,	-	105	0..	37	41
طالقان	Talakan,	- -	98	15..	37	30
فارياب	Fariab,	- -	99	0..	36	45
بلخ	Balkh,	- -	101	0..	36	41
باميان	Bamian,	- -	102	0..	34	35
هلاورد	Helawerd,	- -	101	0..	37	30
بلاساغون	Balasaghun,	-	101	30..	37	40
سمنجان	Semenjan,	- -	102	15..	37	15
قناديان	Konadyan,	- -	102	0..	37	15
ديوالح	Dywaleh,	- -	102	20..	36	0
صغانيان	Saghanyan,	- -	102	40..	38	50
طالغان	Talaghan,	- -	102	50..	37	25
اندراب	Enderab,	- -	103	45..	36	0
بدخشان	Badakhshan,	-	104	25..	37	10
كابل	Kabul,	- -	104	40..	34	30
پنجهر	Penjhir,	- -	104	40..	35	0
لمغان	Lumghan,	- -	——	..	34	15

		Longitude. D.	M.		Latitude. D.	M.
گردیز	Girdez, - -	105	20	..	36	0
حرم	Herem, - -	104	20	..	36	0
کشمیر	Cashmeer, - -	108	0	..	36	15
بلور	Belore, - -	108	0	..	36	0
منبع نهر مهران	Membe Nehr Mehran, the source of the River of Mehran,	126	0	..	36	0
سرفتین	Sireftyn, - -	——		..	——	
هبسه	Hebseh, - -	——		..	——	
حران	Heran, - -	——		..	——	
بیسار	Bysar, - -	——		..	——	
قراده	Keradeh, - -	——		..	——	
فرهان	Farhan, - -	——		..	——	
ملان	Malan, - -	——		..	——	
ابوخیس	Abukhis, - -	——		..	——	
اودمیه	Owdmyeh, - -	——		..	——	
قرماسین	Kermaseen, - -	——		..	——	
دوارق	Dowarek, - -	——		..	——	
دیاربکر	Diyarbekr, - -	——		..	——	
قزنین	Kuzneen, - -	——		..	——	
نینوي	Nenevy, *Niniveh*,	——		..	——	
پلنکان	Pelengan, - -	——		..	——	

			Longitude. D. M.	Latitude D. M.
قیصر Kysir,	-	-	—— ..	——
بجابه Bejabeh,	-	-	—— ..	——
بلنسیه Bulenseyeh,		-	—— ..	——
سامس Samis,	-	-	—— ..	——
ایاس Jyas, -	-	-	—— ..	——
عرقه Erkeh,	-	-	—— ..	——
زقبه Zekbeh,	-	-	—— ..	——
صهیون Sehyoon,	-	-	—— ..	——
حارم Harem,	-	-	—— ..	——
خامیه Khamyeh,	-	-	—— ..	——
شیرزه Sheerzeh,	-	-	—— ..	——
حمات Hemat,	-	-	—— ..	——
مرغش Merghesh,	-	-	—— ..	——
عینتات Aytat,	-	-	—— ..	——
معد Maad,	-	-	—— ..	——
حصن کیف Hesn Kyef,	-	-	—— ..	——
سوت Sowt, -	-	-	—— ..	——
حصن الطاق Hesn al Tak,		-	—— ..	——
کرون Keroon,	-	-	—— ..	——
کیلان Gilan,	-	-	—— ..	——
جوین Jowain,	-	-	—— ..	——
خاجرم Jajerem,	-	-	—— ..	——

		Longitude. D. M.		Latitude. D. M.
معرو	Maru, - -	——	..	——
ترجستان	Kurjistan, - -	——	..	——
کرخ	Kerkh, - -	——	..	——
نسا	Nissa, *in Servia*, -	——	..	——
ابیورد	Abiwerd, - -	——	..	——
شهرستان	Shehristan, - -	——	..	——
اسکاکند	Askakend, - -	——	..	——
فربر	Firbir, - -	——	..	——
فامیاب	Famyab, - -	——	..	——
طمغاج	Timghaj, - -	——	..	——
خلان	Khelan, - -	——	..	——
وخش	Wekhsh, - -	——	..	——
شومان	Shuman, - -	——	..	——

THE FIFTH CLIMATE.

		Longitude D.	M.		Latitude D.	M.
اشبونه	Ashbuneh, *Lisbon*,	36	15	..	42	40
سنترین	Santereen, *Santillana*,	38	0	..	39	0
جزیره وقاس	The Island Wakass, *the Island of Corsica*,	21	12	..	43	50

		Longitude. D.	M.	Latitude. D.	M.
مدينه وليد	The city of Waleed, *in Sudan,* - -	22	50..	29	20
مرقسيه	Merkessiah, *in Ethiopia,*	28	15..	43	15
مدينه سالم	The city of Salem, *Salamanca in Spain,*	29	10..	39	0
دانيه	Daniah, *Dania, a city of Valencia,* -	31	30..	42	30
نطليه	Natleeáh, *Natoli,*	31	30..	40	15
سرقسطه	Sirkestch, *Saragosa,*	31	30..	42	30
طرطوسه	Tertusah, *Tortosa in Castile,* - -	32	30..	43	15
جزيره ميرقه	The Island of Meerekeh, *Majorca,* - -	34	10..	39	40
هيكل	Hykel, - -	34	15..	43	15
برشلونه	Barseluneh, *Barcelona,*	34	3..	42	0
اربونه	Arbuna, *Narbonne,*	36	15..	43	20
طركونه	Terkuneh, *Toulouse,*	38	0..	43	0
جنوه	Genuva, *Genoa,* -	41	0..	41	20
ربوسه	Rabuseh, *Ragusah, on the Gulph of Venice,*	43	40..	41	30
مدينه طبر	The City of Tiberta,	55	12..	43	15
جزيره نغريت	The Island of Nacrit, *Nacaria,*	58	50..	42	15

		Longitude. D. M.	Latitude. D. M.
جزيره مت لنا	The Island of Metlena, *Metelin or Lesbos,*	55 15..	43 15
وسط بحر بنطس	Weset Behr Bontes, *the middle of the Euxine or Black Sea,* - -	55 30..	46 41
غيون اسغرس	Ayun Askurus, -	55 15..	46 51
مقابض لورستانس	Mekabez Luristanis,	36 0..	43 32
علايا	Allaya, - -	62 0..	39 30
عمورية	Ammuryah, -	64 0..	43 0
انكوريه	Enguryeh, *the city of Areyra,* - -	64 40..	41 15
ماقدونيا	Macdoonia, *Macedonia,*	65 0..	41 15
آقا شهر	Acca Shehr, -	65 15..	41 40
قونيا	Kuniyah, *Iconia,* -	66 30..	41 40
قيساريه	Kysaryeh, *Cesarea*	67 15..	40 15
اقسراي	Akserai, - -	67 45..	40 15
سيواس	Siwas, - - -	71 30..	40 10
طرابون	Terabun, - -	73 0..	43 0
شمشاط	Shemshat, - -	73 15..	40 0
ملازجرد	Malazjird, - -	75 15..	39 30
اخلاط	Akhlat, - -	75 50..	39 20

		Longitude. D. M.	Latitude. D. M.
باب الحديد	Babal ul Hedid, *Derbend near the Caspian Sea*, -	76 0.	. 41 0
ارزنجان	Arzenjan, - -	78 0.	. 39 40
ارزن الرم	Arzen al Rum, -	77 0.	. 39 40
بردعه	Bardaah, - -	83 0.	. 40 30
شمكوره	Shemkoreh, -	83 0.	. 41 50
خنكره	Khenkereh, - -	83 0.	. 38 40
ارزندروم	Erzendroom, -	79 0.	. 41 15
تغليس	Teflis, - - -	83 0.	. 43 0
بيلقان	Bilkan, - -	83 30.	. 39 50
باكويه	Bakuyeh, - -	84 30.	. 40 50
شماخي	Shamakhi, - -	—— .	. ——
روميه كبري	Rumyah Kobra, *the city of Rome*, -	55 0.	. 41 50
باب الابواب	Babulabwab, *Derbend*,	89 0.	. 43 0
جزيره سياه كوه	The Island of Syah Kouh, *an Island of the Black Sea*,	89 0.	. 43 30
هشترخان	Heshterkhan, -	—— .	. ——
اغرجه	Agherjeh, - -	—— .	. ——
كات	Kat, - - -	94 0.	. 41 30

		Longitude. D.	M.	Latitude. D.	M.
بوكركانج	Bukerkanj, - -	93	45..	42	30
جرجانيه	Jerjanyeh, - -	94	0..	42	45
كركانج	Kerkanj, *capital of Khavarezm*, -	94	30..	42	17
هزاراسف	Hazarasf, - -	95	20..	41	10
زمخشه	Zemekhsheh, -	94	30..	41	40
درقان	Derkan, - -	96	0..	40	30
بخارا	Bokhara, - -	96	30..	39	10
پيكند	Pikend, - -	96	39..	39	45
طراويس	Terawis, - -	97	40..	39	30
چند	Jend, - - -	97	45..	43	30
نخشب	Nekhsheb, called also Tekhsheb, Neshef and Kershy, -	98	0..	39	0
سمرقند	Summerkund, -	99	0..	40	0
ايلاق	Ilak, - - -	99	10..	43	20
كش	Kash, *a city of Badakhshan*, - -	99	30..	39	30
زامين	Zamin, - -	99	40..	43	40
اسفجاب	Esfijab, *dependent upon Sash*, - -	99	50..	48	30
اسروشنه	Osrushnah, - -	100	0..	41	0

		Longitude. D.	M.	Latitude. D.	M.
اسبانیکت	Asbaneket, *a town of China*, - -	100	30..	40	0
خجند	Khojend, - -	105	35..	41	55
خواقند	Khowakund, -	105	50..	42	50
پنکت	Penket, - -	101	0..	43	25
ترمز	Termiz, - -	101	15..	37	15
اخسیکت	Akhseket, *capital of Farghana*, -	101	30..	42	0
کاشان	Kashan, - -	100	35..	42	0
قبا	Koba, - -	101	50..	42	50
فرغانه	Farghana, *commonly called Andejan*,	102	0..	42	20
روس	Rus, *Russia*, -	102	20..	43	20
ختن	Khoten, - -	107	0..	42	0
چاج	Chaj, *is Shash*, -	109	0..	42	30
تبت	Tibbet, - -	110	0..	40	0
خاجو	Khaju, - -	123	32..	42	15
سوکجو	Sookjoo, - -	124	0..	40	0
تنکباس	Tenkabas, - -	130	0..	39	10
مهدي	Mehdy, - -	140	0..	30	0
نشوي	Nushwee, - -	——	..	——	
کشاینه	Keshayeneh, -	——	..	——	

		Longitude. D. M.		Latitude. D. M.
يومان	Yūman, - -	——	..	——
شير نحاس	The City of Nehās,	——	..	——
رقان	Rakan, - -	——	..	——
كيس	Kiēs, - - -	——	..	——
ابروق	Abrook, - -	——	..	——
افسوس	Efsūs, *Ephesus,* -	——	..	——
بسطة	Bus̆teh, - -	——	..	——
كويا	Kuya, *a city of Russia,*	——	..	——
مقسين	Mūkseen, - -	——	..	——
ختلان	Khētlan, - -	——	..	——
مخلاط	Mekhlat, - -	——	..	——
روم	Rum, - - -	——	..	——
شامش	Shamish, - -	——	..	——
شلب	Shileb, - -	——	..	——
سنتره	Sentereh, - -	——	..	——
قبره	Kubreh, - -	——	..	——
قسطلول	Kustelul, *possibly Castile,* - -	——	..	——
سورقه	Surekeh, - -	——	..	——
مرغزا	Marghcza, - -	——	..	——
سقطيسله	Sektes̆yleh, - -	——	..	——
بطلسوس	Bētelsus, - -	——	..	——

		Longitude. D. M.	Latitude. D. M.
شهر والد	Shehr Walid, -	—— ..	——
مرسيه	Mersyeh, *probably Marseilles,* -	—— ..	——
دانيه	Danyeh, - -	—— ..	——
سالم	Salem, - -	—— ..	——
سرقط	Sirket, - -	—— ..	——
توقاب	Tookab, - -	—— ..	——
موشن	Mushen, - -	—— ..	——
شيران	Sheeran, - -	—— ..	——
ساوه	Saweh, - - -	—— ..	——

THE SIXTH CLIMATE.

حليقه	Helikeh, - -	20	0..	46	0
نبلوقه	Neeblookeh, -	34	15..	45	15
بردال	Berdal, *Bourdeaux,*	30	15..	44	15
كنبرويه	Kembruyeh, *Cambray,*	40	30..	43	15
بندقيه	Bendekyeh, *Venice,*	42	0..	44	0
نيره	Neereh, *Nice or Nizza,*	42	0..	45	0

		Longitude. D.	M.	Latitude. D.	M.
بسرشان	Bisirshan, - -	50	0..	45	0
ابرو	Abroo, - -	59	45..	45	0
بوزنطيه	Buzantyeh, *Byzantium*,	59	50..	45	0
كسلونه	Kusslooneh, -	65	30..	46	20
سنوب	Senoob, - -	64	0..	47	0
هرقله	Herkelch, - -	67	20..	46	30
اماسيه	Amasyeh, - -	67	30..	45	45
سامبنون	Sambenoon, -	69	20..	46	40
فرض الروم	Ferzal Rum, -	74	30..	46	50
سرين آلان	Sereenalan, - -	73	0..	44	0
بلنجر	Belenjer, *the capital of Kherz*, -	85	0..	46	30
كرش	Kersh, - -	87	0..	46	50
بنقي كند	Benkykend, -	97	30..	46	40
طراز	Teraz, - -	99	50..	44	31
فاراب	Farab, - -	98	30..	45	0
بلخ	Balkh, - -	105	30..	44	0
المالق	Almalik, - -	102	30..	44	0
اوزكند	Urkend, - -	102	50..	44	0
كاشغر	Cashghur, - -	106	30..	44	0
اوتن كلوران	Autan Keluran, -	110	0..	46	0
قبالغ	Kabaligh, - -	108	0..	44	0

			Longitude. D. M.		Latitude. D. M.
بیس بالغ	Byshbaligh,	-	111 0	..	44 45
قراقوروم	Karacurem,	- -	115 0	..	46 0
خان بالغ	Khanbaligh,	- -	124 0	..	40 0
ابولده	Abuledeh,	- -	——	..	——
اشت	Asht,	- -	——	..	——
انظرخت	Enzerkhet,	- -	——	..	——
فرتنه	Fertineh,	- -	——	..	——
تطليسه	Tetleeseh,	- -	——	..	——
استوب	Astoob,	- -	——	..	——
سامون	Samun,	- -	——	..	——
طرابزون	Terabizun,	- -	——	..	——
جنده	Jendeh,	- -	——	..	——
سموره	Semooreh,	- -	——	..	——
لنبرويه	Lembiruyeh,	-	——	..	——
برشان	Bershan,	- -	——	..	——
بل خجر	Belkhejer,	- -	——	..	——
جابلستان	Jabulistan,	- -	——	..	——
دشت قپچاق	Desht Kepchak,	-	——	..	——

THE SEVENTH CLIMATE.

		Longitude. D.	M.	Latitude. D.	M.
جزیره طاپانا	The Island of Tapana,	9	0	50	30
سنبتاقو	Sumbatakoo, -	39	0	49	0
صفج	Suffej, - -	48	30	50	30
اقچه کرمان	Akjeh Kerman, -	65	18	49	0
قرقز	Kerkez, - -	67	15	50	0
کفا	Keffa, - -	67	15	48	0
صلعات	Selaat, - -	67	10	50	10
طرتو	Tertoo, - -	67	30	50	45
بلار	Belar, - -	90	0	50	30
ارق	Arek, - -	105	0	48	0
صراي	Saray, - -	106	0	48	0
اكله	Akleh, - -	108	0	49	0
وسط بحره اول جیحون	Weset Behreh Awel Jihun, -	110	0	48	0
باطق	Batek, - -	——		——	
بجنه	Bejenneh, *a city of Turkestan,* -	——		——	
صقلاب	Seklab, *a city of Rum,*	——		——	

		Longitude. D. M.	Latitude. D. M.
معشقه	Mashekeh, - -	—— ..	——
طليه	Telyeh, *Italy*, -	—— ..	——
مرقله	Merkeleh, - -	—— ..	——
ازق	Azek, - -	—— ..	——
كلك	Kelek, - -	—— ..	——
صاري	Sary, - - -	—— ..	——
صقاليه	Sekalyeh, - -	—— ..	——
خابلقا	Jabilka, - -	—— ..	——

THE

THE EXTENT

OF THE

INHABITED EARTH.

THE Greeks ſay, that in the ſame manner as the equinoctial line divides the earth into northern and ſouthern hemiſpheres, ſo does the circle of the natural horizon, by interſecting the equator, form two other hemiſpheres, making altogether four quarters; namely, the upper and the lower northern, and the upper and the lower ſouthern quarters.

The Greeks ſay, that formerly the whole of the ſouthern quarter was land, but that now a great part of it is inundated, among which are the Fortunate Iſlands, part of Greece, and other places. The Hindoos teach that the earth is not inhabited beyond the latitude of 66 deg. 29 min. 43 ſec. no animal being ſuppoſed able to live at a greater diſtance from the equator, on account of the extreme ſeverity of the cold. Others among them ſay, that a ſmall part of the upper ſouthern quarter, which joins to the northern quarter, is land, but not inhabited. Others maintain, that the earth is inhabited as far as ten degrees ſouth.

But thoſe who are better informed ſay, that the ſouth is inhabited as well as the north. And but a ſhort time ago, a very extenſive iſland, with well-inhabited towns, to the ſouth of the equator, was conquered by the Fringies, who have called it the NEW WORLD. Some ſhips were driven there by contrary winds, and one of the crew having mounted his horſe, the natives were ſo aſtoniſhed at the ſtrangeneſs of his appearance, that, thinking the man and beast to be only one animal, they fled before him in terror and consternation, and the country became an easy conquest.

THE HINDOO QUARTERS OF THE EARTH.

Some say, that the Hindoo philosophers divide the earth into nine parts, viz.

The South, *Dekhan*, containing Arabia.
The North, *Ootre*, Turkestan.
The East, *Poorub*, China and Chinese Tartary.
The West, *Putchem*, Egypt and Barbary.
The North-east, *Iyssa* Khatai, Moghul Tartary.
The North-west, *Bayib*, the Turkish dominions and Europe.
The South-west, *Nyrut*, part of Egypt and Barbary, Africa, and Andelusia.
The South-east, *Aknew*.
The centre they call *Muddehdeys*.

I have not seen in any Hindovee book the geographical divisions which I have given above; neither are their learned acquainted with them.

Of

OF NUMERATION.

The Brahmins have only eighteen places in numeration, as follows:

Units, - - - -	Ekhun.
10 - - - -	Dehſhem.
100 - - - -	Shut.
1000 - - - -	Sehſir.
10,000 - - - -	Jyoot.
100,000 - - -	Lukſh, vulgarly lack.
1,000,000 - - -	Purboot.
10,000,000 - - -	Kote, vulgarly krore.
100,000,000 - - -	Arbud.
1,000,000,000 - -	Abuj.
10,000,000,000 - -	Kehrub.
100,000,000,000 - -	Nikhrub.
1,000,000,000,000 -	Mahapuddum.
10,000,000,000,000 -	Sunkh.
100,000,000,000,000 -	Jeldeh.
1,000,000,000,000,000 -	Untee.
10,000,000,000,000,000 -	Moodddeh.
100,000,000,000,000,000 -	Berardeh.

After this they ſay, tens of Berardehs, hundreds of Berardehs, &c.

OF THE JEHATS, OR QUARTERS OF THE WORLD.

The Hindoo philoſophers call a ſide or quarter *Dessa*, and alſo *Deg*. They reckon ten, including the upper and lower ſides of the earth; and they believe that each has its particular guardian ſpirit, to whom they give the general appellation of *Degpaul*.

TABLE OF THE QUARTERS, WITH THEIR GUARDIAN SPIRITS.

Quarter.		Guardian Spirit.
Poorub,	Eaſt,	*Indree.*
Agnee,	South-eaſt,	*Augin.*
Dulchen *com.* Dekhan,	South,	*Jum.*
Nyrut,	South-weſt,	*Benyroot.*
Putchim,	Weſt,	*Wurrun.*
Baybee,	North-weſt,	*Banoo.*
Ootre,	North,	*Kobeir.*
Iyſanee,	North-eaſt,	*Jysan.*
Oordhoo,	Above,	*Birmha.*
Adeh,	Below,	*Nag.*

Some philoſophers alſo make a quarter of the centre between the upper and lower, the guardian ſpirit of which they call Roodre; ſo that, according to this account, there are eleven quarters.

OF THE HINDOOS.

Although it is impoſſible to give, in this abridgment, a circumſtantial account of the ſeveral tribes of Hindoos, their various characters, cuſtoms, and ceremonies, yet ſomething ſhall be ſaid ſummarily on each ſubject.

If a diligent inveſtigator were to examine the temper and diſpoſition of the people of each tribe, he would find every individual differing in ſome reſpect or other. Some among them are virtuous in the higheſt degree, and others carry vice to the greateſt exceſs. But impartiality muſt allow that thoſe among them who dedicate their lives to the worſhip of the Deity, exceed men of every other religion in piety and devotion. They

They are vigorous enemies and faithful friends, and when driven to despair, make no account of their lives. They are renowned for wisdom, disinterested friendship, obedience to their superiors, and many other virtues. But at the same time there are among them men, whose hearts are obdurate and void of shame, turbulent spirits; who, for the merest trifle, will commit the greatest outrages.

In short, some have the disposition of angels, and others are demons.

The Hindoo philosophers divide the human race into Charburren, or four tribes. 1, Brâhmin, more commonly called Brahmin. 2, Chuttree, vulgarly Kehteree. 3, Wiess, vulgarly Biess. 4, Shooder, vulgarly Sooder. At the creation of the world, these four tribes were produced from Brahma. The Brahmins from his mouth; the Kehteree from his arms; the Biess from his thighs; the Sooder from his feet. The other people of the world they call Milleetch, and suppose them to have been first produced from the Cow of Camdhen.

The Brahmins.

These have properly six duties. 1, The study of the Bedes. 2, The study of other sciences. 3, To instruct others. 4, To perform the Jug, or the bestowing of charity for the sake of the Dewtahs, and exciting others to do the same. 5, Giving charity on their own account. 6, Receiving charity from others.

The Kehteree

Are enjoined the performance of three of the abovementioned duties. 1, Study. 2, Performing the Jug. 3, Bestowing charity.—Besides which they have ten other duties. 1, Serving Brahmins. 2, To be rulers of the earth, and receive the reward of their labour or tribute.

tribute. 3, The protection of religion. 4, The exaction of fines from delinquents, and ascertaining the quantity thereof. 5, To punish every one according to his offence. 6, To acquire wealth, and spend it properly. 7, To train elephants, horses, and oxen, and to instruct servants in their respective duties. 8, To be soldiers. 9, Not to receive charity from men. 10, To reward merit.

The Biess.

They also perform the three duties of the Brahmins abovementioned, to which five other offices are added. 1, Servitude. 2, Agriculture. 3, Merchandise. 4, Taking care of oxen. 5, Bearing arms.

And any of the offices abovementioned, for the Kehteree and Biess tribes, may also be performed by Brahmins, previous to their putting on the zenar.

The Sooder.

They cannot perform any of the offices assigned to the other three tribes. But they may serve them, wear their cast-off clothes, and eat any victuals they have left. They may be of any of the following professions: painters, goldsmiths, blacksmiths, carpenters, salt merchants, dealers in honey, milk, buttermilk, ghee, and grain.

The Milleetch

Are infidels, who have not any religion, and of these they reckon Jews and Guebres.

And they say that, by the intermarriages of these four original tribes, sixteen races of men are produced. 1, Brahmin, whose father and mother are both Brahmins. 2, Moordhawaseekut, the father Brahmin and the mother Kehteree. 3, Neshad, the father Brahmin and the mother Sooder. 4, Untelut, the father Brahmin

min and the mother Biefs. 5, Kehteree, both father and mother Kehteree. 6, Sooté, the father Kehteree and the mother Brahminee. 7, Maheys, the father Kehteree and the mother Biefs. 8, Oogur, the father Kehteree and the mother Sooder. 9, Biefs, both father and mother Biefs. 10, Beydeah, the father Biefs and the mother Brahminee. 11, Magdeh, the father Biefs and the mother Kehteree. 12, Kurren, the father Biefs and the mother Sooder. 13, Sooder, both father and mother Sooder. 14, Chundal, the father Sooder and the mother Brahminee. 15, Chutta, the father Sooder and the mother Kehteree. 16, I-ugoee, the father Sooder and the mother Biefs.

Again, by the mixture of thefe fixteen tribes, are produced others without number, each differing in their cuftoms and religious worfhip. The diftinctions, likewife, of country, profeffion, and rank of anceftors, form fuch a variety of branches, as are almoft inconceivable.'

THE BRAHMINS,

Themfelves, are of four tribes according to the refpective doctrine of the four Bedes, each tribe following its own particular book. They alfo differ in the manner of reading them. For the Rig Bede, are eight ways of reading; for the Jijer Bede, eighty-fix; for the Sam Bede, one thoufand; and for the Atehrben Bede, five. And each of thefe readers are divided into diftinct claffes.

There are ten diftinctions according to their manner of employing themfelves. 1, Deo, perform the Howm for themfelves, but not for others. They give charity; but do not receive it. They learn; but do not teach.

2, Mun. They perform not the Howm for themfelves, nor for others. They receive charity, and they teach.

 3, Devij,

3, Devij. These observe twelve rules. 1, Perform the Howm for themselves; 2, and for others; 3, they give charity; 4, they receive charity; 5, they learn; 6, they teach; 7, they bear injuries with patience; 8, they observe temperance of every kind; 9, they inflict on themselves the severest austerities; 10, they believe solely in their respective Bede; 11, they kill not any animal; 12, they do not consider any thing as belonging to themselves.

4, Raja. Perform the same offices as the Kehteree.

5, Biess. Perform the offices of the Biess.

6, Sooder. Do whatever appears advantageous to them.

7, Budaluck. Are mendicants who receive alms from any one.

8, Pusha. Are bound by no rules, and like brutes know not good from evil.

9, Milleetch are infidels; who follow the customs of the Milleetch before described.

10, Chundal. Are vile wretches and eat carrion.

The Kehteree

Were of two original tribes. First Soorujbunsee, who are regarded as descendants of the sun in the following genealogical order. At the creation of the world, Berincheh was produced by the will of Brahma. From whom proceeded Kushup. From whom proceeded the sun. From whom proceeded Biyoorwutchmunnoo. From whom proceeded Ikebako. Then from the nose of Ikebako issued a seed, from whence commenced generation. Of this tribe, three persons were universal monarchs. 1, Rajah Sooker; 2, Rajah Kehtwang; 3, Rajah Rig.

The

The ſecond tribe of Kehteree are called Soombunſee, or deſcendants of the moon, in the following order:

From Brahma was produced Attree, out of whoſe right eye iſſued the moon. The moon produced Mercury, with whom generation commenced. Of this tribe two perſons have been univerſal monarchs. 1, Rajah Jewdiſhter; 2, Rajah Sunnang.

There are now upwards of five hundred different tribes of Kehteree, fifty-two of whom are in eſteem, and twelve are better than the reſt. But at preſent there are ſcarcely any true Kehterees to be found, excepting a few who do not follow the profeſſion of arms.

Thoſe among them, who are ſoldiers, are called Rajpoots. There are near a thouſand different tribes of rajpoots; but I ſhall only mention the moſt famous, who are entertained in his majeſty's ſervice.

The Rahtore, of whom there are ſeveral tribes, are ſixty thouſand cavalry and two hundred thouſand infantry.

The Chowhen, of whom alſo there are ſeveral branches, viz. Soongera, Kehwera, Hada, and Nirya. Fifty thouſand cavalry and two hundred thouſand infantry.

The Punwar. Formerly this tribe was very numerous, and ſome of them were princes of Hindoſtan. At preſent they are twelve thouſand cavalry and ſixty thouſand infantry.

The Jadown. Fifty thouſand cavalry and two hundred thouſand infantry. The Bhatee and Jareeyeh, are branches of this tribe, as are alſo the Jenooheh, who are amongſt the Mewat Khanehzad *.

* Vol. I.

The Gehlote. Twenty thouſand cavalry and three hundred thouſand infantry. The Seeſowdyeh and the Chundrawut are branches of this tribe.

The Cutchwaheh. Twenty thouſand cavalry and one hundred thouſand infantry.

The Soolunkhee. Twenty thouſand cavalry and one hundred thouſand infantry.

The Toonoor, of which tribe there have been ſome kings; ten thouſand cavalry and five thouſand infantry.

The Birjoojir. Ten thouſand cavalry and forty thouſand infantry.

And each of theſe tribes now carry in their hands genealogical tables for ages back.

THE BIESS AND THE SOODER.

They are alſo divided into branches.

It is neither poſſible to deſcribe the extent of the learning of the Hindoos, nor all the branches of their tribes.

There is a branch of the Bieſs tribe, called in the Hindovee language Bunnick, or more commonly Bunnyeh, or grain merchants; and of theſe are no leſs than eighty-four tribes, among whom are mendicants, men of learning, artiſts, magicians, handicrafts, and ſuch expert jugglers, that their tricks paſs for miracles with the vulgar, and impoſe even upon thoſe who are wiſer.

OF

Of the Languages of Hindostan.

ALTHOUGH there are innumerable dialects ſpoken in the different provinces of Hindoſtan, yet for the moſt part they have ſuch an affinity, as to be generally comprehended. The only dialects that are merely local are thoſe of the following places: Dehly, Bengal, Multan, Marwar, Gujerat, Nanek, Sind, Kandahar, Balootch, Telinganeh, and Caſhmeer, the Mahratteh dialect, and that of the Afghans of Shal, which is a place between Sind and Cabul. To which may be added the jargon of the Bunmannis, or wild men of the woods.

The Birds and Beasts of Hindostan.

AFTER this ſummary deſcription of man, the nobleſt animal of the creation, it may not be improper to ſay ſomething of the birds and beaſts of Hindoſtan.

The Bunmannis is an animal of the monkey kind. His face has a near reſemblance to the human; he has no tail, and walks erect. The ſkin of his body is black, and ſlightly covered with hair. One of theſe animals was brought to his majeſty from Bengal. His actions were very aſtoniſhing.

Of the following animals here are great abundance. Elephants, panthers, tigers, lions, bears, wolves, dogs of various ſpecies, monkeys, ſyagoſhes, hyenas, jackals, foxes, otters, cats, white and yellow, and another kind that will fly for a ſhort diſtance.

The ſardole, although ſmaller than the dog, preys upon the larger wild beaſts.

Horſes. In conſequence of the encouragement given

given by his majesty, ſuch are now bred here as equal thoſe of Arabia and Perſia.

The rhinoceros is a ſurpriſing animal. He is almoſt twice as big as a buffalo, and looks like a horſe in armour. His feet and hoofs reſemble thoſe of the elephant, and his tail is like the buffalo's. His forehead is armed with a horn, and his hide is ſo hard that an arrow will not penetrate it. Of the hide are made breaſt-plates, targets, &c. If he meets with a horſe he attacks him and kills him with his horn.

The antelope has two very high horns, and is the moſt beautiful of the deer kind.

The muſk deer is bigger than the fox. His hair is very harſh; he is furniſhed with two tuſks, and has two protuberances in the place of horns. This animal is very common.

The Kataſs cow differs but little from the common cow, excepting in the tail, which is the Kataſs. The people of the country, where they are found, are very expert in joining the hairs of ſeveral tails, ſo as to make them appear of one length.

The civet cat is alſo found in this country.

BIRDS.

The ſharukh imitates the human voice in ſuch an aſtoniſhing manner that, if you do not ſee the bird, you cannot help being deceived.

The myneh is bigger than the ſharukh. The plumage is a dark brown with a little yellow under the tail. The bill and temples are alſo of this laſt colour. It ſpeaks as well as the ſharukh.

Parrots

Parrots are red, white, green, and a variety of other colours.

The koyil refembles the myneh, but is blacker and has red eyes, and a long tail. It is fabled to be enamoured with the rofe, in the fame manner as the nightingale.

The pepeeheh is fmaller and flenderer than the koyil, and the tail is fhorter. This bird fings moft enchantingly about the commencement of the rains, and efpecially during the night, when its lays caufe the old wounds of lovers to bleed afrefh. This bird is now alfo called *Peeyoo*, which, in the Shanfcrit language, fignifies *beloved*.

The baril has a green plumage, with white claws and red eyes, and is fmaller than the pigeon. He never alights upon the ground, and when he wants to drink, he defcends with a fmall twig in his claws, and floats himfelf upon the water.

The biya is about the fize of the fparrow, but yellow. He is very docile, exceedingly fagacious, and may be taught to fetch and carry grains of gold, with fafety. If carried a great diftance from his mafter, he will fly to him immediately upon hearing his voice.

And, from the encouragement given by his majefty, the animals of Turan, Iran, and Cafhmeer, as well game as others, have been tranfplanted here in aftonifhing abundance.

Of WEIGHTS and MEASURES.

The following are those which were used formerly.

Measures.

6 Zerrehs,	make one	Murreetch.
6 Murreetch,	make one	Khurdul.
3 Khurduls,	make one	Mustard seed.
8 Mustard seeds,	make one	Barley corn.
4 Barley corns,	make one	Rutty.
6 Rutties,	make one	Masheh.
4 Mashehs,	make one	Tank.
2 Tanks,	make one	Kowl.
2 Kowls,	make one	Towlcheh.
2 Towlchehs,	make one	Suckut.
2 Suckuts,	make one	Pul.
2 Puls,	make one	Palm.
2 Palms,	make one	Unjil.
2 Unjils,	make one	Manka.
2 Mankas,	make one	Purifteh.
4 Purifteh,	make one	Adhek.
4 Adheks,	make one	Dooroon.
2 Dooroons,	make one	Soorup.
2 Soorups,	make one	Khary.

Jewellers Weights.

20 Bifwehs,	make one	Rutty.
24 Rutties,	make one	Tank.

Formerly they reckoned $2\frac{1}{2}$ bifwahs to the barley-corn; but his majesty has fixed it at 2 bifwehs, or 10 barley-corns to the rutty. In order to prevent frauds, his majesty has farther commanded that the barley-corns shall be made of agate.

The following are the weights which the jewellers always keep ready for use. Bifweh, barley-corn, $\frac{1}{4}$, $\frac{1}{2}$ of a rutty;

a rutty; 1, 2, and 3 rutties; (the laſt being the fourth of a tank,) 1, 2, 5, 10, and 20 tanks, and $\frac{1}{2}$ a tank. And with theſe they compound any weight required.

For the royal uſes, there are alſo in agate from a biſweh to 140 tanks.

Banker's Weights.

$7\frac{1}{2}$ Barley-corns,	make one	Rutty.
8 Rutties,	make one	Maſheh.
12 Maſhehs,	make one	Tolecheh.

Formerly the rutty contained 6 barley-corns.

The following are the weights which the bankers always keep ready for uſe; $\frac{1}{2}$ rutty, 1 and 4 rutties; 1, 2, 4, and 6, maſhehs; 1, 2, 5, 10, 20, 50, 100, 200, and 500 tolechehs.

But in the royal exchequer there are much larger weights.

Other Ordinary Weights.

Formerly, in ſome parts of Hindoſtan, the ſeer contained 18 dams, in others 22 dams; and, in the commencement of the preſent reign, it conſiſted of 28 dams. Now it is fixed at 30 dams, each dam being 5 tanks.

Alſo, formerly in the ſale of coral and camphor, the dam was reckoned at $5\frac{1}{2}$ tanks; but now the price of thoſe articles has been reduced by valuing the dam at 5 tanks.

The following are the weights kept for ordinary uſes, $\frac{1}{8}$, $\frac{1}{4}$, and $\frac{1}{2}$ of a ſeer; 1, 2, 5, 10, 20, and 40 ſeers, or 1 mun, or maund.

The

The Learning of the Hindoos.

THE Hindoos have upwards of three hundred arts and ſciences. The author of this work having aſſociated himſelf intimately with the learned men among them, has heard and comprehended the various doctrines of each ſect and profeſſion. It is impoſſible, in a ſingle volume, to give a particular relation of ſuch a variety of ſubjects; but, for the ſatisfaction of thoſe who are uninformed, I ſhall ſketch out the rudiments of each art and ſcience, without offering any argument for or againſt them. This may prove a uſeful index to ſome future ingenious inveſtigator, who wiſhes to compare their doctrines with thoſe of Plato and Ariſtotle, the Soofees and the commentators on the ſacred text; and, who after having removed the prejudices which obſtruct religious enquiries, will ſeek out for proofs, rejecting the doubts of ignorance, but, at the ſame time, exerciſing his reaſon with caution.

Among the Hindoos there are nine ſects, eight of whom teach of the creation; and of a future ſtate; of the divine eſſence and attributes; of the order of the upper and the lower regions; of the forms of worſhip morality; and of political government.

The ninth ſect deny the exiſtence of a God; and believe neither a beginning nor an end.

All theſe ſects have many books, containing their reſpective creeds, and rules of conduct. They are generally written with an iron ſtyle, either on the leaf of the Taar, or the bark of the Tooz, in the ſame manner as was practiſed by the Greeks before the time of Ariſtotle. The Hindoos write from left to right. Although they now ſometimes write upon paper, yet they never uſe any bindings for their books, but keep them in ſeparate leaves.

3 Their

Their books contain ſublime doctrines and valuable inſtructions. How ſhall I proceed with my ſubject! perplexed every moment with worldly avocations; I am unable to expreſs myſelf, at the ſame time that I earneſtly deſire to be communicative. I know not if this diſtraction is the natural fault of my diſpoſition, or whether it be that truth is ſtruggling to reveal itſelf to me. If I was not thus embarraſſed, I would arrange the Hindoo philoſophy in the ſame manner as that of the Greeks. But I muſt conform to my circumſtances, and the compaſs of my book.

NAMES OF THE NINE ABOVE-MENTIONED SECTS.

1, Neyayek; 2, Beyſheekheh; 3, Beydantee; 4, Meymanſuck; 5, Sankh; 6, Patunjil; 7, Jien; 8, Boodh; 9, Naſtick.

The principles of each ſhall be hereafter particularized and explained.

The Brahmins, however, admit only of the ſix firſt doctrines, and call them *Khutdersun, six modes of knowledge*. The three laſt they conſider as heretical.

The Neyayek and the Beyſheekheh agree in many points, as do the Beydantee and the Meymanſuck. The Sankh and Patenjil have very inconſiderable difference.

THE SCIENCE OF NEEAIY.

GOTEM, the philoſopher, was the firſt who taught this ſcience. It compriſes theology, metaphyſics, mathematics, and logic. According to this doctrine there is only one God, who is incorporeal, neither begetting nor begotten, and free from all other defects belonging to human nature; he is the creator of the universe, himself being eternal, without beginning and without end, the preserver, the true uncompounded spirit. They say that he created a body, and then entered himself into that body, which body is Brahma; and in the same manner as a human body acts from its union with the soul, so does the body of Brahma act from its relation to the deity. And they maintain that this mixture of persons does not in the least defile the holiness of the deity. This opinion nearly corresponds with the faith of the Christians; and agrees with the tenets of the divines *, excepting that the Neyayeks deny the universe to have been from eternity.

They believe that God sent to the people of the earth, by the hands of Brahma, a book, which they call *Bede*, containing upwards of one hundred thousand ashlogues. An ashlogue comprises four cherruns, each of which contains from eight to twenty-six atchers, and an atcher is composed of one or two letters; if it consists of two, the last letter is mute. But in the Bede the cherrun never consists of more than twenty atchers. They also say that one of the celestial spirits, named Byass, divided this book into four sections, viz. 1, Rig; 2, Jejir; 3, Sam; 4, Atehrbun. One sect

* *Elahioun*, the *divines*. The Mahommedans mean by this word the second sect of philosophers, who admitted a first mover of all things, and one spiritual substance detached from every kind of matter. Guzali, in his book entitled *Mockedh*, says, that the philosophers of this second sect were Socrates, Plato, and Aristotle, the inventor of logic, or the art of reasoning, and who reduced science to method. This last, continues he, has pretended to refute Plato, Socrates, and all who went before him of that sect; but he has, nevertheless, supported many of their erroneous sentiments, although he seems in a manner to have abjured them: for he maintains the eternity of the world, which obliges us to reject his opinions as impious, as well as those of all the other philosophers who are called divine. We say the same thing of those amongst the Mussulmen who would philosophise after their manner, as Alfariabi and Ebn Sina (Alfarabius and Avicenna.) D'HERBELOT.

maintains

maintains that Brahma had four mouths, and that he delivered a ſection from each mouth.

Theſe four books are eſteemed to be of divine origin, and they believe that every Brahma who appears, delivers the ſame letter and word, without diminution or addition.

They ſay that God is the abſolute efficient cauſe; and that the actions of men are produced by two cauſes; namely, by the power of God, and by the power of Brahma. They believe that every action is good or bad, as it is deſcribed in the Bede. They believe that there is a hell and a paradiſe. Hell they call *Neruch*, and place it in the inferior regions. Paradiſe they call *Soorug*, and ſay it is in the upper regions. They do not believe either the puniſhments of hell, or the rewards of paradiſe to be everlaſting; but ſay that, according to the degree of wickedneſs committed, men will be puniſhed in hell, and afterwards come out from thence; and, aſſuming other forms, will go into paradiſe; when they will again change their forms, and return into the world; thus going and returning through the three different ſtates, till they have fully received the fruits of their good and bad actions: after which, ſtanding in no further need of either hell or paradiſe, they will become free from joy and ſorrow, in the manner that will be hereafter related.

They believe ſome parts of the univerſe to have exiſted from all eternity, and that others are created, the particulars whereof will be given hereafter.

They reckon eight divine attributes, which they call accidents. 1, *Geeyan*, omniſcience; 2, *Itcha*, omnipotence; 3, *Purreytun*, providence; 4, *Sunkehya*, unity; 5, *Purman*, immenſity, ſince God is believed to be every where; 6, *Purtukhtoo*, analyſis; 7, *Sunjoog*, union,

union, becauſe all things unite in the deity; 8, *Behbaug*, diviſion. Of theſe eight attributes, it is believed that the firſt ſix have been from all eternity, and the other two produced afterwards.

In this ſcience they make uſe of ſixteen predicaments, which compriſe every thing in the univerſe.

THE PREDICAMENTS.

1 Poormanoo, *perfect knowledge.*
2 Purmiey, *comprehension.*
3 Sunſhee, *doubt.*
4 Puryujen, *cause.*
5 Diſhtant, *inference.*
6 Sidhant, *positive proof.*
7 Iyou, *all the parts of a syllogism.*
8 Turrek, *negative proof.*
9 Nirnee, *faith founded on entire proof.*
10 Bad, *controversy with a view to knowledge.*
11 Jelp, *proposition of number.*
12 Betanda, *indirect proposition.*
13 Heetwahbas, *proposition founded on appearance.*
14 Chul, *false proposition.*
15 Jaut, *artful proposition.*
16 Negehriſtin, *proof obtained from the adversary's arguments.*

EXPLANATIONS OF THE PREDICAMENTS.

The first Predicament, POORMANOO,

Signifies true and perfect knowledge, and is of four kinds. 1, *Pertehj*, the five external ſenſes, together with *Mun*, which will be explained hereafter; 2, *Unman*, conjecture; 3, *Owpman*, analogy; 4, *Subdh*, tradition.

The

The second Predicament, PURMIEY, *comprehension, and which is of twelve kinds, viz.*

1 Atma, *soul of the universe.*
2 Sireer, *matter.*
3 Inderee, *sensation.*
4 Ir-th, *substance.*
5 Boodh, *human knowledge.*
6 Mun, *the mind.*
7 Perweert, *voluntary action.*
8 Dowkh, *the cause of prudence.*
9 Pereetbhow, *transmigration of the soul.*
10 Phul, *fruit, reward.*
11 Dookh, *pain.*
12 Apoorukh, *deliverance from pain.*

Atma, a ſubtle eſſence that pervades every part of the univerſe, and is the ſeat of knowledge. And this eſſence is of two kinds, *Jewa Atma,* that which belongs to animals and vegetables; and *Pur Atma,* omniſcience, which is the intelligence poſſeſſed ſolely by the only and eternal God. Beſides *Jewa Atma,* every body has a diſtinct ſpirit, by which it exerciſes the internal and external ſenſes, in conjunction with a third eſſence, called *Mun,* and which will be more particularly explained preſently.

Sireer, matter, and which is of two kinds, 1, *Jewnej,* a body produced by the copulation of male and female; 2, *Ajewnej,* a body which is not produced by theſe means. *Jewnej* is ſubdivided into two kinds, *Jerayooj* viviparous, and *Unduj* oviparus. *Ajewnej* is ſubdivided into four kinds, 1, *Parthu,* terrene; 2, *Apie,* aqueous; 3, *Teyjes,* igneous; 4, *Baiweeya,* aerial.

Indree is the five external ſenſes, together with *Mun,* the mind. This laſt is a ſubtle eſſence which unites more eſpecially with the heart, and upon it depend knowledge, thought, and recollection; but they in general

ral do not believe that this ſenſe pervades the whole body like *Atma*. But, according to the tenets of the *Meymansa*, it is made to be in every part of the body.

Ir-th, ſubſtance, is of ſeven kinds, viz. 1, *Dirb*, ſubſtance in general; 2, *Goon*, ſenſible qualities; 3, *Kurrum*, motion; 4, *Samanee*, ſeparable accident; 5, *Bysekh*, foreign accident; 6, *Sumwaiy*, relation and correllation; 7, *Abhow*, privation.

Dirb, ſubſtance in general, which they conſider as having exiſted from all eternity; but they ſay that, in the four elements, there is an indiviſible particle. The ſubſtances are *Atma*, *Mun*, *Akass*, *the four elements*, *Kal*, time, and *Dessa*. *Atma* and *Mun* have been explained. The *Akass*, ether, is a ſubtle matter which pervades the univerſe, and is the medium of ſound. In the deſcription of the four elements they agree with the Greeks, only that they make air to be the uppermoſt. *Kal*, time, they alſo make a ſubtle matter pervading the univerſe. *Dessa* is a ſide or quarter of the univerſe, which they conſider as being every where. *Goon* is an accident, of which there are ſix kinds; *Kurrum*, motion and progreſſion, of which there are five kinds; 1, circular; 2, upwards; 3, downwards; 4, contraction; 5, expanſion, which laſt they call *Hadit*. *Saman* literally ſignifies whole, entire. This whole they conſider as the compound of ſubſtance and accident. They ſay that nature is from all eternity, and that it is founded on ſubſtance, accident, and motion, which three collectively they term *Jaut Saman*, or inſeparable accident. The ſeparable accident, or *Owpareh Saman*, they ſay is not from all eternity, but may happen to any thing. *Bysekh* is that whoſe exiſtence depends upon ſomething entirely diſtinct from its own nature; and this accident can only proceed from the eternal eſſence. *Sumwaiy* is the connection of five things with their reſpective relatives, viz. 1, The relation between motion and

and its cause; 2, The relation between the substance and the accident; 3, The relation between the materials of which a thing is formed, and the thing itself, as thread and cloth; 4, The relation between the whole and its component parts; 5, The relation between the eternal and other substances; and this relation they consider as having existed from all eternity. They also believe that union is of three kinds, 1, In the manner that has been related; 2, That produced by the union of two substances, which is *Sunjoog*, already mentioned among the attributes; and of this kind of union, they say, there are many. 3, The union of spirit with matter, as the soul with the body. This kind they call *Sooroop*.

Abhow, privation depending upon something foreign, and it is of two kinds, 1, *Sunsirgabhow*, the privation of any one thing. 2, *Anewneeabhow*, the separation of two things, as time and place. *Sunsirgabhow*, is subdivided into three kinds, 1, *Paragabhow*, a negative past; 2, *Perdehnsabhow*, a compound negative; 3, *Attenabhow*, a negative, that does not happen in one place, although it be at one time, as for example, Zied is present on the seashore, and is not in the desert.

The other five sensible qualities are called *Goon*, and are of twenty-four kinds; 1, *Roop*, colour. They reckon five original colours; red, yellow, blue, black, and white; 2, *Russ*, the taste; 3, *Gund*, the smell; 4, *Soopress*, the touch; 5, *Sunkehya*, the order of numerals, and which is after three ways; either one by itself, or two together, or more numbers together; 6, *Purman*, quantity, and which is of four kinds. *Un*, the indivisible particle; 2, *Hirsoo*, the quantity of two particles, which they also call *Denook*; 3, *Deerug*, the quantity of three particles and upwards; 4, *Meht*, the quantity of the akass and the other elements; 7, *Poortuckhtoo*, discrimination, and this accident is entire in its own nature. It is after three ways, as if you

you were to ſay, this one is not like that one; or theſe two are not like thoſe two; or theſe three are not like thoſe three or more; 8, *Sunjoog*, the union of two eternal ſubſtances, which unite together from their mutual motion. But they do not conſider this union to be the ſame as that which they call *Sumwaiy*, relation and correllation; 9, *Behbaug*, diviſion; 10, *Purtoo*, diſtance of time or place; 11, *Apurttoo*, nearneſs of time or place; 12, *Boodh*, human reaſon; 13, *Sookh*, eaſe; 14, *Dookh*, pain; 15, *Itcha*, deſire, will; 16, *Dooweekh*, anger; 17, *Purreytun*, providence; 18, *Gowrtoo*, gravity; 19, *Durwuttoo*, progreſſive motion; 20, *Sunneyah*, fluidity; 21, *Sunskhar*, is an accident whoſe occurrence does not make any alteration in the original ſtate of the ſubſtance, and it is of three kinds; 1, *Beyg*, an accident which is produced by motion, and which becomes the cauſe; as the motion of the arrow after it has left the bow. They include the ſecond motion in the firſt, and certainly this accident is occaſioned by that, and the motion of the arrow becomes the ſecond cauſe; 2, *Bhawna*, is particularly applied to reaſon, being the recollection of ſomething forgotten; and ſince knowledge cannot exiſt without cauſe, action, and effect, they therefore make uſe of this accident, either when the recollection is aſſiſted by ſeeing any thing like what had been forgotten, as when any incidental ſearch after ſomething elſe, whoſe connection with what was forgotten brings it again to memory; 3, *Sootithaig* is that which, after having been twiſted or bent, becomes ſtraight again; or that which from being bent is made ſtraight, and afterwards returns to its primitive ſtate, (action and reaction): 22, *Dherem*, happy conſciouſneſs; 23, *Adherem*, unhappy conſciouſneſs. The followers of this doctrine ſay that men, by means of theſe two laſt accidents, tranſmigrate into different forms, and according to their good or evil deeds are rewarded with happineſs, or puniſhed with ſorrow, 24, *Subd*, ſound.

Divisions of the Accidents.

Accidents of the rational Sense.

1 Boodh.
2 Sookh.
3 Dookh.
4 Itcha.
5 Dooweekh.
6 Pureyten.
7 Dehrem.
8 Adherem.
9 Bhawna.
10 Sunſkar.
11 Sunkehya.
12 Purman.
13 Poortukhtoo.
14 Sunjoog.
15 Behbaug.

The firſt nine belong eſpecially to this ſenſe, being never ſeparated from its eſſence.

Accidents belonging to the Akass.

1 Sunkehya.
2 Poortukhtoo.
3 Sunjoog.
4 Behbaug.
5 Subd.

The laſt belongs eſpecially to the akaſs, being never ſeparated from its eſſence.

Accidents of Kal and Dessa.

1 Sunkehya.
2 Poortukhtoo.
3 Sunjoog.
4 Behbaug.

Accidents of Mun.

1 Sunkehya.
2 Poortukhtoo.
3 Sunjoog.
4 Behbaug.
5 Pertoo.
6 Apertoo.
7 Biyg.
8 Sunſkar.

Accidents of Bad.

1 Sooperſs.
2 Sunkehya.
3 Purman.
4 Poortukhtoo.
5 Sunjoog.
6 Behbaug.
7 Pertoo.

7 Pertoo.
8 Apertoo.
9 Durwuttoo.
10 Biyg.
11 Sunſkar.

Accidents of Fire.

1 Roop.
2 Sooperſs.
3 Sunkehya.
4 Purman.
5 Poortukhtoo.
6 Sunjoog.
7 Behbaug.
8 Pertoo.
9 Apertoo.
10 Gowrtoo.
11 Durwuttoo.
12 Suneyeh.
13 Sunſkar.
14 Kurrum.

Sooperss and *Kurrum* belong eſpecially to fire, being never ſeparated from its eſſence.

Accidents of Water.

1 Roop.
2 Ruſs.
3 Sooperſs.
4 Sunkehya.
5 Purman.
6 Poortukhtoo.
7 Sunjoog.
8 Behbaug.
9 Pertoo.
10 Apertoo.
11 Gowrtoo.
12 Durwuttoo.
13 Suneyeh.
14 Sookh.
15 Sunſkar.

Suneyeh, Kurrum, and Sooperſs, are eſpecial to water, being never ſeparated from its eſſence.

There are many more diviſions of the accidents, but what have been given are ſufficient for my purpoſe. I ſhall now proceed to explain the fifth diviſion of the predicament *Purmiey*.

Boodh. Although this has already been mentioned under the ſecond diviſion of Ir-th, yet it is neceſſary to ſay ſomething more on the ſubject in this place.

Boodh,

Boodh, human knowledge, they divide into two kinds: 1. *Unnebhow*, conjecture or opinion, which is obtained by the means of *Itcha*, or the will; 2. *Soomerut*, is that which having been learnt and forgotten, is recollected through the medium of *Bhonwa*. Again Unnebhow is of two kinds; that which is certain, and that of which there is some doubt. This last is subdivided into three kinds: 1. *Sunshee*, mixed with doubt; 2. *Beeparjee*, mistaking; 3. *Turrek*, the eighth predicament, which will be explained in its proper place.

Mun, already mentioned among the substances, has the following divisions; *Purweert*, the actions of *Mun*, by means of the tongue, and other members, in good and bad deeds. They say that external actions require four things: 1. Knowledge. 2. Inclination. 3. Determination. 4. Motion.

Dookh, is the cause of *Pureytun*, and is of three kinds: 1. *Rakh*, desire, will. 2. *Dooweekh*, anger. 3. *Mowh*, believing that to exist which does not exist.

Pereetbhow, is living after death, and the rational sense entering the body, and dying after living, and breaking the relations between body and soul after the union.

Phul, the fruit, or reward, or punishment of *Dehrem*, or *Adherem*.

Dookh, pain, is the contrary of *Sookh*, ease, happiness. They say that all the comforts of this life are only sorrow, and therefore do not make any account of *Sookh*.

Apoorukh, the deliverance from one pain by such means as will not produce another. They say, there are twenty-one kinds of pain or sorrow; viz. the six senses

ſenſes and their ſix objects, the ſix intelligences which form the ſenſes, and the body, which is the ſtorehouſe of evils, and joy, according to the vulgar opinion; but which, in reality, is ſorrow and abſolute pain. *Doohh* implies whatever is contrary to our inclination, which, if it takes any effect, cauſes uneaſineſs. When a perſon arrives at ſuch a degree of perfection as entirely deſtroys all the twenty-one things above-mentioned, that ſtate is called *Muckut*, when the ſoul becomes perfectly inſenſible, quits its connexion with the body, and never again viſits either paradiſe or hell; becauſe that all the cauſes of ſorrow ariſe from the union of the ſoul with the body. This union of the ſoul with the body they call *Jennum*, birth, and it is produced by *Dehrem*, or *Adherem*. After the union of body and ſoul takes place, the perſon receives in this life the reward of his virtues and the puniſhment of his vices, beſtowed or inflicted in return for *Kurrum*, which in this place ſignifies the performance of any action, whether it be good or bad, joyful or ſorrowful. *Kurrum* is produced by *Jeytun*, which has the ſame ſignification *Pureytun* and *Purweert*, voluntary action, in conſequence of *Rakh*, deſire. *Rakh* is produced by *Meethageeyan*, falſe conception. Through the means of *Bhowna*, recollection, and *Sunskar*, reflection, the ignorant obtain knowledge. Knowledge proceeds from the operations of the ſoul and body, and the proper uſe of good means; knowledge produces worthy reflections: then ſenſual knowledge vaniſhes, true knowledge diſcovers itſelf, and there is an end of tranſmigration.

Some ſay that when, through the means of reaſon, man is arrived at the higheſt degree of perfection, there is an end of miſcomprehenſion, ignorance, deſire, and anger. *Purweert*, voluntary action, ceaſes, and in conſequence, there is an end of *Jennum*, or birth; and from a ceſſation of *Jennum*, there is an end of pain and ſorrow; and everlaſting *Muckut* enſues.

Another

Another feſt ſay, that when the ſtate of everlaſting knowledge is obtained, *Meet-hageeyan* falſe conception, ceaſes, which deſtroys *Itcha*, which deſtroys *Pureytun*, which deſtroys *Kurrum*. The deſtruction of *Kurrum* is followed by that of *Dehrem* and *Adherem*, which puts an end to *Jennum*, and its conſequence *Dookh*.

But the ſtrict followers of the Neeaiy doctrine ſay, that when the elementary body obtains the true light, knowledge alſo ceaſes. And they ſay that this degree of perfection is obtained through the means of three things, *Shirwun*, *Munnun*, and *Nidhassen*. 1. *Shirwun*, hearing and perfectly comprehending the Bedes, and the traditions of the righteous, which cannot be effected without the guidance of one who hath travelled that road. 2. *Munnun*, giving the mind to the performance of whatever is eſtabliſhed by the divine book, and by the doctrines of the righteous, ſo as to have implicit faith in their proofs and arguments. Another ſect maintain that man, after having obtained the perfection above deſcribed, is continually contemplating the ſtate of the ſoul, independent of every thing elſe. 3. *Nidhassen* is that ſtate which is produced by the contemplation and inveſtigation of divine things to ſuch an intenſe degree, that it becomes quite habitual, occupying every thought and governing every action.

Another ſect ſay, that the contemplation of the ſoul will be of ſuch continuance, that the thread will never be broken.

The followers of the Neeaiy believe in *Gaiybeyoh*, which is this: When the light of knowledge ſhines upon a righteous perſon, he becomes acquainted with things paſt and preſent concerning himſelf, knows how many tranſmigrations he muſt undergo; and if he wiſhes them to paſs quickly, the Almighty endows him with

with ſuch power, that he is enabled to perform the various changes in a ſhort ſpace of time, and without paſſing into *Mirtlogue*, but enters into immortal bliſs inſtantly upon quitting the elementary body. They alſo ſay that all mankind will ultimately arrive at the ſtate of *Muckut*. Although they do not allow of any beginning of the world, yet they believe that there will be an end of procreation.

The Third Predicament, SUNSHEE,

Mixed with doubt, and which they make to be of three kinds: 1. That which is produced from beholding compound accidents; as ſeeing ſomething at a diſtance without being able to determine whether it be a tree or a man. 2. When a thing is diſcovered by ſome particular mark; but its age, ſubſtance, and accident, are not known. 3. That doubt which occurs in diſcourſe, as when two learned men diſpute by poſitive or negative arguments.

The Fourth Predicament, PURYUJEN,

The cauſes of which they reckon only three. 1. The efficient cauſe, which they call *Nimutkaren*. 2. The material cauſe, *Sumwaiykaren*. 3. The external or apparent cauſe, *Asmewaiykaren*.—They call the cauſe *Karen*, the effect *Karidj*, and the final cauſe *Samgurree*. The detail is to be found in Hindovee books, where they treat of the firſt predicament.

The Fifth Predicament, DISHTANT,

Inference, or mentioning the place relative to the neceſſity.

The Sixth Predicament, SIDHANT,

Enlightened by proofs.

The Seventh Predicament, IYOU,

Whatever is neceſſary for forming a ſyllogiſm, which

are five, viz. 1. *Pertignya*. 2. *Heeyut*. 3. *Oodakurren*. 4. *Apnee*. 5. *Nigmun*.

1. *Pertignya*, or uttering the proposition; as if you were to say, *there is fire in this mountain*.

2. *Heeyut*, proof by inference; as smoke issuing from the mountain proves fire to be there also. There are three kinds of inference; 1. Positive inference, which they call *Keylewenwee*. 2. Negative inference, *Keywulbitreekee*. 3. Both positive and negative, *Unneweebitreekee*. And they also make five things necessary under this last head to complete the syllogism, viz. *Putchsuttoo*, *Suppitcheesuttoo*, *Beputchasuttoo*, *Abadhpesheetoo*, *Assulpurrutputchtoo*. The first, *Putchsuttoo*, the person who knows the proof, knowing it to be an absolute consequence: 2. *Suppitcheesuttoo*, knowing the place and the necessary consequence; as the kitchen where there are smoke and fire. 3. *Beputchasuttoo*, knowing that in whatever place there is not what is required, there can neither be the consequence; as water, in which there is neither smoke nor fire. 4. *Abadhpesheetoo*, ignorance of the privation of what is required. 5. *Assulpurrutputchtoo*, an appearance resembling what is sought.

3. *Oodakurren*, illustration of the effect.

4. *Apnee*, shewing the cause in the place required.

5. *Nigmun*, the conclusion of a syllogism. Although this is the primary object, yet being obtained by the afore-mentioned means, it is therefore the fifth, by way of conclusion of a syllogism.

The Eighth Predicament, TURREK,

Negative proof. Thus he says to him who denies the

the exiſtence of fire, " if it were ſo, there could not be any ſmoke; that being the effect of fire."

The Ninth Predicament, NIRNEE,

Certain belief founded on proof.

The Tenth Predicament, BAD,

True controverſy, with a view to knowledge.

The Eleventh Predicament, JELP,

Propoſition of number.

The Twelfth Predicament, BEYTANDA,

Indirect propoſition.

The Thirteenth Predicament, HEETWABHAS,

A propoſition founded on appearance, and is of five kinds.

The Fourteenth Predicament, CHUL,

Falſe propoſition.

The Fifteenth Predicament, JAUT,

Giving an uſeleſs anſwer of a bad tendency, but which, through artifice in the delivery, ſucceeds; and this they reckon of twenty-four kinds.

The Sixteenth Predicament, NEGRESTAN,

Is when the adverſary is convicted by his own words; and this they reckon of twenty-two kinds.

Of all theſe ſixteen predicaments, there are various diviſions and explanations.

They believe that whoſoever is perfect in the knowledge and practice of theſe ſixteen predicaments, will immediately arrive at the ſtate of *Muckut.* They ſay that the attainment of this excellence depends on three things,

things, 1. *Owdies*, the knowledge of the names of these sixteen predicaments, and remembering them. 2. *Lutchin*, knowing the true meaning thereof. 3. *Pureytcha*, the practice thereof.

The followers of this doctrine, although they deny that the universe had any beginning, yet believe in its dissolution, which they call *Purlie*. This they say is of two kinds; first, *Kundpurlie*, when a Brahma will arrive at the state of *Muckut*. At this time there will be left only *Dehrem*, *Adherem*, *Bhawana*, *Sunskar* and *Kurrum*. And in every wonderful hundred years, of which something has been said already*, Brahma will arrive at their state. The second at the death of Brahma, when all created beings will be destroyed. The first cause of this dissolution, will be the divine will, at the expiration of an appointed time. At that period, by the will of the Most High, *Dehrem* and *Adherem* will be destroyed; and the indivisible particle will get into motion, whereby *Bhaug* (separation) will become complete, and *Sunjoog* (union) will be destroyed.— Earth, fire, air, and water, will be destroyed one after the other, in the order now mentioned. Thus there will be an end of all created things; and the soul will be in the state of *Muckut*. This dissolution they call *Mohapurlie*.

One sect reckons four dissolutions. Two as now described. At the third there will be an end of virtue, and this they say will be at the end of every four jowgs. The fourth is the dissolution of each particular thing; as first when the spirit *Mun* separates from the soul, which is its *Purlie*. Then the dissolution of the union between the body and the soul, and which is its *Purlie*.

* Vol. 1st.

They call the creation of the world, after its diſſolution, *Seriſhte*, and ſay that by the will of God, after the expiration of a long period, *Dehrem* and *Adherem* will come into action, and the indiviſible particle will obtain motion. Firſt there will be an union of two atoms, which they call *Deenook*, which will be joined by a third atom, which will produce a good mixture called *Tereeſhnook*, and the union of the fourth atom they call *Chutternook*. And thus the union will increaſe gradually, and produce a number of forms; exiſtence changing out of non-exiſtence in the following order, contrary to what they were at firſt: Air, Fire, Water, Earth, Brahma, Biſhen, Mahadeo. But there will not be any viſible appearance of theſe glorious perſons in their own forms, although they will aſſume various others, and beſtow bleſſings upon mankind. From air will be produced aerial bodies, who will inhabit *Baiylogue*, which is the higheſt region. From this element will alſo be produced the touch, wind, and the ſoul, figuratively called *Purran*, and which they reckon to be of five kinds, as will be deſcribed hereafter. From fire will be produced fiery bodies, whoſe ſeat will be *Aditlogue*, which is the region that the ſun travels through; and from this element will alſo proceed ſight, and different degrees of heat. From water will be produced aqueous bodies, whoſe ſeat is in the *Wurrenlogue*. It will alſo produce the taſte, ſeas, and rivers, ſnow, ice, and hail. The region of *Wurrenlogue* they place near the mountain of *Summier*. From earth will be produced earthly bodies, and the ſenſe of ſmelling, together with metals, minerals, plants, and animals. Brahma will firſt create bodies by his own power, without the medium of generation; and in this place they give a wonderful detail.

They ſay that there is one eternal will of God, which creates, and another which deſtroys. The creative will they

they call *Chickeerkha*, and the deſtructive will, *Sunjeerkha*.

Of their Books.

They reckon five gradations: 1. *Sooter*, which is a kind of treatiſe or epitome; 2. *Bhakey*, which is ſomewhat fuller; 3. *Bartick*, more comprehenſive than the former; 4. *Teeka*, which is a commentary on the laſt; 5. *Nebundeh*, is the complete ſyſtem of any ſcience. Others make twelve, inſtead of five degrees. The five aforeſaid; 6. *Biert*, which is a conciſe explanation of the *Sooter; Neerookt*, a detail of the *Subd*, or traditions. They have alſo two modes of writing, one when the letter is not accented, which they call *Dhoon;* and the other when the letter is accented, and which is called *Burren* and *Atcher:* a number of *Atchers* form a *Pud* (word), a number of *Puds* form a *Bakia* (ſentence), and ſeveral *Bakias* make a *Sooter;* a number of *Sooters* make a *Purkurren;* a number of *Purkurrens* make an *Ahinek*, and a number of *Ahineks* make an *Adehya* or *Shaster*. In ſome books, when there is any doubt of the ſignification of a *Pud*, it is alſo explained in the *Shaster*. 8. *Purkurren*, a treatiſe upon one or two caſes; 9. *Ahinek*, is an abridgment that can be read in a day; 10. *Purshisht*, is a treatiſe on any particular ſcience; 11. *Puddhet*, is an illuſtration of the doctrines of the ſix ſects properly arranged; 12. *Sungreh*, treats of the doctrines of the other three ſects.

Theſe books are not confined to the followers of *Neeaiy*. A note or common place book, they call *Birjeah*. In the place of chapters and ſections they make uſe of the following words, *Unk, Utchwass, Surrug, Bisram, Oollass, Puttull, Adeys, Adheen, Tunter*.

The ſcience of *Neeaiy* is compriſed in five *Adehyas;* 1. is a detail of the *Padaruts*, and the praiſes due to each; 2. treats of the *Purmans;* 3. on the firſt ſix kinds

 of

of *Purmiey*; 4. on the remaining kinds of *Purmiey*; 5. on *Jaut* and *Negristan*.

The SCIENCE of BEYSHEEKHEK.

Although Konad taught Beyſheekhek before Gotem introduced Neeaiy, yet as the latter is more comprehenſive, and more generally followed, I have treated of it firſt.

Konad, the philoſopher, was the inventor of Beyſheekhek. It agrees with Neeaiy in ſome points, and differs in others.

The followers of Beyſheekhek, in the place of ſixteen predicaments, make uſe of *Dirb*, *Goon*, *Kurrum*, *Saman*, *Byseekh*, *Sumwaiy*, and *Abhow*.

Purmanoo (perfect knowledge) they divide only into *Pertehj* and *Atma*.

Of the accidents of heat produced by the ſun or fire, they reckon colour, taſte, ſmell, and touch. To theſe four accidents they give the general term *Pakudj*. The Neeayicks maintain that corporeal ſubſtance does not change its ſtate by maturity or immaturity; but theſe ſay that the corporeal particles are ſeparated, and reunited by the divine power. The Neeayicks ſay that *Sumwaiy* (ſimilitude) is diſtinguiſhed by the eye; whilſt Konad aſſerts it to be only conjecture, and parity of reaſoning.

THE

The SCIENCE of MEYMANSA.

This was invented by Jymin, before either Neeaiy or Beysheekhek. He presided over three other sages, Komarul Bhutt, Purbhaker Gooroo, and Morar Missер. It is said by some, that this sect are atheists; and others pretend that they admit a God, but deny a creator, believing all things to be produced by Dehrem and Adherem. But from strict enquiry, and close intimacy with the learned followers of this sect, it evidently appears, that they agree with the two foregoing respecting the Deity; but being sensible of human ignorance, they are silent on the subject, and confine their doctrine to sensible actions. But the ignorance and malice of the world attribute this silence to a denial of the existence of a Supreme Being.

The purmans (quantities), which the Neeayicks use among the accidents for explaining the divine nature, these do not apply to that purpose. They do not, indeed, believe Brahma, Bishen, and Mahadeo to be emanations of the Deity; but say they are human beings, who, through their righteousness, attain to this degree of perfection. They believe most of the effects attributed to the Dewtahs, to be nothing more than magick, and think it to be produced by repeating certain words.

They believe the universe and the elements to be without beginning, and without end. They believe that bodies are only a compound of atoms, and not produced from one substance. They believe *Mun*, like *Atma*, to be every where; and say that men are free agents. They teach of the different degrees of hell and paradise, the transmigration of the soul, and *Muckut*; but deny *Kundpurlie*. They believe Muckut to be produced by the union of knowledge and action.

action. They say that in this state the soul will perpetually enjoy sublime knowledge, and perfect ease.

They make air to be the medium of sound, whereas the Neeayicks attribute this property to the akass.

Sumwaiy (relation) they make to be the second of the three persons (Bishen), eternal from eternity, and accidental from accident; and believe it to be different in every instance.

BHUTT *and* MISSER *use the ten following Predicaments*,

1 Derb.	6 Abhow.
2. Goon.	7 Bysheeshtee.
3 Kurrum.	8 Shuckt.
4 Saman.	9 Sadershee.
5 Tadatmiey.	10 Sunkehya.

Bysheeshtee, the arrival at privation, which they consider as a distinct state; and this is what the Neeayicks call *Sooroop* and *Subdh*, or the dissolution of the accidents.

Shuckt is a property dependent upon something else, and which is invisible. As the property of burning, which is in fire; and the property of water to quench thirst. This they say is twofold; one essential, as has been described; and accidental, which is produced by magick, and such means. But the Neeayicks consider them as merely essential; the property of burning and quenching being in fire, and in water.

Sadershee, a common property between two things.

Sunkehya (number), they do not consider as an accident, but make it a distinct substance.

Purbaker

Purbaker Gooroo reckons only nine predicaments, rejecting *Abhow*, privation.

Komarul Bhutt reckons eleven predicaments; the first nine the same as the Neeayicks, to which he adds *Undkhar*, darkness.—The Neeayicks say that darkness is nothing but the absence of light; but these account it a distinct substance, which spreads its own shade over every thing; and they consider the following to be the accidents of darkness; colour, quantity, divisibility, union, separation, distance, proximity. The 11th *Subdh*, (traditions), these consider to be everlasting and universal. The forms of speech they consider as substances, and excepting *Roop* (colour) give them all the other twenty-one accidents.

Purbaker Gooroo says, that *Subdh* is not a substance, but an accident from all eternity.

Bhutt asserts that knowledge is attained by conjecture; whilst Gooroo says, that by means of knowledge, conjecture is formed, like a lamp, which being lighted, makes itself, as well as other objects, visible. Mirar Misser agrees with the Neeayicks, that knowledge is obtained through the means of *Mun*; but he denies the existence of the two first accidents of *Purmanoo*.

The Neeayicks say, that gold is produced from fire; and the Meymensucks, that it is from earth. *Kal*, time, according to the Neeayicks, is comprehended by conjecture; but these say that it is discovered by the senses. Of the accidents, these make colour to have been from all eternity; and they consider the five colours as only one accident.

General property, they say, is inherent in the substance. *Beyg*, cause of motion, and *Sunskar*, repulsive quality,

quality, they do not admit, but attribute their actions to *Kurrum*, motion.

Bhutt and Miffer ufe fix divifions of *Purmanoo* (perfect knowledge), four of which have been mentioned in Neeaiy; they reckon feven fenfes. The feventh is *Tamisindree*, the perception of darknefs. They deny pofitive and negative inference. Gooroo neither admits of falfe conception. In *Sunshee*, (doubt), and *Beyperjee*, (miftake), they confider two perfect modes of knowledge. The perception of air, which the Neeayicks attribute to conjecture, thefe afcribe to the touch. The 5th, *Irt-hapute*, is advancing the caufe, and requiring the effect. The 6th, *Unpelubdeh*, the ignorance of things. They fay that ignorance is the want of knowledge. But Miffer agrees with the Neeayicks, that this want of knowledge proceeds from defect in the fenfes.

They fay that good and evil depend upon actions, which they reckon of two kinds. *Bhutt*, an action which produces good; and *Nickeddeh*, that which produces evil. The firft is again of four kinds: 1. *Nit*, a duty, whofe continual performance is indifpenfible, and the omiffion bad. 2. *Neemith*, an indifpenfible duty to be performed at a particular feafon; fuch as the ceremonies neceffary to be performed at eclipfes of the fun and moon. 3. *Kamee*, an action which produces the defired effect. 4. *Perayishcht*, expiation of a crime. The firft fix of the nine fects agree in the neceffity of expiating a crime.

The four tribes, following this doctrine, have their refpective ceremonies. But the general doctrine of *Meymansa* is comprifed in twelve *Adheyas*, containing as follows:

1. Of predicaments and purmanoo. 2. Of actions; and

and explanations of many dubious points in the Bede. 3. A ſummary of thoſe great duties, the fruits of which are explained in the Bede; and alſo of the leſſer duties which are dependent on them. 4. On the two uſes for which wealth is acquired, for ſenſual gratification, and for burnt ſacrifice. 5. Rules of conduct. 6. The rewards for good, and puniſhments for bad actions. 7. A particular relation of what is treated ſummarily in the Bede. 8. Illuſtration of ſome points that have been treated ſummarily. 9. Explanation of the incantation that is made in one of the three names; what other name may be ſubſtituted for it; and the ceremonies to be obſerved. 10. Some particulars which cannot be treated ſummarily. 11. Explanation of one good action, which may produce two good effects. 12. Explanation of an action which has but one object.

THE SCIENCE OF BEYDANT.

This doctrine was firſt taught by Byaſs the philoſopher, one of the nine perſons whom the Hindoos ſay are immortal. The following are their names: 1. Loomus; 2. Makiendie; 3. Byaſs; 4. Aſhootaman; 5. Bul; 6. Hunwent; 7. Bibeekhen; 8. Kirpacharij; 9. Purriſſram. Of theſe nine immortal perſons they relate wonderful ſtories.

The followers of this doctrine agree with Bhutt in the pudaruts, purmans, &c. But although they believe in hell, paradiſe, and other viciſſitudes, yet they ſay they are only ideal.

They ſay, that, excepting the Deity, nothing exiſts; the univerſe being only an appearance, without any reality, juſt as a man in a dream ſees imaginary objects, and in that ſtate experiences ideal pleaſure and pain.

So

So that life is nothing but a dream, there being only one resplendent light, which assumes different appearances.

In this science there are six things: 1. Brimmah; 2. Issur; 3. Jeewa; 4. Geeyan; 5. Sumbedeh; 6. Birbede.

The first, *Brimmah*, is God, the sole bestower of justice. Omniscience, Omnipresence, and Rest, which they call *Anund*, are the fountain of his essence They believe Brimmah to be without beginning and without end; and the other five are from eternity.

To *Geeyan* (knowledge) they ascribe two powers; *Pitchutsuckut*, the external, and *Auwerunsuckut*, the internal power of knowledge.

Sumbedeh is the exercise of the external sense of knowledge.

Birbede, the cessation of *Sumbedeh*. *Geeyan*, when it employs *Pitchutsuckut*, is called *Maia;* and *Abedeeya*, when it acts by the means of *Auwerunsuckut*. The divine essence, upon its union with *Maia*, becomes manifest, and is then called *Issur;* and it is not defiled by this union. When the Deity unites with *Abedeeya*, it is called *Jew* and *Jewatma*. Then it retires behind the veil of secrecy, without suffering any impurity. Some among this sect say, that *Abedeeya* is uncompounded, not making any account of *Jew;* and deny that any one has yet arrived at the state of *Muckut*. Others again, and who are numerous, admit both *Jew* and *Muckut*. It is certain that many virtuous men have arrived at this state, which is throwing off *Ageeyan* by the light of sublime knowledge. *Ageeyan* has three accidents; 1. *Sut*, from whence proceed virtue, knowledge, ease, and such like; 2. *Ruj*, from whence proceed desire, sorrow, joy, and such like; 3. *Tum*, from whence proceed anger, ignorance, indolence, and such

ſuch like. When *Issur* unites with *Ruj*, it is called *Brahma*, who is the creator. When it unites with *Sut*, it is called *Bishen*, the preſerver. When it unites with *Tum*, it is called *Mahadeo*, the deſtroyer.

The progreſſion of the creation is from theſe three accidents; and all theſe incorporeal beings are viſible, through the medium of *Ageeyan*.

They agree with the Neeayicks in making five elements; but each of theſe they divide into two kinds: 1. *Sochum*, an inviſible particle, and in that ſtate it is called *Apuncheekeert*, when *Tum* is prevalent. 2. *Lithowl*, a viſible particle, in which ſtate it is called *Puncheekeert*, and is produced by the prevalence of *Ruj*, and a great prevalence of *Ruj* is called *Akass*. They reckon ſound an accident of the *Akass*. By an exceſs of *Ruj*, air is alſo produced, to which they give two accidents, *Subdh* and *Sooperss*. From *Sut* is produced fire, to which they give three accidents, *Subdh*, *Sooperss*, and *Roop*. From an exceſs of *Sut* and *Ruj* is produced water, to which they give four accidents; the three laſt mentioned, and *Russ*. From the exceſs of *Tum* is produced earth, to which they give five accidents, the four laſt mentioned, and *Gundh*.

They ſay that the ſenſe of hearing is produced from the *Akass*; the touch from air; the ſight from fire; the taſte from water; the ſmell from earth. And theſe five ſenſes are occaſioned by the power of *Sut*. Theſe five ſenſes they call *Geeyan Indree*. The *Akass* produces *Bak*, ſpeech; air produces *Ban*, the power of the arms; fire *Pad*, the power of the feet; water *Paiey*, the power of voiding the excrement; earth *Opusteh*, the power of urining. And whoever has the full exerciſe of theſe functions, they call *Kurrum Indree*.

By the exceſs of *Sut* is produced a ſubtle eſſence, called

called *Untahkurrum*, which from its four ſtates has four names: 1. when *Sut* is prevalent, and there is a deſire of deſcriminating and enquiry, it is called *Chit*; 2. when *Ruj* is prevalent, from whence doubt ariſes, it is called *Mun*; 3. when *Sut* is ſo prevalent that certainty enſues, it is called *Bhoodh*; 4. when *Tum* (pride) is prevalent, and aſſumes to itſelf the things that are only lent, it is called *Ahenkar*. *Apuncheekeert*, by the prevalence of *Ruj*, produces five winds: 1. *Purran*, the wind in the mouth and noſe; 2. *Oudan*, the wind in the belly; 3. *Oupan*, the wind in the poſteriors; 4. *Beyan*, the wind in the other parts of the body. *Lingsereer* and *Sowchumsereer*, are general terms for the ten *Inderees*, *Untahkurrum*, and the five airs; making altogether ſixteen things. This *Sowchum*, (body), they ſay, belongs to every animal; but that on account of its ſubtilty it is not diſcernible by the ſenſes, and is loſt in the ſtate of *Muckut*. After that an animal is produced, whoſe body is entirely *Lingseereeree*, which they call *Herenegerbeh* Whatever tranſmigration happens after this has a ſpiritual form.

The production of *Ishthowlsirreer* is after the following manner. Each of the five aforeſaid kinds of *Sowchum* they divide into two parts; and five of theſe ten they ſubdivide again into five others each. Half the *Sowchum Akass*, with four other parts of air, fire, water, and earth, unite together, which produces *Akass Ishthowl*. Half the *Sowchum*, air, with a part of *Akass*, fire, water, and earth, united produce *Badishthowl*. Half of the *Sowchum* fire, united with a part of akaſs, water, fire, and earth, produce the *Ishthowl* fire; the ſame with water and earth. Some ſay that the *Ishthowl Akass*, and *Ishthowl* air are produced without any mixture of fire, water, and earth; but agree reſpecting the reſt, excepting that the *Ishthowl* fire, water, and earth, they divide each into two parts; one of which they leave in its original ſtate, and the other half of each they divide

into

into three parts, which are compounded in the manner before described; which mixture produces the *Ishthowl* fire, water, and earth. And from the five *Ishthowl* elements, by the excess of either of the three accidents, *Sut*, *Ruj*, and *Tum*, the fourteen regions and their inhabitants are produced.

They say that a person will be created, who will be acquainted with the *Ishthowlsereer*, and he will be called *Berat*.

The dissolution of the universe they describe after the following manner. Earth will be destroyed by water, water by fire, fire by air, air by *Akass*, and the *Akass* dissolve into *Maia*. From this dissolution will consequently arise *Ageeyan*, of which they reckon three degrees; 1. *Dinedan*, the expiration of one day of Brahma; 2. *Parakurt*, the dissolution which will then ensue; 3. *Atentick*, the dissolution of *Ageeyan*, when Omniscience will shine forth. Of the first kind a great deal has happened, and is accomplishing. But *Atentick* will only happen once; it being the dissolution of *Ageeyan* and its accidents.

The doctrines of this sect are comprised in four *Adheyas*. The first contains an account of Brimmah; the second of worship; the third how to obtain *Muckut*; the fourth, the nature of *Muckut*.

The learned Hindoos have divided the Bede into three parts; 1. *Kurramkand*, the performance of various duties, and which they call *Poorub Meymensa*; 2. *Geeyankand*, and this they call *Outre Meymansa*, which is more commonly known under the name of *Beydant*; 3. *Opassua*, which they also call *Sunkerkhen Meymansa*. The signification of *Opassua* is, God being conceived under a form, is worshipped. But now this book is very scarce.

They

They ſay, that every one is not fit to be inſtructed in the *Beydant*, neither is every one capable of comprehending it. He who ſeeks this knowledge, muſt be able to diſtinguiſh what is eternal from what is created, muſt deſpiſe the world, ſtudy with intentneſs, not be diſturbed at not finding the non-exiſting comprehenſions, muſt diſregard joy and ſorrow, but daily increaſe in the contemplation of *Muckut*.

THE SCIENCE OF SANK.

The firſt teacher of this ſcience was Kupel, the philoſopher.

Some pretend that this ſect are atheiſts; but they only diſbelieve in a creator, ſaying that the univerſe is from all eternity, and that nothing is annihilated, but only diſappears, the effect being abſorbed in the cauſe; as the tortoiſe draws its legs into its ſhell.

They believe man to be a free agent, and that he is rewarded or puniſhed according to his good or bad actions.

They ſay that, when the time of creation arrives, *Sut* is prevalent, and there appears *Mehtet*, which is the firſt created ſubſtance. Every man has a diſtinct *Mehtet*, and which they alſo call *Boodh*. This ſubſtance compriſes eight things. 1. *Dehrem*. 2. *Adherem*. 3. *Geeyan*. 4. *Ageeyan*. 5. *Berag*, comprehending and deſpiſing the things of this world. 6. *Aberag*, miſcomprehending and eſteeming the things of this world. 7. *Iyshruj*, the operations of the ſoul, by which man comprehends whatever is abſtruſe. 8. *Abiyshruj*, thoſe operations of the ſoul which lead to miſconception. Of theſe eight faculties four are invariable, which are produced by by the prevalence of *Sut;* and four accidental, produced by the prevalence of *Tum.*

The creation of the elements they consider to be of six kinds. 1. *Surglogue,* or the uppermost region, produced by the prevalence of *Sut.* 2. *Meertlogue,* the region inhabited by the human race, produced by the prevalence of *Ruj.* 3. *Patallogue,* beneath the earth, produced by the prevalence of *Tum.* 4. The *Dewtah,* who are produced by *Assut,* the absence of passions. They have power to change their forms, and assume wonderful shapes, whilst from the transparency of their substances, their natural forms are not visible. There are eight orders of *Dewtahs.* 1. *Brahma,* those who inhabit the region of Brahma. 2. *Perajaputty,* the inhabitants of the region of *Perajaput,* a very powerful Dewtah. 3. *Indree,* those who inhabit the region of *Indree.* 4. *Petree,* the inhabitants of the region of *Petree.* They whose ancestors for several generations have been virtuous, when they assume paradisical forms, enter into this region. 5. *Gundherp,* the host of divine choristers. 6. *Jutah,* the inhabitants of the region of *Jutah,* the guardian of the north. 7. *Rackass,* evil *Dewtahs,* who destroy mankind. 8. *Pyacheh,* another race more hurtful than the *Rackass.*

The Elementary Creation continued.

5. *Tirjung,* animals produced by the prevalence of *Ruj,* and who are of five kinds. 1. *Pusk,* domestic quadrupeds. 2. *Moorg,* wild quadrupeds. 3. *Pookh,* birds. 4. *Sirrysirp,* snakes, and all aquatres. 5. *Sithawer,* plants. The sixth *Munnook,* mankind, produced by the prevalence of *Ruj.*

Many believe in the above divisions, and say that, at the dissolution, the universe will be absorbed in the elements, and they in *Akenkher,* which absorption they call *Purkeert.*

Pain

Pain is of three kinds. 1. *Adehyatemk*, envy and ill nature. 2. *Adehdewik*, that which is inflicted by the *Dewtahs*. 3. *Adehbhowtik*, that which is occasioned by any of the elements.

They say, that if man relies solely upon God, he will become a monarch of the upper regions, and there enjoy all his wishes for the space of one hundred thousand *Monunters*, at the expiration of which he will return to this world; and then again for every good action, will receive a suitable reward in the upper regions. Whosoever gives to a Brahmin sufficient ground for a house to stand upon, will enjoy ten *Kulebs* in paradise before he returns again to the earth. And for bestowing one thousand head of cattle, the reward in paradise will be ten thousand years of bliss, before he returns again to this world. After he has undergone many of these transmigrations, he will arrive at *Muckut*, which is the state of sublime knowledge, when transmigration ceases.

The doctrines of this sect are contained in sixty books, which they call *Tunter*.

THE SCIENCE OF PATENJIL.

This doctrine was introduced by the philosopher *Patenjil*. It agrees in every point with *Sank*, excepting that these make God to be the creator; and say that existence and omniscience are the fountain of his essence. These also believe that *Muckut* can only be obtained through the medium of *Jowg*, or a complete victory over the passions, for gaining which they assign various means, some of which I shall here relate, as the information may be serviceable to those who wish to obtain this state. They say, that when *Mehtet* unites

2 with

with the three accidents, *Tum*, *Ruj*, and *Sut*, five ſtates are produced, which they call the five *Bhoom*, viz. 1. *Chipt*, produced by the prevalence of *Ruj*, when the heart is not fixed to any one point. 2. *Mowdh*, from the prevalence of *Tum*, when the heart is ſatisfied, notwithſtanding it does not obtain its wants. 3. *Beychipt*, from the prevalence of *Sut*, when the heart obtains all its deſires, and is a little at reſt. 4. *Eykagur*, when ſo much power is obtained, that on whatever object the heart is ſet, it does not wander. 5. *Nyrodeh*, is the ſtate wherein, from the abſence of thoſe three accidents, all deſires of the heart ceaſe, and it begins to have ſome knowledge. *Jowg* is never obtained, excepting in the two laſt ſtates. In the firſt ſtate, the mind is poſſeſſed by *Adherem*; in the ſecond, by *Ageeyan*; in the third, by *Abyrag* and *Abeyshruj*; in the fourth by *Dehrem*, *Geeyan*, *Birag*, *Isyruj*; and in the fifth all traces of good and bad actions are eraſed, there being an end of *Beert*, or the inclination to do good or bad. *Beert* is of two kinds. 1. *Kullisht*, the inclination to do bad. 2. *Akullisht*, the inclination to do good. And each of theſe is again divided into five kinds. 1. *Purmanbeert*, certain knowledge of things from the prevalence of *Sut*. 2. *Beepeyie*, depraved knowledge, from the abſence of *Sut* and *Tum*. 3. *Biklup*, doubt concerning the Deity, from the abſence of *Sut* and *Tum*. 4. *Nidra*, ſleep, when knowledge vaniſhes, from the abſence of *Tum*. 5. *Sumrut*, recollecting what had been forgotten, from the abſence of *Sut*. When all theſe ſtates are at an end, the bleſſing of *Muckut* is obtained.

The ſtate of *Muckut* is obtained by the twelve following actions. 1. *Iysuropasna*, continual contemplation of the Deity. Thoſe who practiſe this ſay, that by keeping God continually in remembrance, all evil is diſpelled, and the nine following enemies to men are diſperſed. 1. *Beyedeh*, ſickneſs. 2. *Settyan*, diſinclination

nation for good actions. 3. *Sunshee*, doubts of the cauſes and benefits of the *Jowg*. 4. *Purmad*, forgetfulneſs of indiſpenſable duties. 5. *Alsee*, ſlothfulneſs in buſineſs. *Owrut*, unlawful deſires. 7. *Behrantdurshun*, corrupt knowledge. 8. *Alubdhwumkutto*, fickleneſs. 9. *Anoostiktuttoo*, a mind not to be ſatisfied.

The ſecond means of obtaining *Jowg* is *Sidha*, or a hearty inclination to perform the *Jowg;* and conſidering it as the means of obtaining our wiſhes.

The third, *Peyperj*, ſearching after it with ardent deſire.

The fourth, *Somrut*, belief that this work will produce great benefit; and being intent upon the performance of it.

The fifth, *Meytree*, wiſhing well to all mankind.

The ſixth, *Kuma*, being afflicted at the diſtreſſes of others, and ſtriving to relieve them.

The ſeventh, *Moodeh*, taking pleaſure in the virtue of others.

The eighth, *Apeecha*, withdrawing from thoſe who injure us, and doing them neither good nor harm, ſeeing that whoſoever injures another, the ſame will fall upon himſelf.

The ninth, *Samadeh*, making choice of retirement, and thinking only on one object.

The tenth, *Perkeya*, having nothing in the heart but ſublime knowledge, and ſeeking after righteouſneſs.

The

The eleventh, *Byrag*, having the heart alienated from worldly concerns, and inceſſantly ſeeking God.

The twelfth, *Abeehyass*, being ſo perfect in knowledge and good actions, that they become natural.

The *Jowg* is of two kinds. 1. *Sumpergeyat*, which is when the heart, by confining itſelf to one contemplation, arrives at perfection by degrees, and conceives an ideal form of the divinity. 2. *Assumpergeyat*, when the imaginary form of the Deity diſappears from the mind, and nothing remains but the contemplation of his eſſence. Again, *Sumpergeyat* is of three kinds. 1. *Goraheyhsummaput*, when the mind is fixed upon the elements. 2. *Gerhensummaput*, when the mind employs only one of the ſenſes. *Girkittersummaput*, when the mind employs only *Atma*. And alſo *Assumpergeyat* is of two kinds. 1. *Bhoopirtee*, when there remains the power of diſtinguiſhing *Perkeert*, *Atma*, and the elements from each other. 2. *Opaypirtee*, being only able to diſtinguiſh *Atma*; and this is the ſtate of *Muckut*.

The perſon who has arrived at the ſtate of *Jowg*, poſſeſſes theſe four qualities. 1. Advancing in this perilous road with ſtrong inclination and firmneſs; and this ſtate is called *Pirtehmkeleek*. 2. *Mudbhoomick*, ſo ſubduing the heart by virtuous actions, that, like a mirror it may be free from all impurity, and be able to reflect whatever is in the heart of another, and thus to perceive any thing that from its minuteneſs is imperceptible to ordinary viewers. 3. *Pirgeeayajowt*, by diligence, aided by good fortune, gaining victory over the ſenſes and the elements, ſo as to be able to ſee and hear whatever is far or near; and to have power to create and to deſtroy.

They ſay, that the *Jowg Sumpergeyat* is compounded

 of

of eight things. 1. *Jum*. 2. *Neem*. 3. *Assun*. 4. *Purraniyan*. 5. *Perteeyakar*. 6. *Dohama*. 7. *Dehyan*. 8. *Summedeh*.

Jum is of five kinds. 1. *Ahensa*, not to kill or molest any animal; whereby enemies become friends. 2. *Suttee*, to speak nothing but truth; by which means he will obtain his wishes. 3. *Asteeyee*, not to accept of more wealth than what is allowed by law; by which means he will have under his command the keys of the treasures of the world. 4. *Birhumchiry*, not to have any connexion with women, by which means his breath will be so efficacious, that it will light up the lamp of knowledge in the hearts of the ignorant. 5. *Appergerreh*, not holding any worldly possessions, but considering them as the cause of every kind of unhappiness. From this action, past and to come will be revealed unto him.

Neem is also of five kinds. 1. *Sowch*, avoiding all connexion with mankind. By this means the essence *Mun* will become pure, and good desires be the fruit thereof. 2, *Suntowk*, giving up all improper desires, from having no pleasure in them. This action will produce such a happy disposition, that he will not have any relish for worldly pleasures. 3. *Tup*, reconciling the mind and body to cold, heat, hunger, thirst, and silence. From this conduct, distant and hidden things will be revealed to him; he will see behind him, and assume any shape he pleases. 4. *Sewadehyney*, reading the divine books, remembering the divine attributes, and those actions which lead to *Muckut*. If he cannot read, he must always have upon his tongue the word *Unkar*. For these actions, the *Dewtahs*, and other celestial spirits, will associate with him, and give him their âssistance. 5. *Issurpurrendhan*, making all his endeavours tend to the satisfaction of God. From doing thus, he will derive variety of knowledge.

Assun,

Assun, sitting, of which there are eighty-four ways, thirteen of which are esteemed particularly holy, and each has a distinct name. Whosoever practises them, suffers little from cold, heat, hunger, or thirst. They have also for the purposes of the world, thirteen different modes. The author of this work has seen many who practise the austerities of *Assun*, and has been astonished how they could make their muscles, nerves, and bones, so obedient to their command.

Purraniyan, managing the breath; and this is after three ways. 1. *Pooruck*, stopping the left nostril with the right thumb, and inspiring through the right nostril. 2. *Koombuch*, inspiring for a considerable time, and then shutting both nostrils with the thumb and little finger of the right hand. Some of this sect can hold their breath for an incredible length of time. 3. *Reechek*, letting out the breath gently, by removing the thumb from the right, and the little finger from the left nostril; that is, they inspire through the right nostril, and respire through the left. When these three actions are done, one *Purraniyan* is completed. According to some, the breath that goes out of the nostrils does not go above sixteen fingers distance, and others say only twelve. From the performance of these actions, *Mun* obtains rest, and sublime knowledge commences. But these exercises cannot be performed without the instruction of one who is experienced in them. He who performs these exercises must abstain from flesh, spices, acid, and salt, and must content himself with a little milk and rice. He must not cohabit with women, for that would occasion melancholy madness.

Pirteeyehar, the five senses, regaining the exercise of their respective faculties. When *Mun* is at rest, the senses are locked up, and all things involuntarily become revealed to it.

Deherna,

Deherna, the heart desiring solely one object.

Dehyan, not suffering the heart to wander from that object, nor allowing any thing else to enter the heart.

Summadeh, knowledge and reflection being at an end. At this period *Sumpergeeyat* ceases, and *Assumpergeeyat* commences; so that knowledge and *Jowg* are completed.

They say, that *Jum* and *Neem* are like the seed when sown in the earth; *Assun* and *Purraniyan*, when it sprouts above the earth; *Purteeyakar* resembles the flower; and that *Deherna*, *Dehyan*, and *Summadeh*, are the fruit. These three are collectively called *Sunjum*. In this state the person performs wonderful actions, to the astonishment of the beholders. This miraculous power is called *Iyissoorej*, and is of eight kinds. 1. *Uniwa*, making himself so small that he can pass through the eye of a needle. 2. *Meheema*, making himself so tall as to be able to reach his arm to the moon. 3. *Lughema*, making himself so light as to mount by a sun-beam into the upper regions. 4. *Gurrema*, making himself as heavy as he pleases. In some books this is called *Purraput*, signifying that he can unite himself with any thing he pleases. 5. *Purrakamee*, sinking into one part of the earth, and coming out of another, like a diver in water. 6. *Eysittoo*, creating and destroying. 7. *Bistoo*, making the elements, and every thing dependent on them, obedient to his command. 8. *Kammebyayeetoo*, accomplishing whatever he desires.

This relation will not gain credit with men who admit nothing but ordinary appearances; but they who acknowledge the infinite power of God, will not refuse it belief.

The doctrine of *Patenjil* is comprised in one *Adehya*, containing four *Churrens*, viz. 1. Particular relation

tion of the *Jowg*. 2. Caufes thereof. 3. The different kinds of *Iysirrej*. 4. Of *Muckut*.

The SCIENCE of JINE.

The firft teacher of this doctrine was the philofopher *Jun*, whom they alfo call *Arun* and *Arehnut*.

They have the fame idea of the Deity as the profeffors of *Meymansa* and *Sank*. They fay, that man is a free agent; and believe that there are future rewards and punifhments. They make the *Surglogue* to confift of twenty-fix divifions, in the uppermoft of which dwells God's elect, whofe bodies are formed of the indivifible particles. They fay, that the elements are one fubftance. The component parts of the univerfe they believe to have exifted from all eternity, but that the form is new. Some of this fect maintain, that all created beings are from God; others attribute them to time; others to *Poorutkeert*, or the fruit of good works; and others to *Subhow*, or a fpecial caufe. They do not believe that the whole univerfe will fuffer diffolution; but that of every thing fome part will be left, from whence creation will be renovated.

Thefe ufe only two predicaments, viz. 1. *Poorteck*, that knowledge which is derived through the five external fenfes, *Mun* and *Atma*. 2. *Purrookuss*, that which does not depend upon the fenfes. Of thefe they make many fubdivifions; however, I fhall only mention a few that are moft material.

They fay there is a fubtle effence in which knowledge refides and illuminates the body, in the fame manner as a lamp enlightens a houfe. And this knowledge has the power of doing good and evil. This power

power is of two kinds, 1. *Atma*; and, 2. *Jew Atma.* The firſt belongs ſolely to the Deity, to whom they aſcribe four attributes. 1. *Anuntgeyan*, analytic knowledge. 2. *Anuntdirson*, ſynthetic knowledge. 3. *Anuntbeerij*, omnipotence. 4. *Anuntsook*, total reſt.

They do not believe in the *Owtars*, or incarnations of the Deity, but think that men, from their virtuous conduct, become omniſcient, and whatever they ſay on the ſubject of religion or legiſlation ſhould be conſidered as the word of God: ſuch an enlightened perſon they call *Sakapirmeysir*, of whom they reckon twenty-four. The firſt was named *Adnauth*, and the laſt will be called *Mahavede*, and to each they add the appellative *Jun*. Of theſe they relate wonderful ſtories. The Supreme Being they call *Nirgoonpirmeysir*.

The conjunction of ten things produces life, and the abſence of any one of them occaſions death. The general name for theſe ten things is *Peran*. They are the five ſenſes; *Mun*, ſpeech, aſſumption of a body, breathing, and exiſting for a ſpace of time. They reckon four kinds of animals, 1. *Dewtah*. 2. *Munnook*. 3. *Narkee*. 4. *Tirjinj*. The firſt, or *Dewtah*, are luminous ſubſtances, which, by the will of God, are produced without generation. Their bodies have neither fleſh nor bones, and their breath is perfume. They ſuffer not ſickneſs, nor the infirmities of age. They obtain whatever they deſire; can aſſume a thouſand different forms; and walk without touching the earth. Theſe *Dewtahs* are alſo of four kinds, and inhabit the upper regions.

They make the univerſe to be compoſed of three regions. 1. *Munkoologue*, the face of the earth, inhabited by the human race. They ſay, that the ſurface of the earth is one *Raj* in length, and the ſame in breadth; of which four millions five hundred thouſand

jowjuns

jowjuns are inhabited. 2, *Petallogue*, under the earth, and which is ſeven *Raj* in length, and the like in breadth, wanting nine hundred jowjuns. 3, *Surglogue*, the upper region, which is ſomewhat leſs than ſeven *Raj* in breadth and length. This region is Paradiſe, where men, after having aſſumed paradiſical forms, enjoy happineſs. This ſtate they call *Wymanick*. A *Raj* is ſuch a diſtance, that if an iron ball, weighing $3\frac{1}{2}$ Akberee ſeers, were to be let fall, it would be in its deſcent ſix months ſix days and twelve *Ghurries*.

They ſay, that at the diſtance of forty-eight coſe above the uppermoſt region is a place reſembling cryſtal, in length and breadth four millions five hundred thouſand jowjuns, and in height eight jowjuns; and $3\frac{5}{6}$ coſe above this, is the holy habitation of *Muckut*, where men aſſume luminous forms, and are abſorbed in the Deity.

The life of a *Dewtah* is never more than one *Pullowpun*, nor leſs than three *Sagur*. They have all the power of aſſuming different ſhapes. The *Dewtahs* require food, but do not receive nouriſhment through the mouth. Thoſe who are arrived at the age of ten thouſand years, require nouriſhment every other day, and breathe once, during a time that a man in health would breathe forty-nine times. And as their age advances above ten thouſand years, in ſuch proportion of time can they abſtain from food, and retain their breath. All the *Dewtahs* that inhabit the firſt and ſecond ſtages of the upper region have ſenſual commerce, but the females do not conceive. Thoſe in the higher regions have more refined pleaſures. They ſay that men, in reward for their good actions, become *Dewtahs*.

The ſecond claſs of animals is *Munnookh*, who are of two ſpecies. 1, *Sunnya*, thoſe who have the faculty of of *Mun*, or are rational. 2, *Assunnya*, irrational, being animalcule produced in the flesh, blood, and saliva of men, and whose time of existence does not exceed two hours. *Sunnya* is again of two species. 1, Those who inhabit this earth, and receive future rewards and punishments in paradise and hell, in return for their good and evil actions. 2, Those who will be rewarded merely on account of their charitableness, in the manner hereafter described.

In this earth, there are fifteen grand divisions. From its creation to its dissolution comprises twelve *Chuckerwerts*, or universal monarchs, with nine *Bassdeos*, and nine *Buldeos*. The dominions of a *Chuckerwert* consist of thirty-two thousand kingdoms, with sway over thirty-two monarchs. He has also eight millions four hundred thousand elephants, and the like number of cavalry and chariots, together with four thousand viziers, ninety-two millions of infantry, eight millions four hundred thousand philosophers, three hundred thousand cowrburdars, five hundred thousand torch bearers, thirty millions of musicians, sixty-four thousand wives, one hundred and twenty-eight thousand handmaids, besides possessing sixteen thousand mines of precious stones, nineteen thousand gold mines, and one hundred and twenty thousand mines of other metals; and within his empire are sixteen thousand nations of *Mileetch*, and sixteen capital cities; and, to complete the account, three hundred and sixty millions of cooks, three hundred and sixty of whom are for his own particular use. And besides these they give many other distinctions. In the present cycle, the first *Chuckerwert* was Rajah Bhirt, son of Adnaut, some of whose family, in reward for their virtuous conduct, are now enjoying paradise. The nine others, named *Bassdeo*, are only half *Chuckerwerts*, and will go into hell; and of this number they account *Kishen*. The nine called *Buldeo*, will possess only a fourth of a *Chuckerwert*. The whole will be subdued by a person

named

named *Teertehnkit*, who will be ſpoken of particularly preſently.

Beſides the earth inhabited by mankind, there is another very extenſive country, the people of which clothe themſelves with the leaves of trees, and feed upon wild fruits and the earth, which is there very ſweet. They are handſome and well behaved. Their ſtature is from one to three coſe. Every male and female beget a ſon and a daughter, and then die. When this ſon and daughter arrive at years of maturity, they become man and wife. Their lives ſometimes extend to three *Pollowpum*. Whoſoever has not led a perfect virtuous life in this world, but has beſtowed charity, will receive the reward thereof in the territory now deſcribed.

The third ſpecies of animals, *Narkee*, like the *Dewtahs*, can aſſume different ſhapes, and reſemble them in ſeveral other reſpects; but their forms are always hideous; they are inhabitants of the ſix infernal regions, where they torment one another.

The fourth kind of animals, or *Terjenj*, are of three ſpecies, viz. aquatic, terreſtrial, and aerial. The firſt are again of five ſpecies, 1, *Soosmar*, thoſe aquatic animals that reſemble men, elephants, horſes, &c. 2, Every kind of fiſh. 3, Tortoiſes. 4, *Kerrah*, which are animals reſembling rope of different lengths. They faſten about the legs of elephants and other animals, and prevent their getting out of the water. 5, Aligators. The ſecond diviſion, or terreſtrial, are of three ſpecies; viz. quadrupeds; whatever creep upon their bellies, as ſnakes; and thoſe that go ſometimes on two legs, as the *Mongooso*. The third diviſion, or aerials, are of four ſpecies, 1, Domeſtic, and that have feathers, as pigeons. 2, Thoſe whoſe wings are of ſkin, as bats. The 4th and 5th, who are various, fly in the

the regions of *Dewtahs*, and ſurpriſing ſtories are told of them.

They explain a *Pollowpum* in the following manner. Take hairs of a *Chugul* infant (which is 4096 times thicker than the hair of an infant of Dehly,) ſplit them into indiviſible particles, and fill with theſe a well that meaſures four coſe in width, breadth, and depth. At the expiration of every hundred years, take out one of theſe particles, and when the well is emptied, one *Pollowpum* will be completed.

100,000 - -	make one	Lukſh, vulgarly lack.
10 Lacks, -	make one	Kote, vulgarly krore.
100 Krore, - -	make one	Arib.
10 Arib, - -	make one	Khurb.
10 Khurb, - -	make one	Beykhurb.
10 Beykhurb, -	make one	Mahaſerooj, or Puddum.
10 Puddum, -	make one	Sunkh.
10 Sunkh, - -	make one	Summooder.

According to this ſect, *Muckut* cannot be obtained without an union of knowledge and good works, which they exemplify by the following apalogue. "Fire fell upon a houſe in which dwelt a blind man and a cripple, neither of whom could eſcape without the help of the other; therefore the blind man took the cripple upon his back, to avail himſelf of his eyes, and in return gave the cripple the uſe of his legs. Thus, by mutual aſſiſtance, they both got out in ſafety." But theſe may be obtained by attending to the inſtructions of the holy, becauſe through their favour knowledge is gained, which is the ſource of *Byrag*, whereby man becomes attached to a life of auſterity. *Byrag* is of twelve kinds. One in this ſtate muſt obſerve the following rules: Only to eat at appointed times. Formerly they would live nine months, or a year, without eating any thing ſolid, but now they cannot exceed ſix months.

months. To eat ſparingly. Never to aſk food at more than five places; and, when that is obtained, to reſt ſatisfied till next day. To abſtain from eating milk, curds, ghee, Seſamé oil, and ſweetmeats. In order to reduce the body, to cover himſelf with ſand in the heat of the ſun. During the winter to go naked. Drawing up the arms and legs, and ſitting on the poſteriors. Theſe things muſt be practiſed for a long time to produce the deſired effect; but there are many who have not power to ſubmit to ſuch auſterities.

But, by an obſervance of the following rules, a man may ſoon obtain the object of his wiſhes. To pay implicit obedience to his *Peer*. To act as a ſervant unto thoſe who inflict auſterities upon themſelves. To ſtudy with attention the great books. Frequently to recline his head upon his breaſt, for not leſs than two hours continuance. Some of the ancients would keep the head reclined upon the breaſt for an incredible length of time. The way is, to ſtretch the arms down both ſides, and keep the body free from motion. They have forty-five great books, twelve of which they call *Ung*, and which they ſay are divine, viz. 1, *Achar Ung*. 2, *Soorkirta Ung*. 3, *Sutehr Ung*. 4, *Sumwaya Ung*. 5, *Bhegwutty Ung*. 6, *Matadehremhahta Ung*. 7, *Oupasuckdesha Ung*. 8, *Autgulddehdesha Ung*. 9, *Anutturrowdawaiy Ung*. 10, *Purrisnubbeakurren Ung*. 11, *Beepakseth Ung*. 12, *Hudurutty Ung*. There are twelve other books, which they call *Owpa Ung*; four others named *Moolsooter*; ſix others entitled *Jeedgurrunth*; ten others ſtyled *Pyena*; and another which they call *Tundysecter*.

To a proficient in this doctrine they give the title of *Jetty*. A noviciate is called *Sikh*. One who has practiſed the auſterities for ſix months is called *Gunnies Sikh*. *Purwirtekh* is the ſame as *Gunnies Sikh*, excepting that this is hèld in higher eſteem by his *Peer*.

Sithowr assists the last, by punishing the refractory, and aiding the helpless. He is also called *Rutnadehk* and *Punniass*. *Acharij* is a person who, for the sake of God, explains with cheerfulness any difficulty that may occur to the noviciates. *Owpadehaiy* instructs the students in the signification of any difficult words that occur in the divine books, and in other requisites; his office nearly resembling the *Acharij*. All these now mentioned preserve nothing but a few clothes, which will be particularized hereafter. *Gundhir* is one who, by great application, arrives at a high degree of knowledge. He keeps more clothes and books than are necessary for himself, that he may be able to supply students who stand in need of them. He is the representative of the *Jun*; but the *Jun* is far more excellent than he, being possessed of universal knowledge; and he is also called *Teertehnker*. The following is his description: His face is beautiful; his mind superlatively virtuous; and his breath a delightful perfume. His discourse is replete with wisdom. His flesh and blood are white. No one ever sees him eat nor exonerate. He has no bodily infirmity. His hair and nails never grow long. Wherever he resides no noxious animals approach. Neither is there war, drought, pestilence, or famine. And every one of the twenty-four that are to appear will have these qualities.

A *Jetty* never goes within the hearing of a female voice. He neither eats flesh, fruits, nor sweetmeats; nor dresses any food; drinks nothing but warm water; and never eats nor drinks in the night. He never lights a lamp or any fire in his house. If any thing falls from his hand, he never takes it up again. He only washes such parts of his body as happen to be foul. He never suffers himself to joke, or commit any mean or idle action. He never uses more than the following clothes in summer, a sheet, a blanket, and a square piece of cloth of $1\frac{1}{2}$ cubits, which he makes into four

four folds, and when he speaks applies, to his mouth, that no insect may enter it. In the winter he has an additional sheet. He has also a *Dehrimdigh*, which is a broom made of woollen threads, or woollen cloth, fixed in a wooden handle. With this he softly sweeps the ground before he sits down, for fear of killing any insect.

Those of this sect, who engage in the affairs of the world, are called *Serawuck*. They observe the following rules. Never to injure the innocent. Not to tell untruths on the following occasions, as they consider them as great sins. 1, In bearing witness. 2, In breach of trust. 3, In praise, 4, Or dispraise of a virgin. 5, Concerning an ox. Not to soil their hands with dishonesty of any kind. Not to covet another man's wife. To keep only as much wealth as is necessary for the purposes of life, and to bestow the rest in charity. When on a journey, to travel daily only stated distances. To calculate the necessary wants of each day, and live accordingly. Not to go where a woman has been burnt with her husband, nor to a place where a malefactor has suffered death. To set apart two *Ghurries* of every day for devotion. To sleep only during the appointed time. To abstain from food and drink, day and night, on the 8th, 14th, 15th and 28th days of the moon, and the next morning to feed the poor before breaking the fast. Every night before he goes to sleep, to examine himself upon the above eleven points. The following is their description of a virtuous man. He is one that constantly attends to the reading of the divine books; bestows charity; makes it a rule to praise the virtuous; never speaks ill of any one; and is particularly respectful in his conversation concerning princes. He marries one who is his equal. He is ever afraid of doing evil. Wherever he dwells he conforms to the laws of the land. He chooses a habitation that is neither very public, nor totally secluded from society.

His

His houſe hath not more than two or three doors and windows. He ſettles in a good neighbourhood, and aſſociates with the virtuous. He is dutiful to his father and mother. He flies from that city or country which is invaded by foreign troops. He regulates his expences by his income; and dreſſes ſuitable to his rank in life. He ſtudies the divine books, and follows their precepts implicitly. He never eats but at ſtated meals. He is not covetous of riches. He is affable and charitable to a gueſt, a *Jetty*, and thoſe who are ſick. He is not vain of his perſon, nor of his words. He is deſirous of being inſtructed in every profeſſion. He travels not at improper times, nor in a country where he cannot exerciſe his religion. He never engages in a war, without knowing whether he is going againſt his friends or his enemies. He partakes in the misfortunes of his relations. He has a grateful ſenſe of favours conferred on him. His deportment is pleaſing to every one. He is diffident in his manner, courteous to all, and upright in every tranſaction of his life. He exerts himſelf in the affairs of others; and keeps ſenſual gratifications under the command of reaſon.

There are, however, ſome general prohibitions, which are obſerved both by the *Jetty* and the *Serawuck*. To abſtain from fleſh, ſpirituous liquors, honey, butter, opium, ſnow, ice, and hail; every thing that grows beneath the earth; all fruits whoſe names are unknown; and whatever fruits contain ſmall ſeeds; and from eating at night.

The doctrine of *Jine* is alſo of two kinds, *Seweetambir* and *Digneer*. The author of the Ayeen Akbery, having been intimately acquainted with the learned of the *Seweetambir*, has been able to relate their tenets in an ample manner. The ſecond, or *Digneer*, go quite naked. They maintain, that women cannot arrive at the ſtate of *Muckut*. They ſay, that whoſoever obtains

obtains the bleſſing of *Muckut* in this world, ceaſes to require food from that time. They, however, agree with the *Seweetambir* in many points; but as the author had no intimacy with any of this claſs, ſo he has not been able to write any farther account of them.

From the moſt ancient times, down to the preſent, the learning and wiſdom of Hindoſtan has been confined to the *Brahmins* and the followers of *Jine*; but, ignorant of each others merits, they have a mutual averſion. *Kishen*, whom the *Brahmins* worſhip as God, theſe conſider as an infernal ſlave. The *Brahmins* carry their averſion ſo far as to ſay, that it is better to encounter a mad elephant, or a furious lion, than to meet a man of this perſuaſion.

The deſire of eſtabliſhing truth has induced his majeſty to illumine the world with univerſal peace and unanimity; whereby the darkneſs of error being now in ſome degree diſpelled, men of different perſuaſion quit the narrow paths of prejudice, and aſſociate together.

THE DOCTRINE OF BOODH.

BOODH, who firſt taught this religion, has various names, and amongſt them *Shakmun* and *Shakmuny*. His followers believe, that by means of his good actions he gained perfect knowledge: and at length arrived at the ſtate of *Muckut*. His father was Rajah Siddown, prince of Bahar, and his mother, named Mala, was delivered of him through her navel. At his birth there ſhone forth a wonderful light; the earth trembled; and the water of the Ganges roſe and fell in a moſt aſtoniſhing manner. The very hour he was born he walked ſeven ſteps, and diſcourſed with an eloquence that raviſhed the hearts of his hearers. The aſtrologers foretold, that after twenty years and ſeven days, he would become a monarch; but that, deſpiſing the world, he would prefer retirement, and introduce a new religion. In the manner, and preciſely at the time predicted by the aſtrologers, it came to paſs that he turned his mind from the affairs of the world, and made choice of a life of retirement. He viſited Benaris, Rajgird, and ſeveral other fire temples. He then travelled to Caſhmeer, where he made many proſelytes; and he alſo gained for his followers people of Hind, the ſeaports, Tibbet and Khatai. From his birth to this time, which is the 40th year of his majeſty's reign, is a period of 2962 years. They ſay that he had the gift of prophecy; and could change the courſe of nature. He died at the age of one hundred and twenty years. The learned among the Perſians and Arabians call the prieſts of this religion *Bukshee*, and in Tibbet they are ſtyled *Lama*. For a long time paſt there have not been any traces of them, excepting in Peigu, Dehnaſiry, and Tibbet.

The third time that the author followed the imperial ſtirrup to the delightful territory of Caſhmeer, he met with ſome old men of this religion; but he never ſaw any of their learned; nor did he diſcover any thing like what is deſcribed by *Hafez Abroo* and *Benagutty*.

The Brahmins call *Boodh* the ninth Owtar; but aſſert that the religion which is aſcribed to him, is falſe, and fabricated by ſome other perſon.

The following is all that is known of this religion. They believe that God has never been defiled by incarnation; and, like the profeſſors of *Sank*, *Meymansa*, and *Jine*, do not conſider him to be the creator of the univerſe. They ſay that it has neither beginning

2 nor

nor end; but that it vanishes, and then appears again in its original form; and thus time after time.

The priests of this religion shave their heads, and wear dresses of leather and red cloth; they use frequent ablutions; will not refuse any kind of food that is offered them; and whatever dies of itself they consider to be killed by God, and therefore eat it. They have no commerce with women. They will not kill any animal; neither root up nor cut any plant, because they think it has life. They hold six things to be highly meritorious; 1, Subduing anger; 2, Improvement of the understanding; 3, Bestowing money in charity; 4, The study of theology; 5, Boldness in asserting their own rights; 6, Continual contemplation of the Deity. They reckon three things to be the means of good; 1, Knowledge. 2, Disinterestedness. 3, Being pleased at the success of others. They say that good and evil proceed from eleven things, viz. the five senses, and their faculties, and *Mun*.

They use four predicaments in argument, which are collectively called *Arjsutter*.

The first Predicament,

Dookh, and which is of five kinds; 1, *Geeyan*, worldly knowledge; 2, *Weedineh*, receiving reward or punishment; 3, *Sunkeyna*, the names and properties of things; 4, *Sunka*, the conjunction of *Dehrem* and *Adherem*; 5, *Roop*.

The second Predicament,

Is *Summeddeo*, the causes of desire and anger. By means of this power a man says, "*I am, and this is mine.*"

The third Predicament,

Marik, to be accustomed to believe that the universe is continually disappearing and reappearing.

The fourth Predicament,

Nerode, the ſtate of reſt which *Mun* enjoys when it is going to enter into *Muckut*. The following negative and poſitive duties are indiſpenſible towards obtaining this ſtate. Beſtowing charity. Abſtaining from evil, which is killing, moleſting, ſtealing, uncleanneſs, lying, ſpeaking ill to the good, ſeeking what is unprofitable, bad inclinations; and aſſociating with thoſe of a different religion. The following are alſo indiſpenſible duties. Reſpect for his *Peer* and teacher; venerating the idols; neither to be elated by praiſe, nor depreſſed by reproach; to ſit in a particular manner, to frequent the temples, which they call *Chietee;* to place no more than a proper value on the things of the world; and to ſtrive to obtain *Jowg*, in the manner deſcribed in *Patenjil;* to have implicit belief in the words of his *Peer;* to waſte the mind and body by ſuffering auſterities; not to ſuffer the heart to dwell upon any ſubject but the contemplation of the Deity; to improve in knowledge; and perform thoſe exerciſes by which *Muckut* is obtained.

They ſay, that knowledge has two cauſes; 1, Whatever is obtained by means of the ſenſes; 2, Whatever is gained by proofs.

This ſect are of four tribes; 1, *Webhakehk*, who admit the exiſtence of knowledge and things; 2, *Sootranitk*, who conſider all things to be only the imagination of the ſenſes; 3, *Jookaja*, who believe that nothing exiſts but knowledge; things being only the various forms thereof; 4, *Medheemuck*, who call knowledge and things *Sun*, or a cypher; and they never argue upon their exiſtence or non-exiſtence.

The followers of the doctrine of *Boodh* have many books

books on every ſcience, but they value moſt natural philoſophy, ethicks, and theology.

NASTICK.

Charbag, an ignorant Brahmin, was the inventor of this doctrine. The Brahmins call this ſect *Nastick*.

They ſay that nothing exiſts but the elements; and that all knowledge is obtained through the ſenſes. They do not believe in a God. They ſay that paradiſe is man being in that ſtate which is moſt pleaſing to him, and totally independent of every one; and that hell is being ſubject to the command of another.

They ſay that all men deſire only four things; 1, riches; 2, women; 3, a good name; 4, good actions. They admit only of ſuch ſciences as are ſerviceable in this life, and prefer before all others the equitable adminiſtration of good laws.

This doctrine reſembles that of the Greek ſophiſts. They have written many books in reproach of others; but which ſerve as monuments of their own ignorance.

THE EIGHTEEN BIDDYA, OR SCIENCES.

HAVING given a ſummary account of the nine tribes, I ſhall proceed in the ſame manner to treat of what is admitted by the Brahmins, and others of the ſix firſt-mentioned tribes. They ſay that whoſoever is completely verſed in theſe eighteen *Biddya*, has reached the perfection of knowledge.

The four firſt *Biddyas* are, 1, *Rig Bede*; 2, *Jejir Bede*; 3, *Sam Bede*; 4, *Atherbun Bede*. Theſe they conſider to be divine books. Something has been ſaid of of them already. Each of these books contains four things; 1, *Bidh*, whatever is to be done; 1, *Art-hwed*, the praise and reward thereof; 3, *Munter*. The incantations and implorations which are profitable on every occasion; 4, *Mamedehee*, explanation of great and indispensable duties. Each of these again have three objects; 1, *Kurrum*, the approved actions of the visible world. 2, *Owpasna*, faith in God. 3, *Geeyan*, the knowledge of God.

THE FIFTH BIDDYA, OR POORAN.

There are eighteen large books to which they apply this title; and which contain explanations of the *Bedes* under the five following heads; 1, The creation of the universe; 2, The dissolution thereof; 3, The several relations of the different parts of the universe; 4, The nature of the fourteen *Mowmunters*. These are fourteen holy spirits who, during the whole age of Brahma, will appear successively, and govern the world. The length of the life of each will be seven times four Jowgs. A complete revolution of the four Jowgs is four million three hundred and twenty thousand years. And in like manner there will be fourteen *Indres*, their companions. They say that during the life of Brahma, fourteen *Dewtahs* will reign over the upper regions successively. The relation of their exploits, in return for which this high dignity is conferred on them, and the history of the renowned monarchs of the earth, are contained in these *Poorans*.

TITLES OF THE POORANS.

Sutsee; *Maikundee*; *Bhowkee*; *Bhagwut*; *Birlimliyuret*; *Eerhamund*; *Birhum*; *Ba-iy*; *Bamun*; *Bishen*; *Barah*; *Agun*; *Nardeenee*; *Puddum*; *Ling*; *Gowrum*; *Sogund*; and *Kunrer*; all produced by the enlightened wisdom of the philosopher *Byass*.

Owppooran are eighteen commentaries on the *Poorans*. Some give them the following names, *Sunthomar* originally

ginally called *Soor*, from the perſon who compoſed it. *Owppooran* ſignifies what is not in the *Pooran*, therefore each commentary is called after its reſpective *Pooran*; *Narsing*; *Shewdherem*; *Deorwass*: *Kupeel*; *Manies* (called alſo *Bhirmakand*); *Kalee* and *Kalka*; *Maheysir Nard*; *Shamneb*; *Adtee*; *Peraseree*; *Bhagwut*; and *Gowrum*.

The Sixth BIDDYA.

Dehrem Shaster, is the doctrine of virtuous actions. This is extracted from the *Bedes*, and there is a commentary upon it. The *Dehrem Shaster*, which is alſo called *Simrut*, conſiſts of ſixteen parts. There are three principal matters in three books; 1, The reſpective religious worſhip of the four tribes; 2, The art of medicine; 3, The remedies for ſins.

The eighteen Simrut; 1, *Mun*; 2, *Jakun*; 3, *Wulkee*; 4, *Uttre*; 5, *Unkera*; 6, *Ooshna*; 7, *Gotum*; 8, *Purrashir*; 9, *Sunkhlukkut*; 10, *Bishen*; 11, *Hareeynt*; 12, *Beisheesht*; 13, *Jum*; 14, *Kulp*; 15, *Abestump*; 16, *Katbayin*; 17, *Birhisput*; 18, *Byass*; and ſome add *Dutch*.

Names of the eighteen *Owpsimrut*, or commentaries on the *Simrut*; 1, *Unkera*; 2, *Jabal*; 3, *Machukt*; 4, *Sugund*; 5, *Lookaksh*; 6, *Kushup*; 7, *Byass*; 8, *Sunthomar*; 9, *Shuttez*; 10, *Zunk*; 11, *Weeakher*; 12, *Katyayin*; 13, *Zathernee*; 14, *Kuppinjil*; 15, *Boodyayen*; 16, *Kenad*; 17, *Bishwametre*; 18, *Summent*.

The Seventh BIDDYA.

Shiksha, the places of the letters, whether *Guttrals*, *Labials*, &c.

The Eighth BIDDYA.

Kulp is a book containing explanations of the ten ceremonies

ceremonies required to be performed from the day of marriage, till his ſon puts on the cord. They are treated in the following order: 1, The ceremony of marriage. 2, Cohabiting with the wiſe. 3, From the commencement of pregnancy to the fifth month. 4, From the 6th to the 8th month. 5, At the time of birth. 6, Giving the name. 7, Expoſing the child to the ſun. 8, Weaning him. 9, Shaving his head. 10, Giving him the cord. Each of theſe requires particular prayers and ceremonies.

The Ninth BIDDYA.

Veakern, compriſes grammar, ſyntax, and etymology. It alſo treats of the compoſition of letters. They reckon fifty letters, which are divided into three kinds; 1, the fourteen *Sur* (vowel), letters that have diſtinct ſounds of themſelves, and which are alſo uſed to accent other letters; 2, thirty-three letters called *Punchun* (conſonants), which cannot be ſounded alone; 3, five others called *Unusewa*, *Bissergeh*, *Jubhamool*, *Gujkumbhakirt*, and *Ardehbund*. The firſt is like the Perſian کن; the ſecond is like که; the third is between the letters ه and ح and is always a final. The fourth is a mute nearly like ه and is always a medial; the fifth is ſomewhat like a naſal ن.

The Hindoos reckon the following parts for the utterance of letters, the breaſt, the root of the tongue, the teeth, the noſe, the palate, the lips, and the crown of the head.

The Tenth BIDDYA.

Neerkut, the contents of the Bedes.

The Eleventh BIDDYA.

Jowtick, aſtronomy and aſtrology.

The

The Twelfth BIDDYA.

Ch-hund, of the different kinds of verſe. The firſt ſix *Biddyas* are called *Ung*, which ſignifies whatever is neceſſary to be known for comprehending the *Bedes*.

The Thirteenth BIDDYA.

Meymansa, of the three ſects of which ſomething has been ſaid.

The Fourteenth BIDDYA.

Nee-aiy, which has been treated ſummarily among the ſciences. Many believe that the knowledge of theſe fourteen *Biddyas* are ſufficient for obtaining *Muckut*. But ſome add the following.

The Fifteenth BIDDYA.

Iyrbede, the art of preſerving health; and what remedies to apply to different diſeaſes. This is taken from the *Rig*, or firſt Bede.

The Sixteenth BIDDYA.

Dehnerbede, the art of managing the bow and arrow, and other arms. This is taken from the *Jejir*, or ſecond Bede.

The Seventeenth BIDDYA.

Gandhrib, the art of muſic, compriſing compoſition, ſinging, and playing. This is taken from the *Sam*, or third Bede.

The Eighteenth BIDDYA.

Art-h-shaster, how to acquire wealth, and the manner of employing it to advantage. This is taken from the *Atherbun*, or fourth Bede. Theſe laſt five Biddyas are collectively called *Owpbede*.

OTHER

OTHER ARTS.

In the extenſive empire of Hindoſtan there are ſo many arts that they cannot be deſcribed. Something, however, ſhall be ſaid of them, which may prove an acceptable preſent to the curious enquirer, and perhaps excite his further curioſity.

KURREMBEYPAK.

This is a ſurpriſing art, in which all the ſix ſects perfectly agree. By it can be diſcovered whatever was done by men in their former ſtate of exiſtence, and it preſcribes a particular expiation for each crime. This art is of four kinds.

THE FIRST KIND ſhows in what manner a man has conducted himſelf in his former ſtate of exiſtence.

A *Kehteree* who lives virtuouſly, when he is born again tranſmigrates into a *Brahmin*. A *Byess*, who forfeits his life for the ſake of a *Brahmin*, tranſmigrates into a *Kehteree*. A *Sooder*, who lends money without intereſt, and never diſtreſſes his creditor for payment, will be a *Byess*. A *Mileetch* who ſerves a *Brahmin*, and eats of his food till the time of his death, will become a *Sooder*. A *Brahmin* who acts the part of a *Kehteree* will become a *Kehteree*. A *Kehteree*, who deſcends to the offices of a *Byess*, will become a *Byess*; and thus a *Byess* a *Sooder*, and a *Sooder* a *Mileetch*. Alſo, whoſoever accepts of the donation called *Kishnej*, or accepts in alms the bed which a perſon died upon, or a *Buffaloe*, or whatever is beſtowed in the temple of *Kurkhet*, will, in the next life, from being a man, become a woman. And any woman, or *Mileetch*, who ſees the image of *Narayin*, in the temple of *Bidreenarayin*, and performs certain incantations, in the next birth, the woman will become a man, and the *Mileetch*

leetch a *Brahmin*. This temple is in the northern mountains, a great way beyond *Hirdewar*.

THE SECOND KIND. The different diseases of the human body, which are punishments for crimes committed in a former state; and the various ceremonies for procuring health.

Physicians say, that sickness originates in the animal constitution; but those that are skilled in the art we are now treating of, maintain it to be a punishment for crimes committed in a former state. The Hindoo philosophers divide bodily diseases into three kinds; 1, Those that can be cured by medicines; 2, Those to be removed by certain ceremonies; 3, And those that require the application of both methods. In order to discover each, they describe three kinds of crimes, viz. what were done whilst awake intentionally or unintentionally; and what were committed during sleep. They have volumes upon this art which they consult, and consider physicians as useless.

The *Headache* is a punishment for having in a former state spoken irreverently to father or mother. *Cure:* Let him make of two tolahs of gold the images of *Kushup* and *Adit*, and considering them to be the representations of the father and mother of the *Dewtahs*, give them to the needy.

Madness is a punishment for disobedience to father, mother, or *Peer*. *Cure:* Let him perform *Chanderayin*, which is to eat on the first day only one mouthful; two mouthfuls during the second day, and thus continue increasing a mouthful every day, for a month; and then decreasing gradually a mouthful on each day, till he leaves off as he began. Or let him make *Kushup* and *Adit* each of two tolahs of gold, and give them to the poor.

The *Epilepsy* is a punishment for having adminis-

tered

tered poiſon to any one, at the command of his maſter. *Cure:* Beſtowing in charity two ſuch images as laſt deſcribed, together with a cow, thirty-two ſeers of ſeſamé ſeed, and repeating ſome incantations in the name of *Mahadeo.*

Pain in the Eyes is a puniſhment for having coveted another man's wife. *Cure:* Performing the faſt of *Chanderayin.*

Blindness is a puniſhment for having killed his mother. This perſon, before his new birth, will ſuffer many years torments in hell. *Cure:* Performing the ceremony of *Parajaputty*, which is of five kinds. 1, Beſtowing in charity a cow. 2, Or one tolah of gold. 3, Or feeding twelve *Brahmins.* 4, Or throwing into the fire ten thouſand times a mixture of ſeſamé ſeed, ghee, honey, and ſugar. 5, Or going barefooted to a temple, for the diſtance of a *Jowjun.* Or let him make a boat after the following deſcription: the boat of four tolahs of gold, the maſt of ſilver, and ſix oars of copper; and beſtow it in charity. But if it ſhould be a puniſhment for having only acted in contradiction to the commands of his father or mother, let him make the images of *Kushup* and *Adit*, as before deſcribed.

Dumbness is a puniſhment for having killed his ſiſter. *Cure:* Let him form a cow of the following deſcription: the body four tolahs of gold; the hoofs two tolahs of ſilver; the hump two or three maſhas of copper. This, with a veſſel of braſs for the milk, he muſt give in charity, and for one week eat nothing but a mixture of milk, curds, ghee, and cow's urine and dung.

The *Bellyache* is a puniſhment for having eaten with a perſon of a different religion, or with a liar. *Cure:* Faſting three days, and giving away in charity twelve tolahs of ſilver.

The

The *Stone* is a puniſhment for having committed inceſt with his mother. *Cure:* Performing the ceremony of *Mudhoodheen*, which is as follows: he muſt conceive in his imagination that the following articles form a complete cow, viz. that four veſſels, each containing one and a quarter maund, filled with honey, repreſent her body; one tolah of gold her mouth; four ſeers of ſugar-candy her teeth; two pearls her eyes; two pieces of lignum aloes her horns; two plantains her ears; wheat flour her dugs; three ſeers of ſugar-cane for each leg; a white woollen cloth thrown over the whole her hide; ſkeins of ſilk the tail. The hoofs of this cow muſt be of ſilver, and her neck be covered with two pieces of red cloth; in the front muſt be ſet a copper veſſel; and eight ſeers of four different kinds of grain formed into a heap. Near her muſt be placed a veſſel full of honey to repreſent her calf, and copper veſſels full of ſeſamé ſeed. When theſe are completed, he muſt repeat certain incantations, worſhip them, and afterwards beſtow them in charity.

Lameness is a puniſhment for having kicked a *Brahmin*. *Cure:* Let him make one tolah of gold into the form of a horſe, and beſtow it in charity; and give food to one hundred and eight *Bramins*.

A *Fever* is a puniſhment for killing an innocent *Kehteree*. *Cure:* Repeating one hundred times the incantation of *Mahadeo*; feeding thirteen *Brahmins*; and ſprinkling with water the image of *Mahadeo* one hundred times.

A *Cough* is a puniſhment for killing a *Brahmin*. *Cure:* Making a lotus of four tolahs of gold, and, after repeating certain incantations, performing with it the ceremony of *Howm*, and giving it to a righteous *Brahmin*.

Flux

Flux is a punishment for having killed his wife, without her having committed any fault. *Cure:* Performing the ceremony of *Kishnajun*, which is spreading a deer skin, and laying upon it a heap of sesame seed, and one hundred tolahs of gold, or more; repeating certain incantations, and performing the *Howm*. It is considered as a very wicked action to accept of this charity.

The *Asthma* is a punishment for having accepted of the *Kishnajun*. *Cure:* Make a buffaloe of iron, with horns of lead, and the forehead of stone. Load it with keneer flowers, cover it with a black blanket, and give it in charity, together with three and half maunds of mash.

Indigestion is a punishment for having robbed a house. *Cure:* Let him bestow in charity the following articles; a house and furniture; seven kinds of grain; of each thirty-two seers; a hand-mill; a pestle and mortar; drinking vessels; a stove; a broom; a cow; and money according to his circumstances.

THE THIRD KIND, for what crimes committed in a former life; a woman has no children during her present existence; and other particulars.

A woman whose husband dies before her, in her former state was of a great family, which she left to live with a stranger, and when he died, burnt herself with him. *Cure:* She must pass all her life in austerities, or put an end to her existence by burying herself in snow.

A woman who does not menstruate, is punished for the following action: once in a former state when she had her customs, some neighbouring children came into her house to play, but she was angry, and drove them

them away. *Cure:* Let her fill an earthen veſſel with water from one hundred wells, throw into it a beetle-nut, a maſha of gold, and perfumes; and then give it to a *Brahmin.* She muſt alſo give five, or ſeven, or nine, or eleven kinds of fruit to children to eat.

A woman whoſe child dies ſoon after its birth, is puniſhed for having in her former exiſtence expoſed a child, and who died. This, although it be a common practice in Hindoſtan, is nevertheleſs very nefarious. *Cure:* Make a cow, the body of four tolahs of gold, the hoofs of one tolah of ſilver, a jewel for her tail, braſs-bells on her neck; together with a calf of one tolah of gold, and half a tolah of ſilver for its hoofs, then beſtow them in charity.

A woman who has only daughters, is puniſhed for having poſſeſſed a great deal of pride in her former exiſtence, and not ſhowing proper reſpect to her huſband. *Cure:* Let her plate the horns of a white ox with four tolahs of gold, and the hoofs with four tolahs of ſilver, and cover the hump with one and a quarter tolah of copper; which ſhe muſt beſtow in charity, with a veſſel made of two and a half ſeers of braſs; beſides ſatisfying with food one hundred *Brahmins.* Or ſhe muſt make ten maſhas of gold into the form of the Deity, and after performing certain incantations, give it in charity, and feed fifty *Brahmins.*

A woman who has only one ſon, in her former exiſtence took a calf from its parent cow. *Cure:* Giving away a milch cow, with ten tolahs of gold.

A woman whoſe ſon dies, and daughter lives, in her former ſtate killed animals. Some ſay it is only for having killed goats. *Cure:* Performing the faſt of *Chanderayin,* giving away a cow, and feeding fifty *Brahmins.*

A woman

A woman who is pregnapt for ſixteen years, without being delivered, in her former ſtate was burnt when pregnant. *Cure:* Beſtowing the charity of *Hurrenkhereh.*

Being a maid ſervant, is a puniſhment for having had criminal connexion with the huſband of another in her former exiſtence, and having burnt herſelf with him. *Cure:* If ſhe is in the houſe of a *Soodre*, let her go to the houſe of a *Byess*, then paſs to that of a *Kehteree*, and laſt to that of a *Brahmin*, and remain in his ſervice till her death.

THE FOURTH KIND, of riches and poverty, &c. Whoſoever beſtows charity at the appointed times, ſuch as during the eclipſes of the ſun and moon, in his next ſtate of exiſtence will be rich and bountiful. Whoſoever at theſe times goes to any holy place, particularly *Ilahabass*, and there deprives himſelf of life, will poſſeſs great ſtore of wealth in his next ſtate.

Whoſoever, when he is hungry, and has food before him, upon hearing the voice of a beggar, gives the whole to him, will in his next life be very rich, and ſucceſsful in all his undertakings.

But whoſoever refuſes to do ſo, will in the preſent life be poor and unlucky. *Cure:* To whatever tribe he belongs let him religiouſly perform the duties thereof, and alſo during the time of eclipſes viſit *Koorkheyt*, and bury in the ground, by way of oblation, a piece of gold, if it be but one maſha.

On each of the four kinds of this art, they have written books, deſcribing the ſymptoms and remedies. What I have related is only an abſtract.

SUR,

Is the art of predicting events, by obferving in what manner the breath iffues through the noftrils.

The breath comes out of the noftrils after three ways. Firft, when it comes moftly out of the left noftril. This they attribute to the influence of the moon, and call *Adda* and *Chandernaree*. The fecond, when it iffues moft from the right noftril, which they attribute to the influence of the fun, and therefore call *Soorejnaree* and *Pingela*. The third is, when both noftrils breathe equally, which they call *Sookkmurna* and *Soomkhoonaree*.

The following is the order in which the breath ought to pafs through the nofe: from *Perwa* to the third *Teth*, *Chandernaree*, and the fame number of days *Soorejnaree*, alternately throughout the month. Others make it weekly thus, Sunday, Tuefday, Thurfday, and Saturday, *Soorejnaree*; and Monday, Wednefday, and Friday, *Chandernaree*. Others maintain, that it is regulated by the fun's courfe through the zodiack, Aries beginning with *Soorejnaree*, Taurus with *Chandernaree*, and thus alternately through all the figns. All the learned of the Hindoos believe, that if a man breathes differently from one of thefe three ways, fome misfortune will befal him. That if the irregularity lafts two days, a quarrel will enfue. If it continues ten days, fome misfortune will befal his wife. If fifteen days, he will have a fevere fit of ficknefs. If for a month, his brother will die. Others fpeak thus of the irregularities of breathing. If for a day and night *Soorejnaree* is in excefs, the perfon will die at the expiration of a year. If it lafts two days and nights, he will live two years, and fo a year for every day. If the excefs continues for a month, he will die at the end of the enfuing month. For the excefs of *Chandernaree*, they

fay

ſay if it laſts a day and night, that perſon will have a fit of ſickneſs at the expiration of a year, and according to the number of days he will be ſo many years ſick.

The Manner of predicting Events by the Knowledge of this Art.

If any one comes to enquire whether a woman who is pregnant, ſhall be delivered of a boy or a girl, the perſon who is to anſwer muſt examine the noſtrils of the queſtioner. If he breathes more through one noſtril than the other, and ſtands on that ſide, it ſhall foretel a ſon; but if he happens to place himſelf on the oppoſite ſide, it ſhall indicate that it will be a daughter. If he breathes equally through both noſtrils, there will be twins. Some believe that if the queſtioner ſtands on the *Soorejnaree* ſide, it will be a boy; and if on the *Chandernaree*, a daughter; and that if it be *Sookhmunna*, it denotes an hermaphrodite.

If an enquiry is made concerning a perſon who is ſick, if the queſtioner ſtands on the *Soorejnaree* ſide, the ſick perſon will die; but if he ſtands on the *Chandernaree* ſide, he will recover.

If it be enquired whether or not an enemy's army will come, if the queſtioner is *Chandernaree*, and ſtands on that ſide, the army will come; but if he is *Soorejnaree*, and ſtands on that ſide, it will not come.

If he enquires concerning peace and war, *Chandernaree* implies the firſt, and *Soorejnaree* the laſt.

AKUM,

Teaches what incantations are advantageous, and what are hurtful, what will improve the underſtanding, increaſe rank and fortune, cure diſeaſes, ſubdue enemies, cement friendſhip, inſure the conqueſt of countries, and advance the ſucceſs of government.

1 SHOOGUN,

SHOOGUN,

Is the art of difcovering what is now happening, and predicting future events, by obferving the motions of birds. This is an art in which the Hindoos are fkilled.

The learned Hindoos difcover hidden things by means of five things: 1, *Astrology*. 2, *Sur*. 3, *Shoogun*. 4, *Keywul*, which are omens learnt by throwing dice. 5, *Samdirg*, predicting from obferving the form of the members and their motions, the lines and moles on the body.

GARUD,

Is the art of repeating certain incantations, for recovering a perfon who has been ftung by a fcorpion, a fnake, or any other venomous reptile. This is done by repeating his genealogy, and praifing his anceftors, which obliges the animal to prefent itfelf. The following is a wonderful fact. When they have caught an old fnake, of a particular fpecies, they repeat certain incantations, and then make it bite a *Brahmin*. When the poifon takes effect, the *Brahmin* continues for fome time in a ftate of ftupefaction, when, upon any queftions being put to him, he gives anfwers that are invariably found to be true. The Hindoo philofophers believe, that during the revolution of the *Cal Jowg*, nothing is truer than fuch anfwers. And thefe anfwers have been collected together into feveral volumes.

INDERJAL,

Is the arts of Necromancy, Talifmans, and Slight of Hand, in which they are wonderful beyond defcription.

RUSSBIDDYA,

Teaches how to kill quickſilver, gold, ſilver, copper, and other metals; and it alſo compriſes Alchymy.

RUTTENPURETCHA,

Is the art of judging precious ſtones, their properties, and value.

KAM SHASTER,

Treats of the generation of the human race.

SAHTEE,

Is the art of writing with elegance, and the ſkilful uſe of irony. Thus, a woman ſent a handmaid to call her huſband, who, when ſhe came to him, uſed criminal familiarity with her; and ſent back an excuſe to his wife for not coming home. The diſordered ſtate of the girl's dreſs evidently diſcovered what had happened. But the wife, being a woman of prudence, and having regard for her huſband's character, diſguiſed her anger; but reprimanded the girl in the following ironical manner: "You have told a lye; you did not go to my huſband, but idly went and bathed yourſelf in the river; for behold the *Sirmah** is out of your eyes, and the ſandal ointment is no longer upon your body." By this delicate irony, ſhe diſcovered to the girl that ſhe was not ignorant of what had really happened. This art alſo treats of *Nowruss*, or the nine human inclinations. Firſt, *Singarruss*, the friendſhip between man and woman, and the conſequences of connexion and ſeparation. Second, *Hassuruss*, the different kinds of laughter which they ſay is excited either by changes in the body or dreſs, or by actions. Laughter is of three kinds. 1. *Simt*, a little alteration in the cheeks, eyes, and lips. 2, *Wehrut*, opening the mouth. 3.

* A preparation of antimony, with which they tinge the eyebrows, eyelaſhes, and corners of the eyes.

Aphust,

Aphust, loud laughter. Third, *Kurrenruss*, grief. Fourth, *Raoudre*, anger. Fifth, *Veer*, joy. Sixth, *Bheyaneck*, fear. Seventh, *Behbutch*, averſion. Eighth, *Adhowt*, amazement. Ninth, *Sant*, or that kind of happineſs which is obtained by knowledge, when the mind is freed from enmity and partiality. Of theſe they make many ſubdiviſions, which they illuſtrate with delightful ſtories.

SAHTEE,

Alſo contains a deſcription of the different kinds of men and women that excite love and friendſhip. In Turan and Iran, friendſhip is chiefly deſcribed by the poets, as ſubſiſting between men; but in Hindoſtan it is celebrated between man and woman. The Hindoo philoſophers call woman *Naeykha*, and make the ſex to conſiſt of ſeveral kinds. *Sewaya*, a virtuous woman, who loves her huſband: ſhe is ſo modeſt that no man can diſcover her looking at him: ſhe never laughs loud, nor ſmiles ſo as to ſhow her teeth: ſpeaks ſeldom, and always in a low tone; is never in a paſſion; and never goes out of doors, even if ſhe has the opportunity. *Pirkeya*, one who is wanton, but carries on her intrigues with ſecrecy: if ſhe is married, they call her *Purredha*, and if ſingle, *Kunneka*. *Samaneya* has no paſſion but the deſire of wealth.

Sewaya is again divided into three kinds, viz. *Mokdha*, one who, in her youth, betrays ſigns of wantonneſs, but flies from the embraces of her huſband. This happens from eight to eighteen years. *Muddheya*, is modeſt, and has a great affection for her huſband, and never mentions his name in anger. This ſtate laſts to the age of thirty-two years. *Pirgulbha*, makes her own deſires and knowledge ſubſervient to the will of her huſband, and captivates him by her wiſe conduct. This is from thirty-two till fifty. The two laſt mentioned are moreover of three kinds. *Dheera*, if her huſband attaches himſelf to another woman, ſhe becomes jealous and diſturbed, but increaſes her affection and aſſiduity, and thereby reclaims him, by making him aſhamed of himſelf. *Adheena*, diſcovers her uneaſineſs, and attacks her huſband with irony; as, for example. "It is aſtoniſhing, that from your want of ſleep, my eyes ſhould be thus inflamed; and that by your having drank wine, my heart ſhould be intoxicated." *Dheera Adheera*, unites both theſe diſpoſitions.

Pirkeya, is of five kinds. *Goompulta*, conceals her indiſcretions, by feigning plauſible excuſes. Thus, being ſcratched with the nail of her lover, ſhe ſays, "A cat ran over me laſt night in bed, and in attempting to catch a mouſe, gave me this ſcratch." *Weedugdha*, is pleaſing in her converſation, and poſſeſſes every female accompliſhment. *Lecheta*, beſtows her favours without ſhame. *Kuletta*, proſtitutes her perſon, merely for the ſake of vice. *Unneſeyana*, has the inclination to intrigue, but is prevented by timidity.

They alſo claſs women in the following manner. *Pooroukhitbhertika*, one who is inconſolable for the abſence of her huſband, and cannot reſt on account of her apprehenſions for his ſafety. This again is of ſeveral kinds. *Khundita*, is inconſolable for her lover having proved faithleſs. *Bulhentreta*, is ſorry for having diſcovered her paſſion for her lover, and ſtrives to remedy her indiſcretion. *Bebpirlubdha*, is one who goes to an appointed place, and does not find her lover there. *Ootka*, is ſorrowful for the diſappointment, and ſeeks the cauſe of his not having come. *Basuckpja*, is making joyful preparations for the arrival of her lover. *Sewadheenseetka*, is ſhe who hath powerful aſcendency over her lover. *Abhesareeka*, ſhe who calls her lover to her, or goes to him.

The following is another method of claſſing women.

Ootema,

Ootema, whose husband does not love her, whilst she is distractedly fond of him. *Adhima*, the contrary. *Mudhima*, is sometimes in friendship, and sometimes in enmity, with her husband.

Another division. *Pudminnee*, an incomparable beauty, with a good disposition; she is tall, and well-proportioned; has a melodious tone of voice; talks little; her breath resembles a rose; she is chaste; and obedient to her husband. *Chittrunnee*, something inferior to the other in beauty of face; is neither fat nor lean; has a small waist, and full breast. *Sunktnnee*, is fat and short, of a violent temper, and is always quarrelling with her husband. *Hesstenee*, worse in appearance and temper than the last. Of these they treat at length, and allot each to particular kinds of men.

Man, a wife who is disrespectful to her husband; and this they reckon of four kinds. 1. *Lugh*, she who assumes consequence upon her husband showing her a little affection. 2, *Muddhee*, she who, after suffering a little trouble, gives up her affection for him. 3. *Goor*, looses her affection after suffering a great deal. 4, *Russabhess*, who refuses comfort, and lessens her affection.

Man, they call *Nayick*, and describe three kinds. 1. *Put*, one who marries an Hindoo wife. 2, *Owpupt*, he who defiles himself by marrying a woman of another religion. 3, *Bisheyek*, a fornicator. And each of these are again of three kinds. 1, *Unkole*, is he who has only one wife. 2, *Dutchen*, has several wives, but agrees with them all. 3, *Dhisht*, has only one wife, who uses him ill, which only serves to increase his affection.

Sakhee, is a faithful maid-servant, whose master and mistress have perfect reliance upon her fidelity, and take her advice upon all occasions. She amuses her mistress when on a journey, assists in putting on her ornaments,

ornaments, and if there happens any family misunderstanding, she endeavours to effect a reconciliation. Such a mediatrix is called *Dootee*; and if a man, *Doot*.

Sahtee also comprises rules for behaviour, exemplified by pleasing tales, which may be consulted at length by those who are desirous of being farther informed on this head.

SUNGEET,

Is the art of vocal and instrumental music; together with that of dancing.

The rules thereof are comprised in seven books, viz. First, *Soor*, the nature of sound, which is of two kinds; *Annahut*, a sound without any earthly cause, and which they consider to have existed from all eternity, after the following manner. When a man closes the orifices of his ears with his fingers, he perceives an inward noise, to which they give this name. They say this proceeds from *Brahma*, and that it cannot be heard without stopping the ears, till a man is in the state of *Muckut*, when it becomes part of his nature. *Akut*, a sound which proceeds from a cause which, like speech, they consider to be an accident of air, occasioned by percussion. They say that Providence has given every man twenty-two nerves, extending from the belly to the crown of the head, through which the air passes from the navel upwards; and according as these nerves are employed forcibly or weakly, in such degree is the sound uttered. The air does not pass through the fifth, sixth, eighteenth and nineteenth nerves, consequently they are mute; but the sound uttered through the others they divide into seven kinds, in the following order. 1, *Surj*, is like the voice of the peacock, and which is produced by the fourth nerve. 2, *Righbeh*, is like the voice of the *Peepeeheh*, a bird resembling the *Sar*, which sings in the rainy season. It is in compass from the

the ſeventh to the tenth nerve. 3, *Gandhar*, is like the bleating of a goat, and reaches from the ninth to the thirteenth nerve. 4, *Mudhen*, is like the voice of the crane, and reaches from the thirteenth to the ſixteenth nerve. 5, *Punchem*, is like the voice of the bird called the *Koyil*, and reaches the ſeventh nerve. 6, *Dehwut*, is like the voice of the lizard, and reaches from the eighth to the twenty-ſecond. 7, *Nikhad*, is like the noiſe of the elephant, and reaches from the twenty-ſecond to the third.

An air, which contains all theſe ſeven *Soors*, they call *Sunpoorun*. If it has ſix, *Kahdow*; if ſive, *Owdub*; and no air has fewer. But the *Tan* (or ſymphony) may be compoſed of two.

SECOND ADHYA, *Ragbibeehai*, the Modes and their Variations.

They ſay, that ſinging was invented by *Mahadeo* and *Purbutty*. That the firſt had five mouths, from each of which iſſued a muſical mode in the following order: 1, *Sree Rag*; 2, *Bussunt*; 3, *Behrowng*; 4, *Punchem*; 5, *Megh*. To theſe they add *Nutnarain*, which they attribute to *Purbutty*. Theſe ſix modes they call *Rag*, and each has ſeveral variations; but the ſix following are what are moſt common.

Variations of Sree Rag, 1, *Malwee*; 2, *Tirowenee*; 3, *Gowree*; 4, *Keydaree*; 5, *Maddeemadwee*; 6, *Beharee*.

Variations of Buſſunt, 1, *Deysee*; 2, *Deogurree*; 3, *Byratty*; 4, *Towree*; 5, *Lellita*; 6, *Hindowlee*.

Variations of Behrowng, 1, *Behrowng*; 2, *Muddehmad*; 3, *Bihrowee*; 3, *Bungalee*; 4, *Biratka*; 5, *Sindawee*; 6, *Poonargeya*.

Variations

Variations of Punchem, 1, *Beybhass*; 2, *Bhoopalee*; 3, *Kanra*; 4, *Badhunsha*; 5, *Malsree*; 6, *Pudmunjeree*.

Variations of Megh, 1, *Mullar*; 2, *Sowrutty*; 3, *Assawurree*; 4, *Keyseekee*; 5, *Gundhar*; 6, *Hirsingaree*.

Variations of Nuntnarain, 1, *Kammoodee*; 2, *Kulleyen*; 3, *Adheeree*; 4, *Soodhnaut*; 5, *Saluh*; 6, *Nutkummer*.

Some make only four variations of each *Rag*.

Others in the place of *Bussunt*, *Punchem*, and *Megh*, ufe *Malkoosuck*, *Hindowl*, and *Deepuc*, and make five variations of each. Others inftead of *Bussunt*, *Behrowng*, *Punchem*, and *Megh*, ufe *Loodh*, *Behrown*, *Hindowl*, *Deyskar*, and *Soodhnaut*.

There are two kinds of fongs, *Marug* being thofe invented by the *Dewtahs* and the *Rekehsir*, which are the fame every where, and are univerfally held in the higheft veneration. In the *Dekhan* there are many who fing them in different ways, amongft which are the following: 1, *Soorejperkass*; 2, *Penjtalisser*; 3, *Sirbetoobehdir*; 4, *Chanderperkass*; 5, *Raghuddem*; 6, *Shoomra*; and 7. *Surtunnee*.

The other kind of fongs are called *Deysee* (or local), each place having its peculiar ones, as *Dhoorpud* in Agra, Gualiar, Bary, and that neighbourhood. In the reign of Rajah Manfingh at Gualiar, three of his muficians, named Naik Bukhfhoo, Mujhoo, and Bhaunoo, formed a collection of fongs fuited to the tafte of every clafs of people. When Manfingh died, Bukhfhoo and Mujhoo went into the fervice of Sultan Bahader Gujeratty,

ratty, and being highly esteemed by that prince, introduced into his court this kind of songs.

The *Dhoorpud* consists of stanzas of three or four rhymical lines of any length. They are chiefly in praise of men who have been famous for their valour or their virtue. The *Deysee* songs, in the Telingee and Carnatic dialects, are called *Dherow*; the subject is generally love. Those sung in Bengal, are called *Bungeela*. Those of Jownpoor, *Chootkutta*. Those of Dehly, *Kowl* and *Teraneh*. These last were composed by Ameer Khosru of Dehly, with the assistance of Samut and Tetar; they are a delightful mixture of the Persian and Hindovee style. Those of Mehtra are called *Bishenpud*, consisting of stanzas of four or six lines, and are in praise of Kishen. Those of Sind are called *Kamee*, and are on love and friendship. Those in the Terhut language, called *Lehcharee*, were composed by Bedyaput, and are on the violence of the passion of love. Those of Lahore are called *Chund*. Those of Gujerat *Juckree*. The warlike and heroic songs are called *Kirkeh* and *Sadereh*; they are of different measures, and in various dialects. Besides those already mentioned there are many others, amongst which are *Poorbee*, *Dehnasiree*, *Rumkully*, *Koryie*, *Soohoo*, *Deyskar*, and *Deysneck*.

THE THIRD ADHYA, *Purkeerenka*, treats of *Alap*, which is of two kinds. 1, *Ragalap*, the *Tan*, or symphony, which contains the subject of the air. 2, *Roopalap*, the air with the words.

THE FOURTH ADHYA, *Pirbendh*, is the art of composing *Geet* (or song,) and consists of six things. 1, *Soor*. 1, *Bered* (praise). 3, *Pud*, the person praised. 4, *Tinna*, or Amen. 5, *Tuntinna*, or Amen, Amen. 6, *Neehrut*, Time.

Paut

Paut ſignifies the variations of the word *Tuntinna*, from three to twenty ſyllables. This therefore is an exceſs of time.

Taul, or meaſure. If the *Taul* contains ſix *Tuntinnas*, it is called *Meydenee*; if five *Anundenee*; if four *Debnee*; if three *Bhawanee*; if two *Terawely*; and it never conſiſts of fewer.

The four *Adhyas*, above deſcribed, are only diviſions of *Soor*, or melody.

THE FIFTH ADHYA, *Taul*, treats of the nature and quantity of the meaſure.

THE SIXTH ADHYA, *Wadya*, of muſical inſtruments, and which are of four kinds. 1, *Tut*, ſtringed inſtruments. 2, *Tit*, thoſe made of ſkins, ſuch as drums. 3, *Gheen*, any two things that produce ſound by percuſſion. 4, *Sookhir*, wind inſtruments.

STRINGED INSTRUMENTS.

The *Junter* has a neck of hollowed wood, an ell in length, at each end of which is faſtened half of a gourd. On the neck are placed ſixteen wooden frets, over which are ſtrung ſix iron wires, faſtened into both ends of the neck. The tone is varied, by means of the frets.

The *Bheen* reſembles the *Junter*; but has only three ſtrings.

The *Kinner* has a longer neck than the *Bheen*; and has three gourds with two ſtrings.

The *Sirbheen* is like the *Bheen*, excepting that it has not any frets.

The

The *Ambirtee*, the neck of this is ſmaller than that of the *Sirbheen*, and it has only one gourd, which is placed in the middle of the neck underneath, and one iron wire. The changes of the modes are played upon it.

The *Rebab*, in general, has ſix ſtrings of gut; but ſome have twelve, and others eighteen.

The *Sirmendel* reſembles the *Canoon*. It has twenty-one ſtrings, ſome of which are of iron, ſome of braſs, and ſome of gut.

The *Saringee*, called alſo *Soorbutan*, is of the ſhape of a bow, with two hollow cups inverted at each end. It has one ſtring of gut, reſembling a bow-ſtring. They hold under the ſtring a ſmall gourd, and play with a plectrum.

The *Adhowtee* is a gourd with two wires.

The *Kingerah* reſembles the *Bheen*, but has only two ſtrings of gut, and the gourds are ſmaller.

The SECOND KIND of INSTRUMENTS, or DRUMS.

The *Pukawej* is a hollow piece of wood, in the ſhape of a citron, but flat at both ends, which are covered with parchment; and it is held under one arm.

The *Awej* reſembles two falconers drums faſtened together. It is braced with ſtrings of ſilk.

The *Dehl* is another kind of drum, well known.

The *Dheddeh* is ſmaller than the *Dehl*.

The *Irdahwej* is half the ſize of the *Awej*.

The

The *Duff* is another kind of drum, well known.

The *Khenjir* is a little *Duff* hung round with fmall bells.

The THIRD KIND of INSTRUMENTS, thofe of PERCUSSION.

The *Tal* is a pair of brafs cups, with broad mouths.

The *Kut-h Tal* refemble fmall fifh, and are made of wood or ftone. A fet confifts of four.

The SIXTH KIND, or WIND INSTRUMENTS.

The *Shehna* is the fame as the Perfian *Sirna*, or trumpet.

The *Mushk* is compofed of two reeds, perforated according to rule, and joined together in a leather bag. In the Perfian language it is called *Nie Amban*, or the bagpipe.

The *Moorlee* is a kind of flute.

The *Owpunk* is a hollow tube, an ell long, with a hole in the centre, in which is placed a fmall reed.

The SEVENTH ADHYA, *Tirtya*, or the Art of Dancing.

The different kinds of SINGERS.

Thofe who fing the ancient fongs, which are the fame every where, are called *Bykar*; and thofe who teach them *Sehkar*. The *Kerawunt* chiefly fing the *Dhoorpud*.

The *Dharhee* are thofe who fing the Penjaby fongs, which they accompany with the *Dehdeh*, and *Kingerah*. Many of thefe fing in the field of battle the praifes of heroes,

heroes, to excite the troops to valiant actions. The *Kewall* are of this number, but sing chiefly the Dehly airs and Persian songs in the same style. The *Poorkeya*, the men accompany their voices with the *Awej*, and the women with the *Tal*; formerly they sung the *Kirkeh*, but now the *Dhoorpud*, and such like. There are many beautiful women of this class. The *Dufzun* are chiefly Pinjaby women, who play on the *Duff* and *Dehl*, and sing *Dhoorpud*, and the *Sehlah*, or nuptial and birth-day songs. Formerly they appeared only before women; but now they will exhibit in public. The *Sezdehtaly*, the men of this class have large *Duffs*, and one of the women plays at once upon thirteen pair of *Tal*, placing them upon her wrists, backs of the hands, elbows, shoulders, back of the neck, and on the breast. These are mostly natives of Gujerat and Malva. The *Nutwah* dance with graceful motions, and sing and play upon the *Pukawej*, *Rebab*, and *Tal*.

The *Keertunnya* are *Brahmins*, whose instruments are such as were in use amongst the ancients, viz. the *Pukawej*, *Rebab*, and *Tal*. They are boys dressed like women, who sing the praises of Kishen. The *Bhugleyeh*, whose songs are the same as the last; but they change their dresses, and are great mimics. They exhibit at night. The *Bhunweyeh* greatly resemble the last, but exhibit both in day and night. They dance in a surprising manner, in the compass of a brass dish, called, in the Hindovee language, *Talee*. They also sing. The *Bhend* play on the *Dhel* and *Tal*, and sing. They represent different animals. They draw up water through the nostrils. They run an iron spit down their throat into the stomach. They swallow a mixture of different kinds of grain, and then bring them up again separately, with other slights of hand. The *Kunjeree*, the men play on the *Pukawej*, *Rebab*, and *Tal*; and the women sing and dance. His majesty calls them *Kunchenee*. The *Nut* play on the *Dehl* and *Tal*, dance

dance upon the rope, and throw themſelves into ſtrange poſtures. The *Behroopee* exhibit in the day, and change their appearance in ſuch a manner, that old men ſeem to be youths, and youths old men, beyond detection. The jugglers are ſo dexterous, that they will ſeem to cut a man in pieces, and join him together again.

The AKAHREH, *or Private Singing and Dancing.*

This is an entertainment given at night by great people to their own family. The performers are generally women of the houſe, who are inſtructed by proper people.

A ſet conſiſts of four dancers, four ſingers, and four others who play the *Tal*, with two *Pukawej*, two *Owpunks*, one *Rebab*, one *Junter*; and two who ſtand by with torches. They are for the moſt part inſtructed by the *Nutwah*, who ſometimes teach ſlaves of their own, and then ſell them.

His majeſty is exceſſively fond of muſic, and has a perfect knowledge of its principles. This art, which the generality of people uſe as the means of obtaining ſleep, ſerves to amuſe him and keep him awake.

GUJ SHASTER.

A deſcription of elephants, with inſtructions how to diſcover their age and qualities, their diſeaſes and cure.

SALHOWTER.

The art of farriery.

BASTOOK.

The art of building in every branch.

SOOP.

Treats of the various properties of food.

RAJNEET.

RAJNEET.

The art of governing a kingdom.

There are eight cauſes of anger: 1, Deprivation of riches. 2, Ingratitude. 3, Betraying a ſecret. 4, Neglecting a faithful ſervant. 5, Abuſive language. 6, Unjuſt ſuſpicion. 7, Murder. 8, Cenſoriouſneſs.

It is incumbent on a monarch to diveſt himſelf of avarice and anger, by following the counſels of wiſdom, and not to debaſe himſelf by the commiſſion of any of the eight crimes above mentioned. If he unfortunately ſuffers injury from others, it behoves him to be moderate in his reſentments. It is his indiſpenſible duty to fear God; to be juſt and merciful himſelf, and to excite the like diſpoſition in others; to pay particular reſpect to men of exalted rank, and behave with kindneſs and condeſcenſion towards his ſubjects of every deſcription. He ſhould be ambitious to extend his dominions; and protect his ſubjects from the oppreſſions of his officers, from robbers, and other evil doers; proportioning the puniſhment to the offence. In every thing that concerns himſelf he ſhould be patient, and forgiving of injuries. For his intelligencers, he muſt make choice of men of wiſdom and integrity. No enemy is ſo inſignificant as to be beneath his notice; and therefore he ought to be ever on his guard. Neither muſt he be vain of his own wealth or power. A wiſe prince will baniſh from his court all corrupt and deſigning men. The king reſembles a gardener, who plucks up the thorns and briers, and throws them on one ſide, whereby he beautifies his garden, and at the ſame time raiſes a fence, which preſerves his ground from the intruſion of ſtrangers. Thus a monarch employs on his frontiers men of bold and daring diſpoſitions; making them a ſerviceable barrier againſt invaders; and purging his court of turbulence and ſtrife.

 The

The gardener lops off the redundant branches, and plucks away ſuch leaves as would only ſerve to deprive the tree of its ſtrength. In like manner the king detaches from the nobles their too numerous friends, and dangerous dependents. The gardener alſo refreſhes the weak trees with water; and the king ſuſtains his poor ſoldiers by ſeaſonable liberality.

If the king hath not ſufficient ability of mind, or ſtrength of conſtitution, to execute all public affairs himſelf, he muſt ſearch for a man of exemplary piety and approved integrity, and who to theſe valuable qualities adds experience, and activity in buſineſs. Him he muſt conſult on all occaſions with implicit confidence, and intruſt with the executive power. In affairs of moment, it is not adviſable to conſult with many, becauſe that to be qualified to give advice on ſuch occaſions requires fidelity, liberality of ſentiment, valour, and circumſpection; qualities that are ſeldom found united in one perſon. Some ancient monarchs, indeed, made it a rule to conſult men of a contrary deſcription, and to act diametrically oppoſite to their advice. But they were frequently deceived by this method; becauſe it is difficult to eraſe from the mind the bad impreſſions which are received from timid or crafty counſels, ignorance, or malice. They found it the ſafeſt way to join with the prime miniſter a few wiſe and experienced men, and to require each to deliver his opinion in writing, to be ſeparately canvaſſed and debated upon. A prince, moreover, requires a learned aſtrologer, and a ſkilful phyſician. A wiſe king ſelects his friends with judgment; and conciliates the affection of his troops. He fills his treaſury by prudent management. He divides his dominions into proper portions, and commits them to the government of virtuous men, amongſt whom he takes care to preſerve perfect unanimity. He examines the ſtate of the fortreſſes in his dominions; and is ever attentive to the ſecurity and

proſperity

prosperity of his empire. With those princes who are his equals in power, he takes care to maintain peace friendship; and from those who are weaker than himself he exacts tribute. If any monarch is more powerful than himself, he continually strives to sow dissension amongst his troops; and if he is not able to effect this, prudently purchases his friendship. If possible, he preserves peace with every one; but when war is unavoidable, supports his dignity by vigorous and bold operations. The prince whose territory joins to his, although he may be friendly in appearance, yet ought not to be trusted; he should always be prepared to oppose any sudden attack from that quarter. With him whose country lies next beyond the one last mentioned, he should enter into alliance; but no connexion should be formed with those who are more remote. If he finds it necessary to attack his enemy, he should invade his country during the time of harvest.

Besides the *Rajneet*, the Hindoos have many other sensible books upon government.

BEYHAR.

The administration of justice.

The learned Hindoos say, that law is comprised under eighteen heads, viz. 1, Debt. 2, Deposit. 3, Claim of property. 4, Partnership. 5, Gifts. 6, Wages, hire, and rent. 7, Tribute. 8, Buying and selling. 9, Herdsmen. 10, Boundaries. 11, Abusive language. 12, Assault. 13, Theft. 14, Murder. 15, Adultery. 16, Disputes between man and wife. 17, Inheritance. 18, Gaming.

The judge must erect his tribunal facing the east. He must consider it a religious obligation to discharge the duties of his office with impartiality and justice. If he cannot execute all the business himself, he may delegate his authority to men of experience, courage, and activity.

The plaintiff they call *Badee*, and the defendant *Pirtbadee*. When a complaint is preferred to the judge, if the defendant is a debilitated old man, or is under the age of twelve years, or is an idiot, or is insane, or is sick, or is employed on the business of the state, or is a woman without relations, or a woman of family, such an one cannot be summoned before a court of justice; the judge shall commission an intelligent person to interrogate upon the case. But those who do not come under any of the above descriptions, are obliged to attend.

Whatever the plaintiff says, is taken down in writing with the date; and also his genealogy for three descents, with many other particulars. The same is done with the defendant. The judge, after comparing together the charge and the defence, asks the plaintiff what evidence he has in writing, or what witnesses he can produce. According to some there ought not to be fewer than three or four witnesses in every case; but others maintain, that a charge is sufficiently established by the evidence of one person of known veracity.

An infant under five years of age cannot be a witness in any case, neither can a man who is superannuated. The evidence of a Sooder can only be of service to a Sooder, nor of a handicraftsman but for one of his profession. Neither can any of the following bear evidence; one who is blind, lame or deaf; nor an idiot, nor a madman, nor a gambler, nor a notorious sinner; nor one who at the time is suffering hunger or thirst, or is under the influence of passion; or a thief, or any criminal, whom they are carrying to suffer death; nor a woman, excepting in female concerns; nor a friend for a friend; nor an enemy against an enemy. The judge will

will derive collateral proof by the physiognomy, and prevarication of the parties.

The above stipulations are to be observed in all cases, excepting murder, theft, assault, or abusive language.

If neither party can produce any proof in writing, nor bring any witnesses, the judge shall determine according to the best of his judgment. But if the merit of the cause is so doubtful, that he cannot take upon himself to pass a decision, he shall propose the ordeal. According to some the ordeal can only be performed by the plaintiff. Their are eight kinds of ordeal. *The first kind.* They weigh the person in a pair of scales: then they perform certain religious ceremonies and weigh him again, when if he is found to be lighter than he was the first time, his claim is admitted; but if his scale preponderates, or the balance stands even, he is declared a liar. Some books admit of a trifling difference. This kind of ordeal is peculiar to the Brahmins. *The second kind.* They describe seven or nine circles from one centre, with the distance of sixteen fingers breadth between each periphery. Then the person who is to perform the ordeal bathes himself, and performs certain religious ceremonies; after which he rubs over his hands rice bran, and spreading open both palms, lays upon them seven green Peepul leaves, which are bound round seven times with raw silk. Next they place thereon a red hot iron weighing $3\frac{1}{2}$ seers. With this in his hands he walks between the circles, and upon arriving at the last, throws down the iron, when if it has not burnt his hands, he is declared to have gained his cause. If he should chance to let the iron fall before he has passed over all the circles, he must begin again. *The third kind.* The person stands up to the navel in water with his face towards the east. He next dives under the water, when one of the bystanders shoots

ſhoots from a bow, meaſuring 106 fingers breadth, an arrow made of reed, without any iron ſpike, and another perſon runs and fetches it back. If the appellant keeps all this while under water, his cauſe is declared juſt. This ordeal is peculiar to the Byeſs caſt. *The fourth kind.* Deadly poiſon is adminiſtered thus: in *Bussunt* ſeven grains; or in *Kurreykhim* five grains; or in *Burreyka* four grains; or in *Sird* ſix grains; or in *Hyment* and *Shiskar* eight grains. This is to be mixed up with thirty times the quantity of ghee; and after repeating certain incantations, adminiſtered to the perſon who is to be tried. He muſt turn his face to the ſouth, and the perſon who adminiſters it muſt look towards the eaſt, or the north. If it has not any effect during the time that the ſpectators can clap their hands five hundred times, his cauſe is pronounced juſt, and antidotes are given him. This ordeal is peculiar to the Sooder caſt. *The fifth kind.* They waſh an idol with water, and after praying before it, the perſon who is to be tried drinks three handfuls of the water. If no misfortune befals him within fourteen days from that time, his cauſe is pronounced juſt. *The sixth kind.* They put into an earthen veſſel a particular kind of rice, called *Sathee*, and let it ſtand all night. In the morning, after repeating certain incantations, the perſon who is to be tried eats the rice, looking towards the eaſt. He then ſpits upon a leaf of the Peepul tree, or *Bhowjputter*. If the ſaliva is mixed with blood, or the corners of his mouth ſwell, or he trembles, he is declared to be a liar. *The seventh kind.* They put forty dams of ghee, or ſeſamé oil, into an earthen or ſtone veſſel, meaſuring ſixteen fingers in length and breadth, and four fingers deep. This they keep upon the fire, till it boils violently, when they throw in a maſha of gold. If the perſon who is to be tried, takes out the gold between his forefinger and thumb, without ſcalding himſelf, he is declared to be a man of veracity. *The eighth kind.* They write the words *Dehrem* and *Ad-*

 herem,

rem upon plates of filver and lead, or upon pieces of white and black linen, or *Bhowjputter*, and put them into a flaggon, which has never held water. The perfon whofe caufe is to be decided, puts in his hand, and if he draws out the word *Dehrem*, it proves his affertion to be true. This kind of ordeal is common to all the four tribes.

If a caufe cannot be decided in one day, the judge admits the defendant to bail. Till one fuit is decided another cannot be preferred againft the fame perfon.

When a claim is proved, the perfon who gains the fuit is put in poffeffion; and the judge exacts a fine of equal value from the defendant. And if the plaintiff lofes his caufe, he in the like manner pays double the fum fued for.

I fhall now proceed to give a fummary of the Hindoo laws.

D E B T.

If there is a fimple debt, without any depofit, and there is a difpute about the intereft, a Brahmin fhall pay two per cent. per menfem; a Kehteree three; a Byefs four; and a Sooder five.

If there is a collateral fecurity, then only a fourth of the above is recoverable, even although a higher rate had been agreed upon between the parties.

Upon adventures by land, ten per cent. is allowable, and twenty-five per cent. for rifks by fea.

If there had been an agreement for a particular time, and the time fhould be confiderably elapfed, the judge fhall not allow for intereft a fum exceeding the

the principal. In agreements for grain, as far as five times the principle is allowed.

DEPOSIT.

If a perſon has employed a depoſit illegally, and when it is demanded, demurs paying back the money, he ſhall be fined half the principal ſum in addition, for intereſt.

If he defends the ſuit, and the plaintiff cannot produce any writing or witneſs, the judge may privately direct ſome other perſon to depoſit ſomething with the plaintiff, and after ſome time demand it back again, when, if he refuſes, he ſhall be compelled to ſatisfy the firſt claim, or elſe ſubmit to be tried by ordeal.

If a thief ſteals from a truſtee any depoſit; or it is burnt, or is loſt by water, or is taken away by an enemy in plunder; he ſhall not make reſtitution.

If he has diminiſhed it, he ſhall pay the deficiency to the plaintiff, and the like ſum to the judge.

CLAIMS OF PROPERTY.

If the owner proves that his property has been illegally conveyed over to another, it ſhall be reſtored to him, and the money taken back from the ſeller.

If he diſcovers that it is hidden, or ſold under value, or he finds it in the poſſeſſion of a perſon who cannot give an account how he came by it, the judge ſhall reſtore the property to the owner, and exact a fine according to the rank of the offender.

If any perſon diſcovers him who has ſtolen any thing, the informer ſhall not be fined, but the thief.

PART-

PARTNERSHIP.

If partners have a difpute, and it appears that they had entered into a formal agreement of partnerfhip, the judge fhall determine according to the terms of their engagement. But if there was not any particular agreement, the profit and lofs fhall be divided in proportion to the fhare of each in the ftock.

If a partner loofes or injures the property of the partnerfhip, or it has been employed or carried away without the confent of the other partners, he fhall make reftitution.

If one of the partners commits any difhonefty in the management of the partnerfhip, he fhall firft make good the deficiency, and then be ejected from the partnerfhip; and if any fhare of profit is due to him at the time, it fhall be exacted by the judge.

If a partner is fet to guard the joint ftock, and through his neglect any thing is loft or injured, he fhall make reftitution.

GIFTS.

If any thing is given away under the influence of anger, ficknefs, forrow, or fear, or as a bribe, or in jeft, it is allowable to take it back; and alfo whatever has been given by an infant, an idiot, or a madman. But in no other cafes can a gift be refumed.

If any thing has been given with a view of obtaining future reward; or has been exchanged for any thing elfe; it cannot, under any pretence, be taken back.

WAGES, HIRE, AND RENT.

If wages, or hire, or rent, is received in advance, the agreement muft be fulfilled. If it is broken, the offender

offender ſhall be fined in double the ſum. But if he had only entered into an engagement without receiving the money, then for the failure he ſhall only be fined in the ſum agreed for.

If a ſervant loſes his maſter's property, he muſt make reſtitution. But if it was taken from him forcibly, he is not anſwerable.

PUBLIC REVENUE.

If any one fails in the payment of his revenue to government, his property ſhall be ſeized, and he ſhall be baniſhed.

BUYING AND SELLING.

The buyer may return his purchaſe on the day he bought it, without any conſideration; on the ſecond day he may ſend it back, upon forfeiting a twentieth part of the price; but after the ſecond day, he cannot return it. The following are exceptions: A maid ſervant may be ſent back within a month; a ſlave within fifteen days; grain within ten days; a jewel within ſeven days; cattle in general within five days; a milch cow within three days; iron within one day; unleſs there are any particular ſtipulations to the contrary.

The ſeller may take back his goods within the ſame period; but then he muſt ſuſtain the ſame loſs as would have fallen upon the buyer had he returned them.

HERDSMEN.

If, through the neglect of a herdſman, a beaſt is loſt, or dies, or is hurt, he is obliged to repair the injury.

If a beaſt enters a field adjoining to a town, and eats the produce, the herdſman is not anſwerable for the damage, but the man who was ſet to watch the crop. But if it was not through his neglect, then the maſter of of the beaſt ſhall pay it. *Fines exacted by the judge for the above treſpass.* For a buffaloe, camel, or aſs, ſeven maſhas of ſilver. For an ox, three and one half maſhas; for a ſheep or goat, one and three quarters of a maſha. If a beaſt lies down and eats, the fine is doubled. But for beaſts without owners no one is reſponſible. Eleven days after the death of a Brahmin, it is uſual for his family to let looſe eight, or four, or one bull, with a number of cows, which are previouſly branded in a particular manner. The ſame is done thirteen days after the death of a Kehteree; ſixteen days after the death of a Byeſs; and thirty-one days after the death of a Sooder. The cattle are allowed to rove where they pleaſe. Neither can any fine be exacted for a cow, who has juſt calved, and lies down in a field.

BOUNDARIES.

Diſputes concerning boundaries cannot be enquired into during the rains. Huſbandmen generally mark their boundaries by burying thereon aſhes, ſtones, broken tiles, hair, bones, and ſuch other articles as do not ſoon periſh in the ground. Sometimes a tree is a boundary. The judge muſt determine upon theſe proofs, joined to the evidence of at leaſt four huſbandmen, herdſmen, or hunters. The following is the method. Each of the witneſſes muſt be dreſſed in red, with a ſtring of red flowers round his neck, and placing a clod of earth upon his head, he ſhall ſay, "If I ſpeak falſely, my good works ſhall be of no avail unto me." If there are not any witneſſes, nor any marks for diſtinguiſhing the boundary, the judge ſhall decide at his diſcretion.

ABUSIVE LANGUAGE.

This they reckon of three kinds, viz. 1. Abuſing another to his face. 2, Indirect abuſe. 3, Reproaching a man's mother or ſiſter.

For

For the two firſt, if the offender be inferior to him whom he has abuſed, he ſhall be fined 12½ dams; and if they are equal, half that ſum. If a ſuperior offends in ſuch manner againſt his inferior, he ſhall be fined in a fourth of that ſum.

For the third kind, if the offence is committed againſt a ſuperior, the fine is 25 dams. If they are equal, or a Brahmin abuſes a Kehteree, or a Kehteree a Brahmin, the offender ſhall pay 50 dams. If a Byeſs offends in this manner againſt a Brahmin, he ſhall pay 70 dams; but if a Brahmin offends thus againſt a Byeſs, he ſhall pay only 12½ dams. And thus between Byeſs and Sooder.

If any one ſpeaks diſreſpectfully of a Dewtah, of the King, or of a Brahmin who has ſtudied the four Bedes, he ſhall be fined 540 dams. If he abuſes a whole family, he ſhall be fined 270 dams, or if all the inhabitants of a city, 135 dams.

ASSAULT.

This they reckon of four kinds. 1, Throwing at any one clay, earth, or filth. 2, Putting in bodily fear, by threatening a blow with a ſtick, or any other weapon. 3, Striking a blow with the hands, feet, or with any weapon. 4, Wounding with any weapon.

The firſt kind. For ſimply throwing any thing, he ſhall be fined five dams; and if he ſoils him, ten dams; provided the parties are equals. But if the offender is the inferior, he ſhall be fined double, and if he is the ſuperior, only half the ſum.

The ſecond kind. For threatening, five dams, if the parties are equals; but if the offender is the inferior, double; or if he is ſuperior, only half that ſum.

The

The third kind. If the blow occaſions a ſwelling or bruiſe, and the parties are equals, 270 dams. If the offender is the inferior, the offending member ſhall be cut off; or the judge may inflict a ſuitable fine. *The fines are,* A Kehteree againſt a Brahmin 540 dams; a Byeſs againſt a Brahmin 1080; a Sooder againſt a Brahmin 2160. A Byeſs againſt a Kehteree; or a Sooder againſt a Byeſs 540; or a Sooder againſt a Kehteree 1080. But if a Brahmin offends againſt a Kehteree, he pays only 270, or if againſt a Byeſs 135, or a Sooder $67\frac{1}{2}$: and ſo downwards in the other caſts, towards one another.

The fourth kind. Between equals, if the ſkin is ſcratched, fifty dams; if the fleſh is torn, ten tolahs of gold; if a bone is broken, the offender ſhall be baniſhed. If an inferior offends thus againſt a ſuperior, the fine ſhall be double; but if the offender is the ſuperior, it ſhall be only half of what is paid between equals. If any medicine is required, he ſhall pay the expence thereof, and alſo maintain the wounded perſon till cured.

If any one by a blow hurts a ſheep or a goat, he ſhall be fined eight dams; if it is lamed, he ſhall pay its full price to the owner, and 125 dams to the judge; and if it is killed, double the price, and a fine of 250 dams. If a horſe, or camel, or ox, be ſo injured, he ſhall pay double the price to the owner, and to the judge the ſame fine as for a ſheep.

If any valuable vegetables are injured by any perſon, the owner ſhall receive the full price, and the judge exact a fine of ten dams; or if it be of little value, only eight dams.

THEFT.

If any one ſteals one hundred tolahs of gold or ſilver,

ver, or any thing of that value; or a quantity of grain not leſs than 66$\frac{2}{3}$ maunds; or carries away a child, or any one of a family; or another man's wife, he ſhall be puniſhed with death.

For ſtealing leſs than the ſum above-mentioned, they ſhall cut off one of his hands. If it be fifty maſhas or leſs, they ſhall fine him eleven times the ſum. The ſame concerning grain.

In the caſes above-mentioned, whatever has been ſtolen ſhall be reſtored to the owner; and if the criminal is not able to pay the fine, he ſhall be condemned to bondage. For leſſer thefts, the puniſhment ſhall be inflicted at the diſcretion of the judge.

MURDER.

If an inferior kills his ſuperior, he ſhall ſuffer death. If a Brahmin kills a Brahmin, his eſtate ſhall be confiſcated, and the hair of his head cut off; he ſhall be branded in the forehead and baniſhed. If a Brahmin kills a Kehteree, he ſhall be fined 1000 cows and a bull. If a Brahmin kills a Byeſs, he ſhall be fined 100 cows and a bull. If a Brahmin kills a Sooder, he ſhall be fined ten cows and a bull. The ſame fines are inflicted on a Kehteree for killing a Kehteree, and on a Byeſs for killing a Byeſs, &c. If a Sooder kills a Sooder, he is fined 500 cows and a bull.

If the murderer is not diſcovered, the inhabitants of the city, town, or quarter, where the murder was committed, ſhall endeavour to find him; and in default, they are ſubject to whatever fine the judge may think proper to inflict.

ADULTERY.

Whoſoever deflowers a virgin of his own caſt, without her making any reſiſtance, ſhall be compelled to marry

marry her. If he raviſhes her, he ſhall be put to death; but no puniſhment inflicted on the woman. If the offender is a Brahmin, he ſhall only ſuffer baniſhment.

If ſhe was not a virgin, but one who was not uſed to go abroad, and conſented, and they are both of the ſame caſt, he ſhall be fined 270 dams. If he forced her, the fine ſhall be 540 dams. If ſhe is a woman who is uſed to go abroad, and conſented, the fine ſhall be 250 dams, and if forced, 500 dams. If the man is ſuperior in caſt to the woman, the fine, in all theſe caſes, ſhall be 250 dams; but if the man is inferior, he ſhall, in all caſes, be put to death; and they ſhall cut off the woman's ears and noſe.

MAN AND WIFE.

If, immediately after marriage, a man diſcovers any natural defect on his wife, he may part with her without being ſubject to any proſecution; but the father of the woman ſhall be fined.

If a man agrees to give a perſon one daughter in marriage, but afterwards gives him another, he ſhall be obliged to give him both.

If a huſband goes on a pilgrimage, and is abſent beyond the time he had agreed upon, the wife ſhall ſtay at his houſe during the ſpace of eight years, whatever her circumſtances in life may be. If he travels to acquire knowledge, or in queſt of fortune, ſhe ſhall ſtay in his houſe ſix years, waiting his return. If he is gone to marry another woman, three years. After the expiration of the preſcribed period, for each caſe, ſhe is at liberty to leave his houſe in purſuit of her buſineſs. The huſband then has it not in his power to put her away; but if ſhe leaves his houſe before her time, he is at liberty to part with her.

If

If the husband is sick, and the wife does not attend him, he cannot part with her for this neglect; however, he may refuse to speak to her for three months, and he may take back whatever presents he had given her. But after this, he must be reconciled to her.

The Brahmins cannot divorce their wives. But if a husband commits a capital crime, or has any contagious distemper, it is lawful for the wife to separate herself from him.

If a Brahmin has four wives, one of each cast, each shall perform the ceremonies of her own particular cast; but the Brahmin, on all religious occasions, and for anointing his body with oil, &c. can employ only her of his own cast.

INHERITANCE.

If a man dies and leaves behind him a son, or sons, and a widow, they shall inherit his estate equally.

If there be neither sons, nor widow, the daughter who is unmarried is the heir.

If there be neither son, widow, nor unmarried daughter, then the mother of the deceased is the heir.

If he neither leave behind him a mother, then his father shall be the heir.

If he neither leave behind him a father, then his brother shall be the heir.

If he neither leave behind him a brother, then his brother's son shall be the heir.

In default of a brother's son, the estate shall be divided amongst the next of kin.

If

If he leave not any relations, then the estate shall go to his tutor, or if he is not alive, to his school-fellows.

If there be neither any of these, then the king is the heir.

GAMING.

Whosoever plays with false dice, shall be banished.

If any one refuses to pay his game, it shall be forced from him.

The judge is entitled to a tenth of whatever is gained at play.

What I have here delivered is a mere summary of the Hindoo laws. There are a multitude of other cases, with various and contradictory commentaries on each.

CHAR ASHERUM, OR THE FOUR HINDOO DEGREES.

I now proceed to describe the customs and manners of the Hindoos, and their religious ceremonies.

The following are the rules observed by the Brahmins. When a Brahmin is out of his minority, he divides the remainder of his life into four portions, for the performance of the four Asherum, or degrees.

THE FIRST DEGREE, or *Berhemcharee*. The Brahmins regard the *Zenar* as one of the first principles of their religion: indeed none of the three first tribes consider themselves initiated till they have put it on. A Brahmin may put on the *Zenar* at any time between eight and sixteen years of age; a Kehteree, from eleven till twenty-two; a Byess, from twelve to twenty-four; but a Sooder cannot wear it. If any of the three tribes neglects to put on the *Zenar* within the prescribed time for

for each, he is not considered as a Hindoo. A Brahmin receives the *Zenar* from his father or tutor; a Kehteree and a Byess, from the hands of a Brahmin. Only a Brahmin can twist this cord; and that which a Brahmin puts on the first time, must be twisted by his father or tutor. It is made after the following manner: three threads, each measuring ninety-six hands, are twisted together; then they are folded into three, and twisted again, making it to consist of nine threads. This is folded again into three, but without any more twisting, and each end fastened with a knot. This is the *Zenar*, which, being put upon the left shoulder, passes to the right side, and hangs down as far as the fingers can reach. A Brahmin wears four *Zenars* together, and the other two casts only three. Some say that for this purpose cotton thread is used by the Brahmins; worsted by the Kehteree; and hempen thread by the Byess. The first time that they put on the *Zenar*, they hang along with it a slip of deer skin, three fingers breadth; but it is shorter than the *Zenar*. A Brahmin uses antelope skin; a Kehteree any other deer skin; and a Byess goat skin. They, moreover, at this time, wear round the waist a cord, made of a particular kind of grass, called *Moonj*.

He next learns the *Gayteree*, which are certain words in praise of the sun. This they consider like the Kelma of the Mahommedans.

A Brahmin also receives a staff of palass wood; but for a Kehteree, or Byess, it is made of any other wood.

After the performance of these ceremonies, the noviciate is brought from his father's house, and placed under his tutor, to be instructed in the Bedes; beginning first with reading his own particular Bede. They say, that when the philosopher Byass divided the Bede into four parts, he instructed four of his disciples in the respective

ſpective doctrines of each; the deſcendants of which diſciples have followed the tenets of the particular Bede inculcated by the firſt teacher. They never begin to read the Bedes at any of the following times, *Purwa*, *Ashtomeen*, *Pooren Mass*, *Amavuss*; neither in the nights of *Ashtomeen*, nor *Chutturdussy*; nor during an eclipſe. But any other of the ſix above-mentioned ceremonies may be performed at thoſe times.

When a *Berhemcharee* goes to the neceſſary, he hangs the *Zenar* upon his right ear. On this occaſion, in the day time he turns his face to the north, and at night to the ſouth. He afterwards waſhes his privities five times with water, having each time previouſly uſed earth. This is performed with the left hand, which he then cleanſes five times in the ſame manner. Next he waſhes both hands five times; and concludes with waſhing his feet thrice. When he urines, he cleanſes the parts once with earth and water, and then three times with water; uſing his left hand as before; after which he waſhes both hands and feet. This is the number of purifications required from the time of putting on the *Zenar*, till ſixteen years of age, after which period they are doubled. After performing three ablutions, he ſits down upon his haunches looking towards the eaſt or north. Then he takes in his right hand a little water, which he drinks. Then he cleans his teeth with a *Miswak*, uſing a freſh one every day.

The dreſs of a *Berhemcharee* conſiſts of, 1, The *Lungowtee*, which is a piece of clothing for covering the privities. 2, The *Lungee*, another cloth which covers the *Lungowtee*. 3, A ſheet without any ſuture. 4, A linen cap. He bathes every morning before ſun-riſe, without any covering but the *Lungowtee*, and the cord of *Moonj*. He begins with taking up in his right hand a little water, and ſays, "Pardon my offences." After which he throws away the water.

 Then

Then he rubs himſelf all over with earth, and if he is in a river, dives three times, or elſe he throws water thrice over his body, and rubs himſelf with his hands. Next he repeats the name of God, and then thrice takes up in his right hand a little water, which he ſips, and repeats certain prayers, during all which time he ſprinkles water upon his head. Then with his forefinger and thumb he ſtops his noſtrils, and bowing down his face to the ſurface of the water, repeats another prayer, and then dives, or throws water over himſelf thrice. He then ſprinkles ſeven times his forehead, breaſt, and ſhoulders. Then joining his open hands, he fills them eight times with water, and throws it towards the ſun, repeating a particular prayer; after this he ſips a little water, and repeats the *Parayenam*, mentioned under the article *Patenjil*. This they call the ablution, whether it be performed in a river, pond, well, or houſe. He then puts on his clothes, and if he is a follower of *Ram*, makes a mark with aſhes along his forehead. If he is a follower of *Kishen*, he makes twelve kuſhkehs, namely upon his forehead, breaſt, navel, the right and left ſides thereof, the ſhoulders, tips of the ears, the loins, the crown of the head, and the throat. The clay of the Ganges is in the higheſt eſteem for this ceremony; but they ſometimes uſe ſaffron, and other dyes. A Sooder marks only a circle upon his forehead. After this he takes up his ſtaff, and puts over his ſhoulders a leather belt, which faſtens at the navel with a cuſhion. Then he performs the *Sindeyha*, which is ſaying a certain prayer, and drinking and ſprinkling water in a particular manner. Next he performs the *Houm*, or burnt ſacrifice.

When he has performed all theſe ceremonies, he goes and waits upon his tutor, and reads the Bedes. Immediately that the ſun begins to decline, the *Berhemcharee* repeats all the ceremonies above deſcribed, with ſome trifling variation. Then he goes and begs food

food from three, five, or ſeven houſes; but he will not receive any from a Sooder. When he has dreſſed a ſufficient quantity, he carries it to his tutor, and aſks permiſſion to eat. Before he begins to eat, he ſays a prayer, and performs ſome particular ceremonies: and after he has done, repeats another prayer. He never ſpeaks during meals. At the duſk of the evening he repeats the *Sindeyha* and *Howm*. After this he reads two or three hours, and then ſleeps upon the ground on a bed of ſtraw, a tiger's ſkin, deer ſkin, or ſuch like. He abſtains from fleſh, honey, beetle, and perfumes. A *Berhemcharee* wears his head ſhaven, leaving a lock of hair at the back of the crown. The hair of the other parts of the body is ſuffered to grow. He uſes neither *Sirmah* nor oil; and never goes where there is ſinging, dancing, or gaming. He never kills any animal; and has no commerce with women. He never eats of any diſh, till his tutor has taſted it. He is enjoined to abſtain from lying, anger, avarice, and envy; and is forbidden to ſpeak ill of any one, even although he may deſerve it. In ſhort, he is commanded to lead a life of virtue and holineſs. When he prays, he looks towards the eaſt, or the north. He never looks at the ſun at the time of riſing or ſetting. Some continue in the degree of *Berhemcharee* forty-eight years, allowing twelve years for the ſtudy of each Bede. Some paſs through this degree in five years, and others only continue in it till they have learnt the Bedes. Others, again, ſpend all their lives in this ſtate; and in purſuit of *Muckut* inflict upon themſelves great auſterities.

The Second Degree, *Gerihst,h*. When the *Berhemcharee* has finiſhed his ſtudies, if he finds an inclination to devote his life to the ſervice of God, and deſpiſes all worldly enjoyments, nothing can be more meritorious; but if he does not feel ſuch an inclination, he waits upon his tutor, and aſks permiſſion to return to his father's houſe.

He

He then throws aside all his dress, excepting the *Zenar;* but continues the ablutions, and other ceremonies, like a *Berhemcharee.* If he is a Brahmin, he puts on a turban, and a sheet eight cubits long and two broad, which serves to cover his loins and thighs. Another sheet, four cubits long and two broad, he throws over his shoulders; this may have a suture, but the other not. A *Geresht,h* of any of the other casts, wears different kinds of dresses. He now marries, in the manner that will be described hereafter.

The *Gerisht,h* performs certain prayers, and the *Howm*, or burnt-sacrifice, after the following manner. He takes in his hand a branch of a peepul, or palass tree, a cubit in length, and burns it in the *Howm* fire. He then passes into the fire another branch of the same kind, and after having scorched it, takes it out and preserves it against the next *Howm*, which he performs with this stick; and then scorches another in like manner, which he preserves against the time of performing the *Aginhowter.* This is a particular *Howm*, made with peepul wood, and two other sticks, which, by means of a strong cord, are rubbed together till they take fire, when they are put into three earthen vessels. He then makes the figure of a tortoise with one and a fourth of a seer of rice-flour, and sprinkles it with oil. Part of this he throws into the three fires, as an offering to the Dewtahs; and the remainder he gives to the Brahmins, eating some himself. A third part of the fire, he preserves during his whole life, and every day performs the *Howm* with some of it, throwing into the fire as an offering to the Dewtahs, rice, ghee, milk, barley, or any other eatable. And he repeats the *Aginhowter* on every *Purwa*, from the fourth day after his marriage, till he separates from his father, which is the period of this ceremony.

Any of the casts, excepting a Sooder, may be a *Gerisht,h.*

risht,h. At four ghurries before day-break, he riſes in his bed, and prays. He divides his time into eight parts, aſſigning to each a particular duty. Firſt, when the ſun is above the horizon, he firſt looks on it, then on fire, next on water, and laſt on gold. If he is a prince, he firſt looks on the ſun, then on a Brahmin, then on a cow, and laſt on ghee. But if none of theſe eight things are preſent, he muſt look upon the palms of his hands, and perform the *Sindehya*. *The second portion of time*, he employs in ſtudying the Bedes, and other ſciences. *The third*, he paſſes in the ſervice of his prince, and in the tranſaction of his own buſineſs. *The fourth*, in the performance of his family concerns. *The fifth*, which is at noon, he ſpends in ablutions, the *Sindehya*, and in ſprinkling water with his hands, as an offering to the Dewtahs, the *Rekehsir*, and his anceſtors, which ceremony they call *Turpun*, and it is accompanied with certain prayers. *The sixth*, he prays to Biſhen, Mahadeo, the ſun, Durga, and Gunnies. This ceremony, which they call *Deopoojah*, will be more fully treated of hereafter. *The seventh*, he throws into the fire ſome of his food, as a burnt-offering to the Dewtahs. After which he performs the *Atitpoojah*, which is this: he looks out for a perſon who is hungry, and when he has found him, treats him with great attention, and feeds him. Then he eats himſelf, and theſe ceremonies collectively are called *Bysoodeo Pooja*. A Brahmin obtains his food by gleaning the field after the reapers. Or if he does not approve of this method, he may receive it from any of his family. Or if he does not chooſe this, he may receive the voluntary donations of ſtrangers, who are Brahmins, Kehteree, or Byeſs. But if he neither likes this, he may beg. Or if he does not approve of this, he may cultivate land. They think that trade is the worſt means by which he can ſupport himſelf. It is not proper for a Brahmin to keep a greater ſtock than twelve days proviſion; but others may have as large a ſtore as they pleaſe.

please. *The eighth*, he listens to the ancient histories of holy men; and performs the *Sindehya*. If he is hungry, he eats again at this time. He spends the remainder of the evening, till the first watch of the night, in studying philosophy, after which he goes to rest. This they consider to be the proper distribution of time. They observe many particular ceremonies during eclipses, and other holidays; the Kehteree and Byess performing fewer than the Brahmin.

THE THIRD ASHERUM, *Banperisht,h*, is the name also given to the professor, as well as to the degree itself. A Sooder cannot take this degree.

When a Brahmin, Kehteree, or Byess, arrives at old age, or becomes a grandfather, he may give up the management of his family to his son, or some other relation, and bid adieu to the world. He quits the city, and retiring to the desert, there builds himself a cell, where he weans his heart from all worldly concerns, and makes preparation for his last journey. If his wife, through affection, wishes to accompany him in his retirement, it is allowable; but they must subdue all carnal inclinations. Here he preserves the perpetual fire for sacrifice, and covers himself with the leaves or bark of trees; a coarse *Lungowtee* being the only piece of linen that he may wear. He never cuts his hair nor nails. At morning, noon, and evening, he performs his ablutions, with the *Sindehya*; and every morning and evening the *Howm*, in the same manner as is directed for the *Gerisht,h*; but his ablutions are now trebled. He hangs down his head, and observes the other rules prescribed in *Patenjil*. He reads the Bedes, never sleeps in the day-time, and always lies upon the bare ground. In the summer months he sits in the sun, surrounded with four fires. During the four rainy months, he dwells upon a stage raised above the water by four poles, but entirely exposed to the weather.

weather. In the four winter months, he ſits all night in cold water. He inceſſantly performs the faſt of *Chanderaijin*, and eats only at night. It is allowable for him to amaſs a ſtore of proviſions ſufficient for one year; but he receives nothing from any one; and only ſupplies himſelf with wild grain and fruits. He never cooks his victuals; but it is allowable for him to ſoften them in water. When he cannot collect proviſions himſelf, he applies to other *Banperishth's*, or if they cannot ſupply him, he then through neceſſity goes to the next town for food, but remains there no longer than is neceſſary for that purpoſe.

If he is weary of life, he travels towards the eaſt or north, till he expires with the fatigue of the journey, or elſe he throws himſelf into a fire; or precipitates himſelf from an eminence; or drowns himſelf. They think this is the ſure road to paradiſe; but unleſs he had obtained the ſtate of *Sonnyass*, he will not from this action alone be rewarded with *Muckut*.

THE FOURTH ASHERUM, *Sonnyass*. Nothing can exceed the auſterities of this ſtate, which, when properly performed, enſures the reward of *Muckut*. His majeſty calls one of theſe diſciplinarians *Sonnyassy*.

When a man has paſſed through the three degrees above deſcribed, he goes and aſks permiſſion from his tutor to enter into this ſtate, which being obtained, he quits his wife, ſhaves his head and beard, and gives up all worldly concerns. His tutor preſents him a *Lungowtee*, and a ſmall piece of cloth; and accepts ſome trifle in return.

The diſciplinarian then gives up reading, and applies himſelf ſolely to contemplation. He lives alone in the wilds. Every morning, noon, and evening, he performs his ablutions, and purifications, and follows the rules

rules prescribed in *Patenjil*. He has a particular way of performing the *Sindehya*, and continually repeats the word *Awan*, which is the commencement of the *Bedes*. Towards the evening, he goes to the nearest town, and begs his food from three, five, or seven houses, inhabited by Brahmins, repeating the name of God; but he never receives from one house more than a handful. If they give it him in his hand, he eats it immediately; but if they throw it on the ground, he takes it up with his mouth, or collecting it in a cloth, washes it in the river before he makes his meal. Then he retires to a place, where there are not any signs of cooking or eating, or lighting of fires.

He refuses all communication with a *Sooder* or *Mileetch*, and if any person does not supply him immediately with food, he will not wait. Before he eats, he squints upon the end of his nose, and, contemplating, walks on with his head and feet bare, never standing still in one place. He never stays more than three days in a city, nor two in a village. In the rains he dwells in one place; and thus he passes his life.

Some perform all these austerities in the first and second degrees. Some allow twenty-five years for each of the four states.

The second degree, or *Gerisht,h*, may be professed by any of the four tribes. From the first and second, the *Sooder* is excluded. The fourth is peculiar to the Brahmins.

THE WORSHIP OF THE DEITY.

The Hindoo philosophers say, that whosoever seeks to please God, must set aside part of his property for the purpose of divine worship. According to the followers of Nea-iy, Beysheekhek, Meymansa, Beydant, Sank, and Patenjil, there are four kinds of divine worship,

ſhip, namely, Pooja, Juggen, Dan, and Sheradh, which will be explained in their proper order.

THE FIRST KIND OF WORSHIP, OR POOJA.

Issur Pooja. Since they admit that the Almighty occaſionally aſſumes an elementary form, without defiling his holineſs, they make various idols, in gold and other metals, which ſerve to aſſiſt their imaginations whilſt they offer up their prayers to the inviſible Deity. This they call *Pooja*, and divide into ſixteen ceremonies. After he has performed his uſual ablutions, with the *Sindehya* and *Howm*, he ſits down looking towards the eaſt or the north, with his legs drawn up in front. Then taking in his hands a little water and rice, ſprinkles the idol, thinking that he thereby begins the worſhip of God. Next is the *Kulsh Pooja*, when he worſhips the idol's flaggon. Then follows the *Shunkh Pooja*, or the worſhip of the Conch Shell. Laſt is the *Ghunta Pooja*, which is plaſtering the bell with ſandal wood. When he has performed theſe *Poojas*, he throws down a little rice, and wiſhes that God may be manifeſted. Thus far includes the firſt of the ſixteen ceremonies. 2. He places a table of metal, or any thing elſe, as a ſeat for the Deity. 3, He throws water into a veſſel to waſh his footſteps. In Hindoſtan it is the cuſtom, that when a ſuperior enters the houſe of an inferior, he waſhes his feet. 4, He ſprinkles water thrice, to repreſent the idol rinſing his mouth. It is alſo the cuſtom, for an inferior to bring to a ſuperior water, to rinſe his mouth before meals. 5, Sandal, flowers, beetle, and rice, are offered to the idol. 6, The idol and his ſeat are carried to another ſpot. Then he takes in his right hand a white conch ſhell full of water, which he throws over the idol, and with his left hand rings the bell. 7, He dries the idol with a cloth, replaces it upon its ſeat, and dreſſes it. 8, He puts the Zenar upon the idol. 9, He makes the *Kuskeh* upon the idol in twelve places. 10, He throws over the idol flowers, or green leaves.

leaves. 11, He fumigates it with perfumes. 12, He lights a lamp with ghee. 13, He places before the idol trays of food, according to his ability, which are distributed amongst the by-standers as the idol's leavings. 14, They call *Numskar*, which is worshipping God with heart and tongue, and stretching himself at full length with his face towards the ground. This prostration is called *Dundowt*. Then he lays himself in such manner, that his eight members touch the ground; namely, the two knees, two hands, forehead, nose, and cheeks, and this they call *Shashtang*. These kinds of prostration are also performed to great men. 15, He compasses the idol several times. 16, He stands like a slave, with his hands uplifted, and asks permission to depart. There are particular prayers, and many different ways of performing these sixteen ceremonies. Some use more than these sixteen ceremonies; and others believe that only from the 9th to the 13th are indispensible duties. Excepting a Sonnyassy and a Sooder, all other Hindoos perform this *Pooja* thrice every day.

God may be adored in the heart; or in the sun; or in fire; or in water; or in earth; or under the form of an idol.

They also make images of those who have obtained eternal felicity, and consider the worshipping of them as the means of obtaining salvation.

THE SECOND KIND OF WORSHIP.

Juggen, which they also call *Jag*, and it is of three kinds. 1, *Pak Juggen*, making the *Howm* in the name of the Dewtahs, and bestowing charity before he eats. This is of different kinds. 2, *Jup Juggen*, repeating prayers, and reading books of wisdom. And these two are in constant use. 3, *Bidh Juggen*, is also of several kinds, in some of which great sums of money are expended, and a number of animals sacrificed.

One

One kind of *Bidh Juggen* is the *Ashowmeedh Juggen*, which is performed only by great monarchs. When every thing is prepared for the facrifice, they place in the front a white horfe, who has a black right ear, and after repeating certain prayers, the prince fets out upon conqueft, and carries victory wherever he goes. All the monarchs of the earth become tributary to him, and enter into his troops. They fay, that whofoever has performed this ceremony an hundred times, will become a monarch of the upper regions. They pretend that there have been feveral fuch, and relate marvellous ftories of them. If he does not perform that number, he only obtains a comfortable habitation there. *Rassewee Juggen*. At this grand facrifice, all the monarchs of the earth muft be prefent, and they alone can officiate. Whofoever has prefided at fuch a facrifice twice, becomes a monarch of the upper regions, and they fay, that many have obtained this felicity. This facrifice is of various kinds; but the two here given muft fuffice for this volume.

The Third Kind of WORSHIP.

Dan, giving money and goods to the needy. There are various ways of beftowing alms, but the following are moft in eftimation. 1, *Toladan*, weighing himfelf againft gold, filver, and other valuables. 2, *Herngirbh Dan*. An image of Brahma is made with four faces, in each of which are two eyes, two ears, two nofes, and two mouths; it has four hands, and the other parts of the body like an ordinary man. It is of gold, weighing not lefs than thirty-three tolahs and four mafhahs, nor more than 3410 tolahs. The heighth muft be feventy-two fingers, and breadth forty-eight fingers. This is adorned with jewels, and, after the performance of certain ceremonies, given away in alms. 3, *Brahma, und Dan*. An egg is made of gold of two parts, which join together fo as to form a perfect oval. It muft not be fmaller in breadth and heighth than twelve fingers;

gers; nor larger than 110 fingers. The weight from ſixty-ſix tolahs ſix maſhahs, to 3333 tolahs four maſhahs. 4, *Kulptoor Dan*, is the name of a tree, which was one of the fourteen things brought out of the ſea by the *Kowrum Owtar*; which will be deſcribed hereafter. Birds are repreſented ſitting upon the branches. It is made of gold, and muſt not weigh leſs than two tolahs. 5, *Goosihsir Dan*. One thouſand cows, with the points of their horns plated with gold, and their hoofs with ſilver, with bells and kataſſes about their necks. 6, *Herenneeyeh Kamdheen Dan*. A cow and calf made of gold, weighing from 850 to 3400 tolahs. 7. *Herenneeyeh-shew Dan*. A horſe made of gold, weighing from ten tolahs to 3333 tolahs four maſhahs. 8, *Herenneeyeh-shewrith Dan*. A four-wheeled chariot made of gold, with four or eight horſes, weighing from ten tolahs to 6660 tolahs eight maſhahs. 9, *Heemhestrith Dan*. A carriage drawn by four elephants, all of gold, weighing from ſixteen tolahs to 6660 tolahs eight maſhahs. 10, *Penehlongel Dan*. Four ploughs of gold, the ſame weight as the laſt article. 11, *Dehra Dan*. A repreſentation of a piece of land, with mountains and rivers, made of gold, not weighing leſs than ſixteen tolahs eight maſhahs, nor more than 3333 tolahs. 12, *Wishwachucher Dan*. A golden ſphere, weighing from ſixty-ſix tolahs eight maſhahs to 3333 tolahs four maſhahs. 13, *Kulpleta Dan*. A golden vine, weighing from ſixteen tolahs to 3333 tolahs four maſhahs. 14, *Suptsagir Dan*. A repreſentation of the ſeven ſeas in gold, weighing from twenty-three tolahs four maſhahs to 3333 tolahs four maſhahs. 15, *Ruttendheen Dan*. A cow and calf made o fprecious ſtones. 16, *Mahabhootghit Dan*. Is a golden figure, with the head of an elephant, and the other parts human. This is *Gunnies*. Weight from ſixteen tolahs eight maſhahs to 3333 tolahs four maſhahs.

According to ſome books, *Toladan* is the only kind

that is proper, and none of the others ſhould be leſs than 106 tolahs ſix maſhahs, or more than 833 tolahs four maſhahs. There are alſo different opinions about the manner of diſtribution: ſome maintaining that it ought to be firſt given to the *Achareya*, and by them diſtributed to others. An *Achareya*, is one who teaches the Bedes, and other ſciences. Some direct it to be given to other Brahmins.

There are diſtinct ceremonies appointed for each kind of *Dan*; but they may be given at any time, although during eclipſes, and when the ſun enters the ſign Capricorn, and ſome other ſeaſons, are eſteemed more eſpecially meritorious. Great rewards are promiſed to thoſe who are charitable, inſomuch that for the firſt kind of Dan, if he weigh himſelf againſt gold, he will remain in paradiſe for one hundred million kulps; and when he reaſſumes a human form, will be a mighty monarch.

The Fourth Kind of WORSHIP.

Sheradh, giving charity in the name of his anceſtors, and which is done at various times. 1, The day on which he dies, and the anniverſary thereof. 2, On the Tit,h Amavus, of every month. 3, The ſixteenth Tit,h, of the month of Aſſin. 4, Beſtowing charity in their names at ſome public place of worſhip.

The following is the manner of performing the Sheradh. He gives to the Brahmins money, goods, and food, dreſſed and undreſſed, in the name of his father, grandfather, and great-grandfather; and of his mother, grandmother, and great-grandmother.

According to the four tribes, when *Poojah*, *Jug*, *Dan*, and *Sheradh* are performed, the Deity is completely worſhipped.

The

The OWTARS, or Incarnations of the Deity.

The Hindoos of the ſects of Nee-aiy, Beyſheekeh, Beydant, Meymanſa, Sank, and Patenjil, believe that God occaſionally aſſumes an elementary form; which manifeſtation they call *Pooran Owtar.*

Thoſe numberleſs parts of the creation, which by the ray of divinity that they poſſeſs, are endowed with wonderful powers, they call *Unsh Owtar.*

The POORAN OWTARS.

They ſay, that during the four Jowgs, there will be ten Owtars; and that nine have already appeared.

MUTCH OWTAR.

When the Deity was manifeſted under the form of a fiſh, of which they give the following account. In the country of Darawird, ſituated at the extremity of the Dekhan, in the city of Behdrawutty, during the Sut Jowg, in the month of Phagun, on the Tit,h Ekaduſſy, Rajah Mun, who had bid adieu to all worldly deſires, and had ſolely employed himſelf in the worſhip of God, for above a million years, was performing his devotions on the beach of the river Kirtmala: and whilſt he was performing his ablutions, a little fiſh came into his hand and ſaid, "Preſerve me." It remained in his hand the ſpace of a day and night, when having become larger, he put it into an ewer. When this would not contain it, he put it into a jar. But growing too large for it, he threw it into a well; from thence he removed it to a pond; and from thence into the Ganges. But this ſoon becoming too confined for the fiſh, it went into the ocean. When it had filled the ocean, the Rajah diſcovered it to be the Deity, worſhipped it, and prayed to be informed of the cauſe of the manifeſtation. He heard the following anſwer, "I am the only God, and have aſſumed this body for the

the deliverance of yourſelf, and a few more of the elect. After ſeven days, a light ſhall ſhine forth, and the earth ſhall be deluged with water. Embark on board a certain ſhip, taking with you a few righteous perſons, together with the divine books, and the choiceſt medicines; and faſten the ſhip to the horn, which grows out of my head," The deluge laſted one million ſeven hundred and eighteen thouſand years; and when the deluge ceaſed, the fiſh diſappeared.

KOWRUM OWTAR.

In the month of Katick Suckulputch, on the Tit,h Duaduſſy, God appeared in the form of a tortoiſe. The Dewtahs wanted to churn the ocean, in order to make the water of immortality, in the ſame manner as butter is obtained from milk. For this purpoſe they made uſe of the mountain Minder, which is the largeſt in the univerſe, by way of a churn pole. The weight of the mountain was ſo exceſſive, that they could not ſuſtain it, ſo that it ſunk into the ocean, and they were not able to recover it, till God appeared in the form of a tortoiſe, and raiſed it upon his back, when the Dewtahs obtained their wiſh. On this miraculous occaſion, fourteen invaluable treaſures were obtained from the ſea. 1, *Lutchmeen*, riches, appeared like a blooming bride, and beſtowed bleſſings upon mankind. 2, *Kowstubh Mun*, a wonderful reſplendent jewel, of ineſtimable value. 3, *Parjatuckbeeretch*, a tree whoſe flowers never fade, and whoſe odor perfumes the univerſe. According to ſome it is oracular, and beſtows whatever is deſired; which donation is called *Kulpbirkh*. 4, *Soora*, wine. 5, *Dehmunter*, a phyſician who healed the ſick, and raiſed the dead to life. In his right hand he held a leech, and in his left a branch of the Mirabolan tree. His majeſty ſays, that theſe ought to have been reckoned ſeparately, and increaſed the number of bleſſings to ſixteen. 6, *Chunderman*, the moon. 7, *Kamdhen*, a wonderful cow, from whoſe dugs iſſued whatever was wanted. 8, *Iyraput*, a white elephant with four tuſks. 9, *Sunkh*, a wonderful ſounding white conch ſhell, which beſtowed victory upon whomſoever poſſeſſed it. 10, *Amrit*, or the water of immortality. 11, *Bikh*, deadly poiſon. 12, *Rumbha*, a beautiful woman of an amiable diſpoſition. 13, *Assoo*, a horſe with eight heads. 14, *Sarengdhenook*, a bow that never failed to carry an arrow true to the mark.

After theſe diſcoveries, *Kowrum* deſcended into the earth, where they believe he is ſtill exiſting.

BARAH OWTAR,

Or the hog; which incarnation happened at the city of Bermahwert, near Neemkhar, in the Soobah of Owdh, during the Sut Jowg, in the month of Katick, on the Tit,h Pooran Maſſy, after the following manner. One *Hirnakess*, of the race of the Deyts, had paſſed a long life in religious worſhip. One day God revealed himſelf unto him, and aſked him what he wiſhed for. Hirnakeſs, rejoiced at theſe words, enumerated all the noxious animals, and entreated that they might not have power to hurt him; and that he might be univerſal monarch. Shortly after he obtained his wiſhes. When he took upon himſelf the government of the upper regions, he committed the earth to the care of one of his relations. The Dewtahs, accompanied by Brahma, went to Biſhen, and they altogether laid their grievances before the Almighty. Hirnakeſs, in enumerating the noxious animals, had forgotten to include the hog, wherefore they received for anſwer, "I will manifeſt myſelf under that form, and deprive him of life." A ſhort time after, God appeared in that form, and deſtroyed Hirnakeſs. They ſhow the place where this happened, near Soroon.

NIRSINGH

NIRSINGH OWTAR,

Was an animal from the head to the waist like a lion, and the lower parts resembling a man. It appeared at the city of Kerenpoor, now called Herdoun, near Agra, during the Sut Jowg, in the month of Bysakh Suckulputch, on the Tit,h Chutterdussy.

It is related, that one Herenkishp, of the race of the Deyts, having spent many years in austerities, God revealed himself unto him, and asked him what he wanted. He first asked, that his death might neither happen during the day nor night. He then begged that he might be invulnerable from all noxious animals, naming them one by one; and concluded with demanding to be sole monarch of the earth, and of the upper regions. The Dewtahs were accordingly put under his command, and the universe groaned under oppressions. The chiefs of the Dewtahs besought Brahma to be their mediator with God; and he heard their prayer. Herenkishp had a son, named Pirladh, who associated with the Dewtahs in their worship of the Deity, and notwithstanding his father did every thing to molest him, never could be made to swerve from his duty. One evening Herenkishp came to his son, and asked him where the Deity was to be found. He described him as being every where, and in order to explain himself, pointed to a pillar, saying that he was manifested even there. Herenkishp ignorantly struck the pillar; when by the miraculous power of God, there issued from it the animal above described, and tore him in pieces. This happened at the interval between day and night, and not by any animal that he had described. It is said, that *Nirsingh* asked Pirladh what he desired, and that noble minded being asked only for *Jeewun Muckut*, which is everlasting life, free from worldly joy and sorrow. This Owtar continued manifest one hundred years.

BAMUN OWTAR.

In the Tirtya Jowg there lived, at the city of Soonbhedra, on the banks of the Nerbudda, one Kuſht, the ſon of Merech, the ſon of Brahma. In the month of Bhadun, on the Tit,h Duaduſſy, Suckulputch, this Kuſht had a male dwarf by his wife Arwut. This is the Bamun Owtar; and he lived one thouſand years.

A perſon, of the race of the Dyte, named Bul, inflicted upon himſelf many auſterities, in hopes of obtaining for his reward the monarchy of the univerſe. God appeared unto him, and granted his wiſh. When he aſſumed the government, he did not diſpoſſeſs any of the Dewtahs. But although he performed various *Juggens*, he omitted to offer to the Dewtahs their appointed ſhare; whereupon they, through the mediation of Brahma, prevailed upon Biſhen to dethrone him. He by his preſcience foretold what ſhould befall him, and which was accompliſhed to the very minute. When this infant dwarf was of a proper age, they placed him in the ſchool of the philoſopher *Birdewaj*, and he attended that philoſopher at the *Juggen* which the rajah performed at Koorkheyt. The rajah aſked him what he required, and he anſwered, "Give me as much land as I can meaſure with three ſteps." The rajah was angry, and ſaid, "Why aſk you ſuch a trifle from me, ſeeing that I am ſuch a powerful monarch?" However, after a long converſation, he at laſt conſented. The firſt ſtep of *Bamun*, included the earth and *Patall*, and the ſecond ſtep took in all the upper regions. The rajah, in exchange for the third ſtep, delivered himſelf up to him. Becauſe the rajah was naturally good, Bamun, after depriving him of his kingdom, made him monarch of the infernal regions.

PURRISH-

PURRISHRAM OWTAR.

In the Tertya Jowg, in the month of Byſakh Suckulputch, at Rungta, near Agra, in the houſe of Jumdekhen, a Brahmin, there was born this child.

One Deeruj, of the race of the Dyte, who had neither hands nor feet, at that time ſat upon the throne. He was very unhappy at his misfortune, and at length quitting the world, retired to the mountain of Kylaſs. Mahadeo had compaſſion upon him, and gave him a thouſand hands, and made him monarch of the three regions. But he oppreſſed the Dewtahs till, at their prayer, God conſented to put an end to his tyranny. They ſay that Jemdekhen was a deſcendant of Mahadeo, and Runeeka, his wife, of the poſterity of Adit, the mother of the Dewtahs. She had five ſons, of whom Purriſhram was the laſt. He was educated by Mahadeo in the mountain of Kylaſs; and his father Jemdekhen worſhipped in the deſert. Deeruj was one day hunting, and happened to paſs by the cell of Jemdekhen. Being very hungry and thirſty, Jemdekhen ſupplied him with exquiſite viands, and alſo preſented him with dreſſes and jewels befitting a monarch. The rajah was aſtoniſhed, and ſaid, "I will not venture to touch theſe things, till you have informed me in what manner you came by them." He anſwered, "Indre, the monarch of the upper regions, intruſted to my care the cow Khamdheen, and whatever I want ſhe gives me out of her dugs." This account filled the rajah with avarice, and he demanded the cow. Jemdekhen ſaid, that without the order of Indre, he could not comply with his deſire, neither would he be able to take her by force. He was amazed, and having collected together a great number of troops, commenced hoſtilities, but without any effect. At laſt he came ſecretly in the night, and killed Jemdekhen, but could not get any tidings of the cow. Runeeka ſent for her ſon Purriſhram,

ram, and after performing the uſual ceremonies of mourning, according to the cuſtom of her tribe, burnt herſelf, and ſent her ſon to revenge the death of his father. Purriſhram, poſſeſſed of divine power, after twenty battles, ſlew the rajah, and reſtored the kingdom to the Dewtahs. Then having collected together all the riches of the univerſe, he performed the Juggen, and beſtowed the whole in charity; after which he retired from the world. They believe him to be ſtill living, and ſhow his habitation in the mountain of Mehinder in the Koken.

RAM OWTAR.

They ſay that Rawen, of the tribe of the Rakuſs, who was only two deſcents from Brahma, had ten heads and twenty hands. He ſpent ten thouſand years in the mountain of Kylaſs, worſhipping God; and devoted his heads, one after the other, in hopes to obtain for his reward the monarchy of the three regions. God appeared to him, and granted his deſire. The Dewtahs, being oppreſſed by him, implored the Almighty to dethrone him. Their prayer was granted, and Ram appointed to execute the divine will. Ram was born in the Tertya Jowg, in the month of Cheyte Suckulputch, in the ninth Tit,h, in the city of Owdh. His father was Rajah Jeſſerut, and his mother Kooſhelya. In his youth he acquired every art and ſcience, and afterwards deſpiſing worldly enjoyments, traverſed the deſerts, and made pilgrimages to all the holy places. At length he became king of the earth, and deſtroyed Rawen, and introduced many laws.

KISHEN OWTAR.

Above four thouſand years ago, Ogur Sein, of the Jadown tribe, reigned at Mehtrah, but was dethroned by his ſon, Kenſs, who aſſumed the government. At the ſame time Jeraſund, Seis Paul, and other kings of the Dyte caſt, exerciſed unbounded tyranny. The earth,

earth, thus oppreſſed, aſſumed the form of a cow, and accompanied by Brahma, went to Biſhen, and implored him to deliver her from thoſe oppreſſors. He granted their requeſt, and committed the execution of it to Kiſhen The aſtrologers foretold Kenſs, that a perſon ſhould ſoon be born who would deprive him of life, upon which he ordered that all the new born infants ſhould be deſtroyed; and thus every year ſhed the blood of numberleſs innocents. His ſiſter, Deywuckee, juſt now married Buſſdeo, of the Jadown tribe. At this time Kenſs heard a voice ſaying, that the eighth ſon of that marriage would kill him. He therefore threw them both into priſon, and deſtroyed ſeven of their children. But in the beginning of the Kal Jowg, in the month of Bhadun Kiſhenputch, Tit,h Aſhtoomee, Kiſhen was born in the priſon at Mehtra. The guards were fallen aſleep, the fetters fell from the feet of the father and mother, and the doors of the priſon flew open. The infant ſaid, "Croſs the Jumna, and go to the houſe of Nunda Aheer, and while the family are aſleep, bring away his new-born daughter, and leave me in her ſtead." Buſſdeo accordingly forded the river, and leaving Kiſhen in the houſe of Nunda, brought away his new-born daughter in exchange.

Kiſhen, in his ninth year, killed Kenſs, and reſtored Ogur Sein to his kingdom. He then made war upon the other tyrants, and deſtroyed them.

He lived one hundred and five years. He had 16,108 wives, every one of whom brought him ten ſons and a daughter. And every wife thought that ſhe poſſeſſed the whole of Kiſhen's affection.

BOODH OWTAR

Was born to Rajah Sedowdhen, by his wife Maia, in the city of Mokta, in the Kal Jowg, in the month of Byſakh, Tit,h Sutmee Suckulputch.

They,

They say, that on account of the number of animals which were at that time sacrificed in *Juggens*, the Almighty appeared under a human form, to convince mankind of the wickedness of this custom; and that he accordingly manifested himself at the time abovementioned, and live one hundred years. Some account has already been given of him, in describing the doctrine of Boodh.

KULKEE OWTAR

Will be born of Bishenjun Brahmin, by Awejsirdenee, in the city of Sembel, at the end of the Kal Jowg, in the month of Bysakh Tit,h Sutmee Suckulputch. He will live a hundred years.

They say, that the time will come when there will not be a monarch on the earth; when wickedness will be universal; grain scarce, and the life of men will never exceed thirty years; but the greatest number will die before that period. And that God, to remedy all these evils, will assume a human form, and make the world flourish again by justice.

Some add fourteen other Owtars, increasing the number to twenty-four; and have written histories of each, containing wonderful relations.

The Hindoos make images of the Owtars of gold, silver, and other materials, and worship them.

UNCLEAN THINGS.

Wine, blood, all the human excrements; a woman who has not performed her necessary purifications; the flesh of ass, hog, dog, and their bones; also the dust that is shaken out of them, as well as of sheep and goats, and the dust of a broom, or out of a garment. Being touched by a sinner, or a crow, or a cock or hen; or a rat, or a mouse, or an eunuch, or a burnt net,

net, or a wafherman, or a hunter, or a fifherman, or a gamefter, or a diftiller, or an executioner, or a tanner, or a dealer in leather, or a dyer, or an oilman.

PURIFIERS.

Fire, prayer, *Purryanem Sendehya*, funfhine, moonfhine, light of a fire, air, water, earth, afhes, muftard feed, wild grain, fhade of a tree, the hind part of a cow's leg, a plough, milk, milk-curds, ghee, dung, and urine of a cow.

THE MANNER OF PURIFICATION.

The foul is purified by knowledge, and religious worfhip; and when the body is defiled by any improper food, it is cleanfed by *Puryanem*, or *Sindehya*, or by eating wild grain. A drunkard is purified by melted glafs. When the body is defiled by any impurity that proceeds from itfelf, it is purified by earth and water, and by wafhing the teeth and eyes. Water that has been defiled by the fhadow of a chundal, is purified by funfhine, moonfhine or wind. If any filth falls from an animal into a well, they muft draw out fixty jars of water; and if the fame accident happens to a pond, they muft take out one hundred jars. If any filth falls into oil, it muft be boiled. Milk cannot be purified, excepting from the fhadow of a chundal, when it may be boiled. Cotton, molaffes, or grain, after feparating whatever had defiled it, muft be fprinkled with water. Gold, filver, ftone, vegetables, filk, and whatever grows in the earth, are purified by being wafhed in water. If they have been defiled by unclean oil, they muft be wafhed in hot water. Wooden veffels, if touched by a chundal, cannot be purified by any means. But if they are touched by any other unclean thing, or by a Sooder, they may be purified by fcraping. The fame rule is to be obferved for veffels of bone or horn. Any ftone veffel that has been defiled, after being wafhed muft be buried for feven days.

days. A ſieve, or a peſtle and mortar, is purified by being ſprinkled with water. An earthen veſſel is purified by being heated in the fire. The earth is cleanſed by ſweeping, or by waſhing, or by lighting a fire upon it: or if a cow lies down upon it, or walks over it, or in time it will purify itſelf. If a cow touches any food with her mouth, or a hair, a fly, or any other inſect falls therein, it is purified by aſhes or water. If it is defiled by any filth falling off the body of the perſon who is eating, he muſt waſh it with water, or ſcour it with earth, till it is perfectly clean. If he defiles himſelf in the upper parts of the body, excepting the hands, he muſt ſcour himſelf with earth, and bathe. If he defiles himſelf in the lower parts, he is purified by waſhing the parts. If he is defiled by drinking wine, or by having connexion with an impure woman, or by any human excrement, he is purified by waſhing, ſcouring with earth, and waſhing again, if below the navel; but if it happens above the navel, then after the ſecond waſhing, he muſt anoint the parts with ghee, cow's milk and curds, and cow's dung and urine, and he muſt alſo drink three handfuls of river water. If he is defiled by the touch of a waſherman, or a dealer in leather, or an executioner, or a hunter, or a fiſherman, or an oilman, or a tame hog, he is purified by water alone. But if he touches an unclean woman, a ſweeper, a ſinner, a corpſe, a dog, aſs, cat, crow, cock, or hen, or a mouſe, or a camel, or is defiled by the ſmoke of a corpſe that is burning; or by the duſt ſhaken off an aſs, dog, ſheep, or goat, he muſt go into the water with his cloaths on, look at the ſun, and repeat ſome particular prayers. If he touches human fat or bone, he muſt bathe with his clothes on; or drink three handfuls of water; or or look at the ſun; or put his hand upon a cow. If he is ſoiled with the blood of clean animals, he is purified by ſcouring himſelf with earth and water. If a garment of wool or ſilk is polluted by ſuch things as would require a man, if touched, to bathe, it is purified by the wind or ſunſhine.

IMPRO-

IMPROPER DRESS.

It is reckoned indecent for a Brahmin, a Kehteree, or a Byeſs, to wear any part of their dreſs of blue, unleſs it be of ſilk or wool. Excepting a Brahminee at night; and a Kehteree woman, whilſt a bride, or at a feaſt, and a Byeſs woman when performing Sheradh. But they all take it off during meals.

FORBIDDEN FOOD.

Human fleſh, beef, horſe-fleſh, houſe fowls, parrots, ſhahrukh, pigeons, owl, vulture, camelion, kirdanch, ſareſs, pepeehch, water-fowl, frogs, ſnakes, mungooſe, and all animals whoſe claws are joined together. All tame animals, excepting goat, red water fowl, heron, dried fleſh, the five kinds of rohoo fiſh, all carnivorous animals, camel, elephant, rhinoceros, monkey, worms of all kinds, camels and mares milk; and the milk of all animals with parted hoofs; the milk of wild animals, and the milk of a cow for thirteen days after calving. The milk of a cow whoſe calf has died, till ſhe has another; garlic, carrots, onions, grain that has grown in unclean ground; grain that has been touched by the foot of a man, or by the hand of an unclean woman. Any thing that comes from the houſe of an adultreſs, or a thief, or of a carpenter, or of an uſurer, or of a blackſmith, or of a poliſher of metals, or of a goldſmith, or of a waſherman, or of an executioner, or of a dealer in leather, or of a public ſinger or dancer, or of one who ſells arms, or of a diſtiller, or of a phyſician, or of a ſurgeon, or from the houſe of a hunter, or an eunuch. Neither is it lawful to eat any thing that has been dreſſed for the Dewtahs. Nor the food, nor leavings of any perſon who is mourning for a relation, nor the food of an irreligious woman, or of a great ſinner. Cheeſe, and every thing of that kind that is made of milk, is alſo forbidden: and whatever is dreſſed without

without water or oil; and any thing dreſſed over night; or any food that is defiled, and unpurified.

Neither is it allowable to eat before performing ſome ceremonies, which will be now deſcribed.

The Manner of DRESSING FOOD, *and the Ceremonies to be obſerved before* MEALS.

Every time before cooking, if it be in the houſe, the ground and part of the wall muſt be plaſtered with cow-dung and earth. If it be abroad, then as much ground as will contain all the cooking utenſils, muſt be plaſtered in the ſame manner. No perſon, but the cook, muſt enter this place. The cook firſt bathes himſelf, then puts on a Dhowtee, and covers his head. If a piece of paper, a dirty rag, or any filthy thing, falls upon the ground, which has been ſpread with cow-dung and earth, the food is ſpoilt. He muſt then begin again, by plaſtering the ground a-freſh with cow-dung and earth. The cook muſt be either a woman, or a Brahmin, who makes it his particular buſineſs, or a relation; unleſs the maſter of the family cooks himſelf.

Before eating they plaſter the ground with cow-dung and earth. They never ſpread any covering over the ground, but may ſit upon a plank, or a ſtool.

The following ceremonies muſt always be performed before meals, 1, Hearing ſome part of the Bedes. 2, Sprinkling water, as a libation for their anceſtors. 3, Preſenting ſome of the food to their idol. 4, Throwing a little food upon the ground, as an offering to the Dewtahs. 5, Giving ſome part to the poor. When theſe ceremonies are concluded, the children eat firſt, then the man's relations, and laſt of all himſelf. Two cannot eat out of one diſh, not even infants. Only the cook can ſerve up the victuals. He eats after all have done.

done. For drinking, every one has alſo a ſeparate cup. Formerly a Brahmin would eat at the houſe of a Kehteree or a Byeſs, and they were alſo allowed to eat at his. But ſince the commencement of the Kal Jowg, no one will eat but in the houſe of his own particular caſt. Formerly they uſed for their plates and diſhes the leaves of trees, as well as gold, ſilver, braſs, and *roeyeen*, and would not uſe copper, earthen ware, or ſtone. Now they refuſe to eat out of a broken diſh, or from off the leaves of Peepul or Akh. They account it improper to eat more than once in a day, and once in a night.

OF THEIR FASTS.

The first kind. When they neither eat nor drink, for a day and night. There are twenty-nine ſuch faſts in the courſe of the year, that are indiſpenſible, viz. the two Akaduſſys and Duaduſſys of every month. Sewrat, Chutterduſſy Suckulputch of Byſakh, which is the anniverſary of the birth of Nerſingh. The Tertya Suckulputch of Byſakh, or the nativity of Purriſhram. The ninth of the Suckulputch of Cheyte, the nativity of Ram. Aſhtoomee Kiſhenputch of Sawen, the nativity of Kiſhen. Some, at theſe times, abſtain from eating grain, or from particular kinds only.

The second kind. He faſts during the day, and eats at night.

The third kind. He eats nothing but fruits, and drinks milk or water.

The fourth kind. He eats once during the day and night.

The fifth kind. He eats only one particular kind of food, during the day and night; but as often as he pleaſes.

The

The sixth kind, Chanderayin, which has been defcribed.

The seventh kind. He neither eats nor drinks for twelve days.

The eighth kind. This lafts twelve days. The firft three days, he eats a little, once in a day. The next three days, he eats only once in the night. The next three days, he never eats any thing, unlefs it is brought to him. And during the laft three days, he neither eats nor drinks.

The ninth kind. This lafts fifteen days, after the following manner. For three days and nights, he eats only one handful at night. For the next three days and nights, if any one gives him fuch an handful, he eats it, otherwife he does not take any fuftenance. Then he eats nothing for three days and nights. The next three days and nights, he takes only a handful of warm water each day. The next three days and nights, a handful of warm milk each day.

The tenth kind. For three days and nights, he neither eats nor drinks. He lights a fire, and fits at a door where there enters a hot wind, which he draws in with his breath.

The eleventh kind. This alfo lafts fifteen days, thus. Three days and nights, he eats nothing but leaves. Three days and nights, nothing but the Indian fig. Three days and nights, nothing but the feed of the lotus. Three days and nights, nothing but peepul leaves. Three days and nights, the expreffed juice of a particular kind of grafs called *Doobah.*

The twelfth kind The following is his regimen for a week. 1ft day, milk. 2, Milk-curds. 3, Ghee. 4. Cow's

4, Cow's urine. 5, Cow's dung. 6, Water. 7, Nothing.

During every kind of faſt, he abſtains from fleſh, adeſs, lubya, honey, and molaſſes; ſleeps on the ground; plays not at any game; has no connexion with woman; anoints not himſelf with oil; neither ſhaves; and every day he beſtows charity, and performs other good actions.

OF SINS.

They reckon theſe of ſeven degrees.

SINS OF THE FIRST DEGREE.

Killing a Brahmin. 2, Inceſt with his mother. 3, Drinking ſpirituous liquors, excepting the Sooder, with whom ſome kinds is not unlawful. There are three kinds of ſpirits; that diſtilled from rice or other grain; what are obtained from fruits or berries; and what are made from molaſſes and other ſweets. The three are forbidden to the Brahmin, but the Kehteree and Byeſs are only prohibited from the two firſt. 4, Stealing ten maſhahs of gold. 5, Not making expiation for either of theſe ſins for a year.

SINS OF THE SECOND DEGREE.

Lying concerning caſt. Speaking reproachfully of any one to the king. Giving the lie to his tutor. Committing inceſt with his ſiſter. Raviſhing a virgin. Committing adultery with a ſweeper, a dancing girl, a fiſherman's wife, or a friend's wife, or with a daughter-in-law. Forgetting the Bedes. Giving falſe evidence. Selling a relation. Eating any thing that is unlawful. Breach of truſt. Stealing a man, a horſe, jewels, or ſilver. Getting poſſeſſion of land by fraudulent means.

SINS OF THE THIRD DEGREE.

Killing a cow. Committing adultery with any women that are not prohibited in the firſt and ſecond degree. Theft. Killing a woman, or a Kehteree, Byeſs, or Sooder. Practiſing magick. Committing oppreſſion Exacting illegal fines. Being a pimp in any degree. Being a proſtitute. Treating with diſreſpect his tutor or parents. Uſury. A Brahmin or Kehteree trading unleſs they do it through neceſſity: but then he may not deal in the following articles; oil, ſalt, ſweatmeats, dreſſed food, ſeſamé ſeed, red cloths, hempen or linen, or woollen cloths, fruits, medicines, arms, poiſon, fleſh, perfumes, milk, honey, milk-curds, wine, indigo, lack, graſs, or water: nor any thing made of leather. But on no pretence ſhall he neglect to perform *Juggen* to the Dewtahs, and reading the Bedes with his ſpiritual guide.

Other ſins of the third degree are, neglecting to put on the *Zenar* at the proper age; refuſing aſſiſtance to his relations in a manner befitting his circumſtances; ſelling his wife, ſon, garden, or pond. Digging out of the earth any plant that he has not occaſion for; reading books of any other religion. If a Brahmin enters into ſervice, he ſins in this degree. Alſo the younger brother marrying before the elder, is accounted a ſin of the third degree.

SINS OF THE FOURTH DEGREE.

Diſſimulation. Sodomy. Injuring a Brahmin. Smelling at wine, urine, or dung.

SINS OF THE FIFTH DEGREE.

Killing any of the following animals; an elephant, horſe, camel, deer, ſheep, goat, buffalo, neelghaw, and alſo fiſh. Exacting fines from thoſe who are not ſubjected to them by the laws; ſuch as ſweepers, &c. A Byeſs dealing in any of the articles prohibited to a Brahmin or Kehteree in the former degree. Lying. Serving a Sooder.

SINS

SINS OF THE SIXTH DEGREE.

Eating ſmall inſects, ſuch as ants. Eating out of the hand, or veſſel of a wine-bibber.

SINS OF THE SEVENTH DEGREE.

Stealing fruits, flowers, or fire-wood.

And for each ſin there is a particular expiation.

They ſay, that whoſoever kills a Brahmin will tranſmigrate into a deer, dog, camel, or hog; after which he will again become a man; but he will always be ſickly, and die of a violent diſtemper. The only way to avoid this, is to tear off his fleſh by degrees, and throw it into the fire. To quit his family for twelve years, and beg with a human ſkull in his hand, confeſſing his wickedneſs at every door. This is provided he killed him by accident; but if the murder was wilful, he muſt perform this penance for twenty-four years.

OUTWARD SINS.

Theſe are innumerable; but the twelve following are accounted the worſt: 1, *Kerowd*, being under the influence of anger. 2, *Lowbh*, inſatiable avarice. 3, *Dooweekh*, malice. 4, *Rag*, delighting in worldly pleaſures. 5, *Man*, pride. 6, *Mowh*, ignorance. 7, *Mud*, being intoxicated with liquor, riches, youth, power, or knowledge. 8, *Shewh*, affliction at the loſs of riches, or reputation, or for the abſence of friends, 9, *Mumuttoo*, conſidering the things of this world as his own. 10, *Ahenkar*, ſelf-love. 11, *Bhie*, fearing any but God. 12, *Hirkh*, rejoicing at his own virtue, and at his enemy's vice.

It is the endeavour of all men who have a proper ſenſe of the Almighty, to get free from theſe twelve human imperfections, and render themſelves worthy of his divine bleſſing. Some ſay that all evil actions may

 be

be comprifed under ten heads; of which number the three following vitiate the heart: 1, Adopting the evil fentiments of another. 2, Evil inclination. 3, Thinking ill of God's elect. Three corrupt the body, viz. 1, Seizing another's property. 2, Diftreffing the innocent. 3, Adultery. And four pollute the tongue, 1, Abufe; 2, Lying; 3, Slander; 4, Impertinence.

Oh Lord defend us from thefe offences, and fhower down thy mercy upon us.

Places *dedicated to* Divine Worship.

The enlightened part of mankind, are fenfible that true righteoufnefs is an upright heart; and believe that God can only be worfhipped in holinefs of fpirit. But priefts, who know the weaknefs of vulgar minds, have found it neceffary to engage their imagination by the contemplation of vifible objects. With this view they have declared particular places holy, and enjoined pilgrimages; which ferve as a means of profeffing their faith; and the promife of future reward, make men perform the journey with enthufiaftic eheerfulnefs.

They are of four kinds. *The first, called Dive*, are dedicated to Brahma, Bifhen, and Mahadeo. Of thefe the principal are the following twenty-feven rivers, 1, Ganges. 2, Serfooty. 3, Jumna. 4, Nerbudda. 5, Beypaffa, commonly called Beyah. 6, Buttiftah, vulg. Behet. 7, Kowfhekee, near Rohtafs in Penjah; and part of it goes to the weft quarter of Ghurhee. 8, Nundawuttee. 9, Chunderbhaka, vulg. Chinab. 10, Seryoo, vulg. Sirow. 11, Suttewlee. 12, Tapee, vulg. Tipenee; Burhampoor is upon its banks. 13, Purrawuttee. 14, Paffawuttee. 15, Goomtee, near Dewarka. 16, Gundnkee; Sultanpoor, and the Soubah of Owdh are upon its banks. 17, Bahode. 18, Deeka. 19, Gowdaweree; Putten in the Dekhan, ftands on its banks. 20, Tamifpermee, in the extremity of the

the Dekhan; it produces pearls. 21, Chirmenowtee. 22, Owrna, near Benaris. 23, Irawuttee, vulg. Rawee; Lahore is upon its banks. 24, Sutdduroo; Ledyaneh is upon its banks. 25, Bheemruthee, alſo called Bheema, is in the Dekhan. 26, Pernaſowna. 27, Bokhra; is in the Dekhan. 28, Atchmeeya. Some include the river Sind (or Indus). Each of theſe rivers being dedicated to one of the Dewtahs, has particular properties aſcribed to it. There are alſo many places upon the banks of theſe rivers that are held ſacred, amongſt which is the town of Sowroon, on the banks of the Ganges; whither multitudes reſort on the 12th of Aghun.

CITIES *that are called* DIVE, *from being dedicated to* BRAHMA, BISHEN, *or* MAHADEO.

Kaſhee, vulg. Benaris. The city, and round it for five coſe, is held ſacred. Pilgrimages are made to it throughout the year; but on *Sewrat* multitudes flock there from great diſtances. It is conſidered very fortunate to die here. The Hindoos ſay that there are ſeveral kinds of *Muckut*, viz. *Salookee*, paſſing immediately through paradiſe to Kylaſs. They ſay, that after a man has enjoyed paradiſe, he will return into this world, and after undergoing various tranſmigrations, he will at laſt proceed from paradiſe to Kylaſs, from whence he will never return. *Sameepee*, is when a man in return for his righteouſneſs, after breaking the elementary bonds, is admitted into the ſervice of God's elect, and never returns to this world. *Sawyej*, when having paſſed through all the degrees of rewards and puniſhments, he obtains immortal felicity, or the enjoyment of *Muckut*.

Ajewdheya, vulg. Owdh. It is held ſacred ground, to the diſtance of forty coſe north, and twenty coſe ſouth. It is a place of great reſort on the ninth Suckulputch of Cheyte.

Ownitka, vulg. Owjein; all round it for two cofe, is efteemed holy. On the *Sewrat* great numbers of people affemble here.

Kantee, in the Dekhan; all round it for twenty cofe is accounted holy. On the eighth of every Hindoo month, that falls on a Tuefday, this is a place of great religious refort.

Mehtra. All round for the diftance of forty-eight cofe is held holy. The place was held facred before the birth of Kifhen. The grand days at this place are the 23d of Bhadun, and 15th of Katick.

Dowarka. The country for forty cofe in length, and twenty cofe in breadth, is efteemed holy. Pilgrimages are made thither on the feafts of *Dewalee*.

Maya, vulg. Herdewar, on the banks of the Ganges, for eighteen cofe in length, is confidered holy. Great numbers of pilgrims come here on the 10th of Cheyte.

The above feven cities are called the feven *Lowpree*.

Pyag, now called Illahabafs; all round for twenty cofe, is efteemed holy. They fay, that when a man dies at this place, whatever he wifhes for, he will obtain in his next regeneration. Although they believe that fuicide in general will be punifhed with torments hereafter, yet they confider it meritorious for a man to kill himfelf here. This place is vifited by the devout, throughout the year; but more efpecially in the month of Maugh.

Nuggerkote. Round for eight cofe is accounted holy. Great multitudes of pilgrims affemble here on the 8th of Sawun and Cheyte Suckulputch.

Cafhmeer,

Cashmeer is also esteemed holy land, being dedicated to Mahadeo; and some parts are esteemed peculiarly sacred.

Religious places of the second rank, called *Assoor*, are dedicated to the race of Dyte. These, on many occasions, unite with the Dewtahs, but the latter are purer. The Dyte are the source of tum (anger), and assume hideous forms. Their temples are placed in Patall.

Religious places of the third rank, called *Arkh*, are dedicated to the Rehkehser. These are virtuous men, who are rewarded with high rank near the throne of God. Their temples are very numerous, and amongst them are Neemkhar, Phoker, and Khowshub in Budderee.

Religious places of the fourth rank, called *Manook*, who are virtuous men, a degree inferior to the *Rehkhesir*. These have also many temples, amongst which are Koorkeyte, and forty cose round it. Multitudes assemble here during eclipses of the sun and moon.

There are certain rules laid down for each pilgrimage; and various rewards are promised to those who perform them.

O thou, who seekest after knowledge, learn a lesson from these fables! Every atom of the creation is a sublime temple, which the Deity hath erected, that human imagination may not wander in vain pursuits.

Of MARRIAGES.

The Hindoos have eight kinds. 1, *Brahmee*. The virgin's father, or her nearest male relation, goes and brings the bridegroom to the house where she dwells, and makes preparation for the marriage. Then the girl's girl's grandfather, or her brother, or any other male relation, or her mother, faith before the company, "I have betrothed fuch a woman to fuch a man." And the man gives his confent in the prefence of the fame people. Then they perform the Howm, and both parties declare that they have not any bodily imperfection, or infanity of mind. After this, one of the girl's female relations wafhes the feet of the bride and bridegroom. Next the bride and bridegroom mark themfelves with a Khufhkeh. There are placed in the middle of the affembly three veffels, one containing rice, one curds, and the other honey, which, after performing certain prayers, are given to the bride and bridegroom to eat. When all this is done, the couple are dreffed out, and carried to a corner, where they fit with a curtain between them. The father of the woman, with all his fons, looks towards the eaft, whilft a Brahmin repeats fome prayers, after which he gives the bride and bridegroom fome rice, and five beetle-nuts each. Then the curtain is drawn up, and the bride and bridegroom throw the rice and beetle-nuts upon each other. The Brahmin now puts the woman's hands into the man's, and after repeating a prayer, feparates them, and then ties together the hands of each with a flight thread. Then the bride's father takes hold of her hands, and gives her away to the bridegroom, faying, "May there always be a partnerfhip between you, and may it produce benevolence and fatisfaction." To conclude, they light a fire, and carry the couple round it feven times, which ceremony makes them man and wife; and till this performed, it is allowable to break off the match. 2, *Dive*, At a Juggen, all kinds of things are beftowed in charity, at the fame time a virgin is given to a Brahmin; and this is their marriage ceremony. 3, *Arsh*, is when a virgin is given in exchange for a cow and a bull, which ceremony completes their marriage. 4, *Rajeputty*, is when a virgin is married with the ceremonies of *Brahmee*, during the performance of a *Juggen*.

gen. 5, *Assur*, is when a large ſum of money is given to the girl's family by the bridegroom; and which conſtitutes their marriage. 6, *Khandhir*, is when they marry from mutual affection. 7, *Raksh*, is when any one takes away a man's daughter by force to his own houſe, and marries her there. 8, *Pyshatch*, is when a man is obliged by law to marry a girl whom he has raviſhed.

Of theſe eight kinds of marriage, the four firſt are entered into only by Brahmins. The fifth is peculiar to the Byeſs and Sooder. The ſixth and ſeventh for a Kehteree. The eighth is held diſgraceful by all.

The Brahmins never give any dower to their wives. In the former Jowgs, a Brahmin uſed to marry out of all the tribes; but it was not lawful for any one of the others to wed a Brahminee; neither were ſuperiors and inferiors permitted to intermarry. But now no one chooſes to marry out of his own tribe; and even the different branches of each marry only amongſt themſelves.

There are various tribes of Brahmins, but thoſe moſt eſteemed are deſcendants of the ſeven *Rehkehsir*, viz. Kuſhp, Ater, Bhirdewaj, Biſhwametre, Gowtum, Ungera, and Pulleſtee. Each of theſe have many branches, and the deſcendants of each of the ſeven original ſtocks are called *Kull* and *Gowtir*. A man and a woman of the ſame *Gowtir* may not marry together, if their relationſhip be ever ſo diſtant.

The Kehteree, Byeſs, and Sooder, are each obliged to employ a Brahmin of one of the above ſeven *Gowtirs*, to perform their marriage and other ceremonies; and a Brahmin ſo officiating is called *Purrowhit*. It is not lawful for a man and woman to marry, whoſe *Purrowhits* are both belonging to one *Kull* or *Gowtir*.

Upon

Upon marriage, the woman quits her family's *Gowtir*, and goes into that of her husband. A younger brother cannot marry before his elder. They do not hold it commendable for the bride to be younger than eight, nor older than ten years. Twenty-five years they reckon the properest age for the man, and think it a folly for any one to marry after fifty. Excepting a prince, it is not thought right for a man to have more than one wife, unless she proves sickly or barren, or her children die in their infancy. In these cases, he may marry ten wives; but if the tenth prove exceptionable, he may not marry any more. If the first wife is unexceptionable, and yet he wants to marry another, he is obliged to give the first wife one third of his estate.

It was formerly the custom, that when any Rajah wanted to dispose of his daughter in marriage, he invited all the neighbouring princes to a feast, at which his daughter made her appearance, and upon whomsoever she fixed her choice, she put round his neck a string of pearl. This ceremony was called *Sowyembir*.

Of DRESS.

Singhar, signifies to ornament. Man is ornamented by twelve things. 1, Trimming the beard. 2, Cleansing the body by ablution. 3, Making the Kushkeh. 4, Anointing with odoriferous oils. 5, Gold ear-rings. 6, A Jammah *, which is tied on the left side. 7, *Mokt*, the gold tassel or fringe that hangs out of the turban. 8, Sword. 9, Jemdher. 10, Ring. 11, Eating beetle. 12, Mouzah †.

Women are ornamented by sixteen things. 1. Bathing. 2, Anointing with oil. 3, Plaiting the hair. 4, Jewels worn on the top of the head. 5, Anointing

* A long gown. † A kind of boots.

with ſandal. 6, Putting on cloaths, and which are of various kinds. The ſleeves of ſome dreſſes reach below the ends of the fingers, and others come only to the elbow. Moſtly they wear a *Peishwaz*, without any ſhirt, and which is called *Ungeeah*. Inſtead of drawers, ſome put on a *Lengha*, which is a *Lowngee* ſtitched on both ſides, and faſtened with a belt. It is alſo made after various other forms. Some have a *Dunddeya*, which is a long ſheet worn over the *Lengha*; part of it is thrown over the head, and one end faſtens round the waiſt. They alſo ſometimes wear veils, and long drawers. 7, The *Kushkeh*. Some, beſides the Kuſhkeh, ornamented the forehead with jewels. 8, Lampblack, with which they make a beautiful collyrium. 9, Ear-rings. 10, Noſe jewels. 11, Necklace. 12, A ſtring of flowers, or pearl, hanging from the neck. 13, Staining the hands. 14, A belt, ornamented with little bells and jewels. 15, Ornaments for the feet. 16, Beetle. To which may be added ſoft blandiſhments.

JEWELS.

Seisphool, a flower reſembling the marigold, made of gold, and worn on the head. *Mang*, an ornament worn upon the parting of the hair of the head. *Gowtbilladudir*, is an ornament for the forehead, conſiſting of five ſhort points and a long one. *Sehra*, ſeven ſtrings of pearl, or more, interſperſed with natural flowers. This is faſtened to the forehead, and covers the face. It is chiefly worn at marriages, and by a mother on the birth of a ſon. *Teeka*, a jewel in the ſhape of a creſcent, which is worn upon the forehead. *Bindelee*, a round piece of gold ſmaller than a mohur, which is worn upon the forehead. *Khuntehla*, an ear-ring of a conical form. *Kurrenphool*, an ear-ring reſembling a roſe. *Deerbutcha*, another kind of ear-ring. *Peepulputty*, ſmall creſcents, nine, or more, of which are worn in each ear. *Ballee Chumpakullee*, a ſmall golden roſe, worn

worn on the thick part of the ear. *Mowrbhenwir*, an ear-ring in the ſhape of a peacock. *Beyser*, a kind of noſe jewel. *Phoolee*, reſembles a roſebud with a ſtalk, and is worn in the noſe. *Lowng*, is a golden clove, which is worn in the noſe. *Nut,h*, a gold ring, upon which are a ruby and two pearls, or other jewels; it is worn in the noſe. *Goolooband*, a necklace, conſiſting of five or ſeven ſtrings of very ſmall gold roſes. *Har*, a ſtring of pearls and flowers hanging from the neck. *Hans*, a collar *Kungun*, a bracelet. *Gujreh*, a bracelet of pearls and gold. *Jewee*, five gold barley corn ſtrung upon ſilk, and worn round the wriſts. *Choor*, another kind of bracelet. *Bahoo*, a ſmall kind of bracelet. *Chooreen*, another very ſmall kind of bracelet; ſeven of which are worn round each wriſt. *Bazoobund*, ornaments for the arms. *Taar*, a hollow ring, worn upon the arms. *Ungoothee*, rings, which are of various forms. *Choodirghunta*, gold bells, ſtrung upon ſilver wire, and worn round the waiſt. *Kutmekhla*, a gold belt. *Jeeher*, three gold rings for each ankle. *Choora*, two half circles made of gold, which join round the leg. *Doondnhee*, like the *Choora*, but ornamented with engravings. *Mussowree*, differs from the *Doondnhee* in nothing but the engraving. *Payil*, rings worn round the ankles. *Ghoonghroo*, little gold bells ſtrung upon ſilk, which are worn about the ancles, between the Jeeher and Payil. *Bank*, ornaments for the top of the foot, and which are either ſquare or triangular. *Beetcheva*, toe rings, half a golden ball. *Unwut*, is a ring worn upon the great toe.

The jewels above deſcribed are made either plain, or ornamented with jewels; and are of various faſhions. The Hindoo goldſmiths are ſuch exquiſite workmen, that ſometimes they charge a gold mohur for working a tolah of gold. His majeſty has pointed out to them many improvements.

WORKMEN.

WORKMEN.

The jewellers of other countries faſten jewels, in the ſettings, with lack; but thoſe of Hindoſtan make uſe of a kind of gold which they call *Kurden*, and which is ſo malleable, that the ſtory of Parvez's gold which he could mould with his hand like wax, ſeems credible. It is prepared by ſtratifying very thin plates of gold with field cow-dung, and a particular kind of ſalt called *Sambhir*, when it is put into a fire of cow-dung, which is ſuffered to expire. And theſe operations are repeated till the gold is ſufficiently refined. When it is thought to be quite pure, it is put into an earthen veſſel, with lime juice, or ſome other acid, and placed in the fire. After this, it is wound round a ſtick, and if it is not ſufficiently ductile, the ſtratifications are repeated. The goldſmith firſt puts a little lack into the ſocket, and over it a piece of this *Kurden* gold. Then he preſſes down the ſtone upon the gold, and faſtens the ends over the ſides; which fixes the ſtone ſo faſt, that there is no danger of its falling out. A goldſmith charges ſixty-four dams for making a tolah of this *Kurden*.

Zerneshan. He inlays with gold, ſilver, cryſtal, cornelians, or ſteel. For every tolah of gold that is expended he charges 2½ tolahs. If he inlays ivory, fiſh's teeth, or horn, with ſilver, he charges twice the quantity that is expended.

Koftgur. He inlays with gold and ſilver, in a manner that ſomewhat reſembles a file. For a tolah of gold, he charges one hundred dams; for a tolah of ſilver, ſixty dams. This is chiefly uſed for ornamenting arms.

Mienakar, enamels cups, flaggons, rings, &c. He firſt lays on the colour, and after enamelling, puts the metal

metal into the fire two or three times. For a tolah of gold that he enamels, he charges ſixteen dams, and for a tolah of ſilver, ſeven dams.

Sadehkar, a plain worker in gold or ſilver. For one tolah of gold, five dams and half; and for a tolah of ſilver, two dams.

Subkehkar, pierced worker; he is paid double the price of the Sadehkar.

Minubbethar, raiſes flowers, &c. by means of a ſtamp. For a tolah of gold, one dam.

Heremkar, inlays with little grains of gold. For one tolah of gold, one rupee; and for a tolah of ſilver, half a rupee.

Seembaft, makes gold or ſilver lace, which is uſed for ſword belts, &c. For working one tolah of gold twenty-four dams; and for one tolah of ſilver ſixteen dams.

Sewadkhar, fills with *Sewad*, or black varniſh, engravings upon gold or ſilver, and poliſhes the ground. The black varniſh is a compoſition of tutty, ſilver, lead, copper, and brimſtone. For fine work, he charges two rupees for a tolah weight of the thing varniſhed.

Zirkowb, makes gold and ſilver plates.

There are alſo ſtone engravers, lapidaries, founders, and other artiſts, whoſe excellencies cannot be deſcribed here.

CEREMONIES ON THE BIRTH OF A CHILD.

Immediately upon the birth of a child, the father bathes himſelf in cold water, makes offerings to the Dewtahs, and the Sheradh for his anceſtors. After which,

which, he ſtirs with a gold ring ſome honey and ghee, which he puts into the mouth of the infant. Then the midwife cuts the child's navel-ſtring, when the whole family become unclean. Whilſt they continue in this ſtate, they abſtain from performing the Howm, worſhipping the Dewtahs, reading the Gayteree, and all other ceremonies; confining themſelves to inward remembrances of the Deity. If the child's father is a Brahmin, all who are related to him, as far as the fourth degree of conſanguinity, are unclean for ten days. The relations in the fifth degree, for ſix days; thoſe of the ſixth degree, for four days; thoſe of the ſeventh degree, for three days; thoſe of the eighth degree, for one day and one night; thoſe of the ninth degree, for four pehrs. And at the expiration of the above preſcribed periods, they are cleanſed by ablutions. If the father is a Kehteree, the family are unclean for twelve days, and if a Byeſs, or Sooder, fifteen days. The inferior branches of Sooder are unclean for thirty days. During this time ſtrangers will not eat in their houſes. This ſtate is called *Sewtuck*. But a prince is not ſubject to this uncleanneſs, nor any of his attendants; nor a phyſician; nor a cook; but on the ſixth day they perform ſome religious ceremonies, and make rejoicings, and waſh the mother and child.

The next day after the expiration of the *Sewtuck*, they name the child, and draw his horoſcope, to which one of the letters of his name muſt have ſome affinity. This name never conſiſts of more than four letters. At the commencement of the fourth month, they place the child in the ſun; before that time he is never carried out of the houſe. The fifth month, they bore his right ear. The ſixth month, if it is a boy, they place round him various kinds of food, and let him eat whatever he chooſes. If it is a girl, this ceremony is delayed till the ſeventh month. When the child is a year old, they ſhave his head. Some delay this till the third, and

and others till the fifth year. On the fifth year, they make rejoicings, and put the child to ſchool. They always celebrate his birth-day, and every year make a knot on a thread of ſilk. For every one of theſe occaſions, they have particular ceremonies and rejoicings.

HINDOO FESTIVALS.

In the month of Cheyte. 1, *Serishtyad*, the Purwah of Suckulputch. 2, *Nowrat*, the nine firſt nights of the year. This is a great feſtival of Durga, particularly at Nuggerkote. 3, *Sirrypunchemeen*, the fifth Tit,h of Suckulputch. 4, *Asooga Ushtoomeen*, the eighth Tit,h of Suckulputch. 5, *Ramnomeen*, the ninth Tit,h, the birth of Ram. 6, *Chowterduss*, the fourteenth Tit,h. 7, *Poorunmassee*, the fifteenth Tit,h. 8, *Purwa*, the firſt Tit,h of Kiſhenputch.

In the month of Byſakh. 1, *Teej*, the third Tit,h of Suckulputch, the birth of Purriſhram. 2, *Suthmee*, the eighth Tit,h. 3, *Chatterdussy*, the fourteenth Tit,h, the birth of Nirſingh. 4, *Amavus*, the thirtieth Tit,h.

In the month of Jeyte. 1, *Chuttert,hee*, the fourth Tit,h. 2, *Dussmeen*, the tenth Tit,h. This day they call *Dussereh*.

In the month of Aſſar, the ſeventh, eighth, and eleventh Tit,hs; and according to ſome the fifteenth alſo.

In the month of Sawun. 1, *Poorumassee*. 2, The eleventh Tit,h of Suckulputch, which with the Brahmins is the greateſt feſtival throughout the year. On this day they wear round their wriſts the *Rackhee*, which is a thread, ſometimes ornamented with pearls. 3, The fifth Tit,h of Suckulputch.

In the month of Bhadun. The fourth, fifth, ſixth, and

and twenty-third Tit,hs. The laſt is the birth of Kiſh-en. Others place this event on the ſeventh of Sawun.

In the month of Aſſin. The firſt nine nights, which they account very holy; together with the tenth Tit,h, which they alſo call *Dehsereh*. This is the vulgar reckoning; but in their books the *Dehsereh* is placed in the month of Jeyte; and this feſtival is there called *Beyjy Dussmeen*. They dreſs themſelves out on this day, and wear on their heads green barley. On this day every mechanic worſhips his tools, which he conſiders a great ceremony. This is the greateſt holiday for the Kehteree. Others add to the foregoing feſtivals, the *Seradh*, or *Kunnagut*, on the fifteenth Tit,h of Kiſhenputch. During all theſe fifteen days they beſtow charity.

In the month of Katick. *Purwa*. This they call *Bul Raj*, and account it a great feſtival. On this day they dreſs out their cattle. The ſecond, ninth, eleventh, twelfth, and thirtieth Tit,hs are alſo feſtivals. The laſt is the *Dewalee*, which, like the *Sheb Berat* of the Mohammedans, is celebrated with illuminations. It begins on the 29th, which night they reckon lucky for many undertakings, and for playing at dice. This is the greateſt Byeſs feſtival.

In the month of Aghun. The third, ſeventh, eighth, and ninth Tit,hs.

In the month of Poos. The eighth of Suckulputch.

In the month of Maug. The third, fourth, fifth, and ſeventh Tit,hs. The fifth they call *Bussunt*. It is the commencement of ſpring, and they celebrate it with great rejoicings; throwing at one another different coloured powders, and ſinging. In ancient books, the ſeventh

ſeventh Tit,h is accounted the greateſt feſtival in this month.

In the month of Phagun. The eleventh Tit,h of Suckulputch, which they call *Hoolee.* It begins properly on the thirteenth, and continues till the ſeventeenth. It is a ſeaſon of great merriment, which is much increaſed by throwing at one another powders of different colours. On the laſt night, they light fires, and throw into them various things. This is a Sooder feſtival. The twenty-ninth day and night of this month, they call *Sewrat.* They keep awake all night, and account it lucky for particular undertakings.

The Brahmins have alſo the following holidays in every month. 1, Aſhtomeen; 2, Chowturduſſy; 3, Poorunmaſſee; 4, Amavus; 5, Sunkerant; which is the day when the ſun moves from one ſign into another.

THE CEREMONIES WITH THE DEAD.

When a man is ſo ill that his life is deſpaired of, they take him from off his bed, and place him upon the ground; ſhave his head, and waſh his body. The Brahmins repeat certain prayers over him, and his family beſtow charity. Then they plaſter the ground with cow-dung, and ſtrew it over with green graſs. After which they lay him down to ſleep upon the graſs upon his back, with his head towards the north, and his feet towards the ſouth; or if a river or tank be near, they carry him there, and place him up to his middle in water. When his diſſolution approaches, they put into his mouth Ganges water, gold, ruby, diamond, and pearl, and place upon his breaſt a Tulſy-leaf, which the Hindoos eſteem holy; and make a Kuſhkeh upon his forehead with a particular kind of earth. They alſo give away a cow. When he expires, his ſon, his younger brother, his ſcholar, and particular friends, ſhave their heads and beards: ſome defer it till the tenth day. Then they

they drefs the corpfe in a dhowtee, and a winding fheet. If a woman dies during the life of her hufband, they do not fhave her head, but drefs her in her ordinary cloaths. The corpfe is carried to the fide of the river, and laid upon a pile of Palafs wood. A Brahmin then repeats fome prayers, and pours fome ghee into the mouth of the deceafed, and puts fmall grains of gold into his eyes, nofe, ears, and other apertures. If the deceafed leaves a fon, he fets fire to the pile, otherwife his younger brother, or alfo his elder brother. All his wives embrace the corpfe, and notwithftanding their relations advife them againft it, expire in the flames with the greateft cheerfulnefs. The funeral pile for great people, is made of lignum aloes and fandal wood.

A Hindoo wife, who is burnt with her hufband, is either actuated by motives of real affection; or fhe thinks it her duty to conform to cuftom; or fhe confents to avoid reproach; or elfe fhe is forced to it by her relations.

They burn not a Sonnyaffy, nor an infant who has not cut its teeth, but bury them, or throw them into the river. Neither ought any of the following defcriptions to be burnt; one who does not believe in the Bedes; one who acts contrary to his faith; a thief; a woman who has murdered her hufband; one who has committed any of the five deadly fins; nor a drunkard.

If the corpfe cannot be found, they make an effigy of the body with reeds, and cover it with deer fkin and Palafs, and a cocoa nut ferves for the head. This they pray over, and burn.

If a wife is pregnant at the time of her hufband's death, fhe is not allowed to burn herfelf, till after her delivery. If he dies on a journey, the wives burn themfelves along with his clothes, or any thing elfe that

 belonged

belonged to him. Some women who have been prevailed upon, by their relations, or have perfuaded themfelves againft burning with the corpfe, have found themfelves fo unhappy, that they have cheerfully fubmitted to expire in the flames, before the next day.

After the corpfe is burnt, his relations and friends difhevel their hair, reverfe their zenars, and bathe themfelves; each leaving on the fide of the river two handfuls of fefamé feed; and after performing thefe ceremonies, they ftand upon a green fpot. The friends of the deceafed exhort his relations to bear their lofs with patience and refignation, and accompany them home, the young people walking in front. When the relations arrive at the door of the houfe of the deceafed, they tafte a bit of *Neemb* * leaf, and then enter.

The fourth day after the death of a Brahmin; or the fifth day after the death of a Kehteree; or of a Byefs the ninth; or of a Sooder the tenth day; the perfon who put fire to the funeral pile, vifits the fpot and performs certain ceremonies.

The afhes and bones are collected together, and thrown into the Ganges. But if it is at a great diftance, they put them into an earthen veffel, and afterwards inclofe them in a bag made of deer fkin, and convey it to that river; on which occafion other ceremonies are performed.

If the deceafed is a Brahmin, all his relations for ten days fleep on grafs, fpread on the ground, and cook not any victuals, eating only what is fent there, or can be bought at market. For ten days, the perfon who put fire to the pile, makes an offering of boiled rice and milk to the deceafed, for the nourifhment of his

* Which is very bitter.

new

new body. They ſay that when the ſoul quits this earthly body, it animates another ſubtle body, which they call *Pereet.* And they believe, that as long as the ſoul continues in the *Pereet* body, it cannot enter Paradiſe. This *Pereet* body vaniſhes at the expiration of ten days, when certain ceremonies are performed upon the ſoul's entrance into another body, which is admitted into paradiſe. This is for a Brahmin; but the other tribes continue in the *Pereet* body according to the length of their reſpective *Sewtuck.*

Some other ceremonies are alſo performed for Brahmins on the eleventh day; and for other tribes on the twelfth day.

If a Brahmin dies out of his own houſe, and an account of his death is received by his family in leſs than ten days after, whatever time is wanting to complete that ſpace, during that they continue unclean. If the intelligence arrives after ten days, then they are unclean for three days. But his ſon, whenever he receives the intelligence, is unclean for ten days, although he had not put on the zenar. If a child dies before he had cut any teeth, or before the ſeventh month, the family are unclean for one day only, and are purified by ablution. If the deceaſed child was two years old, they are unclean for a day and night. For the death of a child, from the time of ſhaving the head, till eight years of age, the family are unclean for three days and nights. For the death of a daughter, under ten years of age, the family are purified by one ablution. If ſhe dies after that age, until the day ſhe is betrothed, they are unclean one day. If ſhe dies after marriage, her father's and her huſband's family are unclean for three days.

MERITORIOUS KINDS OF SUICIDE.

Theſe are five in number. 1, Starving. 2, Covering himſelf with cow-dung, and ſetting it on fire, conſuming

ſuming himſelf therein. 3, Burying himſelf in ſnow. 4, At the extremity of Bengal, where the Ganges diſcharges itſelf into the ſea, through a thouſand channels, he goes into the water, enumerates his ſins, and prays, till the aligators come and devour him. 5, Cutting his throat at Allahabad, at the confluence of the Ganges and the Jumna.

EXPLANA-

EXPLANATIONS

OF SOME

SANSCRIT WORDS.

A

ABEDEEYA, the exercife of Auwerunfucket, or the internal power of knowledge.

Abhow, privation.

Abadhpefheetoo, ignorance of the privation of what is required.

Aberaj, mifconceiving, and putting a falfe value upon worldly things.

Abeyfhruj, vide Aneyfheruj.

Abeehyafs, habitual virtue.

Abeyfhooruj. Thofe operations of the foul which lead to mifconception.

Acharej, amongft the followers of Jine, is one who explains to the noviciate any difficulties that occur in his ftudies.

Adherem, unhappy confcioufnefs.

Adehyatemk, pain occafioned by envy and ill nature.

Adehbhowtek, pain occafioned by the elements.

Adehdewik, pain inflicted by the Dewtahs.

Adhowt, amazement.

Adit, the fun. The father of the Dewtahs.

Aginhowter, a particular kind of burnt facrifice.

Ageeyan, ignorance.

Ahenkar, worldly defire.

Ahenfa, not to kill or moleft any animal.

Ajewnej, a body that is not produced by generation.

Akafs, ether.

Akullifht, the inclination to do good.

Alfee, floth.

Alubdwumkutto, ficklenefs

Anewneeabhow, feparation of two things.

Anyentabhow, a negative that differs in place, but agrees as to time.

Anoorrektottoo, a mind not to be fatisfied.

Anuntgeyan, analytic knowledge.

Anuntderfun, fynthetic knowledge.

Anuntfook, total reft.

Apoorickh, deliverance from one pain by fuch means as will not produce another.

Apie, aqueous.

Apurttoo, proximity of time or place.

Apnee, fhewing the caufe in the place required.

Apunchekurt, an invifible atom.

Appergench, defpifing and rejecting all worldly poffeffions.

Art.hwed,

Art,hwed, the praiſe and reward of religious duties.

Arjſutter, the four predicaments uſed by the followers of Boodh.

Aſmewaiykaren, external or apparent cauſe.

Aſſulpurrutputchtoo, an appearance reſembling what is ſought.

Aſſeecha, forgiveneſs of injuries.

Aſſempergeyat, when the imaginary form of the Deity vaniſhes from the mind, and nothing remains but the contemplation of his eſſence.

Aſteeyee, not to poſſeſs more wealth than is really uſeful.

Aſſun, ſitting in a particular manner.

Aſunnya, irrational beings.

Aſherum, the four Hindoo degrees of diſcipline.

Aſhowmeedh-Juggen, a ſacrifice performed by great monarchs.

Atma, the ſoul of the univerſe.

Atentick, the diſſolution of ignorance.

Auwerunſuckut, the internal power of knowledge.

B

Bad, controverſy in purſuit of knowledge.

Baiweeya, aerial.

Bede, the divine book revealed to Brahma. It was afterwards divided into four, viz. Rig, Jejer, Sam, and Atehrbun. This diviſion is by ſome attributed to Byaſs; whilſt others maintain that Brahma uttered one from each of his four mouths.

Berhemcharee, the firſt of the four Hindoo degrees of diſcipline.

Betenda, indirect propoſition.

Beyg, an accident produced by motion, and which becomes the cauſe.

Beeputcheeſuttoo, knowing that in whatever place there is not what is required, neither can there be the conſequence.

Beyperjee, miſapprehenſion.

Berag, comprehending and deſpiſing the things of this world.

Beychipt, when the heart is fixed upon one object, and is a little at reſt.

Beapeyee, depraved knowledge.

Birbede, the ceſſation of the exerciſe of the external faculties of knowledge.

Beert, the inclination to do good or bad.

Beyedeh, ſickneſs.

Behrantdurſhun, corrupt knowledge.

Beyperj, ſearching after the Jowg, with earneſt deſire.

Beddya, ſcience, art.

Bhawona, the means by which any thing is forgotten or recollected.

Bhutt, an action which produces good.

Bhoom, five ſtates of the mind, viz. Chipt, Mowdh, Beychipt, Eykagur, Nyrodeh.

Bhoopirtee, the ſtate when the mind

is not able to diftinguifh between the elements and the fenfes.

Bidh Juggen, a very expenfive facrifice of animals; and at which large fums of money are diftributed.

Biklup, doubt concerning the Deity.

Boodh, human knowledge.

Brimmah, God.

Byefs, or Bice, the third of the four Hindoo tribes.

Byfekh, foreign accident.

Byfheefhtee, the arrival at privation, which they reckon a diftinct ftate.

C

Charburren, the four original Hindoo tribes, viz. Brahmin, Kehteree, Bice, and Sooder.

Chickeerkha, the creative will of God.

Chit, defire of knowledge.

Chipt, when the heart is not fixed upon one object.

Chanderayen, a faft explained in p. 443.

Chundal, one whofe father is a Sooder and his mother a Brahminee.

Chul, falfe prepofition.

Chutternook, the union of four atoms.

D

Dan, alms.

Deyet, a race of genii, created from fire.

Derb, fubftance in general.

Denook, the quantity of two atoms.

Derug, the quantity of three atoms.

Denedan, the expiration of one day of Brahma.

Dehema, the heart having only one defire.

Dehyan, keeping the heart fixed upon one object.

Dehremdigh, the broom which a Jine always carries in his hand, to fweep the ground before he fits down, for fear of killing any infect.

Dherem, happy confcioufnefs.

Difhtant, inference.

Digneer, followers of Jine, who go quite naked, and inflict upon themfelves great feverities.

Dowkh, the caufe of prudence.

Dookh, pain.

Dooweekh, anger.

Durwuttoo, progreffive motion.

Dundowt, proftration.

Dhowtee, a piece of cloth worn over the lungowtee.

E

Eykagur, when the paffions are fo far fubdued, that the heart never wanders from its primary object.

Eyfittoo, the power of creating and deftroying.

G

Gaiybeyeh, the knowledge of paft and future events, which the followers of Neeaiy believe may be obtained by mortals, through righteoufnefs.

Geeyan, omnifcience; alfo, worldly

worldly knowledge, and the knowledge of God.

Geeyan Indree, the five ſenſes.

Gerakeyh Summaput, contemplation of the elements.

Girketter Summaput, when the mind employs only Atma.

Girken Summaput, when the mind employs only one of the ſenſes.

Goon, ſenſible qualities.

Gowrtoo, gravity.

Gund, ſmell.

Gundhirp, the heavenly choriſters.

Gunnies Sikh, one who has followed the diſcipline of Jine for ſix months.

H

Hadet, expanſion.

Huſt Joaſh, a compoſition of metals, deſcribed in vol. 1. p. 41

Heeyut, proof by inference.

Herengirbeh, the inviſible body.

Hirſoo, the quantity of two atoms.

Howm, a burnt ſacrifice, to perform which they preſerve perpetual fire.

I

Inderee, ſenſation.

Irt,h, ſubſtance.

Irthapute, advancing the cauſe, and requiring the effect.

Iſſur, the manifeſtation of the Deity.

Iſſur,purrendham, conſtant endeavours to pleaſe God.

Iſhtowſireer, vide Sithowlſireer.

Itcha, omnipotence, will, deſire.

Iyou, all the parts of a ſyllogiſm.

Iyſhruj, thoſe operations of the ſoul which lead to knowledge.

Iyſſurepaſna, continual contemplation of the Deity.

Iyiſſoorej, the power of working miracles.

J

Jaut, artful propoſition.

Jaut Saman, inſeparable accident.

Jelp, propoſition of number.

Jew Atma, animal and vegetable life.

Jewnej, animals produced by generation.

Jerayooj, viviparous.

Jennum, birth, regeneration.

Jeytun, voluntary action.

Jetty, a proficient in the doctrine of Jine.

Jowg, a complete victory over the paſſions.

Jun, amongſt the followers of Jine, is their prophet, and who is alſo called Teertehnker.

K

Kal, time.

Kamee, an action which produces the deſired effect.

Kammebyayeetoo, the power of accompliſhing whatever one deſires.

Keywulbitreekee, negative inference.

Keylaivenwee,

Keylaivenwee, poſitive inference.

Khutderſun, ſix modes of knowledge; the ſix orthodox Shaſters; 1. Neeaiy, 2. Beyſheekhek, 3. Beydant, 4. Meymanſa, 5. Sank, 6. Patenjil.

Khundpurlie, the diſſolution of the univerſe, which will happen when a Brahma is in the ſtate of Muckut.

Kurrum, motion, alſo the approved actions of the viſible world.

Kurrum Indree, a perſon who has the full exerciſe of his bodily faculties.

Kurrumkand, the performance of all the duties enjoined by the Bedes.

Kulliſht, the inclination to do evil.

Kuma, compaſſion, and ſtriving to relieve the diſtreſſed.

Kuſhup, the ſon of Barincheh, the ſon of Brahma, and father of the ſun.

Kuſhkeh, a mark which the Hindoos make upon their foreheads, and different parts of the body, particularly deſcribed in p. 484

L

Lingſireer, a general term for the ten Indrees, Untuhkurrum, and the five kinds of air, making together ſixteen things.

Lutchen, conceiving the meaning of ſixteen predicaments of Nee-aiy.

Lungowtee, a piece of cloth that covers the privities.

Lungee, a piece of cloth worn over the lungowtee.

M

Maia, the exerciſe of Pitchutſuckut, the external power of knowledge.

Mahavede, according to the followers of Jine, will be the laſt inſpired mortal.

Marik, the belief that the world is continually vaniſhing and appearing.

Mamedehee, the explanation of great and indiſpenſible duties.

Mahapurlie, the general diſſolution.

Meht, the quantity of all the elements.

Meehtageeyan, miſcomprehenſion.

Mehtet, according to the followers of Sank, is the firſt created ſubſtance.

Meytree, philanthropy.

Mowh, believing that to exiſt which doth not.

Mowdh, when the heart is contented, notwithſtanding it doth not obtain its wants.

Moodeh, taking pleaſure in the virtue of others.

Mun, the mind.

Muckut, an abſorption in the nature of the Supreme Being.

Munnum, implicit faith in the Bedes, and in the doctrines of the righteous, and conforming to them exactly.

Munnook, mankind.

Mudbhoomich,

Mudbhoomieh, clearing the heart from all impurities.

N

Narkee, the evil ſpirits who inflict torments in hell.
Naſtick, atheiſm.
Nerode, the ſtate of reſt which the ſoul enjoys immediately before it enters iuto Muckut.
Nergoonpirmeyſir, the Supreme Being.
Neruck, hell.
Nerookt, a detail of traditions.
Neemet,h, an indiſpenſible duty.
Neem, vide p. 420.
Nirnee, conviction obtained from the adverſary's arguments.
Nidhaſen, the contemplation of divine things till it becomes habitual.
Nickeddeh, an action which produces evil.
Nidra, ſleep.
Nowruſs, the nine human paſſions.
Nyrodeh, when from having ſubdued the paſſions, the heart begins to have ſome knowledge.

O

Opaypertee, being only able to diſtinguiſh Atma; and this is the ſtate of Muckut.
Owpaſſna, faith in God.

P

Pak Juggen, a burnt ſacrifice to the Dewtahs.
Parayanam, vide p. 421.
Peragabhow, a paſt negative.
Perdehnſebhow, a compound negative.
Pertegnya, uttering the propoſition.
Petree, thoſe whoſe anceſtors for ſeveral generations have been virtuous, when they aſſume paradiſical forms, enter into a region ſo called.
Perkeya, ſeeking after righteouſneſs.
Pertehmkeleek, an earneſt deſire to ſubdue the paſſions.
Peerjeeayajowt, the power of working miracles.
Peerteyehar, the five ſenſes regaining the exerciſe of the faculties, after a holy trance.
Peeran, the cauſe of life.
Peer, ſpiritual guide.
Phul, fruit, reward.
Pingeela, breathing through the right noſtril.
Pitchutſuckut, the external power of knowledge.
Poormanoo, perfect knowledge.
Poorub Meymanſa, the duties preſcribed by the Bedes.
Pooruck, ſtopping the left noſtril, and breathing thro' the right.
Poorutkeert, the fruits of good works.
Poorteah, knowledge obtained through the ſenſes.
Pooran Owtar, incarnation of the Deity.
Pooja, vide p. 491.
Puryujen, cauſe.
Purmiey, comprehenſion.

Purtehj,

Purtehj, the five ſenſes and the mind.
Purweert, voluntary action.
Pur Atma, the intelligence poſſeſſed ſolely by the eternal God.
Purtoo, diſtance of time or place.
Putchſuttoo, the perſon who knows what is ſought to be an abſolute conſequence.
Pureytcha, the performance of the ſixteen predicaments of Nee-aiy.
Purlie, diſſolution.
Purran, the ſoul.
Purakert, the diſſolution which will enſue at the expiration of one day of the life of Brahma.
Purmanbeert, knowledge obtained through Sut.
Purmad, forgetfulneſs of indiſpenſible duties.
Purraniyan, breathing in a particular manner.
Purrookuſs, that knowledge which is not obtained thro' the ſenſes; inſpiration.
Purwertekh, a degree above a Gunnies Sikh, which ſee.
Punniaſs, another name for Sithowl.
Purreetbhow, tranſmigration.
Purreytun, contrivance.

R

Rakh, deſire.
Rakuſs, evil Dewtahs.
Raoudre, anger.
Rajſew Juggen, the great ſacrifice, at which only monarchs can officiate.
Ruj, reſt.
Rutnadekh, another name for Sithowl.

S

Samance, ſeparable accident.
Samwaiy, ſimilitude; relation, and correllation.
Saman, whole, entire.
Samgurree, final cauſe.
Saderſhee, a property common to two things.
Sakapirmeyſir, one who is inſpired.
Sereer, matter.
Seriſhte, the renovation of the world, after its diſſolution.
Serawuck, a follower of Jine, who purſues worldly occupations.
Semadeh, love of retirement.
Sewadehyny, reading the divine books; remembering the divine attributes; and performing thoſe actions that lead to Muckut.
Seweetambir, called alſo Sewreh, vide Jine, p. 432.
Shirwun, hearing and perfectly comprehending the Bedes, and the traditions of the righteous.
Shaſter, a book on any ſubject.
Shuckt, an inviſible property dependent upon ſomething elſe.
Sheradh, in Bengal written Seradh, offering to the manes of their anceſtors, as far back as the third generation.
Sikh, a noviciate in the diſcipline of Jine.
Sidha, earneſt deſire of obtaining the ſtate of the Jowg.

Sithowl,

Sithowl, a viſible atom.
Sithowlſireer, viſible body.
Sindhant, poſitive proof.
Soorug, paradiſe, the ſky.
Sooroop, the union of ſpirit and matter.
Sooperſs, the touch.
Sookh, eaſe, reſt.
Sootethaig, eſteem, veneration.
Soomrut, any thing which had been forgotten, and is recollected.
Sooter, an epitome.
Sootranikt, a ſect of the followers of Boodh, who conſider all things to be only the effect of imagination.
Sochum, an inviſible atom. The followers of Beydant ſay, that every animal has a viſible and an inviſible body. The viſible body they call Sithowlſireer, and the inviſible one Sochum Sireer.
Somrut, belief that the Jowg will prove highly beneficial.
Sowah, avoiding all connection with mankind.
Sunkehya, unity, alſo the order of numbers.
Sunjowg, union,
Sunſhee, doubt, doubtful.
Subdh, tradition.
Sunneyah, fluidity.
Sunſkhar, reflection, repulſive quality. An accident whoſe occurrence does not make any alteration in the original ſtate of the ſubſtance.
Subd, ſound.
Sumbedeh, the ſame as Maia.
Sumwaiykaren, material cauſe.
Suppitcheeſuttoo, knowing the place, and the neceſſary conſequence.
Sunjeerkha, the deſtructive will of God.
Sungreh, the doctrines of the three heretical ſects, Jine, Boodh, and Naſtick.
Subde, the diſſolution of the accidents.
Sunkeyna, the names and proportions of things.
Sunka, the conjunction of good and evil conſciouſneſs.
Summedea, the cauſes of deſire and anger.
Sun, a cypher.
Sut, affection.
Sumrut, recollection.
Suttyan, diſinclination for good actions.
Sumperjeyet, an ideal form of the Deity, obtained by inceſſant contemplation.
Suttee, ſpeaking nothing but truth.
Suntowk, relinquiſhing all improper pleaſures
Summadeh, the extinction of knowledge and reflection.
Subhow, ſpecial cauſe.

T

Tamiſindree, the perception of darkneſs.
Teyjis, igneous.
Tereeſhnowk, the union of three atoms.
Terjung, animals produced by the prevalence of Ruj.
Teertehnkir, the prophet of the followers of Jine.
Tum, anger.
Turrek, negative proof.

Tup,

Tup, reconciling the mind and body to heat, cold, hunger, thirſt, and ſilence.

V

Veer, joy.

U

Un, the indiviſible atom. Monade.

Unebhow, conjecture, opinion.

Undkhar, darkneſs.

Unduj, oviparous.

Unkar, the word directed to be continually repeated, by ſuch of the followers of Patenjil as cannot read the Bedes.

Unneweebitreckee, poſitive and negative inference.

Unman, conjecture.

Unpelubdeh, ignorance of things.

Unſh Owtar, any ſubſtance that is held holy.

Untahkurrem, a ſubtle eſſence, differently modified by Sut, Ruj, and Tum.

W

Weedineh, future rewards and puniſhments.

Wymaneek, paradiſical bliſs.

Z

Zendek, a worſhipper of fire, a follower of the Zend.

Zenar, the thread worn by the three principal Hindoo tribes, p. 481.

LIST

OF

SUBSCRIBERS.

A.

James Peter Auriol, Efq.
William Kerril Amherft, Efq.
John Anderfon, Efq.
Lieutenant Arnot.
Lieutenant Armftrong.
Thomas Adams, Efq.
Captain Anderfon.
John Armftrong, Efq.

B.

John Belli, Efq.
William Bruere, Efq.
Lieutenant William Baillie.
Cornelius Bird, Efq.
John Benn, Efq.
Robert Bathurft, Efq.
W. A. Brooke, Efq.
John Harman Becher, Efq.
John Buller, Efq.
Nathaniel Bateman, Efq. 2 fets.
Major Daniel Butler.
Major Bolton.
Captain Bradfhaw.
Colonel Blair, 3 fets.
Captain Thomas Blair.
George Ball, Efq.
Lieutenant Burril.
Captain Robert Bruce.
T. Brown, Efq.
Captain Robert Blair.
Colonel Brifcoe.
Shearman Bird, Efq.
Colonel Blane.
Captain Jofeph Burnet.
Lieut. William Maffey Baker.
Robert Bruce, Efq.
William Barton, Efq. 3 fets.
Major Balfour.
Francis Balfour, Efq.
G. H. Barlow, Efq.
Hugh Baillie, Efq.
John Burgh, Efq.
Dr. Burn.
Captain Black.
Richard Birch, Efq.
Jofeph Baretto, Efq. 2 fets.
Charles Boddam, Efq.

Thomas

Thomas Boileau, Efq.
The Hon. Hart Rawfon Boddam, *Governor of Bombay.*

C.

Charles Cockerell, Efq.
John Champain, Efq.
Leonard Collins, Efq.
Major Clark.
Lieutenant Comyn.
Philip Coales, Efq.
Robert Collins, Efq.
Lieutenant N. Carnegie.
A. Carnegie, Efq.
Captain W. Cameron.
The Hon. Sir Robert Chambers.
Charles Croftes, Efq. two fets.
Charles Chapman, Efq.
Captain Collins.
Samuel Charters, Efq.
E. Colebrooke, Efq. 2 fets.
H. I. Colebrooke, Efq.
Jofeph Champion, Efq.
William Chambers, Efq.
Colonel Call.
John Craigie, Efq.
Sir John Cumming.
Thomas Crufo, Efq.

D.

H. Douglas, Efq.
Major Duncan.
R. Dalrymple, Efq.
John Dickens, Efq.
P. M. Dacres, Efq. 3 fets.
G. G. Ducarel, Efq.
George Dandridge, Efq.
Jonathan Duncan, Efq.
Colonel Duff.
William Dunkin, Efq.
Simeon Droz, Efq. 2 fets.
Major Dunn.
Sir John D'Oyly, 3 fets.
Samuel Davis, Efq.

E.

George Elliot, Efq.
Major Elleker.
Colonel Edmonfon.
William Elliot, Efq.
Lieutenant Colonel Erfkine.
Lieutenant E. Evelyn.

F.

Francis Fowke, Efq.
E. Fenwick, Efq.
Lieutenant George Fleming.
W. Farquharfon, Efq.
Lieutenant Colonel Fullarton.
Major Farmer.
Lieutenant Fallon.
Captain Frith.

G.

Charles Grant, Efq.
Benjamin Grindall, Efq.
W. F. Gardener, Efq.
Major Gardener.
Richard Goodlad, Efq.
Thomas Gillies, Efq.
T. Green, Efq.
Major Gilpin.
James Graham, Efq.
Captain Lewis Grant.
Robert Grant, Efq.
Charles Græme, Efq.
Captain Grant.
Henry Griffiths, Efq.
James Grant, Efq.
I. Gould, Efq.
George Francis Grand, Efq.
Roger Gale, Efq.
Mr. George Gordon.

Warren

H.

Warren Haſtings, Eſq. 14 ſets.
Edward Hay, Eſq.
Captain Higgins.
Major Henderſon.
Major Hawkins.
Captain R. Hamilton.
Thomas Hamilton, Eſq.
Captain William Hyde.
John Hyde, Eſq. jun.
William Hodges, Eſq.
The Hon. Mr. Juſtice Hyde.
Herbert Harris, Eſq.
S. Haſleby, Eſq.
I. H. Harrington, Eſq.
Captain Hogan.
J. Hodges, Eſq.
Hugh Honeycomb, Eſq.
Arthur Heſilrige, Eſq.
Captain Patrick Hunter.
Major Hardy.
W. Haverkam, Eſq.
John Hollond, Eſq.
I. E. Harrington, Eſq.
Humphry Howarth, Eſq.
Captain Haynes.

I.

James Irwin, Eſq.
Colonel Ironſide.
Lieutenant H. Imlack.
The Hon. Sir Elijah Impey, 3 ſets.

J.

The Rev. Mr. Wm. Johnſon.
Major G. Johnſton.
Richard Johnſon, Eſq.
William Jackſon, Eſq.
The Hon. Sir William Jones.

K.

Lieutenant Colonel Kyd.
Lieutenant W. Keaſberry.
Captain Kennaway.
L. Kelly, Eſq.
J. I. Keighly, Eſq. 2 ſets.
Captain Kirkpatrick, 2 ſets.
David Killican, Eſq.
Richard Kennaway, Eſq.
John Kneller, Eſq.

L.

The Rev. Mr. William Lewis.
Captain Herbert Lloyd.
Lieutenant Lawtie.
Joſeph Loden, Eſq.
Thomas Law, Eſq.
James Laird, Eſq.
Major Lumſdane.
E. G. Lind, Eſq.

M.

The Right Honourable Lord Macartney.
The Hon. John Macpherſon. Eſq. *Governor General.*
Captain Mercer.
Captain Jabez Mackenzie.
Captain John Mawbey.
Colonel Muir.
I. Percy Monk, Eſq.
Colonel Macpherſon.
Lieutenant M'Gregor.
Captain William M'Intoſh.
Captain I. Meredith.
Lieut. Col. Alexander Murray.
Lieut. I. C. Mitchell.
Capt. Dyſon Marſhall.
Major Macdonald.
Lieut. Charles Middleton.

Colonel Martin.
Captain John Mordaunt.
N. Middleton, Efq.
John M'Clary, Efq.
Lieut. Col. Peter Murray.
Major M'Clary.
Sir Thomas Mills.
Captain H. Mordaunt.
John Murray, Efq.
The Rev. Mr. Mackinon.
Captain P. M'Dougal.
C. W. Malet, Efq.

N.

Captain Noke.

P.

Captain Phipps.
Captain Pringle.
John Paterfon, Efq.
John Peiarce, Efq. 2 fets.
John David Paterfon, Efq.
Colonel Pearfe, 2 fets.
John Pringle, Efq.
P. Powel, Efq.
Lewis Perceret, Efq. 2 fets.
Colonel Polier, 2 fets.
Major Palmer, 2 fets.
Charles Purling, Efq.
William Paxton, Efq.
John Petrie, Efq.
Captain James Pringle.
Edward Ephraim Pote, Efq.

R.

Jacob Rider, Efq. 2 fets.
George Roach, Efq.
Major Rawflorne.
Francis Redfearn, Efq.
William Rooke, Efq. 2 fets.
B. Rock, Efq.
Lieutenant John Reed.
John Rawlins, Efq.
Henry Revell, Efq.
James Rofs, Efq.
Captain Reynold.

S.

The Hon. John Stables, Efq. 3 fets.
Major Sands.
Charles Sweedland, Efq.
John Scott, Efq.
James Spottifwood, Efq.
R. O. Smith, Efq.
Jonathan Scott, Efq.
Lieut. Henry Scott.
Lieut. John Stormor.
Captain Charles Scott.
Major Thomas Scott.
William Swainfton, Efq.
Captain John Scott.
General Stibbert.
John Sumner, Efq.
John Shore, Efq. 2 fets.
Peter Speke, Efq.
Major William Scott.
Charles Sealy, Efq.
Lieut. Symes.
Archibald Seaton, Efq.
Henry Scott, Efq.
Ber. Smith, Efq.
James Stark, Efq.

T.

George Templer, Efq.
G. N. Thompfon, Efq.
Dr. Thomas.
I. M. Taylor, Efq.
S. Tolfrey, Efq.
John Taylor, Efq. 3 fets.
Thomas Tront, Efq.

Lieutenan

V.

Lieutenant Charles Vernon.
Henry Vanſittart, Eſq. 2 ſets.
David Vanderheyden, Eſq.
Cornelius Van Citters, Eſq.

U.

David Urquhart, Eſq.
George Udney, Eſq.

W.

Alexander Walker, Eſq.
William Wilkinſon, Eſq.
William Walker, Eſq.
R. Worlidge, Eſq.
Captain John Witherſtone.
Lieutenant I. Winwood.
E. Wells, Eſq.
Major Charles Ware.
Captain Williamſon.
John Wombwell, Eſq.
George Wroughton, Eſq.
John White, Eſq.
Wm. Webber, Eſq. 2 ſets.

Y.

Allen Young, Eſq.

F I N I S.

Printed by J. Swan and Co. Jeruſalem Court, Gracechurch Street.